CCH BUSINESS OWNER'S TOOLKIT

WIN GOVERNMENT CONTRACTS

FOR YOUR SMALL BUSINESS

A *CCH Business Owner's Toolkit* Publication

John DiGiacomo

James Kleckner

CCH INCORPORATED
Chicago

Cover designed by Tim Kaage, Laurel Graphx, Inc.

Books may be purchased at quantity discounts for educational, business or sales promotion use. For more information please contact:

Small Office Home Office Group
CCH INCORPORATED
2700 Lake Cook Road
Riverwoods, Illinois 60015

ISBN 0-8080-0556-1

Printed in the United States of America

THE CCH BUSINESS OWNER'S TOOLKIT TEAM

Alice Magos has over 35 years of experience running the operations of numerous small businesses. She is the author of the *CCH Business Owner's Toolkit*™ online advice column "Ask Alice." Alice is a popular instructor at small business seminars on accounting, financial planning, and using the Internet; is an accountant and a Certified Financial Planner; and holds degrees from Washington University in St. Louis and Northwestern University.

John L. Duoba has more than 13 years of small business experience in book and magazine publishing, fulfilling various roles in editorial and production management. He has been involved in the publication of scores of titles, with multiple editions and issues raising the total well into the hundreds. John is a professional journalist and holds a degree from Northwestern University's Medill School of Journalism.

Joel Handelsman has 20 years of experience writing about business, tax, and financial topics. He has experience with multiple new product and business ventures in the publishing industry, and has held a variety of management positions. Joel is an attorney and holds degrees from Northwestern University and DePaul University.

Susan M. Jacksack is frequently quoted as a small business expert in national publications including *The Wall Street Journal, The New York Times, Money,* and *Worth,* and has made several guest appearances to discuss small business issues on CNBC. She has over 13 years of experience advising and writing for small business owners and consumers on tax, personal finance and other legal topics, and has conducted seminars for new and prospective entrepreneurs on tax issues, business planning, and employment law. Susan is an attorney and a graduate of the University of Illinois, Urbana-Champaign.

Martin Bush has over 15 years of experience providing legal, financial and tax advice to small and large businesses in various industries. He is a frequently quoted small business expert and has appeared on CNBC and National Public Radio. Martin is an attorney and a CPA, and holds degrees from Indiana University, DePaul University, and Northwestern University.

In addition, we would like to thank LaVerne Dellinger, Drew Snider and Linda Lev for their contributions in the production of this book.

ABOUT THE AUTHORS

John DiGiacomo is director of the Procurement Technical Assistance Center (PTAC) at Rock Valley College in Rockford, Illinois, assisting companies in working with the federal government. Under his watch, more than 400 different companies have been awarded over $250 million in contracts. John is a former owner of a business that sold to the government, at both the state and federal levels. After selling his business, he consulted internationally with companies in the U.S., Germany, and England, helping to find, negotiate and win $70 million in contracts. After leaving the private sector, he joined the PTAC and, among other things, has initiated small business workshops and conferences on using e-commerce and EDI to do business with the government, and is in the process of creating an online, real-time video conferencing network within the state of Illinois.

James L. Kleckner is a private consultant specializing in federal government procurement and small business, and also works with the Illinois PTAC program. Prior to starting his own consulting business, James was for 37 years part of various federal procurement activities, including former buyer and staff officer in the Procurement Policy Office of the HQ U.S. Army Weapons Command in Rock Island, Illinois; Small Business Specialist at DCASR Dallas; associate director of Small Business, DCASR Chicago; and deputy for Small Business, DCMAO Chicago. He also was appointed to the Illinois Small Business Council of 100 in 1996, which helps set state policy to foster the growth of small business in Illinois. In all, Jim has worked with over 1200 businesses that were awarded $17.5 million in contracts.

Both authors are Certified Contracting Assistance Specialists with the Association of Government Marketing Assistance Specialists (AGMAS), Certified Business Specialists with the Illinois Small Business Development Association (ISBDA), and members of the National Contract Management Association (NCMA).

DEDICATION

To our wives—Jackie DiGiacomo and Janet Kleckner—and our children—Jonathan and Kyle Martin, Cheri Stanley, Derek Kleckner, and Debra Kleckner Masek—for their patience and support during this new adventure.

Thanks to Linda Lev for being there when we needed her, and to the entire SOHO team at CCH for their support.

A special thanks to LaVerne Dellinger, our editor, who believed in us enough to care. Without her, it wouldn't have been possible.

FOREWORD

If you are a small company, there has never been a better time to do business with the federal government. Recent changes in the laws and regulations that define federal government contracting and the procurement process have made it easier than ever for your business to participate in this $200 billion industry.

Even if you have little or no experience in selling to the federal government and have little or no knowledge of the contracting process, there is no reason you can't share in the opportunities that this huge market offers.

And this guidebook can help you do just that. It is written by expert authors who do what they write about. Together they have 60+ years of experience and have helped over 6,000 businesses in 14 states secure government contracts to the tune of over $2 billion. They take you, step by step, through the process of doing business with the government—from how and where to find government buying opportunities to how to read, price out, and write a successful proposal. They also tell you about the types of resources that are available to help you as you go through the process and provide listings of buying offices, useful web site addresses, and all the other information that you need to make the government your new best customer.

Experience has shown that just about any business with the desire and perseverance can do it. And, with the help of this book, you can too.

A caution and an invitation—the discussions of the laws, web sites, procedures, and other information contained in this book are current as of the date of publication. But remember, things continue to change. To keep abreast of the latest news affecting your business, visit the CCH Business Owner's Toolkit (www.toolkit.cch.com). Take a look at the interactive information and tools that we offer to assist you in running your business. You can also ask follow-up questions of the authors. We welcome and look forward to your questions and comments.

Martin Bush

Publisher, Small Office Home Office Group

Table of Contents

Table of Contents

Table of Contents

Part I

Leap of Faith

You and your business are about to embark on a brand new venture. You are getting ready to enter a new $200 billion market and to pursue a new, rather daunting customer—the federal government of the United States. Seem a bit overwhelming? Not if you understand the rules, the process, what to do and when to do it, and where to go for help. And that's exactly what this book is about.

So, let's get started. In this Part, we will first give you a feel for the magnitude of the opportunity available to small businesses in doing business with the government. Then we will show you how to assess whether you have "what it takes" to take on the government as a customer. Lastly, we will help you understand the government's game plan, the basis of the contracting process, and the rules and the rulebook that you have to know about and abide by.

Chapter 1, What Are the Opportunities?: Find out how much the government spends on the products and services it needs, where it spends its dollars, and whether there is real opportunity for small businesses.

Chapter 2, But Is There Real Opportunity for You?: Here we help answer an important question: What are the chances that the government needs and will buy the product or service that your company offers? We also tell you what government contracting can—and cannot—do for you.

Chapter 3, Subcontracting Alternatives: Many businesses assume that being a government subcontractor would be easier than being a government prime contractor. We tell you why that may not be true. We also tell you what prime contractors look for in a sub and how to improve your chances of getting the job.

Chapter 4, Do You Have What It Takes?: Here's your chance to find out whether you have the "right stuff" to do business with the government. We look at the resources, equipment, technology, and all of the other things that you need to be successful.

Chapter 5, Government Rules You Need To Know: Doing business with the government is really just "selling to a customer"—the same rules of business generally apply. But to minimize any problems, you need to know what the differences are.

Chapter 1

What Are the Opportunities?

How much opportunity is there in doing business with the government? Perhaps these statistics from the 1999 Federal Procurement Report (the most current report available at the time this book went to press) will perk your interest and begin to give you some idea of the magnitude.

In Fiscal Year 1999, the federal government wrote 10.5 million "actions," commonly referred to as "contracts" for products and services that it needed during the year. Of those 10.5 million contracts, 95 percent, or 9.9 million, were between $2,500 and $100,000 in value.

Since any contracts that fall between $2,500 and $100,000 are set aside for small, small disadvantaged, small women-owned, and small service-disabled-owned businesses, that means that *almost 10 million contracts were reserved for small businesses in just one year*! Only 5 percent of the contracts were more than $100,000 in value, and many of those were for major weapon systems, information management services, or large construction projects.

Government Prime Contract Goals

The government has the following designated goals for awarding prime contracts to small businesses:

> *23% to small businesses*
>
> *5% to small disadvantaged businesses*
>
> *5% to small women-owned businesses*
>
> *3% to small service-disabled-owned businesses*

CONTRACTING OPPORTUNITIES

Now let's get a better picture of where the government spends its money.

Fiscal Year 1999 (10/1/98-9/30/99)
Total Federal Actions and Contract Dollars

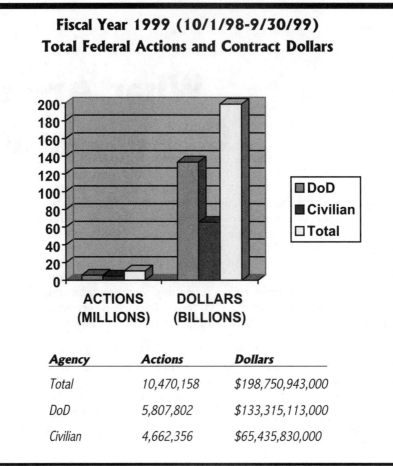

Agency	Actions	Dollars
Total	10,470,158	$198,750,943,000
DoD	5,807,802	$133,315,113,000
Civilian	4,662,356	$65,435,830,000

As you can see, there are two basic areas in which the government spends its contract dollars: the Department of Defense (DoD) and civilian agencies, such as the Veterans Administration and Health and Human Services. And, as you can also see, the government contracted for almost $200 billion in products and services in fiscal 1999 alone. Based on the numbers, it looks like DoD is the biggest opportunity, but remember that many of the dollars went toward major systems and thus to larger companies.

Next let's look at what small businesses have done for the same period.

Fiscal Year 1999 (10/1/98-9/30/99)
Small Business Government Contracting

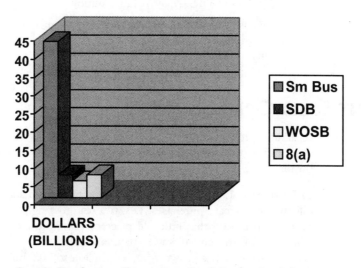

DOLLARS
(BILLIONS)

Small Business Contracts by Method of Award

Noncompetitive	Restricted Competition	Open Competition
* $7,026,692,000	* $8,025,492,000	* $15,825,071,000

These figures do not add up to the total figure of $45 billion because they do not reflect buys for under $25,000, which amounted to $14,631,940,000 and are automatically reserved for small businesses.

As this graph shows, small businesses, overall, did very well at almost $45 billion. It also shows that businesses that can be classified as small disadvantaged businesses (SDB) or as women-owned small businesses (WOSB) have a lot of room to grow.

It is also interesting to note that one-third of the total dollars awarded to small business (i.e., $15 billion of the total $45 billion) was received in open competition. In other words, the little guys and gals beat out the big ones for $15 billion in government contracts. Not a bad return for the effort!

And how many small businesses were new to the game? In fiscal 1999, a total of 7847 small businesses received their first federal contract with the government. These businesses were either women-owned or disadvantaged-owned, and were split almost 50/50 between female and male ownership.

Complete statistics on government contracting are available in hard copy for free or on CD-ROM for a nominal charge. Just call or write and ask for the *Fiscal Year Federal Procurement Report.*

> Federal Procurement Data Center
> U.S. General Services Administration
> 7th and D Street, S.W., Room 5652
> Washington, D.C. 20407
> Telephone: 202-401-1529

CREDIT CARD OPPORTUNITIES

In addition to government contracting, there is a whole new area of opportunity that isn't included in the figures above—credit card buying, often referred to as "micro-purchasing."

In Fiscal Year 1999, the federal government spent an additional $10.2 billion in credit card purchases. Yes, you read that right, $10.2 *billion* in business just using that little old piece of plastic money. Since 1984, when credit card purchases were first authorized, the number of credit card transactions has grown from 4.2 million to 20.6 million in Fiscal Year 1999. This means that, on average, over 56,000 transactions were placed each day. The amount of dollars spent with credit cards by government personnel—not just official government buyers—grew from $1.6 billion to almost $10.2 billion.

Although the biggest credit card users were the Department of Defense and the Veterans Administration, accounting for $6.5 billion, every government office utilizes the credit card for almost everything it needs. That means that you can potentially have a government customer right next door. Does your company accept credit cards? If not, you might want to think about the advantages of offering credit card purchasing as a part of your business strategy. Remember that the private sector is also increasing its use of the credit card.

Chapter 2

But Is There Real Opportunity for *You?*

Although you may be starting to get an idea of the magnitude of government contracting opportunities for small businesses, you may be wondering—and possibly even doubting—whether the government has any need for *your* particular product or service. Of course, we can't tell you with certainty that it does, but what we can tell you is that the government needs—and stands ready to buy— more types of products and services than you can imagine.

WHAT THE GOVERNMENT NEEDS

To make a point, here are some unusual, but real, examples to show that the government needs *all* types of products and services—from junk cars to pork rinds to shooting pigs! They also show that there is every chance that you provide—*or have the capability to provide*—a product or service that the government is looking for right now.

- What use would the government have for old wrecked cars? A small business owner who owns a junkyard near an Air Force base used to think that same question and actually found out. He was awarded a repeat contract for his junk cars, which were used to train Air Force rescue personnel in the use of the "jaws of life" and other emergency situations.

- Just a few years ago, an artist in Oregon was awarded an indefinite federal contract for wildlife artist services by the Department of Interior, U.S. Fish and Wildlife Service. This contract was awarded for various paintings portraying a variety of subjects.

- How about pork rinds? A small business received a contract for manufacturing and providing pork rinds—tasty treats that lots of people love—to several military base stores that needed someone to supply them. The owner won the contract based on price, delivery, and his status as a minority business contractor. And this was all before President Bush made them famous.

- What's that about shooting pigs? An avid bow hunter who sold archery supplies and organized hunting trips won a bid from the Tennessee Valley Authority to get rid of the wild pigs that were living in and around the site and creating a safety problem. (Wild pigs tend to be a bit grouchy!) Instead of bidding against firms that were going to charge and have employees do the work, he bid $1.00 and then scheduled hunters to go out and do the job. After clearing the hunters with the government to enter the area, he made his profit by charging the hunters just as he did for any other hunting trip to any other wilderness area.

- The Fish & Wildlife Services in Atlanta, Georgia awarded a federal contract for walking the beach, specifically "PR for Beach Patrol of Leatherback Sea Turtles." If you're going to walk on the beach anyway, you may as well get paid for it.

WHAT CONTRACTING CAN DO FOR YOU

So, just maybe, the government might want to buy what you have to offer. But will a government contract really be worth the trouble? What can it really do for your business?

While winning a federal contract is not akin to winning the lotto, as some would have you believe, in some cases, it can help you accomplish other goals, from jump-starting your business to helping to finance your retirement.

- In just a few years, a small Midwest business that we know of went from being a one-man operation with a couple of thousand dollars in contracts per year to almost 30 employees with more than $75 million in contracts per year. The owner was able to take his expertise in MRO items (Maintenance, Repair and Operations materials) and win a major supply distribution contract from the Defense Department.

- A larger business that manufactured wood products had tried for some time, although unsuccessfully, to get a government contract for wooden handles for stretchers. The owners even bought a special machine that could put out hundreds of handles a day. But a one-man operation—a semi-retired wood maker who worked just a few hours each day making the handles—won the contract and accomplished his goal of keeping busy while earning extra retirement money. He put out a quality product that the government was happy with and, because he had virtually no overhead, was able to quote a much more competitive price.

- A small business owner who distributed diesel engines and engine parts, and was knowledgeable in government procedures, started a thriving business out of his dining room. He started with one client who wanted to supply the government, but didn't want to deal with the government. So he cut a deal with the client to do the government paperwork, organize the packing and shipping, take care of the problems with the government and become, in fact, the client's "contracting office." He now has several clients that supply different types of goods and works to various government agencies to the tune of several million dollars a year.

But even if your results are not as dramatic, getting a government contract can work to your advantage. What it can do is level out the hills and valleys during the business year. The usual margin of profit is never large, but if you utilize that portion of your business with the government for paying the overhead (i.e. lights, heat, a/c, etc.), you will find that the other contracts you have will be much more profitable. This is a very basic principle: If you can pay your costs with a government contract—which always remains stable—you can be more selective with other, higher margin contracts.

WHAT CONTRACTING CAN'T DO FOR YOU

On the other hand, if your company has fallen on hard times and is in financial trouble, a government contract will not be able to save you. In fact, a contract could push you over the edge and put you completely out of business if you cannot fulfill its requirements.

You also need to keep in mind that the government does not finance contractors, and only rarely makes advance payments. To receive advance payments, there must be a compelling reason, such as a national security issue, and not just the fact that a contractor needs money to stay in business. The best you can hope for is some form of "progress payments."

Work Smart

Contrary to some late night talk show advice, the government does not have loads of free money to give to you that will set you up in any old business you want. It does have some programs that will help you find low interest loans, but that's a different book. (See CCH Business Owner's Toolkit Online: www.toolkit.cch.com.)

Chapter 3

Subcontracting Alternatives

Performing work on government contracts doesn't have to mean working directly with a government agency. There is an alternative: You can do work for a government prime contractor as a subcontractor.

The prime contractor is a commercial company that has won a contract with the federal government for a product or service. The government has no contractual relationship with subcontractors to its prime contractors. Therefore, as a subcontractor, your contractual agreement is with the prime contractor, not with the government agency that the prime has contracted with.

REQUIREMENTS MAY FLOW DOWN

However, if right now, you are thinking, "Great! If I have no contractual relationship with the government, I won't have to deal with all that government paperwork and all those rules and requirements," you'd better think again. If the subcontract is complex, you could actually be required to put up with the same paperwork, rules and obligations as the prime under what is called a "flow down" clause in your subcontract.

Flow-down clauses are especially common in government and construction subcontracts. The government, recognizing the need to assure that important federal policies are followed throughout performance, sometimes will require specific prime contract requirements to flow down to subcontractors and be incorporated into their subcontracts.

The usual flow-down clause will incorporate, by reference, parts of the prime contract into the subcontract. Such clauses bind the subcontractor to the prime to the same extent that the prime is bound to the government. In effect, the prime contractor's duties and obligations "flow down" to the subcontractor. What was that about no paperwork?

WHAT A PRIME LOOKS FOR IN A SUB

Becoming a subcontractor takes hard work, persistence and a thick skin for rejection. Even when you do everything "right," you may still be passed over simply because you don't fit the profile of what the prime is looking for.

In deciding whether to use a sub, and which sub is right for the job, primes look at a variety of issues. Should they make or buy? Is it going to be less expensive for them to go out of plant to get the work done? Are there union issues? Is the technology such that they can only buy or use the sub? Does the potential subcontractor have the needed technical ability and qualifications to do the work? Are there socio-economic considerations in making a decision, like using small minority- and/or women-owned businesses?

Work Smart

Most government contracts over $500,000 in value contain a requirement that the prime must develop a "plan" for using minority business enterprises (MBEs) and women business enterprises (WBEs). This plan must be written by the contractor and approved by the contracting office.

And, finally, did we mention price? This market is very competitive and primes are looking for quality products or services at a very good price.

How To Improve Your Chances as a Sub

In addition to looking for a quality product at a reasonable price, primes are looking for a sub that can help them hold up their end of the bargain and make the contract go smoothly.

You can greatly improve your chances of getting the job if you can show that you are willing and able to learn the protocols, do the required conferencing and follow-ups, and familiarize yourself with any required contract details and forms. As a sub, timing is crucial and communication is essential. Let the prime know that you are aware of this and are ready to satisfy these areas.

Opportunities for Subs

There is an entire market available to you as a subcontractor for a prime. Primes are always looking for "good" vendors. For example:

- *AlliedSignal, consistently among the top 25 prime contractors, depends on materials and components from 7,500 to 10,000 suppliers who accounted for 60 percent of its defense contract costs in 1993.*

- *Sixty percent of the dollar value of Pratt & Whitney's military aircraft engines goes to suppliers.*

- *To build the inertial guidance system for the MX missile, Northrop relied on more than 500 subcontractors to make 19,000 parts.*

- *At Lockheed/Fort Worth, subcontracts consumed 75 percent of the cost of making the F-16 aircraft.*

You can find information about subcontracting opportunities with prime contractors who work for the Department of Defense (DoD) in a publication entitled "Subcontracting Opportunities with DoD Major Prime Contractors."

It is issued annually by the Office of Small and Disadvantaged Business Utilization and lists, by state, those DoD prime contractors with established plans and goals for subcontracting with small businesses and small disadvantaged businesses. For each contractor, the directory provides the address, the product or service line, and the name and telephone number of the company's small business liaison officer. You can download this publication by going to http://www.acq.osd.mil/sadbu and clicking on "Publications."

Chapter 4

Do You Have What It Takes?

So, are you ready to begin doing business with the government? Do you have the "right" resources, finances, equipment, computer skills and whatever else it may take? Here's a chance to find out. We'll tell you what you need and then give you the opportunity to rate yourself so that you can better see where you stand and in which direction you need to be moving.

ARE YOU BIG ENOUGH?

One question that often plagues small business owners at the start is, "Is my business big enough to handle a government contract?" Actually, there are many companies with fewer than five employees that have received a contract. In fact, some companies that have only one person in their entire operation have been awarded a contract. In one case, mentioned earlier, it kept the owner busy for an entire year and amounted to his total year's salary.

In other words, size is not necessarily important. Any business—regardless of size—has the potential to get a contract with the government. But which companies stand the best chance of actually getting a contract? The answer is simple—any business that sells a product or service and is:

- responsible

- competitive

- patient in dealing with the bureaucratic process

- committed to invest and apply the resources that are needed to market to the government.

How Small Is Small?

What constitutes a "small business" by federal government criteria? Generally speaking, if the company provides a product (i.e., actually manufactures an item), then size is determined by the average number of employees over a 12-month period. Currently, that number may range from 1 to 1,500 employees, depending on the type of product(s) manufactured.

However, if the company provides a service, then size is based on average annual sales over a three-year period. Currently, the cap on the three-year average ranges from $0.5 million to $20 million, depending on industry.

The Small Business Administration is responsible for setting size standards, based on industry. The table, below, summarizes the current size standards:

SBA Small Business Size Standards

Type of Business	Criteria
Manufacturing	The maximum number of employees may range from 500 to 1,500, depending on the type of product that is manufactured.
Wholesaling	The total number of employees may not exceed 100.
Providers of Services	Annual receipts may not exceed $3.5M to $20M, depending on the type of service.
Retailing	Annual receipts may not exceed $5M to $20M, depending on the type of service.
Construction	Annual receipts may not exceed $13.5M to $17M, depending on the type of service.
Special Trade Construction	Annual receipts may not exceed $7M.
Agricultural	Annual receipts may not exceed $.5M to $5M, depending on the type of service.

The SBA size standards are available on the Internet at http://www.sba.gov/regulations/siccodes. You will notice that the specific products and services are classified by a government code, called a SIC (Standard Industrial Classification) code. The SBA uses SIC codes to identify the industrial categories and make size determinations. SIC codes, as well as other government coding systems, are discussed in detail in Part II.

Work Smart

While you can use these general standards to make an educated assessment, only the Small Business Administration has the authority to make an official size determination. Anyone can challenge a company's size declaration, but it is the SBA that will settle the issue.

Again, the important thing to remember is that it doesn't matter whether a company is classified as large or small. The companies that successfully sell to the government are the ones that do their homework and "keep at it," while companies that just "give it a try" almost never get a contract.

DO YOU HAVE THE FINANCIAL RESOURCES?

What is the financial situation of your business? Is your business financially stable or are you just starting out and short on cash flow? Are you able to make payroll and other payments with no problem? In other words, is your business financially healthy?

As we mentioned earlier, if you are in financial trouble, a government contract would be more likely to put you out of business than to save your business.

Example

Small business owners primarily look to their own personal resources for capital. The predominant sources of financing are:

Small business owners themselves	*41%*
Cash advances from personal credit cards	*36%*
Personal lines of credit	*25%*

DO YOU HAVE A QUALITY ASSURANCE PROGRAM?

The terms of a government contract generally require you to assure the quality of the product or service that your business will be providing. To do that, you need to show that you have some kind of formal, documented quality control plan in place.

Your plan could consist of anything from a general quality assurance manual to a full quality assurance program that complies with a recognized commercial quality standard, a government standard, or the international ISO standard for your industry. (See Part III of this book for a detailed explanation of quality standards.)

IS YOUR OFFICE UP TO SPEED?

To be ready for the government, you need to be sure you have the proper office skills. You need to be organized, maintain accurate files and records, document important transactions and meetings, know where everything is, and generally be able to keep things humming.

DO YOU HAVE THE TECHNOLOGY?

We can't stress enough the importance of this area. Simply put, if you are not capable of doing business using Electronic Data Interchange (EDI) or some kind of e-commerce, you will not be doing business with the government.

Why? Because, in an effort to go paperless, the law requires the government to use electronic means to issue and award small business contracts, specifically those between $2,500 and $100,000. (By the way, if at this point, you are scratching your head and wondering what EDI is, see the discussion below.)

To be EDI-capable, you need to have the following:

- A personal computer, Pentium or higher, using a Windows 95/98 or Macintosh operating system. The faster and more RAM you have in your computer, the better off you will be. If you are in the process of shopping, we encourage you to buy as much "oomph" (otherwise known as RAM and memory) as you can afford, but don't get carried away with "goodies" you don't need for business,

- A modem with a minimum speed of 56K that uses V.90 technology. The faster your modem, the faster you can transmit and receive bid information.

- A dedicated telephone line. It's really hard to do business and send/receive information when you have only one regular line. Check out a DSL line or cable if available in your area. Satellite may be an option as well.

- A connection to the Internet. These days, there are many providers to choose from. There are three things to remember in choosing one: (1) you want connection when you want it, (2) you need quality hook-up, and (3) the connection is for business, not pleasure.

Work Smart

If you are waiting for the next "best" or "latest" thing before you buy, grit your teeth and go ahead and get the one that's best for you now. There will always be something better or newer. And while you wait, opportunity passes you by.

Example

According to recent statistics, the technology most widely used by small businesses is the fax machine, with 82 percent of small business owners saying they regularly depended on it in their operations. Seventy-one percent routinely use cell phones. Fifty-four percent use the Internet for obtaining business information, while 45 percent use the Internet to communicate with others.

What Is EDI?

EDI, which stands for Electronic Data Interchange, is the paperless, computer-to-computer exchange of business information using electronic tools such as e-mail, Electronic Funds Transfer (EFT), and the Internet. EDI is a part of what is referred to as electronic commerce (e-commerce). It is just one part, but it is an important one.

EDI allows businesses to exchange information and documents, such as invoices, forms, bids, requests for quotes, purchase orders and a whole wealth of other business information more quickly, easily (most of the time), cheaply and accurately. EDI permits the electronic equivalents of common business documents to be transmitted electronically between the computers of what are called "trading partners." A trading partner can be the federal government, a prime contractor, or another commercial business.

How Does EDI Work?

The computers of trading partners are given a standard format and numbers, referred to as ANSI X12 Standards, so that these computers can "talk to" and understand each other.

Value Added Networks (VANs) provide connectivity between trading partners. Most VANs can provide you with many services, but you must be very careful about which VAN you choose—costs vary and sometimes what seems to be very affordable can end up being very expensive. For example, if the VAN you choose doesn't transmit often enough, you can lose out on bidding opportunities by being late for the opening. In choosing, you need to check out all the details and determine exactly what it provides.

What Can EDI Do for You?

Here are just some of the advantages of being EDI-capable:

- Increased business opportunities, not only with the government but also with prime contractors and other private-sector trading partners.

- Faster and more accurate processing of orders, resulting in improved inventory management and, best of all, greater customer satisfaction.

- Faster billing. Since orders are filled and delivered sooner, billing and closeout can occur sooner.

- Lower mailing costs, a reduction in mailroom sorting/distribution time and elimination of lost documents.

- Improvements in overall quality through better recordkeeping and fewer errors in data.

- Better information for decision-making. EDI provides accurate information and audit trails of transactions, enabling you to identify the areas offering the greatest potential for efficiency improvement or cost reduction.

Going Paperless

EDI and e-commerce were not the ideas of the federal government. Their roots actually started in the transportation industry. One of the first non-transportation companies to use EDI with its distributors was Apple Computers, although they didn't call it EDI back then.

We remember, some years ago, watching a friend who owned an Apple store working intently at his computer. When we asked what he was doing, he explained that he was ordering supplies from his manufacturer. We watched him enter product numbers, quantities and other information, and when he hit the Enter key, he said, "Well I just ordered 30 computers, 7 hard drives, 4 modems, and repair parts." What a concept, we thought! What a way to do business—and that was in 1985.

Today it is EDI—in very sophisticated form—that lets you go to the Federal Express web site to look up the status of a shipped package. And, in the future, if you are working with Ford or Chrysler, it is EDI that will allow tracking of the whole process. It very well may be able to look into the manufacturing plant to see where your order is and determine how long it's going to take to finish, who the shipper is, and what the ship date will be.

Today, many companies do business that way and the government is finally catching up with the commercial marketplace and modern technology. You can now get government bids automatically sent to you via e-mail, decide which ones you want to bid on, download the technical information from the Internet, and then bid on the requirement without using one sheet of hard paper.

DO YOU KNOW HOW TO USE THE INTERNET?

Folks, we are not talking here about knowing how to play games or surf the World Wide Web looking for sports scores. We are talking about knowing how to use search engines, download *and* upload files, use viewers like Adobe Acrobat, and communicate via e-mail.

You also need to know how to access a CD-ROM file so you can look at government bids. (We used to get a box the size of an orange crate with bids from the Corps of Engineers every other day. Now we get one CD with all the information, and it's so nice! It's easy to keep track of all the bids because all the information is in one place.)

Rate Your Readiness To Be a Contractor

This "quiz" is not meant to be a serious scientific assessment. Its main purpose is to get you thinking about the government market, what areas you may need to work on, and what will be expected of you and your company. So, with that in mind, here are the categories for scoring:

Criteria	Score
Size of Business	
If you have 1-500 employees and are committed to winning a government contract and willing to do your homework, **give yourself +10**. If you get impatient quickly or plan on making only a half-hearted attempt to win a contract, **give yourself -10**.	
Financial Capability	
If you are financially capable of performing a contract and are going after the government market in order to increase or stabilize sales, **give yourself +10**. If you are going after a contract just to stay in business, **give yourself -20**.	
Quality Assurance Program	
If you have a general QA manual, **give yourself +5**. If your manual complies with a commercial quality or government standard, **give yourself +10**. If your quality assurance program complies with the international standard (referred to as an ISO standard) for your industry, **give yourself +25**. If you have no formal, documented quality assurance program, **give yourself -10**.	

Office Efficiency	
If you keep good records and have an efficient way of finding information, **give yourself +10**. *If it takes you a while to put your hands on a piece of needed information and you run your office on the "I know it's here somewhere" principle,* **give yourself -10**.	
EDI and E-Commerce	
If you have the necessary equipment for doing business using e-commerce, **give yourself +25**. *If you don't have a computer and modem, count yourself temporarily out of the game. Start shopping now.* **Lose all points!**	
Internet	
If you know how to do all the tasks we just talked about, **give yourself +10**. *If you can only play games,* **give yourself −10**. *If you lose to your kids,* **subtract another -5 points**. *If you know enough to go to your teenager and get some help,* **give yourself 5 points**.	
Bonus Points	
Do you know how to get "specs & stds"? If you think that getting "specs & stds" means getting something out of your eye, **give yourself -10**. *If you know that a spec is a specification or standard for a specific product or service,* **give yourself +10**. *Do you believe that all you have to do is send in a bid and no matter what price you quote, it will be approved (like that $300 hammer you heard about 25 years ago)? If you do,* **give yourself -25**. *If you believe that your price needs to be competitive,* **give yourself +25**.	

OK, now for the rating.

If you scored 0-50, you might want to either rethink your idea for getting a government contract or work on acquiring the necessary resources and skills.

If you scored 51-75, you are heading in the right direction and probably just need a little assistance.

If you scored 76-100, you are ripe and ready to go after a government contract.

If you scored 100+, you have everything you need to start winning contracts. (If your score fell into this range, please call us. We might have some money to invest!)

Chapter 5

Government Rules You Need to Know

You've heard it said many times, "Government contracting seems hard—so many rules and regulations. And, if you don't follow them, the government is just waiting to take you down!"

Actually, nothing could be further from the truth. The government not only actively seeks out small business participation when it buys products and services, but it also goes to great lengths and spends lots of money in outreach programs to find good, qualified small businesses to be its suppliers. For example, it will provide information that will help you bid with minimal risk. Just for the asking, you can find out how much the government bought the last 5 to 10 times, who they bought from, and how much they paid. Try asking for that kind of information from your commercial customers and see what they say!

In reality, there are many similarities in selling your products or services to commercial customers and selling them to the federal government—the same basic business principles and strategies generally apply. Both want a quality product or service at a reasonable price, delivered on time. And in both cases, you need to know your customers' needs, how they buy and who buys what.

However, although the approach to the commercial and government market is similar, the procedures and rules of doing business in the government arena are different—and if these differences are not understood, it is here that problems can occur.

However, all of these problems can be minimized if you take the time to gain some basic knowledge of these procedures and rules and to learn how the process works. (Note that we said "minimized," not "avoided," because Murphy's law is always out there waiting to pop up.)

GOVERNMENT PROCEDURES

Let's get started by looking at some of the differences in procedures. First of all, the federal government conducts its business through authorized agents, called contracting officers:

- The Procurement Contracting Officer (referred to as the "PCO") places contracts and handles contract terminations when the contractor defaults.

- The Administrative Contracting Officer (referred to as the "ACO") administers the contracts.

- The Termination Contracting Officer (referred to as the "TCO") handles contract terminations when the government terminates for its convenience.

Depending on the situation, the same person may be all three.

Because the government is a sovereign entity (in other words, it is the ruling power), it has rights that commercial businesses do not have. For example, the government has the right to unilaterally revise the contract, so long as changes are within the parameters of the contract.

This means the government can change the quantity it is contracting for, or how it is packaged or how it is being shipped. The contractor is entitled to equitable cost adjustment, but must comply with the changes. The government also has the right to cancel the contract if the need for the product or service no longer exists. Here again, the contractor would be entitled to reimbursement for costs incurred.

Because taxpayer dollars are being spent, the government can impose extensive audit and surveillance requirements under the terms of a contract. However, extensive and stringent requirements are usually imposed only on higher priced contracts (i.e., contracts of $100,000 or more in value) and thus are not usually applicable to contracts with small businesses.

One of the big fears that small business owners have is that the government will come in and audit their books, go through their files with a vacuum cleaner, and tell them how to run their business. That fear is totally unfounded and far from the truth.

GOVERNMENT LAWS AND REGULATIONS

Now let's take a closer look at the laws and regulations that will affect you when you do business with the government. Maybe the easiest way to begin is with a brief history lesson.

Before the earliest law was passed, private individuals furnished from their own resources whatever supplies and materials the government needed. (How well do you think that would work today?) But that all changed with the Purveyor of Public Affairs Act of 1795, which allowed the government to buy needed supplies and materials.

At the beginning of the Civil War, which created monumental needs for the federal government, the Civil Sundry Appropriations Act of 1861 became law, and this continued the principle of advertised procurements for the next 86 years.

When it became apparent that small companies and their labor force needed protection, the Sherman Antitrust Act of 1890 was enacted.

Finally, the Armed Services Procurement Act, signed into law in 1947, continued the sealed bid as the preferred method of procurement, with specific exceptions. It also attempted to place procurement rules in one location. The result was the Armed Services Procurement Regulation (ASPR).

In addition, there are many other laws and Executive Orders that affect how you must conduct your business if you want to contract with the federal government.

For example, the Eight-Hour Work Law of 1892 set the eight-hour workday. The Davis-Bacon Act of 1931 set the minimum wage on the construction site at the local prevailing wage. In 1933, the Buy American Act required the government to buy only American products. The Walsh-Healey Public Contracts Act of 1936, drastically changed in 1994, required a supplier to certify that it was the manufacturer or a regular dealer. This was an attempt to do away with the broker.

Later on, the Small Business Act of 1953 was passed, which established the Small Business Administration. The Truth in Negotiation Act of 1962 required both prime and subcontractors on contracts over $500,000 to certify the cost data submitted under the solicitation. Public Law 95-507, which amended the Small Business Act of 1978, formalized the Small Business Subcontracting Plan requirement in contracts over $500,000 to large businesses. At that time, this law was considered a significant change in government procurement practices.

Now we come to the recent laws. The Federal Acquisition Streamlining Act of 1994 (FASA) was revolutionary in its impact on the federal acquisition process. It repealed or substantially modified more than 225 statutes and pushed the contracting process into the 21st century.

Among other things, it simplified the federal procurement process, reduced paperwork burdens, and transformed the simplified acquisition process to electronic commerce. Before the law could be fully implemented, the Federal Acquisition Reform Act of 1996 (FARA, also known as the Clinger-Cohen Act) was passed to correct some deficiencies in the earlier legislation and to make more changes. These last two laws were significant events because of the vast changes they made in the way that the government conducts it business. The system is continuing to make adjustments to the new, more open environment.

Example

What prompted the changes in the procurement process as contained in FASA and FARA? The story goes that Motorola was contacted by the Defense Department to supply mobile communication devices to be used by our military in "Desert Storm." The company was more than willing to supply the product, and the price quoted was not an issue.

However, at that time, the law did not allow the government to contract for a basically commercial item. Motorola told the government to take the product and give them a check for the amount agreed upon. The government couldn't do that without a signed contract, an impasse. As hard as the government tried to remove the problem clauses, it couldn't do it.

An ally country, supposedly Japan, came to the rescue. They bought the product and then furnished it to the U.S. government as part of its support of Desert Storm.

After all of this, the powers in Washington finally realized that the procurement process needed some major changes to get in step with the marketplace.

For your easy reference, we have created a chart summarizing the most significant laws and their provisions at the end of this chapter.

How FASA Affects You

What was so significant about FASA to the interests of small businesses? Here are some of the specific changes that this law made:

- Changed the small purchase level from $25,000 and under to between $2,500 and $100,000, and provided that all these purchases can enjoy "simplified acquisition procedures," which in effect reserves all of these purchases for small business. Two of the main purposes of the simplified acquisition procedures are to reduce administrative costs and to improve contract opportunities for small, small disadvantaged, small service-disabled-veteran, and small women-owned businesses.

- The government was mandated to use electronic means to issue and award small purchases (termed by the law as "Simplified

Acquisition Purchases" or "SAP"). That means that for contracts under $100,000, there is now a tremendous effort by the government to go "paperless." What does paperless mean? Well, it simply means that the government is entering the era of electronic commerce and technology for doing business. So much for the myth of being buried by government paperwork and red tape.

- Encouraged government buying offices to use credit cards on all requirements under $2,500. Basically, the intent was to get these "nuisance" buys out of the buying office and simply let the government user buy what was needed quickly and efficiently. This means two things for small businesses: minimal paperwork and a real opportunity for any business that accepts credit cards to increase its business. As we mentioned earlier, in 1999 alone, the federal government spent almost $10.2 billion in credit card purchases in the under-$2500 range. The government now just goes to a local store and buys what it needs.

- Established commercial items as the preferred products for the government to buy if they meet the government need; to do otherwise requires a justification as to why it is necessary. This last little change is having a major impact on the process. First of all, it has meant a reduction in government personnel that small businesses have to deal with. The more the government buys commercial items, the less it will need buyers, production specialists, pricing specialists, quality assurance specialists and other personnel that were required when the government designed to its own specifications. Second, it has meant that only if the commercial market cannot satisfy the government's need can the government buyer require that items be built to government specifications. In other words, most government specifications and standards will be used only with contracts greater than $100,000, so you, the small business contractor, will have fewer government requirements to worry about.

Government Purchasing Thresholds

Micro-purchases (credit cards)	*for contracts up to $2,500*
Simplified Acquisition Procedures (SAP)	*for contracts for $2,501 to $100,000*
Simplified Commercial	*for contracts $100,000 to $5,000,000*
Commercial Off the Shelf (COTS)	*no dollar limits, any dollar size contract*
Commercial Items	*for contracts over $2,500*
Sealed Bids/Negotiations	*FAR Parts 14 & 15 apply for contracts $100,000 and up*

Laws that Affect Government Contracting

Public Law	Result
Purveyor of Public Affairs Act of 1795	Allowed the government to buy needed supplies and materials to perform government functions.
Civil Sundry Appropriations Act of 1861	Continued the principle of advertised procurements for the next 86 years.
Sherman Antitrust Act of 1890	Protected small companies and their labor force from large business.
Armed Services Procurement Act of 1947	Continued the sealed bid as the preferred method of procurement, placed procurement rules in one location and gave us the Armed Services Procurement Regulation (ASPR), which was the beginnings of today's rulebook, the FAR.
Eight-Hour Work Law of 1892	Set the eight-hour workday.
The Davis-Bacon Act of 1931	Set the minimum wage on the construction site at the local prevailing wage.
Buy American Act	Required the government to buy only American products.
Walsh-Healey Public Contracts Act of 1936 (note that this law was drastically changed in 1994)	Required a supplier to certify that it was the manufacturer or a regular dealer. This was an attempt to do away with the "broker."
Small Business Act of 1953	Established the Small Business Administration.
Truth in Negotiation Act of 1962	Required both prime and subcontractors on contracts over $500,000 to certify the cost data submitted under the solicitation.
Public Law 95-507, Amendment to the Small Business Act (1978)	Formalized the Small Business Subcontracting Plan requirement in contracts over $500,000 to large businesses. Set goals for large primes.
Federal Acquisition Streamlining Act of 1994 (FASA)	Revolutionary in its impact on the federal acquisition process. It repealed or substantially modified more than 225 statutes and pushed the contracting process into the 21st century. Among other things, it simplified the federal procurement process, reduced paperwork burdens, and transformed the simplified acquisition process to electronic commerce.
Federal Acquisition Reform Act of 1996 (FARA) or (Clinger-Cohen Act)	Before FASA could be fully implemented, this Act became law and corrected some deficiencies in the earlier legislation and made more changes.

THE RULEBOOK AND BIBLE—THE FAR

No discussion of government procedures and rules is complete without talking about the basic rulebook for government contracts: the Federal Acquisition Regulation, commonly known as "the FAR."

The FAR, which had its beginnings in the Armed Services Procurement Regulation established in 1947, is considered the Bible for federal government contracting. The FAR contains all the rules governing the contracting process as well as all the forms and clauses used in contracts.

The FAR has recently gone through a significant rewrite to reflect and implement all of the changes made by all the recent laws. In order to do business with the federal government, you definitely need to have a basic knowledge of what is in the FAR and how to use it. (See Appendix 5 for a general Table of Contents for the FAR.)

Work Smart

The FAR is designed to be a guide, not a limiting rulebook. Under recent changes in the law, contracting officers can use "good business practices" that make sense in making decisions and in negotiating terms instead of having to consult a rulebook on each decision.

The FAR is divided into 53 parts, each part dealing with a separate aspect of the acquisition process. The first six parts deal with general government acquisition matters and the next six parts deal with aspects of acquisition planning. The rest of the FAR deals with other topics, such as simplified acquisition threshold (formerly known as small purchases), large dollar value buys, labor laws, contract administration, applicable clauses and forms.

Relevant parts for small businesses include Part 19, Small Business Programs, and Part 52, which contains the standard terms and conditions contained in a government contract.

Although the FAR is the primary acquisition regulation for the federal government, each government agency may issue an agency acquisition supplement to the FAR. We therefore have the Defense Federal Acquisition Regulation Supplement (DFARS), the General Services Acquisition Regulation Supplement (GSARS), and the National Aeronautics Space Administration FAR Supplement (NASFARS), just to name a few. Many of these are on the Internet at the agency's web site (see Appendix 3 for a list of web sites that you might find useful).

All of these supplements are not stand-alone documents, but must be read in conjunction with the FAR. The FAR has more than 1000 pages and a supplement may be another 1000 pages, but only a relatively small portion is used in any single contract. That is why it's important, when dealing with a government office, to ask which regulation governs their acquisition procedures. Make sure that you read any changes to the rule before you quote. Don't assume, ask!

You can buy a copy of the FAR in hard copy from the Government Printing Office (GPO), read it on the Internet at http://farsite.hill.af.mil, or buy it from a third party like CCH, Incorporated.

Work Smart

 If you order the FAR from the Government Printing Office, make sure that the price includes all updates, as they occur, so you will always have current information when you prepare a proposal. Updates are important because of the potential impact on the way you will bid. It could change the cost and therefore your quote!

When you view the FAR on the Internet, make sure that you check the update date for the same reason. The softbound type, such as the CCH version, is current until the next update.

Just remember that the government is ready to do business, on a competitive basis, with competent, qualified companies that can supply the products or services it requires at a reasonable price. You, the new contractor, must know what their game plan is. Once you have some understanding of the federal buying process, you can enter this market with greater confidence and be successful and profitable.

Part II

Go For It!

OK, so what do you have to do to actually sign that first deal with the government? We have broken down the actions you need to take into ten steps. In the following chapters, we will guide you through the process of completing each one.

Caution

Although we are presenting the actions you need to take in a step-by-step fashion, it does not mean that they need to be done one at a time. They can be done simultaneously or in a different order, depending on your circumstances.

Chapter 6, Think Like the Government: Start thinking about your business the same way the government does—as the provider of an end product. By thinking in terms of output, and not process, you'll be more likely to make a connection leading to a deal.

Chapter 7, Identify Your Customers: The buying offices of the federal government don't know you're out there, but you can find them if you know where to look.

Chapter 8, Get Registered: Before you can start bidding on contracts, the government needs to know who you are and what you do. A mistake or omission at this point could severely hurt your chances of landing a contract, so we'll tell you what to do step-by-step, including how to decipher all the government codes involved in such a process.

Chapter 9, Find Bid Leads: The government is required by law to inform all potential contractors of what they're looking for, but are you listening? There are a number of outlets for this information, and one is best for you and your company.

Chapter 10, Get the Bid Package: You've got the lead, now you need to get your hands on the specifics. Find out how to get the bid package and how to understand its particular pricing arrangement.

Chapter 11, Review the Bid: The solicitation you've just received has the potential to be a binding contract. Know what to read and how to read it to maximize your chances for success.

Chapter 12, Get Technical Data: To successfully complete your bid, you'll need to do some research. Learn what types of specs may apply and how to get the correct data to comply with the order.

Chapter 13, Price It Out: In a competitive bidding process, price is the determining factor. And if your bid is accepted, it will literally make or break your company—so know what factors to consider.

Chapter 14, Write Your Proposal: This is a formal procedure that must be completed exactly. We take you through it line-by-line, explaining it all.

Chapter 15, Submit Your Bid: Submission of your bid is the final step in a contracting process full of fine print. Know the best ways to keep your bid from being kicked out at the last second.

Chapter 6

Think Like
The Government

You are now ready to get started. You might imagine that the first thing you should do is get out there out and look for all those government buyers and bid opportunities, right?

Not so fast. Before you take any action at all, there is one thing you need to do that will greatly increase your rate of success in finding opportunities and winning contracts: Learn to think the same way the government does when it does business.

When the government buys, it thinks in terms of the end item that it needs—for example, a can, a spring, a bolt, a pencil, etc. It does not think in terms of the process of manufacturing an item. And when the government looks for contractors, it looks for companies that can produce that item. It does not look, for example, for a plastic molder or welder or metal finisher.

Example

At a recent Congressionally sponsored government procurement conference, the owners of a company that made various items for the railroad industry were telling us how disappointed they were in the event, because there were no government offices at the conference that bought railroad items.

After talking with them a while, we got them to realize that they could use their same equipment and skills to make items for the military, such as tanks and off-road vehicles. They went over to the Army booth and found there were indeed some opportunities for them to support the Army's needs for heavy equipment. It turned out to be a good conference after all!

As you look for contracting opportunities, it is crucial that you think the same way. Think of your business in terms of your output—the products or items that you make and, perhaps more importantly, the items that you are capable of making. Think of how you can use your same equipment and process to make things that the government needs and wants—perhaps things you never even considered before.

If you think in terms of your process—for example, if you think of your company as a screw machine shop—you will be facing a much bigger challenge in trying to find government opportunities. Why? Because the government does not purchase items described as "screw machine products"—it buys nuts, bolts and screws.

How you think of your business can affect your success more than you imagine! What are your company's capabilities?

Chapter 7

Identify Your Customers

Now that you are thinking of your business in terms of the end items that you are capable of providing, you are ready to identify prospective customers—the buying offices within the federal government that have a need for your product or service.

A simple rule of thumb is that if the item is a commercial-type or general-purpose item, there is a good chance that the General Services Administration (GSA) buys it for both the military and civilian offices. Think of the GSA as the "Sears and Roebuck" of the government. This doesn't mean that the military or a civilian office won't be using the product; it just means that the GSA may issue the contract, and other government offices—both military and civilian—can buy off of that contract.

There are a number of ways to find the appropriate buying offices:

- Search *Commerce Business Daily*

- Use the personal touch

- Subscribe to a bid-matching service

- Work with a Procurement Technical Assistance Center (PTAC)

SEARCH *COMMERCE BUSINESS DAILY*

One way to locate potential government customers is through the *Commerce Business Daily* (*CBD*), a publication that lists notices of proposed government procurement actions, contract awards, and other information. Published every business day by the Department of Commerce, each edition contains approximately 500-1000 notices, and each notice lists the buying agency interested in buying that particular product or service.

A "classified ad section" for the government, *Commerce Business Daily* is available in hard copy and on the Internet. Although you can skim through the hard copy to find government buying offices, it is usually much easier to let your computer do the work. All you have to do is feed it "good" keywords. Here's how to proceed:

1. Go to http://cbdnet.gpo.gov on the Internet.

2. Arrow down to "Simple Search of the CBD" located under "CBDNet — The CBD Database Online via GPO Access."

3. On the new screen, click on "Simple-Search."

4. On the next screen, change "40" in the block next to "Maximum Records Returned" to "350". (Even though the screen says that you are limited to 200 hits, 350 will work and may save you time.)

5. Next to "Database to Search," check "Archive of Notices" as well as "Active Notices." Including both databases will give you both current and historical information for identifying potential customers.

6. Move down further to the "Search Terms" box. Here is where you will type the keywords that describe your product or service, and therefore here is where you also need to be creative. For example, the government might call a "washer" a "spacer." A "pencil" could be called a "writing instrument." And how about "people elevator" instead of the commonly known "step ladder" (a term actually used in an Air Force bid). Another tip: When you type your keywords, remember to follow the search rules that appear on the screen under the "Search Terms" box, including setting your keywords in quotes.

7. Click "SUBMIT" for your list of results. As you go through the documents on your list, you should be able to identify a buying office and possibly a contact person. (If the document is an award, you will also get other useful information, such as who received it, what and how many were bought, etc.)

8. Finally, contact the buying office(s) that you have identified as prospects for buying your product or service and talk to them about how you can receive opportunities to bid.

CBD is discussed further in Chapter 9.

USE THE PERSONAL TOUCH

One way to locate government buying offices is to pick up your local phone book, search the blue or yellow pages under "Government, federal," and then look for a listing for the purchasing office or small business office. If neither of these offices is identified, then call the office(s) listed and make an appointment to meet with them.

Once there, introduce yourself and your company, and provide the buyer with your business card and a listing of the supplies and services you can offer. If you have one, also provide the URL of your business web page. This gives buyers another opportunity to see who you are and what you can do.

Don't be afraid to ask questions. Find out what products and services they buy. If they don't buy the product or service that you are offering, ask them to refer you to an office and a person that does.

Then later, use the first contact as a referral to the next. For example: "I recently talked to Joe/Mary and they suggested I talk to you for help in bidding on government contracts. What products and/or services do you buy?" This helps establish credibility with the new contact. It is important to get names and numbers for future use.

If you have already registered your business with the government (see Chapter 8), let the buyer know that. Over time, be sure to follow-up with the buyer to see if there are any new solicitations you can bid on and, in addition, to ingrain your company's name in the buyer's mind.

SUBSCRIBE TO A BID-MATCHING SERVICE

Instead of doing the work yourself, you can subscribe to a "bid matching" service to provide you with leads on bids and prospective customers. The bid service, with your help, will develop a company profile using keywords and government product and service codes to help match your company's capabilities to the needs of the government.

Using that profile to screen for suitable leads, the bid service will then search on the Internet for opportunities and will also get bid opportunity information directly from the government. You will receive the leads by e-mail, and all you have to do is decide whether to bid. However, keep in mind that this service only provides the leads; it will not help you understand a particular bid.

You can locate a bid-matching service by searching on the Internet under "bid matching" or "bid matching service," or by asking for a referral from the small business specialist in the government buying office or from your local PTAC. Since bid lead services are usually not close by, contact is by phone or e-mail.

WORK WITH A PTAC

This method works much the same way as a bid-matching service, but costs you nothing (you are already paying for it with your tax dollars). Stop in the Procurement Technical Assistance Center nearest you, sign up to be a client, and get your prospective buyers and bid leads through the PTAC.

As you go through the process, the PTAC will be available to answer your questions or will refer you to someone who can. It can also get copies of specifications and standards for you at minimum cost and do some market research. In addition, it offers training in government procurement practices through seminars and conferences and assistance in understanding e-commerce. To locate the PTAC nearest you, go to http://www.agmas.org or see Appendix 4. To learn more about the services that PTACs provide, see Part IV.

Work Smart

Using a bid-matching service or a PTAC actually identifies customers and gets bid leads in one step. Some leads will not prove to be biddable for a variety of reasons, but the leads themselves will give you a lot of useful information on an item, including the buying office. It "jump starts" you in the process.

As you identify government buyers, keep in mind that there are two parts of the federal government to look at: the Department of Defense (DoD) and the Civilian Agencies. As we mentioned earlier, the DoD is the largest buyer, but you may not fit there. Don't worry if you don't; remember that "green is green."

A list of the major government buying offices, both military and civilian, is included in Appendix 2.

Chapter **8**

Get Registered

One of the most important things you need to do early in the process is to let the government know that you are ready and able to provide the products or services it needs. To do this, you must register your company with various agencies and programs within the federal government.

There are two primary places—both Internet databases—at which you must register:

1.   Central Contractor Registration

2.   PRO-*Net*

In order to register, you must use a personal computer and have access to the Internet. If you don't have access, you may use a personal computer at a Procurement Technical Assistance Center, Small Business Administration office, Federal Procurement Office, or your local library.

As you prepare for registration, you'll no doubt be overwhelmed by the endless litany of codes used by government contractors. When so many goods and services change hands every year, some type of "shorthand" language is needed to keep track of it all. A complete understanding of these codes is absolutely necessary if you hope to successfully compete for the government's business, and we'll cover what you need to know.

REGISTERING WITH THE CCR

Any company, large or small, wishing to do business with the Federal government must register in the Central Contractor Registration (CCR), the central databank for government contractors.

To register, access the database at http://www.ccr2000.com and fill out the form with information about your company. The CCR form contains both mandatory and optional fields, and although your application will be considered complete if you fill out just the mandatory fields, we strongly recommend that you fill out *all* fields. Since government buying offices use the CCR database to help them identify companies that might be able to provide the goods and services they need, it is your advantage to provide a complete picture of your company's capabilities and qualifications.

We also recommend that you gather all the required information and have it at hand before you go into the database and fill out the form. It is important that you enter the correct information the first time. Getting back in to change the information is, to say the least, not an easy task, and you will end up spending a great amount of time trying to fix it. (In the case of one small company, it took us more than three weeks to fix the errors!)

Because proper CCR registration is so important, we are going to review some of the information that you will need to register, below. We also give you tips to help make sure that you enter the information correctly.

The complete CCR form is reproduced in Appendix 6. If you have questions regarding CCR registration, call the Registration Assistance Center at 1-888-227-2423 (1-616-961-4725 internationally).

Information You Will Need to Register in CCR

Please note that we are not going to review every piece of information included on the CCR form. Instead, we are going to discuss what we consider the essential information for small businesses.

We have organized the information that you will need into the following categories:

- Identification numbers

  — Data Universal Numbering System (DUNS) Number

  — DUNS +4 Number

  — CAGE Code

  — U.S. Federal TIN

- General information about your company

- Classification codes for your products and/or services

— SIC codes

— FSC codes

- Information about electronic funds transfer

- Registration acknowledgment and point of contact information

For your convenience, we have provided a space next to each item so you can, if you wish, jot down the correct information for your company and have it handy when you fill out the electronic form.

We want to remind you that when you enter the information on the CCR web site, you must fill in all the fields designated as mandatory or your application will be considered incomplete and your registration will not be accepted. And, again, we encourage you to fill in the optional fields as well.

Identification Numbers

Data Universal Numbering System (DUNS) Number _____
The Data Universal Numbering System (DUNS) number is a unique nine-character identification number provided by The Dun & Bradstreet Corporation (D&B). If you do not have a DUNS number, call Dun and Bradstreet at 1-800-333-0505 or 610-882-7000 to request one. Be prepared to provide an address, telephone number, business start date, and type of business. The process takes about 10 minutes and is free of charge. The number will be issued within three working days. If you already have a DUNS number, the D&B representative will advise you over the phone.

If you have access to the Internet, you can submit your business's request for a DUNS number through D&B's web site at www.dnb.com/dunsno/whereduns.htm.

Work Smart

When entering your DUNS number on the CCR Web site, enter only the numbers— do not enter the dashes.

DUNS +4 _____
The CCR process allows businesses to assign an additional 4 characters to their DUNS number to uniquely identify an affiliate or division at the same physical location. For example, a business might want to have two records for itself at the same physical location to identify two separate bank accounts. Either a DUNS or a DUNS +4

number can be used to successfully complete the registration process.

Vendors wishing to register their subsidiaries and other entities should make sure that each additional location obtains a separate DUNS number from Dun & Bradstreet at 1-800-333-0505. If you have questions regarding the use of DUNS +4, contact the CCR Assistance Center at 1-888-227-2423.

CAGE Code

The Commercial and Government Entity (CAGE) code is a five-character ID number used extensively within the Department of Defense to identify specific companies.

If you don't have a CAGE code and your company has a U.S. address, you may submit the CCR registration form without it and one will automatically be assigned and filled in for you as part of the CCR registration process.

However, if you are a foreign vendor (i.e., your company does not have a U.S. address), you must include an NCAGE code on the registration or it will be considered incomplete.

U.S. Federal TIN

The U.S. Federal TIN (Tax Identification Number) is the nine-digit number that companies use for income tax purposes. If you do not know your TIN, contact the Internal Revenue Service at 1-800-829-1040. If you operate as an individual sole proprietorship, you must enter your Social Security number in the provided space.

If your business is located in the United States and you do not fill in this field, your application will be considered incomplete and your registration will not be accepted. If you are located outside the United States, you are not required to provide a TIN.

Work Smart

When entering your TIN or SSN on the CCR web site, enter only the numbers—do not enter the dashes. (Example: 123456789, not 123-45-6789)

General Information about Your Company

Legal Business Name and Doing Business As

Your legal business name is the name under which you are incorporated and pay taxes. If you commonly use another name for normal operations, such as a franchise or licensee name, then include that in the space below the "Legal Business Name" field.

Work Smart

Your legal business name and street address, as entered on the CCR registration, must match the legal business name under which you are registered with Dun & Bradstreet. If the information does not match, your registration may be rejected during processing.

Street Address _____

You must provide a valid street address where your business is located. A Post Office Box or c/o may not be used in this space. If you use a P.O. Box for correspondence, you may include it in the space allocated under the tab "Address Info."

Street Address 2 _____

If necessary, use this space to continue your physical street address.

City, State, Zip _____

The nine-digit zip code is preferred, although your application will be accepted with a five-digit zip.

Work Smart

When entering the nine-digit zip code on the CCR web site, enter the numbers only—do not include the dash. (Example: 123456789, not 12345-6789)

Country _____

Choose the appropriate country code abbreviation from the list provided.

Date Business Started _____

Enter the date your business was started in its present form. This may be used to distinguish your business from others with similar names. Use the format mm/dd/yyyy. (Example: 01/01/1995)

Close of Business _____

This field calls for the month and day on which you close your fiscal year. For example, if you operate on the calendar year, enter 12/31. In any case, use the format mm/dd.

Average # of Employees and Average Annual Revenue _____

You must provide accurate information about the number of employees and three-year average annual receipts for your business since these values are used to determine your business size classification. These values cannot be zero.

Work Smart

When entering revenue information on the CCR web site, enter numbers only—do not enter dollar signs or commas.

Corporate Status (check one):

You must choose one of the following boxes to indicate the corporate status of your business. If you are a Limited Liability Partners Company or S-Corporation, choose "Corporation."

☐ **Sole Proprietorship**

If you choose Sole Proprietorship as your status, you must complete "Owner Information" located in the "Registration Name" tab at the top of your screen.

☐ **Corporation**

If you choose Corporation as your status, you must enter the state of incorporation if your business is incorporated in the United States. If you are incorporated outside of the United States, you must enter the country of incorporation and check "Foreign Supplier Federal Agency" under business types (see below).

☐ **Partnership**

☐ **Hospital or Extended Care (choose one below):**

☐ **Corporation providing health care services**

If you choose Corporation providing health care services as your status, you must enter the state of incorporation if your business is incorporated in the United States. If you are incorporated outside of the United States, you must provide the country of incorporation and check "Foreign Supplier Federal Agency" under business types (see below).

☐ **Not applicable**

Only a government agency may choose "Not Applicable" as its Corporate Status.

Business Types (check one or more)

Check all the descriptions that apply to your business—you must choose at least one for your application to be complete. If you are unsure as to whether you qualify under a category, contact your local Small Business Administration (SBA) office for the appropriate guidelines or visit their web site at www.sba.gov. If none of the choices applies to you, you may check Emerging Business/Other Unlisted Type.

- ☐ Tribal Government Educational Institution

- ☐ Research Institute Municipality

- ☐ Sheltered Workshop

- ☐ Emerging Business/Other Unlisted Type

- ☐ Nonprofit Institution

- ☐ Construction Firm

- ☐ Historically Black College/University

- ☐ Federal, State, County, or City Facility

- ☐ Foreign Supplier Federal Agency

- ☐ 8(a) Program Participant (If you check 8(a) Program Participant, you will be required to provide the name and address of the certifying party in the address section.)

- ☐ Minority Owned Business

- ☐ Service Location

- ☐ Woman-Owned Business

- ☐ Manufacturer of Goods

- ☐ Small Disadvantaged Business

- ☐ Surplus Dealer Veteran Owned

- ☐ Subgroup American Indian Owned

- ☐ Labor Surplus Area Firm

- ☐ Limited Liability Company

- ☐ S-Corporation

Classification Codes for Your Products/Services

Standard Industrial Classification (SIC) Codes _____

The Department of Commerce publishes a manual that identifies the economic base of the country (i.e., products and services) by types of industry, such as manufacturing, construction, agricultural, service group, etc., through a coding system. This system enables the government to obtain the data it needs to analyze economic trends and similar information. SIC codes can be four or eight digits.

Although you have to enter only one valid SIC code for your registration to be complete, *be sure to list all codes that apply to your products and services.* This could help government buying offices identify your company as one that provides needed goods or services.

You can access the SIC manual on the Internet through the Small Business Administration's home page (www.sba.gov) or in hard copy through your public library.

If you are using a print copy of the manual, you can find your SIC Code by looking for your industry and then going down the list to see where you fit. Or you may search for your products and services by keyword on the Internet at http://www.census.gov/epcd/www/naics.html.

Note: When you set up your company, particularly if you incorporated, chances are that it was classified with a SIC code because that's one of the things that's asked for in the incorporation papers.

Work Smart

When entering your SIC or FSC codes on the CCR web site, separate the codes with a comma and a space, not just a space. (Example: 1234, 5231, 9012)

Federal Supply Classification (FSC) Codes _____
FSC codes are similar to SIC codes, but are used by the buying offices to identify products/services. Although they are not required for your registration to be considered complete, we strongly recommend that you include all that apply to your business because it gives buying offices a better understanding of your capabilities.

You may search for applicable FSC codes by keyword on the Internet at www.ecrc.uofs.edu/fsc-codes/fsc.html.

Electronic Funds Transfer

Under recent law, the government is legally mandated to use Electronic Funds Transfer (EFT) for all contract payments. Therefore, all registrants must complete this section. (There are exceptions: foreign vendors doing business outside the United States, utility companies, and government agencies do not have to supply this information.)

If you need help with the required information, your bank or financial institution should be able to help you. If you are unsure as to whether your registration requires EFT information, call the

Registration Assistance Center at (888) 227-2423 or (616) 961-4725 internationally.

Financial Institution _____

Provide the name of the bank that you use for business banking purposes.

ABA Routing Number _____

The ABA Routing Number is the American Banking Association's 9-digit routing transit number for your financial institution. You can obtain the routing number by contacting your financial institution or you may find it on one of your checks. It usually appears as the first nine digits in the lower left-hand corner.

Account Number, Type, & Lock Box Number _____

Enter the account number to which you want your EFT payments deposited and check the proper box to indicate whether it is a checking or savings account. If you prefer to use a lock box service, enter the appropriate account number in the space provided. If you use a lock box for your banking purposes, you must also check "checking" under account type.

Authorization Date _____

Enter the date when EFT information submitted on this form is valid and in effect. This form may be used to initiate future changes in EFT/banking deposit information (for example, if you change banks or accounts), and the authorization date identifies the effective date for the EFT data furnished.

Work Smart

When entering the date on the CCR web site, you must enter it as mm/dd/yyyy. No date earlier than the date of registration may be entered.

Automated Clearing House _____

Enter the appropriate contact information for your bank's Automated Clearing House (ACH) coordinator. The ACH will serve as the contact if problems occur with your EFT transfer. Note that e-mail addresses requested under the contact entries refer to Internet e-mail addresses, not local area network e-mail addresses within your office.

Work Smart

When entering the phone numbers on the CCR web site, enter the numbers only, not dashes or parentheses. (Example: 9995551212, not (999) 555-1212)

Address Information _____

Enter the address of your bank (i.e., the physical address, not the e-mail address).

Remittance Information _____

Enter the address where you would like a paper check mailed in the event that an EFT transfer does not work. On the name line, enter to whom the check should be mailed and fill in the appropriate information. If you use a lock box and want checks mailed directly to the bank, enter the bank name and address here.

Registration Acknowledgment and Point of Contact Information

Registrant Name _____

Enter the name of the person that acknowledges that the information provided in the registration is current, accurate, and complete. The person named here will be the _only_ person within the registering company to receive the Trading Partner Identification Number (TPIN) via U.S. mail. (The TPIN is a password to protect access to your registration and banking information on the CCR. That's why it is sent by mail.)

The Registrant and the Alternate Contact (see below) are the only people authorized to share information with CCR Assistance Center personnel. It is important that the person named here have knowledge about the CCR registration.

Correspondence Check Boxes _____

_____ US Mail _____ FAX _____ E-mail

To promote prompt receipt of information, e-mail or faxes are definitely the preferred modes of communication. At the time this book went to press, CCR correspondence was being conducted through the U.S. Postal Service.

Alternate Contact _____

Enter the name and phone number for another person at your company in case questions arise when the primary contact is not available.

Accounts Receivable _____

Provide contact information for the accounts receivable person at your company. This is the contact provided to the Defense Finance and Accounting Service regarding EFT payments on your government contracts. Note that this contact is not authorized to receive and/or release information regarding the CCR registration to any Registration Assistance Center personnel. It may be beneficial to have the accounts receivable contact also act as the alternate contact for the registration.

Owner Information _____

If you have checked "Sole Proprietorship" as your business type, you must provide the name and phone number of the owner of the business.

REGISTERING IN PRO-*NET*

The second place that small businesses must register is in PRO-*Net*. PRO-*Net* is an Internet database containing profiles of more than 171,000 small, disadvantaged, 8(a), veteran, and women-owned businesses. It is open to all small firms seeking federal, state and private contracts. It is a search engine for contracting officers and a marketing tool for small companies looking to do business with government, commercial and international customers. It also provides access and is linked to *Commerce Business Daily* (*CBD*), agency home pages, and other sources of procurement opportunities.

Although small businesses technically are not required to register here, we strongly feel, from a practical point of view, that all small businesses *absolutely must* register with PRO-*Net*. (We have been told that, in the near future, searching on PRO-*Net* could become the primary way government buyers seek out prospective contractors!)

You can access the PRO-*Net* database by going to the SBA's home page (www.sba.gov) and clicking on PRO-*Net*. The PRO-*Net* registration form is similar to the CCR form and contains both mandatory and optional fields. And, as we did with CCR, we strongly recommend that you fill in *all* fields, so that buying offices will have a complete picture of your business.

As part of your registration, you will fill out a profile about your company. This profile, which is structured like an executive business summary, will allow you to enter information about the capabilities of your business and a short history of some of your successful jobs. Government buyers can search the businesses profiled on the Pro-*Net* system by SIC codes, keywords, location, quality certifications, business type, ownership race and gender, EDI capability, etc. In addition, if your company has its own web site, you can link your site to your PRO-*Net* profile. Then if buyers like what they see in your profile, they can go directly to your business web site and find out more details.

Once complete, the SBA will review your registration and, if acceptable, will activate it to become available in searches. Keep in mind that you are responsible for updating your profile and keeping the information current. If you don't update your profile within 18 months, the system makes it invisible for market searches until updated. This could prevent you from being offered an opportunity, so remember to stay current on PRO-*Net*.

Information You Will Need to Register with PRO-*Net*

Following is a list of what we consider the essential information fields, with a space next to each so you can pencil in the correct information and have it handy when you fill out the electronic form. When you enter the information on the PRO-*Net* web site, you must fill in all the fields designated as mandatory or your registration will not be considered complete. Note that much of the data required for CCR and PRO-*Net* registration is the same.

Name of Firm _____
Enter up to 80 characters.

EIN_____
The Employer Identification Number (EIN) is the nine-digit number that companies use for income tax purposes and is the same as the U.S. Federal TIN called for on the CCR form. Answers to questions about EIN numbers can be obtained from the IRS at http://www.irs.ustreas.gov/prod/bus_info/pub1635.html.

Caution

When entering the EIN on the PRO-Net web site, use the format: 99-9999999. Also, be careful when entering your EIN because, once entered, you cannot change it without contacting the SBA.

Main Office or Branch Office _____
You can have only one main office in PRO-*Net*, but you can register multiple branch offices with different addresses, phone numbers, etc. Be careful when indicating whether the profile is for a main office or a branch office because, once entered, you cannot change it without contacting the SBA. If you're not sure whether you are already registered in PRO-*Net*, you can search before registering.

Address _____
Enter up to 60 characters.

City _____
Enter up to 30 characters.

State _____
Select from the drop down list on the form

Zip Code _____
Use the format: 999999 or 99999-9999

Phone Number _____

Use the format: 999-999-9999

Fax Number _____

Enter either your fax number or e-mail, up to 50 characters in either case. For fax number, use the format: 999-999-9999

SIC Codes _____

To look up codes pertinent to your business, see the discussion of SIC codes under CCR registration.

Enter up to 25 SIC codes, each up to 4 numeric digits, separated by a comma and a space, not just a space.

NAICS Codes _____

Beginning October 1, 2000, NAICS codes will replace SIC codes. They are basically the same types of codes, except NAICS codes take in the economic data of all of North America, including Canada, Mexico and the United States.

Although the PRO-*Net* system will still use SIC codes for some time during the transition, we recommend that you begin using the NAICS codes after October 1, 2000.

Enter up to 25 NAICS codes, each up to 6 numeric digits, separated by a comma and a space, not just a space.

Keywords _____

Remember that buying offices will be searching by keyword to identify prospective contractors that are capable of matching their needs. Therefore, try to think like the government buying offices think and use words that describe the end products or services your company provides and is capable of providing.

Enter up to 25 words, each up to 20 characters, separated by a comma and a space. (Example: ELECTRICAL, PLUMBING, INSTALLATION, REPAIR.)

Password _____

The password must be a minimum of 6 and a maximum of 30 characters long. Your password can include any printable character, including spaces and punctuation characters. However, it may not include the double-quote.

DECIPHERING GOVERNMENT CODES

Anyone who does business with the government can't help but be confused at times by the different types of codes that the government uses to identify, classify and inventory the products and services that it uses. However, it is important for you to understand the importance and purpose of each type.

Federal Supply Code

The FSC (Federal Supply Code) is a four-digit code used by government buying offices to classify and identify the products, supplies, and services that the government uses and buys. An understanding of which FSCs apply to your products or services is crucial to finding opportunities. For instance, you will need to know the FSCs that apply to your products in order to register to do business with the government.

And since government buyers often use the registration databases to identify the companies that can meet their needs for products and services, it is important that you know all of the FSCs that apply to your company's end products so buyers can find you. Knowing the appropriate FSCs will also help you identify which buying offices issue contracts for the item.

In addition, you can do marketing research based on the FSC when reviewing the buying forecasts that the buying office issues. All four digits of a product code are numeric, for example 1015. In this example, 10 designates a weapon item. The second two numbers, 15, identify the size of the weapon item—in this instance, 75mm through 125mm.

Service codes are alpha/numeric, from "A" to "Z," with "I" and "O" not used. Three numbers are added to the alpha to further define what type of service is needed. For example, in the service code D308, the D3 indicates that the general type of service is Automatic Data Processing and Telecommunication Services, and the 08 indicates that the specific service is Programming Services. In another example—R608—the R means that the general type of service is Professional, Administrative and Management Support Services, and the 608 means that the specific service is Translation and Interpreting Services (including sign language).

Work Smart

Need help finding the FSC codes that apply to your products and services? The government issues a manual called the "Product and Services Codes Manual" that lists all the service and product codes. Look up your end product(s) in the manual and make a note of the code(s). Knowing the codes that apply to your capabilities will not only help you identify the government buying offices that have a need for your product or service, but will also help you register and search for bid opportunities.

The Product and Services Codes Manual is free. Just call the Federal Procurement Data Center at 202-401-1529 to request a copy.

You may also search for applicable FSC codes by keyword on the Internet at www.ecrc.uofs.edu/fsc-codes/fsc.html.

National Stock Number

The NSN (National Stock Number) is the 13-digit number that the federal government assigns, for purposes of identification and inventory control, to every piece of supply, equipment and material that it uses and buys. You can think of the NSNs as a federal cataloging system based on the concept of one NSN for any one item and one single item manager for each particular class of product. (Note that, because services are not inventoried, services don't fit this model. For services, only the first four digits are used—see discussion of FSCs, above.)

In a typical NSN—for example, 4720-00-101-9817—the first four numbers are the Federal Supply Code (FSC), which places the item in a specific category. In this example, 4720 is Pipe, Tubing, Hose, and Fittings because it starts with 47. The second two numbers, 20, identify the item as Hose and Flexible Tubing, which includes air duct, metallic, nonmetallic, and textile fiber hoses and their assemblies, etc. The next two numbers—in our example, 00—identify the country that buys the item; 00 or 01 is the code for the U.S. The remaining numbers of the NSN—101-9817—are referred to as the National Item Identification Number (NIIN) and are used to index NSNs.

How does all of this help you? Understanding the NSN, while at first somewhat of a challenge, is one of the keys that will open up some doors of opportunity for you. The NSN classification system helps to identify the offices and agencies that have control over the item and/or buy that item. Remember for this to be useful, you must know the complete NSN.

If you know the NSN, searching on the NIIN can assist you in finding previous buying trends, previous supplies, and procurement history. Also, if the NSN "gets lost," you can sometimes use the NIIN to locate where it was reassigned since the NIIN tends to remain with an item over time.

You can do an Internet search based on NSNs at http://www.dscc.dla.mil/search/NSN. A search site based on both NSNs and NIINs is at http://www.dodbusopps.com.

SIC and NAICS

The SIC (Standard Industrial Classification Code) and NAICS (North American Industry Classification System, pronounced "nakes") codes identify products and services by type of industry. They are used by the government to evaluate economic performance. The SIC is currently used to analyze economic performance in the United States, while the NAICS, which replace the SICs effective October 1, 2000, will establish a standard to be used to compare economic data for the United States, Canada, and Mexico. The standards are established by the Department of Commerce and utilized by other government offices to gather and analyze the information.

You will need to know the codes that apply to your business in order to register with the government. Being able to identify all the SIC codes that apply to your capabilities is important to your success in doing business with the government. For example, government buyers looking for contractors use the SIC codes of the products and services they wish to buy when searching for businesses profiled on the Pro-*Net* system.

You can access the SIC manual on the Internet through the Small Business Administration's home page (www.sba.gov) or through your public library.

To find your SIC code, look for your industry and then go down the list to see where you fit. Or you may search for your products and services by keyword on the Internet at http://www.census.gov/epcd/www/naics.html.

Officially, NAICS codes should be used after October 1, 2000, although SIC codes will probably be used for some time during the transition.

Chapter 9

Find Bid Leads

OK, let's get down to the nitty gritty. How do you go about finding leads on all those millions of contracts that the federal government awards each year? We discuss several ways:

- Read the *Commerce Business Daily*

- Get included on Solicitation Mailing Lists

- Search SUB-*Net*

- Use Electronic Bulletin Boards

- Check agency bid boards

- Submit an unsolicited proposal

- Get registered on qualification lists

READ *COMMERCE BUSINESS DAILY*

When looking for bid leads, keep in mind that the government is actually required to help you. The Federal Acquisition Regulation (FAR) requires the government to inform all prospective contractors of contracting opportunities and specifies several methods of doing so. One of the most common ways in which the government meets this requirement is by posting notices in *Commerce Business Daily* (*CBD*), and, therefore, one of the main ways prospective contractors can find out about contracting opportunities is to religiously read the *CBD*.

Published by the Department of Commerce, *CBD* lists notices of proposed government procurement actions, contract awards, sales of government property, and other procurement information. A new edition of *CBD* is issued every business day. Each edition contains approximately 500-1000 notices, and each notice appears in *CBD* only once.

All federal procurement offices are required to announce in *CBD*, at least 15 days before issuance of a solicitation, virtually all proposed procurement actions over $25,000. Government agencies are also required to publish information on subcontracting opportunities, including the names and addresses of firms awarded contracts over $25,000 that are likely to result in subcontracts. The solicitations must allow at least 30 days for prospective contractors to respond (45 days to respond to research and development proposals).

There are exceptions to the notice requirements. For example, *CBD* usually does not list procurement notices when the supplies or services are classified or are required immediately due to an emergency.

Many procurement announcements are reserved for—or "set aside"— for small businesses, minority-owned businesses, and women-owned firms, and they are listed as such.

CBD announcements cover both services and supplies that the federal government wants to purchase, plus the information you need to make an informed offer, including:

- the specific service or product wanted

- the buying agency

- the due date for offers

- the phone number of the agency contact

- the addresses for obtaining complete specifications

- any web page information available.

Classification Codes

Notices of contract opportunities that appear in *CBD* are arranged by Federal Supply Codes (FSC). Classification codes are divided into two groups:

1. service codes (alpha or alpha/numeric)

2. supplies, equipment and material codes (numeric)

The contracting officer, not *CBD*, determines the appropriate classification code for a particular notice. Therefore, the contracting officer is the one held responsible if a notice of a contract is misclassified and, as a result, fails to effectively notify the firms most likely to respond.

The list of service and supply codes can be found on the Internet at http://www.dlsc.dla.mil. It includes titles and examples for all codes.

Numbered Notes

When you read a notice in *CBD*, you will often see references to numbered notes within the text. (For example, you may see such phrases as "Notes 12 and 26 apply" or "See Note(s) 22 and 23.")

The purpose of these numbered notes, which are similar to footnotes, is to avoid the unnecessary repetition of information in various announcements. Whenever a numbered note is included in a notice, the note referred to must be read as part of the item or section in which it appears.

A complete listing of numbered notes and their meaning is included in Appendix 7.

Work Smart

Remember as you look through bid leads in Commerce Business Daily *that each one identifies a buying office and a personal contact. What a great marketing tool! If the item or service isn't exactly what you sell, you still have a contact to call to learn more about the buyer's needs.*

Also, be sure and check out the "Award Notices" section of CBD. *This section will give you several pieces of valuable information: a buying office, what was bought, the value paid, and who received the contract. In other words, it gives you a government buying office to contact, an idea of the price paid so you know how competitive you need to be, and the name of your competition and/or subcontract lead.*

Potential Sources Sought

Look for the "Potential Sources Sought" heading in *CBD* to find special *advance* notices of particular procurement opportunities.

These synopses provide you with an opportunity to submit information that will permit your capabilities to be evaluated while allowing the government to gauge interest in possible contracts. Responding is very important if a particular community (e.g., small businesses, minority-owned small businesses, women-owned small businesses, or historically black colleges and universities/minority institutions, etc.) desires a set-aside. The decision to set a project aside is often made on the basis of responses received to these Potential Sources Sought synopses.

Business News

To find out about important upcoming meetings and conferences dealing with federal procurement activities, including pre-proposal and bidders' conferences, look for the "Business News" heading in *CBD*. These meetings are great places to market your capabilities, identify the competition and structure potential teaming arrangements.

Three Forms of *CBD*: Print vs. Electronic vs. Internet

Commerce Business Daily *is the primary source used to identify business opportunities from the government and is available in hard copy (print), electronic and Internet form.*

***Print* CBD** — *If you use the hard copy of* CBD, *you will basically have to read it from cover to cover, or at least scan all of the product and service codes of interest to you. The print is small, so it can be a tough job. An annual subscription to the print version will cost you several hundred dollars.*

To subscribe to a hard copy of CBD, *contact:*

> *Commerce Business Daily*
> *Superintendent of Documents*
> *U.S. Government Printing Office*
> *Washington, DC 20402-9371*
> *Telephone: (202) 512-1800*
> *Fax: (202) 512-2250*

The print CBD is also available at many public libraries in their "Business Reference" section.

***Electronic* CBD** — *If you use the electronic version of* CBD, *you can limit your research time by searching in only those areas of interest. But probably the best way to use the electronic version is to use a Procurement Technical Assistance Center (PTAC) and receive bid leads and award information based upon a profile of your company's interests. The PTAC uses a combination of federal supply/service codes and appropriate keywords to locate bid leads, and then uses the profile information to decide which ones should go to you. Your profile may need to be adjusted from time to time to make sure you are receiving the leads you are interested in.*

You can get the electronic version for a small registration fee.

***Internet* CBD** — *The entire* Commerce Business Daily *is now available on the Internet at several sites. (Search for* "Commerce Business Daily" *to locate them.) You or anybody in your organization can search* CBD *even before it has been published in hard copy. Search every day, once a week, or whenever you wish—a full year's worth is available online. And the "search routines" are designed specifically for* CBD, *so your searches are simple and effective.*

The Internet version is available for a small registration fee.

CBD *is also available online at many public libraries, local business development centers, and Procurement Technical Assistance Centers.*

GET INCLUDED ON SOLICITATION MAILING LISTS

Another way of receiving bid leads is to get your company included on the Solicitation Mailing List (SML) of the specific buying offices likely to have a need for your product or service. The SML database lists the capabilities of businesses interested in selling to the government, and thus enables a buying office to find potential sources to meet its needs for products and services.

We have been told that this method is being used more now, given the recent changes in rules and regulations that require the use of simplified acquisition procedures or micro-purchasing procedures for contracts between $2,500 and $25,000.

Once again, using the target list of prospective customers that you put together in Chapter 7, make an effort to contact them. Be sure to contact the small business specialist at each agency to make sure you do what is necessary to be listed on the appropriate SML.

When the SML is extremely long, the purchasing agency may use only a portion of it for a particular acquisition and rotate the other segments of the list for other acquisitions. In such situations, the regulations require that a prorated number of small businesses be solicited.

Work Smart

Contracting for architect-engineering (A-E) and construction services follows a special procedure and does not use SMLs. For government contracts, A-E firms are selected on the basis of the professional qualifications necessary to perform the required services satisfactorily. Construction companies are selected in a similar manner. Firms interested in such work should file Form SF 254, "Architect-Engineer and Related Services Questionnaire" (attainable from any federal government buying office or PTAC), with the agency responsible for the geographic area(s) or specialized area of construction in which the firm desires to work.

Remember that sometimes there is a geographical limit on who will be considered for an award.

SEARCH SUB-*NET*

SUB-*Net* is a relatively new Small Business Administration web site on which large businesses, government agencies, and other prime contractors post solicitations and bid opportunities.

This is a good place for small businesses to search and view bid opportunities. Small businesses may also register in this area to post a bid opportunity, but only if they are seeking teaming partners or subcontractors for a specific procurement that they would not be able to perform alone.

To access SUB-*Net*, click on "Subcontracting Opportunities" on the SBA PRO-*Net* home page at http://pro-net.sba.gov/.

When searching, again remember to think like the government. Choose search terms that have to do with your end products, not your process.

USE ELECTRONIC BULLETIN BOARDS

The Departments of the Army, Navy and Air Force, as well as various other Department of Defense (DoD) organizations and agencies, use electronic bulletin boards (EBBs) to inform the public about contracting opportunities, provide details of government solicitations, and respond to questions about solicitations. EBBs also permit electronic submission of bids and proposals.

Unfortunately, to use EBBs, you will have to register at each particular site. So bear with the redundancy for now. As the government gets the Central Contractor Registration (CCR) running up to speed, the need to register again and again hopefully will fade. (Note: For now, you will need your tax ID, DUNS and CAGE numbers, as well as other information to register at DoD sites.)

In a typical bulletin board, the government posts a Request for Quote. Interested businesses can submit standard paper quotes or, in some cases, electronic quotes for the buyer to review. Most of the remaining documentation is still on paper. When this book went to press, there were still some agencies that were using electronic bulletin boards, but except for smaller buying offices, we believe that they will eventually become a thing of the past and will be replaced with an Internet version.

Example

The EBB was the original system for transmitting information via computer and modem connecting to a special network through the use of telephone lines. The use of EBBs was largely the result of the Federal Acquisition Streamlining Act of 1994, which required the government to convert from an acquisition process driven by paperwork to an expedited process based on electronic data interchange (EDI).

CHECK AGENCY BID BOARDS

Bid boards, while still used by some buying agencies to post bid opportunities, are becoming a thing of the past, as the Internet becomes more a part of business life.

In the "old days," every DoD buying office maintained, in a public place, a bid board on which it displayed a copy of each small purchase solicitation it issued for contracts valued at less than $25,000. Every notice was posted on the bid board for seven calendar days. If it was impractical to post a copy of the entire solicitation, the bid board notice offered a brief description and the location of the full text version.

There are still agencies that use bid boards, and you can hire an individual in the area to visit the bid board and monitor it for you. That individual can either send you everything on the board or pick and choose for you. At one time, we had twelve of these prospectors getting bids for our clients. It worked, but was expensive and time-consuming.

SUBMIT AN UNSOLICITED PROPOSAL

Sometimes you can create your own contracting opportunities by submitting an unsolicited proposal. Such a proposal is a written offer to the government to perform a task or effort that you initiate. To be considered, an unsolicited proposal must offer a unique and innovative concept to the government. You can learn about an agency's research and development (R&D) needs from advance notices in *CBD* and from informal contacts with agency personnel.

The FAR provides general guidance for submitting an unsolicited proposal. The proposal should contain an abstract of the proposed effort, the method of approach, and the extent of the effort. It should also include a proposed price or estimated cost. You should clearly mark any proprietary data you wish to protect from possible release to others.

These regulations allow the government to use other-than-competitive procurement procedures when they receive a favorably evaluated unsolicited proposal. They also require that the prospective contractors be notified of government's intentions regarding the proposal.

If you're not sure what specific buying office might be really interested in the item or service, then send it to the headquarters operation in Washington, D.C. For example, for the Department of Army, instead of sending a proposal to the electronics command, send it to headquarters, U.S. Army in Washington. For the civilian side, it would be similar. For example, instead of sending a proposal to the Chicago regional area of the FAA, send it to FAA Operations in Washington, D.C.

GET REGISTERED ON QUALIFICATION LISTS

A less common way to receive bid leads is by getting registered on a qualified product list (QPL), a qualified manufacturers list (QML), or a qualified bidders list. Qualification lists are used only for products that require lengthy or costly testing to determine whether they meet the government's requirements. The lists identify the specifications and the manufacturers or distributors of each qualified item. When the government wishes to procure a product for which a qualification list exists, bids or proposals are usually accepted only for specific products or from companies on the list.

To have your product or your company included on a qualification list, contact the small business specialist responsible for qualification at the buying office identified in the product specification.

If all else fails, you can always get help from a bid-matching service or your local PTAC office. These methods are discussed in detail in Chapter 7.

Chapter 10

Get the Bid Package

Once you have found a bid that you are interested in, the next step is to get the bid package (it is also sometimes referred to as a solicitation package). Getting the bid package is often as easy as downloading something off the Internet.

GETTING THE SPECIFICS

To get the package, you can do one of the following:

- Contact the buyer and request the bid package. The buyer's name, address, phone number, and e-mail address are listed on the bid notice. When you request the bid package, also ask for any amendments that might have been issued.

- Locate the web page address in the bid notice and download the bid package off the Internet. A word of caution: Before you start downloading, double-check the number of the bid contract you have selected for download to make sure it's the right one. (The solicitation number will be something like: DAA123-00-R-1234. Or it may say: SOL: or SOL Number.) Proceed carefully; all of the numbers sometimes start to look the same.

CONTRACTS AND PRICING ARRANGEMENTS

When requesting a bid package, you need to be familiar with the types of contracts—or pricing arrangements—that the government uses in buying a product or service. The type of contract used is determined by the circumstances of the acquisition and the extent to which the government wishes to accept the cost risks. The contract type used will have an important effect on the way you price out the contract (see Chapter 13). These pricing arrangements reflect the risk involved in contract performance.

There are three basic categories of contracts:

1. fixed-price

2. cost-reimbursement

3. special situation

Fixed-Price Contracts

These are the types of contracts that small businesses will, for the most part, be dealing with. Under the fixed-price arrangement, the final price is basically determined before the work is performed. There are various types of fixed-price contracts:

- **Firm fixed-price:** The price is not subject to adjustment. The contractor is obligated to perform the contract at the awarded price and accepts 100 percent of the profit or loss of performing the contract within that price.

- **Fixed-price with economic price adjustment:** The price may be adjusted upward or downward based upon the occurrence of contractually specified economic contingencies that are clearly outside the contractor's control.

- **Fixed-price incentive:** The profit is adjusted and the final price is established by a formula based on the relationship of the final negotiated cost to the target cost.

- **Firm fixed-price, level-of-effort:** A fixed price is established for a specified level of effort over a stated time frame. If the level varies beyond specified thresholds, the price may be adjusted.

Cost-Reimbursement Contracts

Cost-reimbursement contracts provide for the final price to be determined either when the work is finished or at some interim point during contract performance. If a contract is cost-reimbursable, the contractor can legally stop work when all contract funds are spent. Thus, the cost risk is essentially shifted to the government. There are various types of cost-reimbursement contracts:

- **Cost:** Reimbursement consists of allowable cost; there is no fee provision.

- **Cost-sharing:** An agreed portion of allowable cost is reimbursed.

- **Cost-plus-fixed-fee:** Reimbursement is based on allowable cost plus a fixed fee.

- **Cost-plus-incentive-fee:** Reimbursement consists of allowable cost incurred and a fee adjusted by a formula based on the relationship of the allowable cost to the target cost.

- **Cost-plus-award fee:** Reimbursement consists of allowable cost incurred and a two-part fee (a fixed amount and an award amount based on an evaluation of the quality of contract performance).

Special Situation Contracts

There are also special types of contracts, including:

- **Time and material:** Direct labor hours expended are reimbursed at fixed hourly rates, which usually include direct labor costs, indirect expenses and profit. Material costs are reimbursed at actual cost plus a handling charge, if applicable.

- **Labor hour:** Direct labor hours expended are reimbursed at a fixed hourly rate, usually including all cost and profit.

- **Definite-quantity:** The contract quantity is defined, but the delivery schedule is flexible. Payment is made on some form of fixed-price basis.

- **Requirements:** Actual delivery schedules and quantities are flexible during the contract period. Payment is based on a predetermined fixed-price basis.

Chapter 11

Review the Bid

Here is where you get to look at your first bid package. And here is where we let you in on the secret to winning and making a profit on the contract you are bidding on:

Read the bid. Then read it again. And after you think you're finished, read it again.

Why is this so important? In most cases, when you submit your bid, all you have to do is fill in some of the blanks on the forms contained in the package and send the package back to the government. But here's the catch: Even though the government itself generated and provided the package, when you send it back to the government, it becomes *your* offer, and the government will look at it as if you had put the entire package together yourself and as if they had never seen it before.

Therefore, you need to understand what's in the bid package because it is more than a solicitation for a bid—if and when the government signs it, it is also your *binding contract*. That means that you must carefully check out *all* portions of the contract, not just the description and specification portion. That also means that you can't just gloss over parts that you do not completely understand—you need to take notes as you go so you can address those parts later on.

The package contains all the information you need in order to bid intelligently—all you need to do is read it.

Example

A small safety equipment company had been doing government work for the military and doing quite well at it. When the owner died unexpectedly, the owner's widow and son continued running the business. Later, they received a bid package for a stretcher for the Navy, and since this was an item that they supplied, they submitted a bid and won the small dollar purchase order.

When the inspector came out to check the stretchers before shipment, the owners discovered that they had made a very serious error. The requirement in the contract called for more than a stretcher—it also called for the stretcher to be enclosed in a hanging unit for use on the wall of a ship—a requirement that they had missed because they didn't read the bid carefully. And since their bid reflected the cost of the stretcher, not the added cost of the hanging unit, completion of the contract at the price quoted would have broken their company.

We recommended that they try to plead their case to the commander at the buying office and ask to be let out of the contract. Luckily for them, the commander must have been having a good day and cancelled the contract—a very rare occurrence for the government.

So, not reading the bid carefully could have cost the owners their business. They were lucky, but you may not be if you fail to carefully review the contract.

Types of Bids/Solicitations

Solicitation packages usually range anywhere from 10 to 50 or more pages, depending on dollar value, the Statement of Work and other requirements. They will include clauses and instructions and other information that will tell you the who, what, where and how of the contract.

The first six positions of a solicitation number (e.g., DAA123-00-R-1234) identify the department or agency issuing the document, the next two positions (e.g., 00) are the last two digits of the fiscal year issued, and the single alpha character (e.g., R) identifies the type of solicitation. For example, B= Invitation for Bid, P= Purchase Order, C= Contract, Q= Request for Quote, R= Request for Proposal, etc. The last four positions identify the sequential order for a particular solicitation.

Bids with an alpha of Q or T are for requirements under $100,000. Usually T bids do not have technical data packages included with them, so if you want to bid on them you are looking at reverse engineering a product or trying to go to the original manufacturer and getting the technical data from them . . . lot's of luck!

The bid package you receive will most likely come in one of three forms:

- **Invitation for Bid (IFB)** — An IFB is an advertised contract, also referred to as a "Sealed bid." There are no discussions, and the bid package is considered complete for bidding purposes. The price is a major consideration, and the signing of the solicitation form—Standard Form 33 (SF 33)—by the bidder and by the government creates a binding document. The solicitation number will look something like DAAE20-00-B-1234, with the "B" in the number indicating it is a sealed bid. It is competitive and the low bid will get it. Also, it is probably worth more than $100,000 in value.

- **Request for Proposal (RFP)** — An RFP is a negotiated contract. There will be discussions, and the bidder may get the opportunity to change bid pricing, technical requirements, etc. As with the IFB, above, the SF 33 is the form that will be used and, again, becomes a binding contract when both the bidder and the government sign. The solicitation number will look something like N00023-00-R-1234, with the "R" in the number indicating it is a negotiated solicitation. Price and other factors will determine the winner. Here again the value is probably more than $100,000.

- **Request for Quote (RFQ)** — An RFQ is a request for information that may include price, but is not a binding contract or document. This is also considered a negotiated bid because the government will want to talk over the information obtained. The number will look something like F62509-00-Q-1234, with the "Q" indicating the solicitation is for information and prices. It is negotiated and may be valued at greater than $100,000. If a contract is made, the government will use a Standard Form 26, Award/Contract.

Common Government Forms

Here are some of the more common forms that you may encounter in bidding on government work. (In Chapter 14, we'll help you fill out some of these forms.)

DD Form 1707, **Information to Offerors or Quoters**, *is a form used by the Defense Department along with the SF 33. It is used by bidders to indicate no response to the solicitation and provides the buying office with various pieces of information such as why you are not bidding.*

Standard Form 33, **Solicitation, Offer and Award**, *is a solicitation/contract form used by the federal government not only to solicit offers but also to award a contract since it is a bi-lateral (i.e., two-signature) document. This means that the bidder signs the document and submits it to the government and, upon acceptance of the bid, the government signs the same document and a binding contract is established. This form is used for either sealed bids or negotiated contracts valued at $100,000 or more.*

Standard Form 26, **Award/Contract**, *is a form used by the federal government to award a contract, usually as the result of a Request for Quotation. Both parties sign, but it requires references to the basic solicitation and/or other documents. In general, the SF 26 and SF 33 ask for similar information to be filled in, but the SF 26 requires some certification information that is not required on the SF 33.*

Standard Form 30, **Amendment of Solicitation/Modification of Contract**, *is a form used to do what its title implies: amend a solicitation before it closes or modify a contract that has been awarded. Normally this form is filled out by the government and is then sent to the bidder or contractor for signature.*

Standard Form 18, **Request for Quotation**, *is used to obtain information and quotations, but the responses are not considered offers. A SF 26 is sometimes used to award a contract resulting from the use of a SF 18.*

Standard Form 1449, **Solicitation /Contract/Order for Commercial Items**, *is used to buy commercial items when the simplified acquisition procedures are used. It can also be used to ship and receive product.*

HOW TO READ A TYPICAL BID

Let's take a closer look at a typical bid using a common form as an example—Standard Form 33 (SF 33)—and we'll show you how to look for what is important.

The SF 33 is divided into four major parts:

- **Blocks 1-8** — The first part contains basic information about the solicitation and is filled in by the government buying office. (Block 2, the contract number, is not filled in by the government until award is made.)

- **Blocks 9-11** — The second part is the Solicitation area. Block 11, Table of Contents, is very important. The sections of Block 11, *when taken together*, make up the whole solicitation and resulting contract. For example, it contains specific information about the solicitation and also the place where you will enter your bid price.

- **Blocks 12-18** — The third part is the Offer area and is filled in and signed by the bidder before returning the offer to the buying office.

- **Blocks 19-28** — The fourth part is the Award area and is completed and signed by the government when it makes the award.

Caution

We strongly recommend that, when reading a bid, you read it in a particular order. Certain sections are related to each other, and it will be much more efficient and understandable if you read them together.

Here is the order we recommend for reading SF 33:

Identify which sections of the form apply to the particular bid. We begin our reading of the bid by first taking a careful look at Block 11, Table of Contents. We begin here because the Table of Contents identifies all the applicable sections that will make up the contents of the subsequent contract. For instance, Section B (see below) of Block 11 tells you what is being bought and provides the place where you will put your bid price.

Note that the Table of Contents is divided into the following four parts:

Part I	The Schedule
Part II	Contract Clauses
Part III	List of Documents, Exhibits, and Other Attachments
Part IV	Representations and Instructions

Each Part is further broken out into several sections. Here is a sample Table of Contents for Part I. *Note that all the various sections may or may not apply; a check mark or "x" in the left column will let you know which do.*

Section A	Solicitation/Contract Form
Section B	Supplies or Services and Prices/Costs
Section C	Description/Specification/Work Statement
Section E	Inspection and Acceptance
Section F	Deliveries or Performance
Section G	Contract Administration Data
Section H	Special Contract Requirements
Section I	Contract Clauses
Section K	Representations, Certifications and Other Statements of Offerors
Section L	Instructions, Conditions and Notices to Offerors
Section M	Evaluation Factors for Award

Note that the majority of pages consist of the Part I The Schedule, Table of Contents; and Part II Contract Clauses. Part III List of Documents itemizes all the attachments included with the solicitation. Part IV Representations and Instructions contains the solicitation provisions that require completion by the bidder, and the information and instructions to guide bidders in preparing proposals, such as evaluation factors for award.

Find out the government's needs and specs. The first—and most important—sections you should review are Part I Section B (Supplies or Services and Prices/Costs) and Part IV Section L (Instructions, Conditions and Notices to Offerors). These sections are crucial, so read them together carefully and check out the information to see whether this is a product or service that you can provide, and whether you comply with the requirements. Take notes!

Assess the evaluation factors. Next, read Part IV, Section L (Instructions, Conditions and Notices to Offerors) and Section M (Evaluation Factors for Award). (Note that you just read Section L in the preceding step, but you need to read it a second time in conjunction with Section M.) These sections tell you which factors the government is going to use in evaluating the bids and making its decision for award, such as key personnel, technical capability, or financial or transportation resources. Check the factors carefully to see whether your company is deficient in any area. If it is, correct the problem before you send in the bid or do not bid on the solicitation. Remember that you must consider all the factors in the contract, not just some. Take notes!

Determine the general and specific requirements of the contract. The next areas to review are Part I, Section C (Description, Specifications and Work Statement), and Part I, Section J (List of Attachments). Section C gives you the general specifications of what the government is looking for. Check the specs carefully; you must be able to comply with all of them. Note that sometimes you may find some inconsistencies between the requirements in Section C and the requirements in Section J. That's because Section J contains the attachments to the bid, which could include changes that affect the work statement in Section C. In general, Section C contains the general requirements for the contract, while Section J contains the specific requirements. It is imperative that you read *both* sections carefully! Be sure to take notes!

If you have any questions, you must address them before award of the contract or, if issued under sealed bid procedures, before the bid opening. If you sign the contract in the hopes that the government will accept something else afterward, you are betting on a really dead horse.

Check out the technical and special requirements. Now read Part II Section I (Contract Clauses); and Part I Section H (Special Contract Requirements), Section D (Packaging and Marking), Section E (Inspection and Acceptance), Section F (Deliveries or Performance) and Section G (Contract Administration Data). These sections provide all the technical requirements on which you will need to perform. Check the packaging requirements in Section D carefully and, if necessary, work with someone knowledgeable in government packaging and marking. Some of the requirements might sound extreme, but remember (especially if the part, product or assembly is for the military) that the item may have to withstand extreme conditions (e.g., battlefield, being dropped out of a plane, hitting a beach at 30 miles per hour, etc).

In some cases, both the military and civilian offices have recently loosened up on some of their special packaging and packing requirements. Packaging standards in the commercial market are often just as good or better than government standards, so commercial items are now often accepted as they come from the supplier. Also, the government is moving toward an "as needed basis" mentality – in other words, the government no longer stocks items as it did in the past, which permits less stringent packaging requirements.

Read the certification provisions. Finally, read Part IV, Section K (Representations, Certifications and Other Statements of Offerors). Here is where you certify that you are a small, minority, or women-owned business; that you have not been debarred by the government; that you are an Equal Employment Opportunity business; and that you agree to certain other policies or programs of the government.

Remember that you must read each and every applicable section of each and every Part, word for word, and understand the information contained in each in order to be able to bid intelligently on the solicitation.

Chapter 12

Get Technical Data

Now that you have reviewed and understand the contents of the bid package, it's time to start gathering information needed to complete the offer, including the technical data related to a particular bid.

Technical data is comprised of the specifications and standards, such as engineering design and manufacturing documents and drawings, that describe the requirements for a material, product or service. It also includes the criteria for determining whether those requirements are met.

Under federal regulations, the specs cover only the government's actual minimum needs in a manner to encourage maximum practicable competition. The government uses a spec only when it knows exactly what it wants and needs. With the recent changes in acquisition policy, more requirements will be based on commercial specifications and standards.

TYPES OF GOVERNMENT SPECS

There are two categories of government specifications:

- **Federal Specifications** — These cover materials, products or services used by more then two federal agencies. They are issued by the General Services Administration (GSA) and must be used by all federal agencies. Federal specifications can be obtained from a GSA Business Center near you. See Appendix 2 to locate one.

- **Military Specifications** — These cover items or services that are intrinsically military in character or commercial items modified to meet special requirements of the military. They are distributed by Naval Publications and Forms Center (NPFC), located in Philadelphia, PA. NPFC stocks and issues

Department of Defense printed and digital matter without charge to federal agencies and the general public. Documents distributed by NPFC include military specifications and standards, federal specifications and standards, Qualified Product Lists (QPLs), Military Handbooks, and Departmental Documents.

GETTING CORRECT SPECS

These days, finding specs and standards can be as easy as logging onto a subscription service on the Internet. Subscription services can get you the specs quickly and easily, but at a hefty price tag. On the other hand, your local Procurement Technical Assistance Center (PTAC) can provide you with the specs you need and, in most cases, will either charge only a small fee or provide them for free. Either way, it ensures that you get the specs required by the solicitation.

Caution

If there appears to be a conflict or question about what specs are required, get it resolved immediately. Whatever you do, don't try to second-guess the government. We can cite case after case where a contractor made a wrong assumption about a spec and it ended up costing the contractor big money.

Normally when you order the solicitation from the buying office, it will send the necessary technical data package with it unless the documents are considered common and are only referenced. If the buying office doesn't send the tech information, then you will have to contact the resource identified in the solicitation. Because of the government's shift to the Internet and e-commerce environment, the solicitation may include a web site where you can download the necessary documents and the appropriate readers for the drawings.

One web site to check out for information on specs and standards is the Department of Defense Business Opportunities site at http://dodbusopps.com. This site serves as a gateway for DoD requirements and is trying to be the Internet site of preference for getting bids, specs, technical packages, and other information that you need to bid on DoD contracts.

(We want to note that there are some great things about this site, but the government puts out literally millions of bids each year and we don't know whether any one site can handle all of that information. We think that, in the future, there may be a number of "portal" sites that will have the info you need.)

Work Smart

You may also want to think about developing your own library of the specs and standards that you use most often, either in hard copy or electronic format. When you find a good site on the Internet for specs and standards, remember to bookmark it for later visits. Government specifications are required on a large number of items. Check out what is required on the bids that interest you and start to build your library. It will be very helpful to you in the long run.

Chapter 13

Price It Out

This is the one step in the contracting process where you are the expert and we are not. Given that there are so many different types of businesses out there and so many different ways of pricing, our best advice is to be as competitive as possible.

The old stories of $200 toilet seats and $300 hammers are simply that—old history—and you better believe that you have to sharpen your pencil as much as possible in order to be competitive.

COMMON PRICING FACTORS

At the same time, however, you also need to make sure that you cover all of your costs and protect your profit. Here are some things to consider in determining your price:

- **Consider Pricing History** — You can often get pricing history from the buying office by asking the Point of Contact identified in the contract (Block 10 if you are using Form SF 33). You can also contact a Procurement Technical Assistance Center and ask it to run a computer review of pricing history for an item. If you are bidding on a service, it becomes more difficult to get good pricing history. You need to know the previous contract number and then make sure the statement of work is the same.

- **Cost Out All Special Requirements** — The buyer may ask for many costly extras. Especially watch out for packaging requirements—they can be expensive. Don't just stick on a percentage of the cost of the item to cover packaging.

- **Think Carefully about Quality Requirements** — Will any of the certifications and acknowledgments add on extra costs?

- **Factor in Bidding Costs** — Some offers are rather simple and straightforward, but as the value of the contract increases, more time and labor are usually required. As a general rule of thumb, you can estimate that the cost of putting together an offer will run 3 to 4 percent of the value of the proposed contract. Make sure current finances can handle that cost.

- **Don't Forget Overhead and Profit** — Make sure your profit is reasonable. Remember that the bidding process is very competitive. You are free to figure in as high a profit as you wish, but you must win the contract to enjoy it. Never bid if it doesn't make good business sense.

Caution

Federal Acquisition Regulation (FAR) Part 15 discusses negotiations and costs for contracts of $100,000 or more and looks at allowable and allocable costs. If you are going to be submitting a proposal over $100,000, either bone up on the FAR in this area or get an accountant who is familiar with government contracting.

Again, we want to remind you to carefully read the solicitation and make notes on points you don't understand. Then go ask the questions. Go to the buyer or Point of Contact identified in the contract, the small business specialist at the buying office, or a Procurement Technical Assistance Center. But please ask someone! The answers could significantly affect your price—and your profit.

Chapter 14

Write Your Proposal

Once you have reviewed the bid, received the specs, gotten pricing history, and priced out the items or services, you are ready to put it all together and write your proposal.

There are two situations that you should be prepared for:

- Writing a proposal when the solicitation is an Invitation for Bid

- Writing a proposal when the solicitation is a negotiated bid, such as a Request for Proposal.

WRITING A PROPOSAL FOR AN IFB

When the solicitation is an Invitation for Bid, which is the case most of the time for small businesses, writing your proposal will consist of filling out the forms that you received from the government in the bid package and sending them in.

But it's not as simple as it sounds. Even though all you basically have to do is fill in some blanks on forms that the government has provided and send back the bid package, you must still be very careful. As we pointed out earlier, *when you send back the bid package, the government will look at it as if you had put it together yourself and as if they are seeing it for the first time.*

To give you a first-hand look at some of the standard forms that you can expect to see with an IFB, we are reproducing some of the more common ones, along with a line-by-line explanation of how to fill them in.

Filling out DD Form 1707

The first form that we will look at is DD Form 1707, *Information to Offerors or Quoters*. This is the cover sheet that accompanies the solicitation itself and is mainly informational. One of its main purposes is to gather information on why a company does not want to bid. This form is used for most Department of Defense (DoD) large dollar solicitations, which are those over $100,000.

Let's start with the cover page and proceed block by block.

Block 1: Solicitation Number — We are using the example number SP0700-00-Q-HE22. This is the number that will identify this specific solicitation throughout the life of the buying action. Any amendments to the solicitation will use this number plus the amendment number as the identifier.

SP0700, the first six alpha/numeric sequence, identifies the buying office where the order originates. The second grouping—00—is the fiscal year the solicitation was issued. The single alpha character Q indicates what type of solicitation it is. For example, B= Invitation for Bid, P= Purchase Order, C= Contract, Q= Request for Quote, R= Request for Proposal, etc. The last alpha/numeric sequence— HE22—is the sequential order number for that solicitation.

Block 2: Type of Solicitation — As previously mentioned, there are three types of bid packages:

- *Invitation for Bid (IFB)* — This is a method of contracting that consists of competitive bids, public opening of bids (yes, you can be there when they are opened), and award. Most of these bids are for buys over $100,000. With this type of bid, the government knows specifically what it wants, how many it wants, and where it wants them sent. The award is based on price and price-related factors.

- *Request for Proposal (RFP)* — The government uses this type of contracting when it is not sure of what it wants and is looking for a way to talk to you on how you plan to fulfill their need for the item or service. This type of bid may be competitive or non-competitive.

- *Request for Quote (RFQ)* — This method is often used to solicit prices or market information. The quote submitted does not constitute an offer. Therefore, it cannot be accepted by the government to form a binding contract. An SF 26, which is a two-signature document, would have to be used.

Form DD 1707

INFORMATION TO OFFERORS OR QUOTERS SECTION A - COVER SHEET	Form Approved OMB No. 9000-0002 Expires Sep 30, 2000

The public reporting burden for this collection of information is estimated to average 35 minutes per response, including the time for reviewing instructions, searching existing data sources, gathering and maintaining the data needed, and completing and reviewing the collection of information. Send comments regarding this burden estimate or any other aspect of this collection of information, including suggestions for reducing the burden, to Department of Defense, Washington Headquarters Services, Directorate for Information Operations and Reports (9000-0002), 1215 Jefferson Davis Highway, Suite 1204, Arlington VA 22202-4302. Respondents should be aware that notwithstanding any other provision of law, no person shall be subject to any penalty for failing to comply with a collection of information if it does not display a currently valid OMB control number.

PLEASE DO NOT RETURN YOUR FORM TO THE ABOVE ADDRESS. RETURN COMPLETED FORM TO THE ADDRESS IN BLOCK 4 BELOW.

1. SOLICITATION NUMBER	2. *(X one)*	3. DATE/TIME RESPONSE DUE
	a. INVITATION FOR BID (IFB)	
	b. REQUEST FOR PROPOSAL (RFP)	
	c. REQUEST FOR QUOTATION (RFQ)	

INSTRUCTIONS

NOTE: The provision entitled "Required Central Contractor Registration" is applicable to most solicitations.

1. If you are not submitting a response, complete the information in Blocks 9 through 11 and return to the issuing office in Block 4 unless a different return address is indicated in Block 7.

2. Responses must set forth full, accurate, and complete information as required by this solicitation (including attachments). "Fill-ins" are provided on Standard Form 18, Standard Form 33, and other solicitation documents. Examine the entire solicitation carefully. The penalty for making false statements is prescribed in 18 U.S.C. 1001.

3. Responses must be plainly marked with the Solicitation Number and the date and local time set forth for bid opening or receipt of proposals in the solicitation document.

4. Information regarding the timeliness of response is addressed in the provision of this solicitation entitled either "Late Submission, Modification and Withdrawal of Bid" or "Instructions to Offerors - Competitive Acquisitions".

4. ISSUING OFFICE *(Complete mailing address, including ZIP Code)*	5. ITEMS TO BE PURCHASED *(Brief description)*

6. PROCUREMENT INFORMATION *(X and complete as applicable)*

a. THIS PROCUREMENT IS UNRESTRICTED	
b. THIS PROCUREMENT IS _____ % SET-ASIDE FOR SMALL BUSINESS. THE APPLICABLE SIC CODE IS:	
c. THIS PROCUREMENT IS _____ % SET-ASIDE FOR HUB ZONE CONCERNS. THE APPLICABLE SIC CODE IS:	
d. THIS PROCUREMENT IS RESTRICTED TO FIRMS ELIGIBLE UNDER SECTION 8(a) OF THE SMALL BUSINESS ACT.	

7. ADDITIONAL INFORMATION

8. POINT OF CONTACT FOR INFORMATION

a. NAME *(Last, First, Middle Initial)*	b. ADDRESS *(Include Zip Code)*
c. TELEPHONE NUMBER *(Include Area Code and Extension)*	d. E-MAIL ADDRESS	

9. REASONS FOR NO RESPONSE *(X all that apply)*

a. CANNOT COMPLY WITH SPECIFICATIONS	d. DO NOT REGULARLY MANUFACTURE OR SELL THE TYPE OF ITEMS INVOLVED
b. UNABLE TO IDENTIFY THE ITEM(S)	e. OTHER *(Specify)*
c. CANNOT MEET DELIVERY REQUIREMENT	

10. MAILING LIST INFORMATION *(X one)*

WE [ ] DO [ ] DO NOT DESIRE TO BE RETAINED ON THE MAILING LIST FOR FUTURE PROCUREMENT OF THE TYPE INVOLVED.

11a. COMPANY NAME	b. ADDRESS *(Include Zip Code)*

c. ACTION OFFICER

(1) TYPED OR PRINTED NAME *(Last, First, Middle Initial)*	(2) TITLE
(3) SIGNATURE	(4) DATE SIGNED *(YYYYMMDD)*

DD FORM 1707, FEB 1999 (EG)   PREVIOUS EDITION IS OBSOLETE.   WHS/DIOR, Feb 99

Block 3: Date/Time Response Due — This information, supplied by the buying office, tells you when you need to have your offer into the buying office.

The next section titled "Instructions" contains information about responding.

Block 4: Issuing Office — This is the office that issued the solicitation.

Block 5: Item To Be Purchased — This is a brief description of what is needed.

Block 6: Procurement Information — This is where you will find out which, if any, restrictions or set-asides apply to this solicitation. It will be marked either "restricted" or "unrestricted." If it is marked "unrestricted," that means that any business—large, small, or in between—can bid on it. If it is marked "restricted," that means it is earmarked as a set-aside for either Small Business or Hub Zone Concerns, or restricted to 8(a) firms.

Block 7: Additional Information — In this block you will usually find any additional information needed to bid on the contract, such as where to send the bid, when it has to be received, who to contact or what web site to visit.

Block 8: Point of Contact Information — Here will be listed the buyer's name, address and telephone number. We should also add that, these days, you may only get an e-mail address for the buyer, and it's likely that the buyer might accept inquiries only in that form.

Block 9: Reason for No Response — As previously mentioned, if you are not going to bid on the solicitation, for whatever reason, be sure to fill out this block and send the form back to the buyer. This is very important! If you don't, you will probably be dropped from the buyer's bidders list and have to start all over again.

Caution

Most forms include a "Reason for No Response" section or block. (For example, in the case of DD Form 1707, this section is in Block 9.) If you decide not to bid on a solicitation, for whatever reason, be sure to fill out the "Reason for No Response" section of the form and send the form in anyway. The government buyer will thank you and, better yet, you will not be dropped off the bidders' list the next time an opportunity comes up. Some buyers give you only one chance. If you don't send in the form to indicate that you are not responding to a bid, you go back to "Go" and start over.

If the buyer gives you an e-mail address, you may send in your response that way, but remember to identify your company with your name, the company name, and your CAGE Code.

Block 10: Mailing List Information — Here you indicate whether you want to be left on future mailing lists for an item. Respond either yes or no.

Block 11: Responding Firm — This is you! This is where you fill in your information, including your bid price. (If necessary, review the discussion of Block 11 in Chapter 11: Review the Bid. You need to read and understand all the applicable sections.) Remember that the sections of Block 11, when taken *together*, make up the whole solicitation and resulting contract.

Back Side of Form — The back side of the form is set up as a fold-over mailer. Just address it, put your stamp on it, and drop it in the mail.

Filling out Standard Form 33 (SF 33)

Next, let's look at the Standard Form 33: *Solicitation, Offer and Award*. This is the form that is used to solicit offers and award contracts. It is referred to as a bi-lateral or two-signature document. You sign the form in Block 17, and the government signs the same form in Block 27. That establishes a binding contract.

Before you start going through our line-by-line explanation, this may be a good time to go back to Chapter 11, where we showed you how to read a contract and included an explanation of the general layout of the SF 33. The top portion, Blocks 1-11, is the Solicitation area and is filled in by the government with information about the solicitation. Blocks 12-18, the Offer area, are filled in by you before returning the offer to the buying office. The last portion, Blocks 19-28, is the Award area and is completed by the government and sent back to you, if and when you are awarded the contract.

Work Smart

Note the paging format "Page 1 of ##." Check your page numbers and if there are any missing, call the buying office immediately. You can't submit an accurate bid if there is information missing. More than one company has been caught in this situation. When sending out millions of bids a year, as the government does, these things can happen.

Solicitation Section (filled in by the government)

Block 1: Contract is a Rated Order — A rated contract is one that has a specific classification for how "hot" the need is. Although these days you will hardly ever see activation of rated procedures, it is there in case the need arises. About the only time you might see a rated bid is during time of national emergency or war.

Block 2: Contract Number — The government will not fill in this number until it awards the contract. The numbering will be similar to the number in Block 3, the Solicitation Number, but it will have a "C" instead of an "R" in the number sequence.

Block 3: Solicitation Number — This is the number we discussed in the DD Form 1707 explanation (Block 1), above.

Block 4: Type of Solicitation — This block will identify whether this is a Sealed Bid IFB (Invitation for Bid) or an RFP (Request for Proposal).

Block 5: Date Issued — This is the date that this contract "hit the street" and became a live requirement.

Block 6: Requisition/Purchase Number — This number is an internal document number used by the requisition people for tracking the item or service to be purchased. This is the original number for that "need," and there might be multiple requisition numbers against a solicitation number.

Block 7: Issued By — This block identifies the government office that is doing the buying. Make special note of the information here. Remember that you might be dealing with a "buying agency" that is physically located very far from the actual end user. You can spend a lot of time with the end user, convincing the user that you are the answer to all their problems, and still lose the whole deal by not checking out where the buy is going to be made.

Example

We dealt with a company that was talking to the end user every week, had developed a one-on-one relationship, but never thought to ask where the buying office was located. The company missed the issue date and only found out that the bid had gone out when it came through a distributor. The company did not lose the contract, but by going through the distributor, it had to pay a commission it wouldn't have had to pay if it had gotten the contract directly.

Block 8: Address Offer To — This block gives you information on where to submit your offer.

Block 9: Additional Info — This block will tell you whether the buying office wants additional copies of the offer for evaluation purposes and where to bring the offer if you hand-carry it to the buying office. This block also tells you the time and date when you need to have the offer in.

Standard Form 33

SOLICITATION, OFFER AND AWARD	1. THIS CONTRACT IS A RATED ORDER UNDER DPAS (15 CFR 700)	RATING	PAGE	OF	PAGES

2. CONTRACT NUMBER	3. SOLICITATION NUMBER	4. TYPE OF SOLICITATION	5. DATE ISSUED	6. REQUISITION/PURCHASE NUMBER
		☐ SEALED BID (IFB) ☐ NEGOTIATED (RFP)		

7. ISSUED BY	CODE	8. ADDRESS OFFER TO (If other than Item 7)

NOTE: In sealed bid solicitations "offer" and "offeror" mean "bid" and "bidder".

SOLICITATION

9. Sealed offers in original and _____ copies for furnishing the supplies or services in the Schedule will be received at the place specified in Item 8, or if handcarried, in the depository located in _____ until _____ local time _____
(Hour)   (Date)

CAUTION - LATE Submissions, Modifications, and Withdrawals: See Section L, Provision No. 52.214-7 or 52.215-1. All offers are subject to all terms and conditions contained in this solicitation.

10. FOR INFORMATION CALL:	A. NAME	B. TELEPHONE (NO COLLECT CALLS)			C. E-MAIL ADDRESS
		AREA CODE	NUMBER	EXT.	

11. TABLE OF CONTENTS

(X)	SEC.	DESCRIPTION	PAGE(S)	(X)	SEC.	DESCRIPTION	PAGE(S)
		PART I - THE SCHEDULE				**PART II - CONTRACT CLAUSES**	
	A	SOLICITATION/CONTRACT FORM			I	CONTRACT CLAUSES	
	B	SUPPLIES OR SERVICES AND PRICES/COSTS				**PART III - LIST OF DOCUMENTS, EXHIBITS AND OTHER ATTACH.**	
	C	DESCRIPTION/SPECS./WORK STATEMENT			J	LIST OF ATTACHMENTS	
	D	PACKAGING AND MARKING				**PART IV - REPRESENTATIONS AND INSTRUCTIONS**	
	E	INSPECTION AND ACCEPTANCE			K	REPRESENTATIONS, CERTIFICATIONS AND OTHER STATEMENTS OF OFFERORS	
	F	DELIVERIES OR PERFORMANCE					
	G	CONTRACT ADMINISTRATION DATA			L	INSTRS., CONDS., AND NOTICES TO OFFERORS	
	H	SPECIAL CONTRACT REQUIREMENTS			M	EVALUATION FACTORS FOR AWARD	

OFFER (Must be fully completed by offeror)

NOTE: Item 12 does not apply if the solicitation includes the provisions at 52.214-16, Minimum Bid Acceptance Period.

12. In compliance with the above, the undersigned agrees, if this offer is accepted within _____ calendar days (60 calendar days unless a different period is inserted by the offeror) from the date for receipt of offers specified above, to furnish any or all items upon which prices are offered at the price set opposite each item, delivered at the designated point(s), within the time specified in the schedule.

13. DISCOUNT FOR PROMPT PAYMENT (See Section I, Clause No. 52.232-8)	10 CALENDAR DAYS (%)	20 CALENDAR DAYS (%)	30 CALENDAR DAYS (%)	CALENDAR DAYS (%)

14. ACKNOWLEDGMENT OF AMEND-MENTS (The offeror acknowledges receipt of amendments to the SOLICITATION for offerors and related documents numbered and dated):	AMENDMENT NO.	DATE	AMENDMENT NO.	DATE

15A. NAME AND ADDRESS OF OFFER-OR	CODE	FACILITY	16. NAME AND TITLE OF PERSON AUTHORIZED TO SIGN OFFER (Type or print)

15B. TELEPHONE NUMBER			15C. CHECK IF REMITTANCE ADDRESS IS DIFFERENT FROM ABOVE - ENTER SUCH ADDRESS IN SCHEDULE.	17. SIGNATURE	18. OFFER DATE
AREA CODE	NUMBER	EXT.	☐		

AWARD (To be completed by Government)

19. ACCEPTED AS TO ITEMS NUMBERED	20. AMOUNT	21. ACCOUNTING AND APPROPRIATION

22. AUTHORITY FOR USING OTHER THAN FULL AND OPEN COMPETITION: ☐ 10 U.S.C. 2304(c) ( ) ☐ 41 U.S.C. 253(c) ( )	23. SUBMIT INVOICES TO ADDRESS SHOWN IN (4 copies unless otherwise specified)	ITEM

24. ADMINISTERED BY (If other than Item 7)	CODE	25. PAYMENT WILL BE MADE BY	CODE

26. NAME OF CONTRACTING OFFICER (Type or print)	27. UNITED STATES OF AMERICA (Signature of Contracting Officer)	28. AWARD DATE

IMPORTANT - Award will be made on this Form, or on Standard Form 26, or by other authorized official written notice.

AUTHORIZED FOR LOCAL REPRODUCTION
Previous edition is unusable

STANDARD FORM 33 (REV. 9-97)
Prescribed by GSA - FAR (48 CFR) 53.214(c)

Block 10: For Information Call — This block identifies the person that you will contact for information on this specific bid, including phone number and e-mail address, if available.

Block 11: Table of Contents — This should be the same as the "TOC" page, but without the "Appendices." Some buying offices will do both, some will not. Make sure they match. This section will also give you the page counts for each section. If it says that there are 25 pages in Section C: Description/specs/work statement and you have only 23 pages, you had better call the buyer and find out what's missing. Don't assume that you will automatically be sent the missing material. And, again, keep in mind that the sections of Block 11, when taken *together*, make up the whole solicitation and resulting contract.

Offer Section (completed by the bidder)

Block 12: Acceptance Period — This block will give you the opportunity to mark how long your bid will be good for. If you don't put in a specific number, it will default to 60 days.

Block 13: Discounts for Prompt Payment — This block is where you will put the size of the discount, if any, that you will give the government if it pays you promptly.

One important catch with the Prompt Payment Act: The clock on this Act starts only if your invoice, when received, is correct. If your invoice is not correct, it gets kicked back until it is corrected and received by the government. Therefore, the definition of "prompt" under this Act is directly tied to the accuracy of your invoice.

Block 14: Acknowledgments of Amendments — In this block you will let the buyer know that you have received all the amendments that it sent out. If the buyer mailed out four and you list only three, the buyer will throw out your bid as non-responsive if the omitted amendment impacts on the material aspects of the solicitation.

Block 15a: Name and Address of Offeror — Here is where you will enter your company name, address and, in the little box marked "code," your Cage Code and your facility code, if you have one.

Block 15b: Telephone Number — Enter the appropriate phone number.

Block 15c: Remittance Address — If you want the government to send the check for payment to an address different from the one you provided in Block 15a, mark this box and enter the address on the schedule.

Block 16: Name and Title of Person Authorized To Sign Offer — In this block enter the name and title of the person "authorized" to sign the contracts. Please don't have someone sign the contract if they are not listed in CCR (Central Contractor Registration) as the "authorized signor." You will lose the award.

Block 17: Signature — This is where the authorized person must sign the contract.

Caution

More than a few companies that carefully prepared their bid lost out just because the contract was not signed. Don't forget to sign the contract.

Block 18: Offer Date — Enter the date on which you are sending the contract.

Award Section (completed by the government)

After you fill in Block 18, above, you have completed your portion of Form 33. If you see the SF 33 coming back in the mail with the Award section filled in by the government, guess what? You won the contract! You are now a prime contractor!

Block 19: Accepted as to Items Numbered — Government will identify which specific items have been awarded to you.

Block 20: Amount — This is the dollar amount of the contract. The cash!

Block 21: Accounting and Appropriation — The government will fill in the appropriate accounting and appropriation codes. (In general, you don't have to concern yourself with this information.)

Block 22: Authority for Using Other Than Full and Open Competition — This field is informational only.

Block 23: Submit Invoice to Address Shown in — The government will tell you where to look in the contract for the appropriate address.

Block 24: Administered By — This is the office that will administer the contract. Note that the office listed here may be different than the one putting out the bid.

Block 25: Payment Will Be Made By — This is the paying office, the office from which you will receive your money.

Block 26: Name of the Contracting Officer — The name of the Contracting Officer is typed here. You will see this person's name only if you win the contract.

Block 27: United States of America — This is the block where the Contracting Officer will sign that you have an active, actual, real government contract.

Block 28: Award Date — This is the date the government contracting officer signs the award.

Work Smart

Award can be made on the SF 33; on another form, such as the SF 26; or by any other authorized official written notice. Be watching for it, check on who won, for how much, and what the details of the award were. Ask questions . . . that's how you find out what you did right or wrong. There are two ways to do this: Either call the buyer and ask for the information or get award notices from the CBD.

Amendments to Solicitation — Standard Form 30

When there is a need to change or modify the quantity, specifications, delivery or any other part of a solicitation, or if there is some part of the solicitation that is defective or incorrect, those changes will be made by an amendment to the solicitation using

Form SF 30, *Amendment of Solicitation/Modification of Contract*. The form itself is completed by the government and sent to prospective bidders.

Work Smart

If the solicitation is an Invitation for Bid, you must bid the requirement as presented. To do otherwise will probably result in your bid being "kicked out." If you think a change is necessary, call the buyer before the bid opening date and explain why it needs to be changed. If the buyer agrees, the bid will be modified or cancelled and re-bid with the changes. Of course, everyone else will get to bid the change also.

If the solicitation is negotiated, you may be able to bid the changes explaining why this is in the best interest of the government. Read the solicitation carefully to make sure that this approach is allowed. If you are not sure, talk to the buyer to get the answer.

As we mentioned above, you will be asked to list any and all amendments that you have received on the bid form before you send it in. If you fail to do this or if you omit an amendment, your bid will be considered non-responsive. That means that your bid could be thrown out, even if you are the low bidder. Therefore, if you received Amendment number 0001 and 0003 and you have not received 0002, you need to call the buyer and find out what the missing amendment is.

If there is a change that will affect the bid opening, the government will extend the bid opening date (BOD) and send a notice to all prospective bidders. And, again, you must acknowledge this amendment in your bid.

WRITING A PROPOSAL FOR AN RFP OR RFQ

As we discussed above, when the solicitation you are responding to is an Invitation for Bid, writing your proposal will basically consist of filling out the forms that the government provides. However, when the solicitation is a negotiated solicitation, such as a Request for Proposal or Request for Quote, things are different.

In addition to filling out the required forms, you will have to provide clear and complete documentation explaining your plan for meeting the government's particular need. You may be required to work up your own drawings, biographies on personnel, management plans, and other types of documents.

Tips on Writing a Proposal

Your proposal should, at the same time, adequately address the government's requirements, be clearly written, and be persuasive. Here are some pointers:

- **Write your proposal like a sales document.** Your proposal must sell your company's ability to meet the requirements, to fulfill all of the stated conditions, and to deliver on time. Be specific and direct—being vague will only demonstrate that you do not understand the requirement and will create questions in the minds of the evaluators. Substantiate your promises and assertions with facts and details. Your goal is to persuade evaluators that your offer is superior to those of competing companies and to prove that your company can do the job.

- **Demonstrate a complete understanding of the stated requirement or problem.** This may sometimes be a challenge. While, in some cases, the government buying office will know exactly what it needs, in other cases, it may not know or may use conflicting or vague terminology. In either event, it is *your* responsibility to demonstrate your understanding of the requirement; it is not the responsibility of the buying officer to interpret your understanding. If your proposal does not respond to the stated requirement or responds to only part of the requirement, it will not be considered for a contract award and may not even receive a complete evaluation.

- **Demonstrate that you are qualified.** This means that not only must you demonstrate your understanding of the problem or requirement, you must also demonstrate your ability to solve or meet it. Include your staff's qualifications, relevant facilities and equipment, as well as any other qualifications that are specific to the project you are bidding on. Your proposal should clearly communicate your ability to successfully perform the contract. Documentation of successful fulfillment of past contracts may also help prove your point.

- **Respond to the stated evaluation criteria.** Section M of the solicitation identifies the factors that the buying office will look at when evaluating your proposal. Cost is but one factor. If your proposal does not respond to these criteria, it will be judged to be technically unacceptable and will not be considered for contract award.

- **Follow the required proposal format.** Section L of the solicitation specifies which topics should be covered in your proposal as well as the order in which they should be presented. If you do not follow the required content format and organization, you risk neglecting or omitting important information, which will result in rejection of your proposal.

- **Provide adequate management and cost information.** Demonstrate your ability to manage the work and account for all of the costs involved in performing the contract. Also provide adequate cost and pricing data.

- **Proofread and critique your proposal.** Writing an effective proposal requires time, patience, and care. Be prepared to write, evaluate, and rewrite, as necessary. Rewriting gives you the chance to improve the quality and responsiveness of your proposal. Pay attention to detail. Good grammar and spelling count. If necessary, ask another person with those skills to proofread the final draft for you.

- **Attend a writing proposal workshop.** There are a number of good ones offered through Procurement Technical Assistance Centers. (For more information on PTACs, see Part IV.)

Chapter 15

Submit Your Bid

Congratulations, you have arrived at the last step—submitting your bid. You can do this via the U.S. mail, UPS, RIP, or another carrier. However, it is important to keep in mind that if your bid is late, the U.S. mail is the only carrier that the government will recognize for consideration of a late bid.

But before you seal up that envelope and send it in, take a few minutes to go through our final checklist to help make sure that you have done everything you need to do.

Final Bid Checklist

☐ *Have you placed your name on the bidder's list for supplies and/or services that you are qualified to provide? This means going to the CCR web page and filling out all the fields (see Chapter 8).*

☐ *Have you read the solicitation carefully? If you wait to read it until after you get an award, you might be in for some severe shocks. For example, you may find out that the packaging costs are greater than the unit cost. How are you going to handle that? (See Chapter 11.)*

☐ *Have you carefully read the specifications and standards that apply to this contract? Remember: It's your responsibility to find and get the specs before you bid. Where applicable, you must also get the tech package, which contains the drawings. More than a few companies that have bid on contracts without seeing a print have been in for a sad awakening when the inspector refused to sign off because they didn't meet contract requirements. (See Chapter 12.)*

☐ *Did you bid on the exact parts that the buyer is looking for and do you propose to furnish material in exact accordance with the specifications, drawings, and description as are in the contract solicitation? If not, you better tell the government how you propose to deviate and make sure that you will still be furnishing what they want. If you plan on bidding with an exception, then you need to explain why as well as how the government* will benefit. Be careful because you can only do this on a negotiated solicitation. If the solicitation is a sealed bid you must bid the requirement first, then an alternative. The government can only consider the alternative if your offer is the low one.

☐ If the product that you bid on requires qualification approval (i.e., a QPL), have you made sure that the approval number that you have entered is correct, and current and was issued to the plant location where the product will be produced?

☐ Have you checked out all packaging and marking requirements? The government has some special packaging requirements that the commercial market does not have. Sometimes the packaging costs can exceed the unit product cost.

☐ Have you checked and verified the unit prices for the contract? Check your math carefully—you don't want to lose the bid or lose money because of a simple arithmetic error.

☐ Is your bid for delivery in exact accordance with the delivery requirements specified in the solicitation? If the buyer is looking for delivery in 45 days or less, do your proposed dates fall within their requirements?

☐ Does your acceptance time conform to the requirements in the solicitation?

☐ Have you requested any information or clarification on points that are not clear to you? Have you gotten them in writing? (If you don't have them in writing, then you don't have them.)

☐ Have you properly completed the "Representations, certifications and acknowledgments" portion of the bid? Remember that if you are a Women-Owned Small Business, you are not a Small Disadvantaged Owned Business. Or if you are owned by a large business, you are not a small business just because you have only 40 workers at your location.

☐ Have you entered your discounts correctly? (Note: You don't have to offer a discount.)

☐ Have you signed the contract? We are serious here! Go back and make sure. Is the person who signed the contract authorized to do so? Your assistant cannot sign for you unless he or she is authorized.

☐ Have you read the whole contract . . . a second and even a third time?

☐ Have you acknowledged all amendments on the bid? The buyer will automatically kick your bid out if you haven't.

☐ Did you include any condition that would modify the requirements? In this regard, be careful of any transmittal or cover letters. If your normal company letterhead contains any statement about terms, price, time of delivery, or anything else that goes to the substance of the bid, it will negate your offer as "nonresponsive" because you have taken exception to the terms and conditions of the solicitation and your bid will be thrown out. All the government wants you to do is provide accurate and complete information on the forms that have been provided to you. But, if you are responding to an RFP, you may have exceptions and need to use a transmittal letter. However, make sure it doesn't have special terms and conditions on it.

☐ *Did you include the correct number of copies? Make sure all of the copies are collated correctly, with no pages missing or out of order.* Also make sure you keep a copy for yourself.

☐ *Did you put enough postage on the bid?*

☐ *If you are submitting a sealed bid, did you put the "Sealed Bid" label on the envelope and not on the bid itself?*

☐ *Have you given yourself enough time to mail or overnight the bid to the purchasing office? UPS and RIP are not the U.S. mail. Bids sent by these methods, if they are received late, do not qualify for consideration under the "late bid procedures" regulation. Isn't it nice to be able to blame it on the mailman?*

O.K., that's it! Run down to the post office and get your bid in the mail!

Part III

After the Bid

Well done! You have completed the work, gone through the steps and submitted your first bid. Now what happens?

Basically, once you are finished with your part of the process, it is time for the government buyer to take over and do its part. Once all of the bids are in, the buyer will begin evaluating all of the offers and ultimately make a final decision on which company will be awarded the contract.

And what if your company is the one that is awarded the contract? What should you be doing and thinking about?

In this Part, we will try to answer some of these questions and look at what comes next. We will first look at how the evaluation process works and the factors that could influence who will win the award. We will also offer some pointers on what to do immediately upon receiving a contract.

We will then discuss the importance of quality assurance standards and provide a checklist for getting you started on setting up an effective quality assurance program for your company. Finally, we will discuss contract terminations and one of the most important and interesting things of all . . . getting paid.

Chapter 16, Bid Evaluation and Award: We tell you what government buyers look for when they evaluate your bid against others and how they decide on the winner. If you are being considered for award, the government may want to perform a pre-award survey to make sure you are capable—we tell you how to prepare. Finally, we provide a checklist of things you need to do right away if you are the winner.

Chapter 17, Quality Assurance Standards: Quality assurance is a crucial part of doing business with the government. How can you assure buyers that you will provide a quality product? We explain the different levels of quality standards and tell you what you need to do to develop a good quality control program for your company.

Chapter 18, Contract Terminations: Most federal contracts allow the government to terminate a contract for its own convenience or for default. We explain both types of terminations and tell you what to expect if this happens to you.

Chapter 19, Getting Paid: Find out how you can help ensure prompt payment and what constitutes a "proper invoice." Also learn about the forms of payment: electronic funds transfer and the government credit card.

Chapter **16**

Bid Evaluation
and Award

Once the government buyer receives all the bids, the evaluation and award process begins. Here is an outline of what happens.

Non-Negotiated Bids (IFBs). If the solicitation is an Invitation for Bid (IFB)—a non-negotiated, sealed bid situation where lowest qualified bidder wins—the bid is opened and the information is recorded on what is referred to as a "bid abstract." This will be used as the bid history database. The abstract contains, in order of opening, the names of the bidding companies, the items being bid, the prices quoted, and any other information that the bidding officer deems relevant.

This is important information that could prove to be very useful to you, whether you get the bid or not. And since the information contained in the bid abstract is considered public information, you can get it just by asking. The government buying office will send you a copy of the abstract if you enclose a self-addressed stamped envelope along with your bid. You should also include a letter stating that you are requesting the bid abstract under the Freedom of Information Act. (See now, isn't the government helpful? You probably won't be able to get similar information from the private business sector at any time in the near future.)

With this information in hand, you can see where you stand in the bidding process. If your price quote is in the upper third of the price ranking, you are outside the competitive range. If you find yourself in the middle third, you're getting there. If you are in the lower third, you are in the right place.

Remember that you will not win all bids. Figure that after you become an old hand at bidding, your rate will be, on average, about three out of ten.

Negotiated Bids (RFPs or RFQs). If the solicitation is negotiated—in other words, if it is a Request for Proposal or Request for Quote—the information on bidding companies, pricing, etc. is not public information. When the award is made, the name of the successful bidder and the contract price become public information.

FACTORS INFLUENCING BID OUTCOME

Which factors do government buyers consider in looking at your bid and finally awarding the contract? Here are some of the most important:

Does Your Bid Meet All Essential Requirements?

One of the first things that government buyers will do is make sure that your bid conforms to all essential requirements of the solicitation. This includes exact conformance to all the specifications, drawings, descriptions, and standards specified in the contract solicitation, as well as materials, delivery dates, packaging and marking requirements, etc.

Are You Capable?

Buyers will also consider whether you are capable of performing and delivering on the contract. Just because you know in your heart that you can do the work is not enough for buyers. They will be looking at your technical capability and trying to make sure that you have the experience and know-how to do the work.

Do you have the production capability? If the contract calls for 100,000 widgets and you have one drill press and a milling machine and a part-time retired guy . . . well, they might see a problem and you probably won't get the contract. Do you have a real place of operation? If you are manufacturing items out of your garage, then that could also be a handicap in getting a contract.

Here's a major consideration: financial capability. For some reason, reasonable business people think that if they are in financial trouble, a government contract will be able to fix the situation and get them financially healthy again. Sorry, but if your business is in trouble, the last thing you want is a contract where the margins are tight and you might have trouble getting financial help to do the work.

What's Your Performance Record?

Another important consideration for buyers is your past performance record. If you didn't meet a deadline on your first contract or if you have a history of late deliveries on contracts, the government will not want to work with you. The government operates on strict schedules and when you don't meet one, the government tends to get very upset and never forget. Even in cases where price is a deciding factor, the government now factors in past performance in figuring out the real cost for an item.

Do You Have Adequate Quality Control?

Government buyers want assurance that you will provide a quality product. You may not need to go all out and get certified under strict international quality standards, but you should have a good, well-documented quality control program that tells all of your customers, including the government, how you guarantee that you will provide quality products and services.

(Quality assurance is such a crucial part of any government contract that we are going to expand on this topic in a separate chapter later in this Part.)

PRE-AWARD SURVEY

The government's responsibility in evaluating a bid is to determine, first of all, the responsiveness of an offer to the solicitation. This is more of a technical process and consists of checking all the paperwork and making sure there are no unacceptable deviations. The government must then determine whether the proposed winner is responsible and capable enough to handle the contract.

To help make this determination, the government might perform what is called a Pre-Award Survey (PAS). The PAS is made in sufficient depth to assure that the proposed award winner has the ability to meet the requirements of the solicitation. It may involve a full government team coming out to check a company's capabilities first-hand, or it may entail nothing more than taking a look at the pertinent information about the company to determine if it is able to go ahead with the contract.

How to Prepare for the Pre-Award Survey

If you are the proposed winner of a government contract, there are certain things you can do to prepare for the Pre-Award Survey to help ensure a favorable outcome for your company:

- Select the person who will meet with the government survey team. This person should be empowered to speak for the company and should be completely familiar with the details of the solicitation and of your company's offer.

- If relevant, make available one or more technicians to answer questions.

- Identify any disparities that may exist between the solicitation and your company's offer that should be resolved during the initial meeting with the survey team.

- Think about how you can demonstrate actual technical capability, or the development of technical capability, on the proposed contract.

- Get your production plan ready and available for review by the survey team.

- Make sure your plant facilities and equipment are available and operable. If they are not, be prepared to demonstrate that they can be developed or acquired in time to meet proposed contract requirements.

- Be prepared to show that you can meet the transportation, packaging, packing and preservation conditions of the solicitation.

- If industrial security clearance is required under the proposed contract, be prepared to show it.

- Make sure that your labor resources have the proper skills or that personnel with the needed skills can be hired expeditiously.

- Gather and make available to the survey team documentation, such as previous government contracts or subcontracts or commercial orders, to demonstrate a past satisfactory performance record with regard to delivery, quality and finances.

- Look over your production plan and make sure that you can demonstrate a capability to meet contract schedules.

- Gather financial documentation for the team financial analyst, including the company's current profit and loss summary, balance sheet, cash flow chart and other pertinent financial information.

- Prepare a listing of available tools and equipment for the team production specialist.

- Make sure that plans are in place for vendor supplies and materials or subcontracts to assure that the final delivery schedule can be met. Make sure that these plans are verifiable.

- Review any technical data and publications that may be required under the proposed contract and make sure you understand them.

- If the contract is a type other than a firm-fixed price or if you have requested progress payments, prepare adequate accounting documentation for review by the audit agency representative of the team.

- Review your quality control program and make sure that it is workable and consistent with the quality requirements stated in the contract. Be prepared to go over the details with the survey team.

- If government-furnished equipment, property or material is involved in the proposed contract, make sure you have established procedures in accord with the regulation stated in the contract.

- Prepare any other information or data that might be pertinent in assisting the government team.

Work Smart

What if you get turned down? There may be a "second bite of the apple" for you if your company is a small business and gets turned down on the Pre-Award Survey. If you can convince the Small Business Administration that you can do the work, the SBA could decide to back you and issue you another pre-award, known as a Certificate of Competency. The Certificate of Competency is like a bond and will allow you to receive the contract.

YOU WON IT! NOW WHAT?

Now, to the big question: What happens next if your company is the one that is awarded the contract? After you have congratulated yourself, what should you be doing and thinking about? Simply put, it is now up to you to fulfill the requirements of the contract, whether it's to produce a product, provide a service or build a structure.

Although it is impossible to cover the infinite variety of situations that might be involved in any given contract, we can offer a checklist of the actions you need to take immediately upon receiving a contract. The items on the checklist may seem obvious to you, but most companies get into trouble simply because they fail to do the obvious.

Contract Performance Checklist

☐ **Reread the Contract.** *You probably hoped that you had heard the last of this, but here we go again. The first thing you should do upon being awarded a contract is to read, read, read the provisions. Recheck your delivery dates, packaging requirements, reports you may be required to submit, and delivery destination. Make sure you haven't missed something -- you may be surprised at what you may find.*

☐ **Record Important Contacts.** *Look on the face of the contract and jot down the name, address, telephone number, and e-mail address of the following contacts so you will have the information handy for on-going reference:*

— *Procuring Contracting Officer (PCO)*

— *Administrative Contracting Officer (ACO)*

— *Paying Office*

— *Government Inspector (You should be contacted by this individual. This might be a local person who will work with you to get the contract completed. If it is a military contract, the local Defense Contract Management Agency (DCMA) should be a big help to you. Think of these people as part of your management team to help complete the contract.)*

☐ **Don't Take Unnecessary Actions.** *If the PCO or the ACO directs you to take a specific action, you must do so. But don't act on anyone else's direction! If you do, you will be liable for any costs or consequences that may result. Only the PCO, ACO, Contracting Officer's Representative (COR) or the contract itself can authorize you to take any action.*

☐ **Resolve Any Questions.** *If you have any questions about what a specific provision means or if you find any inconsistencies in your contract, contact the Contracting Officer (CO) immediately and ask for a meeting or "post-award conference." Open the lines of communication and develop a good working relationship right away. If you are really new to the process, ask for all the assistance that the CO is willing to give you. There is no question that is too "dumb" or "embarrassing"; what is really embarrassing is not performing on the contract. Address any problem right away before it gets out of hand.*

☐ **Keep accurate, timely and well documented records.** *Even in this paperless society, a paper trail is important. You have no case if you can't prove what was said and done. We have found that simple misunderstandings can easily degenerate into a "he said, she said" sort of situation where no one wins and the relationship with the government people becomes, shall we say, "touchy."*

☐ **Determine internal responsibilities.** *Make sure your people understand what is to be done and in what time frame. This will help ensure that everything goes smoothly and that delivery is made in accordance with the terms of the contract.*

☐ **Issue orders and plan production.** *Place any long lead items on contract immediately to ensure that there will be no holdup with production.*

☐ ***Produce/provide the service.*** *If everything was planned out properly, this part should go relatively smoothly. If not, don't forget to keep the Contracting Officer informed. If you see that delivery under the contract may be affected, seek an extension before the due date to avoid being delinquent.*

☐ ***Review your quality control program.*** *Make sure procedures are in place and are adequate to guarantee that the quality of the item will meet government requirements. If necessary, update your procedures and your manual.*

Chapter 17

Quality Assurance Standards

One of the main things that any customer wants is a quality product—and the government is no exception.

When the government purchases products or services from your company, you will be subjected to a very definite standard of quality as specified in your contract. The level and type of quality standard that you will be required to meet will depend on the product or service being purchased. For example, an extensive quality requirement would probably not be imposed if you are producing a non-complex item, since simple measurement or testing would be able to determine whether it conforms to contract requirements.

To assure the government, as well as other prospective customers, that you will provide a quality product, you need to have a well documented quality assurance (QA) program in place. Your program should provide a systematic approach for evaluation, inspection, testing, calibration or whatever is needed to monitor and assure the quality of your product. And, most importantly, that approach should be written down.

From the government's point of view, the purpose of a quality program is to provide a way to assure that an item complies with contract specifications. From your point of view, the purpose is twofold: It will attract and assure government buyers, and perhaps even more importantly, it will also save you money by providing you with the necessary indicators and tools to identify problem areas and the means for correcting those areas. It will make you look at every aspect and phase of your manufacturing and operating processes as well as the results of those processes. If a process results in a bad output, you will be able to identify where changes need to be made to produce an acceptable product.

Example

The owners of a small company in the Midwest that manufactured items for the government had no quality control system, but they did have a 100-percent acceptance rate with the government inspectors. However, they were losing money and couldn't figure out why.

Their approach was to scrap all the items that didn't meet government specs, let the government see only the "good" items, and simply buy enough materials to accommodate the high scrap rate. While this approach resulted in a high acceptance rate, the high cost of materials ate into their profits and hurt the company financially. A good quality control system would have helped them identify the real problem, reduce the amount of scrap, and cut the cost of materials.

Set up a good quality control system and it will pay for itself by reducing material and operational costs, and will make your company more attractive to prospective customers. Remember that the government, like any customer, wants a quality product, on time and at a reasonable price. No more, no less.

A high-quality QA program will also assure that the reliability and quality of the product are maintained throughout the life of the product. Companies that do business with the government need reliability assurance, since the government now requires guarantees on some of their purchases. Also, an aggressive quality control program will prevent product degradation below some minimum requirement that you set.

The government assures quality by reviewing a contractor's inspection system, quality program, or any method used by the contractor to assure compliance with the contract requirements. But, regardless of the government's quality assurance actions, the contractor is responsible for inspecting and controlling product quality, and for offering to the government only materials that conform to contract requirements, either as an individual item or in conjunction with any other item.

Caution

All government quality assurance requirements are spelled out in Part 46 of the Federal Acquisition Regulation (FAR). Any language that you will see in a bid or contract related to quality control consists of clauses extracted from this Part.

CONTRACT QUALITY REQUIREMENTS

When the contracting officer issues a sealed bid (IFB) or a request for proposal (RFP), the solicitation will specify the quality provisions that will be required by the government. Every solicitation or bid will include one of four basic categories of QA coverage for assuring conformance of products and services to contract requirements:

1. **Contractor's existing quality assurance system (applicable to contracts for commercial items).** When the government buys commercial items, it may rely on the contractor's existing quality assurance system, without government inspection and testing. However, if customary market practices for the commercial item being bought include in-process inspection, then the government may do some inspection and testing by its own personnel. Any in-process inspection conducted by the government must be conducted in a manner consistent with commercial practice.

2. **Inspection by the contractor (applicable to contracts for non-commercial items $100,000 or less).** When a contract for non-commercial items (i.e., items built to government specs) is expected not to exceed the simplified acquisition threshold of $100,000 or less, the government may specify that the contractor is responsible for performing all inspections and tests necessary to substantiate that supplies or services furnished conform to contract quality requirements. However, the government may impose stricter requirements if it has special needs that require a greater degree of quality assurance.

3. **Standard inspection requirements (applicable to contracts for non-commercial items over $100,000).** When a contract for non-commercial items is expected to exceed $100,000, the government may require the contractor to provide and maintain an inspection system that is acceptable to the government. The government also has the right to conduct inspections and tests while work is in progress and to require the contractor to keep and make available to the government complete records of its inspection work. Here we are talking about more complex items, such as sub-assemblies, minor components, or items critical to function or safety.

4. **Higher-level quality standards (applicable to complex or critical items—contacts may be for less than $100,000).** When a contract is for complex or critical items, higher-level requirements are applicable. The contracting officer is responsible for identifying the higher-level standard(s) that will satisfy the government's requirement. Examples of higher-level standards that the contracting officer may cite are ISO 9001, 9002, or 9003; ANSI/ASQC Q9001, Q9002, or Q9003; QS-9000; AS-9000; ANSI/ASQC E4; and ANSI/ASME NQA-1. (We discuss some of these standards in more detail, below.) This quality level would be required

when it is important for control of work operations, in-process controls, and inspection or attention to such factors as organization, planning, work instructions, documentation control, etc.

HIGHER-LEVEL INTERNATIONAL STANDARDS

ISO international standards, developed by the International Organization for Standardization (ISO) based in Geneva, Switzerland, are considered among the world's strictest and highest quality standards. The ISO, a non-governmental organization established in 1947, comprises a worldwide federation of national standards bodies from each of 100 countries. The organization aims to facilitate the international exchange of goods and services by establishing international standards and reconciling regulatory differences between countries.

ISO standards contain precise criteria for the features and characteristics of products and services to ensure that these products and services are fit for their purpose. For example, the format of credit cards is derived from an ISO international standard. Complying with an international standard, which defines such features as the optimal thickness (0.76 mm) of each card, means that the cards can be used worldwide.

International standards thus contribute to making life simpler and to increasing the reliability and effectiveness of the goods and services that we use. Coordinated standards for similar technologies in different countries or regions can also effectively remove so-called "technical barriers to trade."

The scope of ISO covers all technical fields, except electrical and electronic engineering, which is the responsibility of the International Electrotechnical Commission (IEC). The IEC is the international standards and conformity assessment body for all fields of electrotechnology. The work in the field of information technology is carried out by a joint ISO/IEC technical committee.

The ISO issues the certifications and certifies individuals that work with companies in setting up ISO standards in their business. ISO certification is very pricey—on average, it runs between $20,000-$35,000 per year. A company can't say that it is ISO unless a certified ISO auditor has declared it so.

ISO 9000

ISO 9000 is a set of five universal standards for a Quality Assurance system that is accepted around the world. Ninety countries have adopted ISO 9000 as national standards, and the federal government is moving closer to having ISO as the one, so to speak, standard to replace its major systems standard, MIL-Q-9858.

When a customer, such as the government, purchases a product or service from a company that is registered to the appropriate ISO 9000 standard, the customer has important assurances that the quality of what it receives will be as it expects.

ISO 9000 registration is rapidly becoming a must for any company that does business with the government or overseas involving complex or critical items. Many industrial companies require registration by their own subcontractors, so there is a growing trend toward universal acceptance of ISO 9000 as an international standard.

The most comprehensive of the 9000 set of standards is ISO 9001. It applies to industries involved in the design and development, manufacturing, installation and servicing of products or services. The standards apply uniformly to companies in any industry and of any size.

Many companies require their suppliers to become registered to ISO 9001, and because of this, registered companies have found that their market opportunities have increased. Registered companies have also had dramatic reductions in customer complaints, significant reductions in operating costs and increased demand for their products and services.

A company in compliance with ISO 9001 ensures that it has a sound Quality Assurance system, and that's good business. ISO 9002 is almost identical to ISO 9001, except that the provisions on "Design Control" are only applicable to 9001. Therefore, ISO 9001 is the appropriate standard if your organization carries out the innovative design of products or services; otherwise ISO 9002 is applicable.

ISO 9001 or ISO 9002?

ISO 9001, entitled "Quality System — Model for quality assurance in design/development, production, installation and servicing," applies in situations when:

1. *design is required and the product requirements are stated principally in performance terms, or they need to be established, and*

2. *confidence in product conformance can be attained by adequate demonstration of a supplier's capabilities in design, development, production, installation and servicing.*

ISO 9002, entitled "Quality System — Model for quality assurance in production, installation and servicing," applies in situations when:

1. *the specified requirements for the product are stated in terms of an established design or specification, and*

2. *confidence in product conformance can be attained by adequate demonstration of a supplier's capabilities in production, installation, and servicing.*

ISO 14001

Before we end our discussion of ISO standards, we want to mention ISO 14001, an emerging international standard for environmental management systems (EMS). The ISO 14000 series is a voluntary set of standards intended to encourage organizations to systematically address the environmental impacts of their activities. The goal is to establish a common approach to environmental management systems that is internationally recognized, leading to improved environmental protection and reducing barriers to international trade.

ISO 14000 is a management system standard, not a performance standard. It is intended to be applicable to firms of all shapes and sizes around the world. The standard does not require specific environmental goals.

Instead, it provides a general framework for organizing the tasks necessary for effective environmental management, including planning, implementation and operations, checking and corrective action, and management review. The series of documents that encompasses ISO 14000 includes components such as environmental management systems, environmental auditing, environmental labeling and product life cycle assessment.

The ISO 14001 standard, which lays out requirements for establishing an EMS, is the centerpiece of the series. In order to qualify for ISO certification, firms must meet the requirements laid out in the ISO 14001. All of the other standards in the ISO 14000 series provide supporting guidance.

ISO 14001 is currently the subject of heated debate. Proponents of ISO 14001 argue that the new standard will be an effective tool for improving industrial environmental performance and help to ease burdens on environmental regulators. At the same time, many in the environmental community worry that compliance with ISO 14000 does not guarantee environmental improvements.

Work Smart

There are several web cites that offer information about ISO standards—search for "ISO" or "ISO standards" to get a list. You can also receive information by contacting:

American National Standards Institute
11 East 42nd St.
New York, NY 10036
Phone: 1-212-642-4900 Fax: 1-212-302-1286

HIGHER-LEVEL U.S. STANDARDS

In the previous discussion, we mentioned that the U.S. government is moving closer to having ISO as the one, so to speak, standard to replace its major quality assurance standard for complex military systems and hardware, MIL-Q-9858. But a funny thing about the government, particularly the military, is that old habits die hard. Two quality assurance standards, MIL-I-45208 (An Inspection System) and MIL-Q-9858A (A Quality Program), have been cancelled, but live on in contract terminology.

MIL-I-45208

Entitled "An Inspection System," this quality specification pertaining to military items sets forth the objectives and essential elements of an inspection system, and was referenced in a contract whenever an inspection system was required for the item. This system was used when technical requirements required in-process as well as final end item inspection, including control of measuring and testing equipment, drawing and changes, and documentation and records.

This requirement impacted both large and small businesses alike. In simple terms, it meant that you had to document your inspection system to assure continuity.

This spec was cancelled a few years ago, along with MIL-STD-45662 (calibration standard), but there are many contracting officers and contracts that still require it, but don't use the name.

MIL-Q-9858A

Entitled "A Quality Program," these requirements are sometimes still referenced whenever the technical requirements of a contract require such things as control of work operations, in-process control, inspection, organization, work instructions, documentation control and advanced metrology. This specification is intended for use in contracts that involve complex types of military hardware and systems.

Folks, this is not for the faint of heart. Don't try to put one of these together yourself. Our best advice is to get an expert to help you. By the way, this standard has also been cancelled and mostly replaced by the ISO series

CERTIFICATE OF CONFORMANCE

A Certificate of Conformance may be used in certain instances instead of source inspection at the discretion of the contracting officer. When a Certificate of Conformance is provided for in the contract, it gives the Contract Administration Office an option to allow material to be accepted and shipped without being inspected.

However, this option is exercised only when product quality history is excellent. When it is exercised, contractors are notified in writing by the inspector that the Certificate of Conformance procedure is applicable and the company can ship. Without this written notification, the contractor must expect regular inspection of product before shipment. Remember that the Certificate of Conformance is for the convenience of the government, not the contractor.

How to Read Specs and Standards

Federal specifications — The titles of federal specifications begin with a series of letters, followed by another letter and a serial number, and possibly a letter indicating the latest revision of the specification. The letter A represents the first revision, B represents the second revision, and so on. For example, A-A-104 is a federal spec for toothpaste. A-A-104B is the second revision of this spec.

Military specifications — The titles of military specifications begin with the letters MIL, MS, or DOD, followed by the first letter in the first word of the title, a serial number, and possibly a letter indicating the latest revision of the specification. It may also be followed by a number in parentheses indicating the last amendment to the specification.

"Revisions" represent major changes to a specification, and a revised specification supersedes all of the earlier versions. The letter A represents the first revision, B represents the second revision, and so on. "Amendments" represent minor changes to a specification, and an amended specification supplements, but does not replace, the latest revision and all earlier amendments.

For example, MIL-C-85322 is a military spec for "Coating, Elastomere, Polyurethane, Rain Erosion Resistant, For Exterior Aircraft Use." DOD-L-85336 is a military spec for "Lubricant, All Weather (Automatic Weapons)." DOD-L-85336A represents the first revision of DOD-L-85336. MIL-L-85314A (1) is a military spec for "Light Systems, Aircraft, Anti-Collision, Strobe." MIL-L-85314A represents the first revision of MIL-L-85314. This first revision has been amended one time [indicated by the (1)].

Industry-wide standards — *The titles of industry-wide standards begin with the letters in the abbreviation of the appropriate association, institute or society, followed by identifying letters and/or numbers. For example AWS A6.I -66 is an industry-wide safety standard for "Gas Shielded Arc Welding" from the American Welding Society (AWS). ANSI B4.1-67 is an industry-wide standard for "Cylindrical Parts, Preferred Limits and Fits for" from the American National Standards Institute (ANSI).*

Quality Requirements for Subcontractors

Right about now, you may be thinking to yourself, "If I am just a subcontractor, I won't have to do all this quality stuff, will I?" Guess again.

In many instances, a prime contractor will find it necessary or desirable to pass along the quality requirements to the subcontractor. Why? The prime contractor is responsible for the quality of materials supplied by the subcontractors or suppliers, and it is in its best interest to assure that all suppliers are capable of providing the materials and meeting the quality requirements of the prime contract.

The only way that the prime can assure itself that you can do quality work, on time and within budget, is to inspect your systems and get them approved. The day of the "pal" or "buddy" at the prime level that will issue a contract just on an owner's assurance that the company can deliver the required product is becoming a thing of the past. Many a small business that had this type of relationship has found, to their woe, that it must still have some kind of quality control system in place.

To the surprise of many contractors and subcontractors, government contract quality assurance at the subcontractor level does not relieve the prime contractor of any responsibilities under the contract nor does it establish a contractual relationship between the government and the subcontractor. So, if you think that you are getting out of some of the quality "stuff" by being a sub, think again.

The prime might, under a special exception or for a particular job, let you slide by without a QA program for a while, but it will eventually want to see a formal program in place or it won't want to work with you. Therefore, you may as well start creating your own program now, and do it to your satisfaction, without having the pressure of having to create one on the eve of a bid contract that you really want.

Assuring Measuring and Testing Requirements

Some years ago, there was a really nice spec, MIL-STD-45662, that thoroughly explained the how and why of what you needed to do to establish and maintain a system of all measurement and test equipment used in the contract. Now you must use Calibration Systems Requirements (ISO 10012-1, ANSI/NCSL Z540-1), which replaced the old 45662 standard.

Although the new spec is shorter, we miss the way that the 45662 explained what was needed. It was a great help for new contractors that had never had a calibration system and, for the most part, was easy to follow.

You may be able to get a copy of the old 45662 standard by contacting the Information Handling Services Group Inc. at www.ihs.com and ordering the historical files from them. They will charge a fee, but you might find it a good first step in creating your QA system.

Assuring Packaging and Shipping Requirements

As we have already mentioned, packaging requirements are a big deal when you do business with the government. They need to be carefully considered and analyzed, not only in pricing out a bid, but also in implementing a QA program. To aid your understanding, we think it would be helpful to define the terms "packaging" and "packing" the way the government defines them.

"Packaging," as defined in the Governments Contract Dictionary, is:

1. "an all-inclusive term covering cleaning, preserving, packaging, packing, and marking required to protect items during every phase of shipment, handling, and storage.

2. "The methods and materials used to protect material from deterioration or damage. This includes cleaning, drying, preserving, packing, marking and unitization." (Unitization is a government term that defines the "unit" of shipment and refers to a grouping of items for shipment.)

"Packing" is:

1. "the assembling of items into a unit, intermediate, or exterior pack with necessary blocking, bracing, cushioning, weatherproofing and reinforcement."

The reason that we defined these terms is that some companies might think that if they produce a quality part, all they need to do when they ship is drop it in a box with some of those "peanuts" and send for UPS. As the definitions imply, there is more to it—a lot more. To further illustrate, let's look at what might be required in the packaging of a part that might be used by the Army.

Assume that your company was contracted by the Army to manufacture a simple, inexpensive item, specifically a "block" consisting of a metal piece approximately 2x4 inches made of a specified material that will withstand high pressure.

So how would you have to package this little block? Under typical government packaging requirements for such a product, the block must first be packed into a plastic package. The plastic package must then be put into another pack that is cushioned and reinforced. A water/vapor seal is then put over the entire package. The sealed package is then packed into a shipping container.

Sounds like a lot for just one item, right? Well, that little block is part of a 155 mm howitzer cannon and is used to fire rounds (those big pointy things that explode when they land). And although this may seem a somewhat roundabout and melodramatic way to show the importance of packaging, the typical civilian usually does not realize how the part he or she is working on will be used or delivered to its ultimate destination. The little block might be headed for a 10,000-mile flight, dropped out of a plane at 5,000 feet, and must be ready to work the first time, and every time, when it lands.

In addition, as electronic technology becomes more complex, expensive and sensitive to damage, protecting electronic products and the work environment is a key government goal. And one place this is reflected is in packaging standards.

So although packaging requirements on a government contract can sometimes seem complex and difficult, if you're smart and do your homework, you can be successful at meeting the challenge.

Packaging Levels and Specs

The government uses 3 levels of packing and protection:

1. *Level A, Maximum Protection, is used for the most severe shipment, handling or storage conditions, or for unknown transportation or storage conditions. Examples: All-wood boxes, sheathed crates, plastic or metal specialty containers.*

2. *Level B, Intermediate Protection, is used for known and favorable shipment, handling and storage conditions. Examples: Single-, double-, or triple-walled, weather-resistant fiberboard, sealed at all openings.*

3. *Level C, Minimum Protection, is used for known and most favorable shipment, handling and storage conditions. Example: Domestic fiberboard or paperboard.*

To give you an overview of what is involved in "packaging," we are listing three packaging specifications, below. But because this area is so complex, we recommend that you get an expert to help you.

You can contact the government office administering your contract and request help from a government packaging specialist. Or, better yet, you can find a packager that has experience in working with the government and form a partnership with that company. Then you, the packager, and the government will all come out fine.

Number:	MIL-STD-2073-1
Title:	DOD MATERIEL PROCEDURES FOR DEVELOPMENT AND APPLICATION OF PACKAGING REQUIREMENTS
Price:	$94.00
Revision/Edition:	D
Date1:	12/15/1999
# Pages:	212

Number:	MIL-STD-2073-2
Title:	PACKAGING REQUIREMENT CODES
Price:	$48.00
Revision/Edition:	C
Date1:	10/01/1996
# Pages:	85

Number:	MIL-STD-726
Title:	PACKAGING REQUIREMENT CODES
Price:	$93.00
Revision/Edition:	H
Date1:	06/23/1993
# Pages:	208

HOW TO DEVELOP YOUR OWN QA PROGRAM

These days, if you don't have a good, well-documented quality control program in place, you are really limiting your business. We can't emphasize its importance enough, not just in the government market, but in the commercial market as well.

The goal of your quality assurance initiative is to create written procedures that will assure full compliance with all contract requirements. Formal, written documentation provides the government and your other customers better assurance that there will be consistency in the process and that, if a mistake is made, the cause can be traced to a specific spot and then corrected. The government wants the who, what, where, when and how of your quality control, so you need to specify the details: Who is responsible, for what specific function, at what stage of the process, etc.

Begin creating your program by first assessing where you are in your company with regard to quality control. There is a good chance that you already have effective procedures in place, but that they are not formally written. You don't have to reinvent the wheel; just document the way you do your work and then organize the material into a manual or handbook.

Tips on Establishing QA Procedures

Here are some things to consider as you start planning and developing your own Quality Assurance program -- whether you are looking to set up a full system to fulfill high-level military or international standards or to establish quality standards for a non-complex item.

As you establish quality assurance procedures and policies, be sure to write them down. This documentation will form the basis of your company's quality assurance manual.

☐ *Review the work rules and quality control policies and procedures that you and/or your employees already follow, but that up to now have just been verbalized. Start writing them down. Also write down any "defect prevention" rules that your company may have.*

☐ *Take a fresh look at your operation end to end, and identify every function and activity that affects the quality of your product or services. Look for possible quality trouble spots in every phase of the production, inspection and shipping cycle.*

☐ *If you don't already have them, set acceptance/rejection standards, procedures for controlling products that have been accepted/rejected, and a means of using failure information to improve the quality of your product or service.*

☐ *Establish procedures to ensure supplier product quality control. Watch purchases to make sure that the people you buy from know and observe your quality requirements, as well as any technical specifications.*

☐ *Set up procedures to ensure that any necessary measurement and test equipment is properly calibrated to the proper standard.*

☐ *Create procedures to spot defects as early in production as possible—for example, nonconforming material control.*

☐ *Decide which records and reports will be required to track all steps of the production, inspection and shipping cycles to identify existing and potential problem areas.*

☐ *Assign responsibility for administration and supervision of the various stages of your quality control program.*

☐ *Let your government inspector provide some assistance. Contact the office administering your contract and ask for help.*

Tips on Creating Your QA Manual

It is easier than you think to create your own quality assurance manual. We can't write it for you, but we can offer some tips:

- Please don't go out and copy a generic manual word for word from "Quality Control for Dummies"or get a manual from your Uncle Ned. It will not work for the government, and, more importantly, it will not work for you. Many community colleges offer courses on quality assurance and show you how to build your own documentation. Plus, the purpose of preparing written procedures and instructions is to establish a quality system that is effective for *your* company.

- Create your manual in a loose-leaf format so it will be easy to correct and update.

- Organize your manual by process. In other words, create separate sections for each operation, such as materials purchased, manufacturing, inspection, packing and shipping, etc.

- Include a Table of Contents to make it easier for you, your employees, and your customers to find what they need.

- Include an Introduction page briefly describing the purpose of the manual and the person(s) responsible for administering and supervising the QA program. Also clearly state the procedure that must be followed if and when any changes to your quality program and the manual are made. Finally, include the date the manual was prepared or last revised.

- Include any charts, forms, etc. that may be relevant to quality control.

Remember that the best manual in the world won't do any good unless all your employees, not just those responsible for quality assurance, know that producing quality products is your company's prime goal.

Chapter 18

Contract Terminations

Almost every federal contract contains a clause allowing termination for the convenience of the government. In addition, most contracts in excess of $25,000 contain a clause covering terminations for default. Let's take a look at both types of terminations.

TERMINATION FOR CONVENIENCE

A termination for convenience (T for C) allows the federal government to terminate all or part of a contract for its convenience. This type of termination protects the government's interests by allowing cancellation of contracts for products that become obsolete or unneeded. The termination does not arise from any fault on the part of the contractor.

If the federal government terminates your contract for its convenience, it must notify you in writing. The notice of termination must contain the effective date of the termination, the extent of the termination, and any special instructions.

The contract termination notice and clause generally require a contractor to stop work immediately on the terminated portion, to terminate all affected subcontracts, to perform any specified unterminated portions of the contract, and to proceed promptly to settle termination claims, both its own and those of its subcontractors.

If you receive a termination notice and fail to follow these directions, you do so at your own risk and expense. You should also receive detailed instructions as to the protection and preservation of all property that is, or may become, government-owned.

After termination, the government is required to make a fair and prompt settlement with you. Generally speaking, settlement takes the form of a negotiated agreement between the parties. The idea is to agree on an amount that will compensate you fully and fairly for the work you have done and for any preparation you have made for the terminated portion of the contract. A reasonable allowance for profit is also included. Settlement of cost-reimbursement contracts is somewhat simpler than that of fixed-price contracts, since you will have been reimbursed on a cost basis from the beginning of the contract.

You are entitled to recover all allowable costs incurred in settling a termination for convenience. Those costs may include the following:

- Preparation and presentation of claims

- Termination and settlement of subcontracts

- Storage, transportation, protection and disposition of property acquired or produced for the contract

- Other termination activities

The federal government retains the right to approve or ratify any settlements made with subcontractors. When you and the government agree to all or part of your claim for compensation as a result of the termination, a written amendment (known as a settlement agreement) is made to the contract.

Generally, termination halts regular payments to you under the contract. However, since you may have money tied up in finished and unfinished products, materials and labor, most termination clauses provide you with interim financing through partial payments.

TERMINATION FOR DEFAULT

A termination for default (T for D) means that the government believes that you, the contractor, have not performed in accordance with the terms of the contract.

The government may terminate all or part of a contract for anything that was done that was not in the interest of the government, including:

- Attempted fraud

- Failure to meet quality requirements

- Failure to deliver the supplies or perform the services within the time specified in the contract

- Failure to make progress and that failure endangers performance of the contract

- Failure to perform any other provisions of the contract.

Cure Notice

Before terminating a contract for default because of your failure to make progress or to perform, the contracting officer will usually give you a written notice, called a "cure notice." That notice allows you at least 10 days to cure any defects. Unless the failure to perform is cured within the 10 days, the contracting officer may issue a notice of termination for default.

Show-Cause Notice

If there is not sufficient time for a cure, the contracting officer will usually send a show-cause notice. That notice directs you to show why your contract should not be terminated for default. It ensures that you understand your predicament, and your answer can be used in evaluating whether circumstances justify default action.

Upon termination for default, you are entitled to payment on the contract only for items accepted by the government. *Under a default clause, the government has the right to repurchase the item elsewhere and charge any excess re-procurement costs to the contractor.*

Excusable Failure to Perform

If you can show that your failure to perform the contract is excusable, your contract cannot be terminated for default. To be excusable, the failure must be beyond your control and not caused by your fault or negligence.

Examples of excusable failure include:

- Acts of God

- Acts of a public enemy

- Acts of government

- Fires

- Floods

- Epidemics

- Quarantine restrictions

- Strikes

- Freight embargoes

- Unusually severe weather

Here is a happy thought! If, after termination, you are found not to be in default or the default is found to be excusable, the termination will be treated as one for the convenience of the government. This means that not only will you have removed the tarnished image that a T for D gives a contractor, but you will also get some of your money back as well!

Chapter 19

Getting Paid

Now we turn to every business owner's favorite topic: getting paid. After you have delivered, and the government has accepted, the contracted product or service, all you have to do is submit a proper invoice to the billing office specified in your contract. Under law, the government is required to pay you within 30 days.

Caution

For all of the conditions and requirements for payment, refer to Federal Acquisition Regulation (FAR) 52.232-25.

PROMPT PAYMENT AND A "PROPER" INVOICE

The Prompt Payment Act, which was enacted in the mid-'80s, requires the government to pay a small business within 30 days after receipt of the invoice, if the business completes its end of the contract. However, as you might expect, there is an important catch. The clock on this Act starts only if your invoice, as received, is deemed "proper" under the law.

If your invoice is not deemed "proper," it will get sent back to you within seven days after the billing office received it, with a statement of the reasons why it is not considered proper. You will then have to correct it, resubmit it to the government, and restart the 30-day wait. Therefore, "prompt payment" by the government is directly tied to the "properness" of your invoice.

To make sure that your invoice is correct and proper the first time around, include the following items:

- The name and address of your company.

- Invoice date. You are encouraged to date invoices as close as possible to the date of mailing or transmitting the invoice.

- Contract number or other authorization for supplies delivered or services performed. Be sure to also include the order number and contract line item number.

- Description, quantity, unit of measure, unit price and extended price of supplies delivered or services performed.

- Shipping and payment terms, such as shipment number and date of shipment, prompt payment discount terms, etc. Bill of lading number and weight of shipment will be shown for shipments on government bills of lading.

- The name and address of the person at your company to whom payment is to be sent. This must be the same person specified in the contract or in a proper notice of assignment.

- Name, title, phone number and mailing address of the person to be notified in the event of a defective invoice.

- Any other information or documentation required by the contract, such as evidence of shipment.

- While not required, you are strongly encouraged to assign an identification number to each invoice.

In addition, your invoice may be deemed not proper, for purposes of prompt payment, if the information you furnished in the CCR (Central Contractor Registration) database regarding EFT (electronic funds transfer) is incorrect or not current. (For details on CCR, see Chapter 8: Get Registered.)

INTEREST PENALTY

The law requires the government to pay a small business within 30 days after receipt of a proper invoice. Payment is considered as being made on the day a check is dated or on the date of an electronic funds transfer. An interest penalty will automatically be paid to the contractor if payment is not made by the due date and if the following conditions are met:

- A proper invoice was received by the designated billing office.

- A receiving report or other government documentation authorizing payment was processed, and there was no disagreement over quantity, quality or compliance by the contractor with any contract term or condition.

- The amount due was not subject to further contract settlement actions between the government and the contractor.

GOVERNMENT INVOICE FORM

You may use your own invoice to bill the government, but you must make sure that it meets all of the requirements previously discussed. If it doesn't, you will only slow up payment. Sometimes you might find it easier to use a government form. One common form that is used with military contracts is the DD Form 250, *Material Inspection and Receiving Report.*

The DD Form 250 is basically a material inspection and receiving report (MIRR) that can be used by the government to document contract compliance and by the contractor to submit an invoice. The contractor is responsible for preparing the MIRR, except for entries that an authorized government representative is required to complete.

Specifically, this multi-purpose report is used for the following:

- Evidence of government contract quality assurance at origin or destination

- Evidence of acceptance at origin or destination

- Packing lists

- Receiving

- Shipping

- Contractor invoice

- Commercial invoice support

Work Smart

The DD Form 250 applies to supplies or services acquired by the Department of Defense when the clause at DFARS 252.246-7000, Material Inspection and Receiving Report, is included in the contract.

Subcontractors do not use the DD Form 250 for shipments to their primes unless specified in their subcontract.

ELECTRONIC FUNDS TRANSFER

It is now government policy to pay all contractors by EFT, electronic funds transfer, whenever feasible. In making EFT payments, the government uses the information contained in the Central Contractor Registration (CCR) database.

This policy underscores the need to get your company registered in the CCR database, and to make sure that the information that you have entered is correct and current (for details, see Chapter 8: Get Registered in Part II). If the EFT information in the CCR database is incorrect, then the government may suspend payment until correct information is entered. Remember that if your EFT information changes, *you* are responsible for seeing that the information in the CCR database is updated.

If you have more than one remittance address and/or EFT information set in the CCR database, you must remember to notify the government of the payment receiving point applicable to the contract you are working on. Otherwise, the government will automatically make payment to the first address.

If an incomplete or erroneous transfer occurs because the government used a contractor's EFT information incorrectly, the government is responsible for making a correct payment, paying any prompt payment penalty and recovering any erroneously directed funds.

The government has two mechanisms for making EFT payment: the Automated Clearing House (ACH) network or the Fedwire Transfer System. If the government is unable to release one or more payments by EFT, you will be paid by check or some other mutually agreeable method of payment, or you may request the government to extend the payment due date until such time as the government can make payment by EFT.

Under certain specific circumstances, payment by electronic funds transfer may be made through other than the CCR database. In this case, the contractor will be required to provide the EFT information directly to the office(s) and by the date designated in the contract. And, again, if the EFT information changes, the contractor is responsible for providing the updated information to the designated office(s).

The EFT information that the contractor must provide to the designated office(s) includes:

- The contract number (or other procurement identification number).

- The contractor's name and remittance address, as stated in the contract(s).

- The signature (manual or electronic, as appropriate), title, and telephone number of the contractor official authorized to provide this information.

- The name, address, and 9-digit Routing Transit Number of the contractor's financial agent.

- The contractor's account number and the type of account (checking, saving or lockbox).

- If applicable, the Fedwire Transfer System telegraphic abbreviation of the contractor's financial agent.

Caution

All government requirements pertaining to electronic funds transfer are spelled out in the Federal Acquisition Regulation (FAR 32.1110 and FAR 52.232-33 and –34). Any language that you will see in a bid or contract related to EFT consists of clauses extracted from these sections.

Note that the government is required to protect against improper disclosure of all contractors' EFT information.

EFT Includes Government Credit Card

Under recent legislative requirements, the term "electronic funds transfer" now includes a governmentwide commercial purchase card. Under the law, the government purchase may be used as a means to meet the requirement to pay by EFT.

A governmentwide commercial purchase card is similar in nature to a commercial credit card and is used by the government to make financing and delivery payments for supplies and services. A government purchase card charge authorizes the third party (e.g., financial institution) that issued the purchase card to make immediate payment to the contractor.

The contract will identify the third party and the particular purchase card to be used, but will not include the purchase card account number. The purchase card account number is provided separately to the contractor.

The provisions related to EFT payment will be specified in your contract. Complete details on electronic funds transfer are included in FAR 32.1110 and FAR 52.232-33 and -34.

Part IV

Who Will Help Me?

Firms, both large and small, interested in doing business with the federal government must help themselves by learning how the federal government conducts its business and by identifying and seeking out those purchasing offices that buy the products and services they can supply.

However, additional help and advice are available to you as you work through this maze called government contracting. In this Part, we will describe the general areas from which you can get assistance as you go through the contracting process:

- Directly from the government

- From government-sponsored and commercial counseling services

- From professional associations

Each one has its strengths and weaknesses. Depending on your situation and circumstances, you will have to determine which one or which combination works best for you.

We also describe another area of assistance that is available to you: the special federal programs and initiatives designed to benefit small businesses.

Chapter 20, Help from the Government: The government stands ready to help you during the contracting process. Learn about the different types of small business specialists that have been hired to work with, and advocate for, small businesses during the contracting process. We also tell you which government web sites and publications are most helpful for small businesses and where to find out about procurement conferences, which provide a great way to network with government buyers and large prime contractors.

Chapter 21, Help from Counseling Services: Personalized assistance and advice are available to you through both government-sponsored and commercial counseling services and from professional associations. We explain the services they offer and tell you how to find them.

Chapter 22, Special Small Business Programs: There are several federal programs that are designed to encourage participation by small businesses in the government contracting process, including small businesses owned by certain minority and disadvantaged groups. Find out what benefits they offer and what you need to do to qualify.

Chapter **20**

Help from the Government

There are several ways in which the federal government tries to assist you in finding opportunities and doing business with it:

- Government web sites

- Specialized government personnel

- Government procurement conferences

- Government publications

GOVERNMENT WEB SITES

The federal government has more than 4,300 web sites, according to a recent GAO report. Fortunately, if you're looking for contract opportunities, you don't have to cover all of those sites.

In order to help companies identify government opportunities and buyers, the government is making a strong effort to reduce the number of locations and to create a more uniform format to simplify the process. The government is looking to establish "gateways" (i.e., web sites with multiple links) to make your search easier. There are several already in existence that are being used more and more to post and find opportunities.

Following is a list of the better ones (as of the time this book went to press). Remember that these sites will help you find the opportunities, but once you do, you—not the government—will have to do the work.

- **Federal Business Opportunities (FedBizOpps)** — The

current plan is that this site will eventually have all government opportunities posted here—the "one face to industry" approach. Let's hope this happens; it would surely make life easier. (http://www.fedbizopps.gov)

- **DoD Bus Opps** — The Department of Defense calls this web site "Your Direct Link to DoD Business Opportunities" and plans to eventually post all DoD opportunities here. Don't let the ".com" in the web address mislead you. This is a government site, even though .com, not .gov, is used in the address. The .com is used to give the site a more commercial feel. (http://www.dodbusopps.com)

- **Small Business Administration (SBA)** — This site has a wide range of information pertaining to small businesses as well as SBA-*Net*, a gateway to resources, opportunities, and networking. Most importantly, it has a direct connect to PRO-*Net*, which is fast becoming the sole database used by government buyers to locate potential small business contractors. (http://www.sba.gov)

- **Commerce Business Daily (CBD)** — This is the site to visit over and over again to locate new opportunities and search out potential new customers. Searching by keywords is simple, as long as you can spell. (http://cbdnet.gpo.gov)

- **Procurement Gateway** — This is the Defense Logistics Agency site for all opportunities from its buying offices. (http://progate.daps.mil)

- **Federal Acquisition Jumpstation** —Although not a place where opportunities are posted, it has most links to the federal sites that small business owners would have an interest in. (http://nais.nasa.gov/fedproc)

SPECIALIZED GOVERNMENT PERSONNEL

There are several types of government employees whose main job is to help you do business with the government.

- **Small Business Specialists (SBS)** — By law, every government buying location must have a Small Business Specialist to work with small businesses trying to do business with that office. Major government buying offices have a full-time staff, while smaller offices have a part-time person assigned to that task. These specialists can be a valuable resource for you on the inside. Get to know them.

- **Competition Advocate** — This individual is assigned at a high management level at major buying offices and is responsible for promoting the acquisition of commercial items and for promoting full and open competition. To that end, Competition Advocates challenge barriers to the acquisition of commercial items and to full and open competition, such as unnecessarily restrictive statements of work, unnecessarily detailed specifications, and unnecessarily burdensome contract clauses. They also look at requirements for a specific item to see what can be done to expand competition for the item, challenging any requirements that are not stated in terms of required performance or essential physical characteristics.

- **SBA Procurement Center Representative (PCR)** — Procurement Center Representatives work for the Small Business Administration, but are often located at a major government buying office. Their job is to identify items and services that could be produced or provided by small businesses and try to get them "set aside" for small businesses (i.e., only small businesses can bid on them). If the buying office is small, the PCR may work out of an SBA District office and travel to the buying office.

- **SBA Commercial Marketing Representative (CMR)** — Commercial Marketing Representatives monitor the performance of large companies under their large government contracts and can help you get subcontract work from large prime contractors.

PROCUREMENT CONFERENCES

The government, as well as other non-government sponsors, hold conferences to help you in your quest. Procurement conferences are a good way to meet and speak with government buyers and large prime contractors. Some areas of the country have several conferences per year; other parts have only a few.

Usually you won't get a contract at one, but you can make valuable contacts. The "News" area of the *Commerce Business Daily* will often announce these events and tell you whom to contact. Many government web sites post these conferences on their calendars as well.

GOVERNMENT PUBLICATIONS

The government issues a large number of publications to assist small businesses, but we're only going to mention the most useful ones. You can order these from the Government Printing Office for a fee or you can go to a government web site and read or print it. If you go to a web site, try looking under "publications" or "helps" to see what they have to offer.

- *Selling to the Military* — This publication covers general information about items purchased by the military. It also gives locations of the buying offices and a phone number for the Small Business Office. You can download this publication by going to http://www.acq.osd.mil/sadbu and clicking on "Publications."

- *Small Business Specialists for DoD* — Here is a listing of names, addresses, and phone numbers for all the resources you need to do business with the Department of Defense. See above for web address.

- *Doing Business with the General Services Administration* — This publication covers general information about items purchased by GSA and tells you where the buying offices are located. Go to http://www.pueblo.gsa.gov/smbus.htm. This site has other interesting information as well. Take some time to browse it.

- *Directory of Small Business Specialists for NASA* — If you always wanted to do business with NASA, but didn't know how to go about it, this publication is for you. Go to http://www.hq.nasa.gov/office/codek/director.htm.

- *Participating in VA Acquisition Program* — Here is a fact sheet that covers general information about how and what the Veterans Administration buys. Check it out at http://www.va.gov/OSDBU/factsheets/participate.htm.

Chapter **21**

Help from Counseling Services

If you need more personalized, ongoing assistance and advice, you can get it through government-sponsored or commercial counseling services. You can also get answers to questions and problems your business may be facing by joining a professional association.

PROCUREMENT TECHNICAL ASSISTANCE CENTERS

The Procurement Technical Assistance Program started in 1985 to help the Department of Defense place contracts in areas of the country that needed an influx of federal dollars. Although it has never been called an economic development program, it works like one to some extent.

Through cooperative agreements, the federal government enters into a cost-sharing arrangement with a state or local government or not-for-profit organization to provide general counseling services to businesses seeking government contracts. Its original purpose was only to help with military contracting and with areas of high unemployment, but over the years it has expanded to provide assistance to businesses wanting to do or doing business at the federal, state or local level.

It is a well-run and very cost-effective program with counselors with a high level of expertise.

The Procurement Technical Assistance Center (PTAC) will help you identify contractual opportunities with the government; help locate potential marketing opportunities; help prepare proposals, financial, and contractual forms; and provide guidance with regard to quality assurance, production, and/or the resolution of engineering, financial, quality or production problems. It will also provide you with assistance on e-commerce issues.

While most services are free, some PTACs may charge a nominal fee for certain services such as electronic bid matching or for getting copies of specifications and standards. You can contact one of the regional directors for the national organization, Association of Government Marketing Assistance Specialists (AGMAS), listed below, and the director will put you in contact with the appropriate local center. To find out more about the national organization, visit its web site at http://www.agmas.org.

AGMAS Regional Directors

Region 1	Richard Alexander
CT, ME, MA	Phone: 207-942-6398
NH, RI, VT	Fax: 207-942-3548
Bangor, ME	E-mail: raxlexander@emdc.org

Region 2	Fred Bender
DE, NJ, NY	Phone: 631-853-4803
Hauppauge, NY	Fax: 631-853-4888
	E-mail: Fred.Bender@co.suffolk.ny.us

Region 3	Richard Spanard
MD, OH, PA,	Phone: 304-376-0770
WV	Fax: 304-367-0775
Fairmont, WV	E-mail: spanard@access.mountain.net

Region 4	Pat Phillips
AL, FL, GA,	Phone: 256-765-4668
MS, NC, PR, SC	Fax: 256-765-4813
Florence, AL	E-mail: pphillip@unanov.una.edu

Region 5	Glenda Calver
DC, KY, TN,	Phone: 540-964-7334
VA	Fax: 540-964-7575
Richlands, VA	E-mail: glenda_calver@sw.cc.va.us

Region 6	James Kleckner
IN, IL, MI,	Phone: 630-942-2178
MN, WI	Fax: 630-942-3789
Glen Ellyn, IL	E-mail: kleckner@cdnet.cod.edu

Region 7   Morris Hudson
IA, KS, MO,   Phone: 573-882-3597
NE, ND, SD   Fax: 573-884-4297
Columbia, MO   E-mail: hudsonm@missouri.edu

Region 8   Elizabeth Johnson
AR, LA,   Phone: 334-482-5790
NM, OK, TX   Fax: 334-262-5472
Lafayette, LA   E-mail: egj3510@louisiana.edu

Region 9 Director   Larry Demirelli
AZ, CO, ID,   phone: 208-334-2470
MT, UT, WY   Fax: 208-334-2631
Boise, ID   E-mail: ldemirel@idoc.state.id.us

Region 10 Director   Donna Kirkpatrick
AK, CA, HI, NV   phone: 360-405-5447
Bremerton, WA   Fax: 360-478-0225
                             E-mail: kirkpatd@ctc.com

COMMERCIAL COUNSELING SERVICES

Hiring a private commercial counseling service is another way to get help in doing business with the government. The good ones can offer great personalized assistance, but will cost you some kind of money, flat fee, percentage of contract, retainer plus costs, or some combination.

If you decide to use this method, try to find a service that is accustomed to working with small companies. And remember: Buyer beware. If a service tells you that it can guarantee you contracts, keep looking. Check references and talk to some of the government people that the service has worked with.

You can find a commercial counseling service through word of mouth or by searching on the Internet. Sometimes a Small Business Specialist will be able to recommend a good one.

NATIONAL CONTRACTS MANAGEMENT ASSOCIATION

The National Contracts Management Association (NCMA) is a government-supported organization that was started years ago (1959) because of the lack of good help for companies doing business with the federal government.

Over the years, it has grown in numbers and effectiveness. It is recognized for its member certification program, educational seminars, and monthly magazine, "Contract Management," which alone is worth the price of membership. The new membership fee is about $105; the annual renewal fee thereafter is about $85.

Membership also entitles you access to its members-only site on the Internet, where you can get answers and advice on contract-related questions and problems, read and download "Contract Management" magazine articles all the way back to January 1980, and get a list of web sites that are helpful to contractors.

Besides the national organization, there are local chapters in many parts of the country.

To find out more about the organization, visit its web site at http://www.ncmahq.org.

Chapter 22

Special Small Business Programs

Traditionally, the government has used the federal acquisition process as a tool to implement and further its programs and initiatives for social and economic change, and this trend continues.

There are several important initiatives that are intended to benefit businesses, particularly small business. These programs, which include incentive, set-aside, and preference programs, give small businesses and small businesses owned by special minority and disadvantaged groups advantages in bidding on federal contracts. Following are some of the more important federal programs that are designed to benefit small businesses.

Caution

Under federal law (15 U.S.C. 645(d)), any person who misrepresents a firm's status as a small, small disadvantaged, or women-owned small business concern in order to obtain a contract to be awarded under the small business preference programs established under federal law is subject to:

- *the imposition of fines, imprisonment, or both*

- *administrative remedies, including suspension and debarment*

- *ineligibility for participation in programs conducted under the authority of the Small Business Act.*

SMALL BUSINESS SET-ASIDE PROGRAM

This first program is probably one of the oldest, if not the original, program set up to help small businesses win government contracts. The Small Business Set-Aside Program (SBSA) helps assure that small businesses are awarded a fair proportion of government contracts by reserving (i.e., "setting aside") certain government purchases exclusively for participation by small business concerns.

The determination to make a small business set-aside is usually made unilaterally by the Contracting Officer. However, this determination may also be joint. In this case, it is recommended by the Small Business Administration procurement center representative (PCR) and agreed to by the Contracting Officer. The regulations specify that, to the extent practicable, unilateral determinations initiated by a Contracting Officer, rather than joint determinations, should be used as the basis for small business set-asides.

- **Contracts of $2,500-$100,000** — Under the set-aside program, every acquisition of supplies or services that has an anticipated dollar value between $2,500 and $100,000 (except for those acquisitions set aside for very small business concerns, as described below) is automatically reserved exclusively for small businesses. However, every set-aside must meet the "Rule of Two," which requires that there must be a reasonable expectation that offers will be obtained from two or more small business concerns that are competitive in terms of market prices, quality, and delivery. If only one acceptable offer is received from a responsible small business concern in response to a set-aside, the Contracting Officer is required to make an award to that firm. If no acceptable offers are received from responsible small business concerns, the set-aside will be withdrawn and the product or service, if still valid, will be solicited on an unrestricted basis.

- **Contracts over $100,000** — In addition, the Contracting Officer is required to set aside any contract over $100,000 for small businesses when there is a reasonable expectation that offers will be obtained from at least two responsible small business concerns offering the products of different small business concerns and that award will be made at fair market prices.

- **Partial Set-Asides** — A small business set-aside of a single acquisition or a class of acquisitions may be total or partial. The Contracting Officer is required to set aside a portion of an acquisition, except for construction, for exclusive small business participation when:

— A total set-aside is not appropriate.

— The government's purchase requirement is severable into two or more economic production runs or reasonable lots.

— One or more small business concerns are expected to have the technical competence and productive capacity to satisfy the set-aside portion of the requirement at a fair market price.

— The acquisition is not subject to simplified acquisition procedures.

VERY SMALL BUSINESS PILOT PROGRAM

The purpose of the Very Small Business (VSB) Pilot Program is to improve access to government contract opportunities for "very small business concerns" by reserving certain acquisitions for competition among such concerns. (This program was scheduled to expire on September 30, 2000. At press time, it seemed likely that it would be extended, although this was not yet known for sure.)

A "very small business concern" is defined as a business that has no more than 15 employees and average annual receipts of less than $1 million and that has headquarters located within one of the following ten designated SBA districts:

1. Albuquerque, NM (serving New Mexico)

2. Los Angeles, CA (serving the following counties in California: Los Angeles, Santa Barbara, and Ventura)

3. Boston, MA (serving Massachusetts)

4. Louisville, KY (serving Kentucky)

5. Columbus, OH (serving the following counties in Ohio: Adams, Allen, Ashland, Athens, Auglaize, Belmont, Brown, Butler, Champaign, Clark, Clermont, Clinton, Coshocton, Crawford, Darke, Delaware, Fairfield, Fayette, Franklin, Gallia, Greene, Guernsey, Hamilton, Hancock, Hardin, Highland, Hocking, Holmes, Jackson, Knox, Lawrence, Licking, Logan, Madison, Marion, Meigs, Mercer, Miami, Monroe, Montgomery, Morgan, Morrow, Muskingum, Noble, Paulding, Perry, Pickaway, Pike, Preble, Putnam, Richland, Ross, Scioto, Shelby, Union, Van Wert, Vinton, Warren, Washington, and Wyandot)

6. New Orleans, LA (serving Louisiana)

7. Detroit, MI (serving Michigan)

8. Philadelphia, PA (serving the State of Delaware and the following counties in Pennsylvania: Adams, Berks, Bradford, Bucks, Carbon, Chester, Clinton, Columbia, Cumberland, Dauphin, Delaware, Franklin, Fulton, Huntington, Juniata, Lackawanna, Lancaster, Lebanon, Lehigh, Luzern, Lyocming, Mifflin, Monroe, Montgomery, Montour, Northampton, Northumberland, Philadelphia, Perry, Pike, Potter, Schuylkill, Snyder, Sullivan, Susquehanna, Tioga, Union, Wayne, Wyoming, and York)

9. El Paso, TX (serving the following counties in Texas: Brewster, Culberson, El Paso, Hudspeth, Jeff Davis, Pecos, Presidio, Reeves, and Terrell)

10. Santa Ana, CA (serving the following counties in California: Orange, Riverside, and San Bernadino)

Under the VSB program, a Contracting Officer must set aside for very small business concerns any acquisition that has an anticipated value exceeding $2,500 but not greater than $50,000 if there is a reasonable expectation of obtaining offers from two or more responsible very small business concerns that are competitive in terms of market prices, quality, and delivery. In addition, the businesses must be headquartered within the geographical area served by the designated SBA district.

If only one acceptable offer is received from a responsible very small business concern in response to a very small business set-aside, the Contracting Officer is required to make an award to that firm. If no acceptable offers are received from responsible very small business concerns, the Contracting Officer is authorized to cancel the "very small business set-aside" and proceed with the acquisition as a "small business set-aside."

The VSB program does not apply to contracts awarded pursuant to the 8(a) Program (see below), which pertains to small disadvantaged business concerns (see below). It also does not apply to any government purchase requirement that is subject to the Small Business Competitiveness Demonstration Program.

SMALL BUSINESS R&D FUNDING PROGRAMS

The government sponsors two programs, the Small Business Innovation Research (SBIR) Program and the Small Business Technical Transfer (STTR) Program, which have proven very effective in releasing the "innovative juices" of the research and development minds of the small business community. Although they were resisted at first by government buying offices, they are now very popular with both the buying offices and Congress.

Small Business Innovation Research Program

The SBIR program is a highly competitive program that encourages small businesses to explore their technological potential while providing the incentive to profit from its commercialization. SBIR funds the critical startup and development phases of R&D projects that serve a government need and have the potential for commercialization in private sector and/or government markets. Although the risk and expense of conducting serious R&D efforts are often beyond the means of many small businesses, by reserving a specific percentage of federal R&D funds for small business, SBIR protects the small business and enables it to compete on the same level as larger businesses.

The program, which was funded at $1.2 billion in Fiscal Year 2000, is administered by the following ten federal agencies:

1. Department of Agriculture

2. Department of Commerce

3. Department of Defense

4. Department of Education

5. Department of Energy

6. Department of Health and Human Services

7. Department of Transportation

8. Environmental Protection Agency

9. National Aeronautics and Space Administration

10. National Science Foundation

The government agencies issue a SBIR solicitation once or twice a year, depending on the size of the agency's budget, describing its R&D needs and inviting R&D proposals. Only small, for-profit, American-owned, independently operated businesses can apply under the program. (To be considered "small" under SBIR, the business must have 500 or fewer employees, including all affiliates and/or subsidiaries.) In addition, the principal researcher must be employed by the business.

Companies apply first for a six-month Phase I award of $50,000 to $100,000 to test the scientific, technical and commercial merit and feasibility of a particular concept. If Phase I proves successful, the company may be invited to apply for a two-year Phase II award of $500,000 to $750,000 to further develop the concept, usually to the prototype stage. Proposals are judged competitively on the basis of scientific, technical and commercial merit. Following completion of Phase II, small companies are expected to obtain funding from the private sector and/or non-SBIR government sources for Phase III, which is to develop the concept into a product for sale in private sector and/or government markets.

Since its enactment in 1982, as part of the Small Business Innovation Development Act, SBIR has helped thousands of small businesses to compete for federal research and development awards. Their contributions have enhanced the nation's defense, protected the environment, advanced health care, and improved the management and manipulation of information and data.

Small Business Technical Transfer Program

Although similar in structure to SBIR, the Small Business Technical Transfer Program (STTR) funds cooperative R&D projects involving a small business and a non-profit research institution (i.e., a university, federally funded R&D center, or non-profit research institution). Established by Congress in 1992, the purpose of STTR was to create an effective vehicle for moving ideas from the nation's research institutions to the market, where they can benefit both private sector and government customers. The government STTR program was funded for $62 million in Fiscal Year 2000.

The STTR program is administered by the following five federal agencies:

1. Department of Defense

2. Department of Energy

3. National Aeronautics and Space Administration

4. Department of Health and Human Services

5. National Science Foundation

Just like the SBIR, there are three phases to the program. Phase I is the startup phase for the exploration of the scientific, technical and commercial feasibility of an idea or technology. Awards for Phase I are for up to one year and up to $100,000. Phase II is the expansion phase of Phase I results. During this period, the R&D work is performed and the developer begins to consider commercialization potential. Awards for Phase II are for up to two years and up to $500,000. Phase III is the period during which Phase II innovation moves from the laboratory into the marketplace; there is no STTR funding of this phase.

Example

Historically, about 15 percent of SBIR and STTR proposals are awarded a Phase I contract, and approximately 40 percent of Phase I projects are subsequently awarded a Phase II contract. However, in recent solicitations, a much higher percentage of STTR Phase I proposals was awarded a Phase I contract.

The qualifications for companies applying for STTR are similar to those for STIR. Only small for-profit businesses can apply under the program. In addition, the business must be American-owned and independently operated, with size limited to 500 employees. Although a company does not have to be an established business when it bids, *it must be an established business when the award is made.*

There is no size limit for the research institution partner. In other words, small businesses can team up with some rather large operations to work along with them to get an idea to market.

Since this program consists of developing and bringing a new idea or technology to market, it is important that the future rights to projects are determined at an early stage. The small business and the research institution must develop a written agreement prior to a Phase I award. This agreement must then be submitted to the awarding agency if requested.

For more information on the SBIR and STTR programs, contact your local PTAC office or:

> Small Business Administration Office of Technology
> 409 Third Street, SW
> Washington, DC 20416
> (202) 205-6450

Getting Started in SBIR and STTR

To get started in the SBIR or STTR programs, you must first obtain the current solicitation, which lists all the research topics under which government agency is seeking Phase I proposals and contains detailed information on how to submit a proposal.

The DoD issues two SBIR solicitations and one STTR solicitation each year. The first SBIR solicitation is issued in May and closed in August. The second SBIR solicitation is issued in October and closed in January of the following year. The STTR solicitation is issued in January and closed in April.

To receive hard copies of current and future SBIR and STTR solicitations, place your name and address on the SBIR/STTR mailing list by calling 800-382-4634 or by registering online at http://www.acq.osd.mil/sadbu/sbir. You can also access the SBIR and STTR solicitations electronically through this web site.

After receiving the solicitation, resolve any questions you may have. If you have a technical question about a specific research topic listed in the solicitation, you can talk by telephone with the Topic Author, whose name and phone number will be listed in the solicitation topic. (Keep in mind that Topic Authors will be listed, and telephone questions will be accepted, only during the two months following public release of the solicitation on the web site and before the government begins accepting proposals.) Or you can submit a written question through the SBIR/STTR Interactive Topic Information System (SITIS), in which the questioner and respondent remain anonymous and all questions and answers are posted electronically for general viewing until the solicitation closes.

If you have a general question about the SBIR or STTR programs, contact the government agency SBIR/STTR Help Desk by e-mail at SBIRHELP@us.teltech.com or by telephone at 800-382-4634.

DoD SBIR/STTR "Fast Track"

The "Fast Track" is a special program for the Department of Defense SBIR and STTP programs that offers a significantly higher chance of SBIR/STTR award, and continuous funding, to small companies that can attract outside investors. Small companies retain the intellectual property rights to technologies that they develop under these programs. Funding is awarded competitively, but the process is more streamlined and easier.

Projects that obtain such outside investments and thereby qualify for the Fast Track will, subject to qualifications described in the solicitation, be evaluated for Phase II award under a separate, expedited process and be eligible to receive interim funding of $30,000 to $50,000 between Phases I and II. They will be selected for Phase II award provided they meet or exceed a threshold of "technically sufficient" and have substantially met their Phase I technical goals.

Thus far, over 90 percent of projects qualifying for the Fast Track have received interim funding and been selected for Phase II award. As of April 2000, 156 projects are on the Fast Track, and under these projects, $110 million in DoD SBIR funds has directly leveraged at least $50 million in matching cash from outside investors.

Caution

To qualify for Fast Track, small companies and outside investors must follow the procedures and rules detailed in section 4.5 of the SBIR/STTR solicitation. This discussion only summarizes the most important requirements.

Many small companies have found the Fast Track policy to be an effective tool for leveraging their SBIR (or STTR) funds to obtain additional funds from outside investors. This is because, under the

Fast Track, a small company can offer an investor the opportunity to obtain a match of between $1 and $4 in DoD SBIR (or STTR) funds for every $1 the investor puts in.

Toward the end of a small company's Phase I SBIR or STTR project, the company and its investor must submit a Fast Track application stating, among other things, that the investor will match both interim and Phase II SBIR or STTR funding, in cash, contingent on the company's selection for Phase II award. The matching rates needed to qualify for the Fast Track are as follows:

- For small companies that have never before received a Phase II SBIR or STTR award from DoD or any other federal agency, the matching rate is 25 cents for every SBIR or STTR dollar. (For example, if such a company receives interim and Phase II SBIR funding that totals $750,000, it must obtain matching funds from the investor of $187,500.)

- For all other companies, the matching rate is $1 for every SBIR or STTR dollar. (For example, if such a company receives interim and Phase II SBIR funding that totals $750,000, it must obtain matching funds from the investor of $750,000.)

The matching funds may pay for additional R&D on the company's SBIR or STTR project or, alternatively, they may pay for other activities (e.g., marketing) that further the development and/or commercialization of the technology.

In the application, the company and its investor must certify that the outside funding qualifies as a "Fast Track investment," and that the investor qualifies as an "outside investor." Outside investors may include such entities as another company, a venture capital firm, an individual "angel" investor, or a non-SBIR or non-STTR government program. Outside investors may not include the owners of the small business, their family members, and/or affiliates of the small business.

DoD will notify each Fast Track company, no later than 10 weeks after the end of Phase I, whether it has been selected for Phase II award. Once notified, the company and investor must certify, within 45 days, that the entire amount of the matching funds from the outside investor has been transferred to the company.

If you need assistance regarding Fast Track, you can visit DoD's STIR/STTR web site at http://www.acq.osd.mil/sadbu/sbir/homepg.htm for complete details on the program. The site also contains a list of private-sector sources of early-stage technology financing as well as a list of ongoing Phase I SBIR and STTR projects.

You can also contact the SBIR/STTR Help Desk by e-mail at SBIRHELP@us.teltech.com or by telephone at 800-382-4634.

SBA PROGRAMS

The Small Business Administration administers several programs that are designed to help small businesses market to both large business and government procurements:

- **The Small Disadvantaged Business (SDB) Certification Program** is designed to treat small companies equitably and empower them to pursue business in both the private and public sector contract arenas by providing them specific advantages in the procurement process.

- **The 8(a) Business Development Program** provides on-going personalized business assistance and counseling to certified 8(a) small disadvantaged businesses in expanding their business, fostering profitable business relationships and becoming more effective in both the large business and government sectors.

- **The HUBZone Empowerment Contracting Program** is designed to stimulate economic development and create jobs in urban and rural communities. The program provides contracting opportunities to small businesses located in, and hiring employees from, Historically Underutilized Business Zones.

- **The 8(a) BD Mentor-Protégé Program** is a new public-private partnership sponsored by the SBA that seeks to grow disadvantaged startup businesses with the help of experienced ones.

- **The Veterans Entrepreneurship Program** is another recently launched program that provides assistance to veterans owning small businesses, especially those who are service-disabled.

Small businesses cannot receive benefits from these programs unless the SBA certifies that they meet the specific criteria applicable for the particular program and that they qualify to participate.

SDB Certification Program

The Small Disadvantaged Business Certification Program (SBD Program) is administered by SBA and designed to help small disadvantaged businesses compete in the American economy by providing specific advantages and benefits in the federal procurement process.

(Note that companies that are certified as 8(a) firms automatically qualify for SDB certification. The 8(a) program is explained below.)

Benefits of SDB Program

If you can qualify as a small disadvantaged business (SBD), then you are entitled to participate in special preference programs aimed at encouraging participation by SBDs in government business.

SDB certified companies may benefit in two main ways. First, SDBs are eligible for special bidding benefits. An SDB can qualify for a price evaluation adjustment of up to 10 percent when bidding on federal contracts in certain industries or services where the U.S. Department of Commerce has determined that SDBs are underrepresented because of the effects of ongoing discrimination.

Work Smart

As of October 1, 1998, SDBs are eligible to receive the price credit when competing in the following industry categories:

Industries:	Services:
Agriculture	Electric
Fishing	Gas
Forestry	Sanitary services
Construction	Wholesale trade
Mining	Retail trade
Manufacturing	Finance
Transportation	Insurance
Communications	Real estate services

Second, the program also provides evaluation credits to prime contractors who achieve SDB subcontracting targets, which in turn boosts subcontracting opportunities for SDBs. All prime contractors are encouraged to use certified SDBs as subcontractors through mandated evaluation factors and optional monetary incentives. The program is intended to help federal agencies achieve the government-wide goal of 5 percent SDB participation in prime contracting.

To receive this credit, a contractor must confirm that a joint venture partner, team member, or subcontractor representing itself as a small disadvantaged business concern is, in fact, identified as a certified small disadvantaged business. Confirmation may be made by checking the database maintained by the Small Business Administration (PRO-*Net*) or by contacting the SBA's Office of Small Disadvantaged Business Certification and Eligibility.

The extent of participation of SDB concerns is evaluated in competitive, negotiated acquisitions expected to exceed $500,000 ($1,000,000 for construction). The SDB preference program does not apply in small business set-asides, 8(a) acquisitions, negotiated acquisitions where the lowest price technically acceptable source selection process is used, or contract actions that will be performed entirely outside of the United States.

Note that this price credit does not apply to government procurements that are below the simplified acquisition threshold of $100,000, procurements that are set aside for small business (i.e., small business set asides, HUBZone set asides and procurements under the SBA 8(a) program).

We also want to mention a new benefit. Under recent federal procurement regulations, the SBA certifies SDBs for participation in federal procurements aimed at overcoming the effects of discrimination.

Eligibility Requirements

Any small business wanting to take advantage of the SDB Program must be certified by the SBA that it meets specific social, economic, ownership, and control eligibility criteria. To qualify as a Small Disadvantaged Business (SDB), the business must be a small business concern that is at least 51 percent owned and controlled by one or more individuals who are both socially and economically disadvantaged.

Social disadvantage. Socially disadvantaged individuals are those who have been subjected to racial or ethnic prejudice or cultural bias within American society because of their identities as members of groups and without regard to their individual qualities. The social disadvantage must stem from circumstances beyond their control.

Caution

To receive the benefits of the SBD Program, a small business must be certified by SBA that it meets all of the requirements.

The U.S. population is broken down into two groups: designated groups and non-designated groups. For designated groups, the law allows for a presumption of discrimination. However, keep in mind that the presumption of discrimination may be rebutted.

Businesses whose owners are members of one of the following groups are presumed to qualify:

- African American

- Hispanic American

- Native American (American Indians, Eskimos, Aleuts, or Native Hawaiians)

- Asian-Pacific American (persons with origins from Burma, Thailand, Malaysia, Indonesia, Singapore, Brunei, Japan, China, Taiwan, Laos, Cambodia (Kampuchea), Vietnam, Korea, The Philippines, U.S. Trust Territory of the Pacific Islands (Republic of Palau), Republic of the Marshall Islands, Federated States of Micronesia, the Commonwealth of the Northern Mariana Islands, Guam, Samoa, Macao, Hong Kong, Fiji, Tonga, Kiribati, Tuvalu, or Nauru)

- Subcontinent Asian (Asian-Indian) (American persons with origins from India, Pakistan, Bangladesh, Sri Lanka, Bhutan, the Maldives Islands, or Nepal)

Individuals in non-designated groups can qualify if they can successfully make an argument for discrimination based on certain types of evidence, which include all of the following:

- At least one objective distinguishing feature that has contributed to social disadvantage such as gender disability, sexual orientation, or living in an economically isolated community

- Personal experiences of substantial and chronic social disadvantage

- Negative impact on one's education, employment entry, and advancement in the business world.

Economic disadvantage. Economically disadvantaged individuals are socially disadvantaged individuals whose ability to compete in the free enterprise system has been impaired due to diminished capital and credit opportunities as compared to others in the same or similar line of business who are not socially disadvantaged.

In assessing the personal financial condition of an individual claiming economic disadvantage, his or her net worth may not exceed the limit set by law. All individuals must have a net worth of less than $750,000, excluding the equity of the business and primary residence.

Successful applicants must also meet applicable size standards for small businesses in their industry.

Once certified, the firm is added to an online registry of SDB-certified firms maintained in the PRO-*Net* database (see Part II, Chapter 8 for details). Certified firms remain on the list for three years.

Contracting Officers and large business prime contractors may search this online registry for potential suppliers.

Application and Certification

To begin the certification process, you need to obtain two documents: an application form and the SDB Certification Checklist. You must provide all of the information required on both of these documents for your application to be considered complete.

Application forms and the SDB Certification Checklist may be requested from your local SBA district office or may be downloaded on SBA's web site at http://www.sba.gov.

Application form. There are four different application forms for the various types of business legal structures: sole proprietorship, partnership, limited liability company, and corporation. Make sure you get the proper application form. If you are obtaining it through the SBA office, tell the person you contact that you are one of the following:

- sole proprietorship

- partnership

- limited liability company

- corporation

- community development corporation

- Alaska Native Corporation or Indian Tribe.

If you are obtaining the form from SBA's web site, make sure you download the correct one.

SDB Certification Checklist. In addition to the application, make sure you also request or download the SDB Certification Checklist, which contains a list of additional documents that you must submit, along with your application, to be considered for SDB certification. These documents include, but are not limited to:

- ☐ SBA Form 355 Application for Small Business Size Determination

- ☐ SBA Form 413 Personal Financial Statement

- ☐ IRS Form 4506 SBA Request for Copy or Transcript of Tax Form

- ☐ Copies of licenses and permits

- ☐ History of business

- ☐ Resumes and profiles of principals and employees

- ☐ Lease/rental/trust deed for business site/office

- ☐ Business bank account information

- ☐ Three recent federal tax returns

- ☐ Current and prior balance sheet and profit and loss statements

- ☐ Personal income tax returns

- ☐ Copies of franchise or trust agreements

- ☐ Any and all additional documentation that may be required on the checklist for your particular type of business entity.

Caution: Look at each item on the checklist carefully. You will not be considered for certification as an SDB unless all the required documentation specified on the checklist for your type of business is submitted along with the completed application form.

Help Getting Certified

You can work directly with SBA in completing your application and providing the required documentation, but if there is something wrong with your paperwork, you will be denied certification and given 45 days in which to respond to the rejection. If you don't satisfactorily address the deficiencies within that time frame, you will have to wait a year to reapply.

You also have the option of working with a private third-party certifier selected by the SBA to help in the certification process. If you choose to do it this way, you can go back to the certifier as often as you wish to get your paperwork correct. However, you will be charged a fee for that service, which can range from several hundred dollars to $1,500.00.

There are also several computer programs available that can provide you some additional assistance in filling out the forms.

Keep in mind that, no matter how you choose to complete your paperwork and application, *you* are the one ultimately responsible for making sure that all questions are addressed and all required information is provided.

For further information on the SDB program, call 202-619-1850 or 800-558-0884 or e-mail the SBA at SDB@sba.gov.

8(a) Business Development Program

The 8(a) Business Development Program, like the Small Disadvantaged Business Certification Program described above, is administered by SBA and designed to help small disadvantaged businesses compete in the American economy. Note that companies that are certified as 8(a) firms automatically qualify for SDB certification.

Example

The 8(a) Business Development Program was named for a section of the Small Business Act. In fiscal year 1998, more than 6,100 firms participated in the 8(a) program and were awarded $6.4 billion in federal contract awards.

In addition to the federal procurement benefits available through the SDB Program, for which 8(a) firms automatically qualify, 8(a) firms receive a broad scope of assistance, including one-on-one assistance and coaching from a Business Opportunity Specialist to help them grow and expand their businesses. Under this program, 8(a) businesses enter into a nine-year partnering relationship with the SBA—a four-year developmental stage and a five-year transition stage.

During the developmental stage, businesses are offered help in expanding their business and fostering meaningful business relationships. During the transitional stage, businesses are helped to become more effective in both the large business and government sector market in dealing with complex business deals and to prepare for post-8(a) program expansion and development.

The overall goal of the program goal is to graduate firms that will go on to thrive in a competitive business environment. To achieve this end, SBA district offices monitor and measure the progress of participants through annual reviews, business planning, and systematic evaluations.

At any time during a firm's term, the SBA may terminate a firm's participation in the 8(a) program for non-compliance with program requirements and regulations.

Benefits of 8(a) Program

In addition to the on-going personal counseling services, the program offers specialized business training, marketing assistance, and high-level executive development provided by the SBA and its resource partners. Businesses may also be eligible for assistance in obtaining access to surplus government property and supplies, SBA-guaranteed loans and bonding assistance.

Moreover, recent regulations permit 8(a) companies to form beneficial teaming partnerships and allow federal agencies to streamline the contracting process. In addition, the recent rules make it easier for non-minority firms to participate by proving their social disadvantage. Specifically:

- Participants can receive sole-source contracts, up to a ceiling of $3 million for goods and services and $5 million for manufacturing. There is also a limit on the total dollar value of sole-source contracts that an individual participant can receive while in the program: $100 million or five times the value of its primary SIC code (SIC codes are explained in Part II).

- Federal acquisition policies encourage federal agencies to award a certain percentage of their contracts to SDBs. To speed up the award process, the SBA has signed Memorandums of Understanding with 25 federal agencies allowing them to contract directly with certified 8(a) firms.

- Recent changes permit 8(a) firms to form joint ventures and teams to bid on contracts. This enhances the ability of 8(a) firms to perform larger prime contracts and overcome the effects of contract bundling (the combining of two or more contracts together into one large contract).

Eligibility Requirements

To qualify for the 8(a) program, a small business must be owned and controlled by a socially *and* economically disadvantaged individual; in other words, a disadvantaged owner must be involved on a full-time basis. Certain minority groups are presumed to qualify as socially disadvantaged and include African Americans, Hispanic Americans, Asian Pacific Americans, and Subcontinent Asian Americans.

However, an individual does not qualify automatically as socially disadvantaged just because he or she belongs to one of the named groups. SBA may challenge an individual's claim of social disadvantage if there is substantial evidence that the individual has not experienced, or has overcome, the traditional discriminatory social attitudes, racial prejudice and stereotyping that have created serious obstacles for many members of these groups when they attempt to obtain equal access to financing, markets and resources necessary to establish, maintain or expand small businesses.

Individuals who are not members of the named minority groups can be admitted to the program if they can show through a "preponderance of the evidence" that they are disadvantaged because of race, ethnic origin, gender, physical handicap, or geographic environment isolated from the mainstream of American society. The individual must demonstrate personal suffering and not merely claim membership in a non-designated group.

To qualify for the 8(a) program, a socially disadvantaged applicant must also be economically disadvantaged. In order to meet the economic disadvantage test, individuals must have a net worth of less than $250,000 for initial 8(a) eligibility, excluding the value of the business and personal residence. For continued 8(a) eligibility after admission to the program, net worth must be less than $750,000. This determination is made on the individuals and not jointly if spouses are involved. Separate personal financial statements on spouses are required.

Caution

To receive the benefits of the 8(a) Program, a small business must be certified by SBA that it meets all of the requirements.

In determining economic disadvantage, the SBA will determine whether the applicant has suffered diminished credit and capital opportunities, based on the following: personal and business assets; personal and business net worth; personal and business income and profits; success in obtaining adequate financing, adequate bonding and outside equity credit; and other economic disadvantages.

Successful applicants must also meet applicable size standards for small business concerns, be in business for at least two years, display reasonable success potential and display good character. Although the two-year requirement may be waived, firms must continue to comply with various requirements while in the program.

Application and Certification

To start the application process, contact the local SBA district office serving your area. An SBA representative will answer general questions over the telephone. Most district offices have regularly scheduled 8(a) orientation workshops designed to explain the 8(a) Business Development Program, the eligibility requirements and to review various SBA forms. An application will be provided at the informational session, along with filing instructions.

You will be notified by mail as to whether you have met eligibility requirements and your company has been approved to participate in the 8(a) program. If you fail to meet eligibility requirements, you will also be notified of the reasons why your application was declined and given 45 days to request a reconsideration of the decision. If your application is reconsidered and declined again, you must wait twelve months to reapply.

For further information, call the SBA Division of Program Certification & Eligibility at (202) 205-6417.

Women-Owned Small Businesses

Federal regulations require that women-owned small businesses (WOSB) have the maximum practicable opportunity to participate in performing contracts awarded by any federal agency. The regulations direct federal agencies to reach out to women-owned small businesses and make sure that they understand the process and are offered contract opportunities. As of this writing, there were no specific preference programs in this area.

However, if you are a women-owned small business and feel that you have been hindered in your efforts to do business, you can apply for certification as a socially and economically disadvantaged business under the SBA 8(a) program. See your local SBA office to discuss this issue.

One word of caution: If you are a male-owned business and you make your wife or another woman owner of 51 percent of the stock in order to qualify for 8(a) benefits, you are spinning your wheels. The SBA auditor will know what you are doing—51 percent ownership is a red flag. Similarly, if the auditor comes to your office and sees that the male office is bigger than the female's, you are not going to be certified. You must be able to show that the business is managed and controlled on a daily basis by a woman, and that the woman is the person who makes the life and death decisions of the company.

Work Smart

If you are looking for information about opportunities for women-owned small businesses, a good place to start is at http://www.womenbiz.gov.

HUBZone Program

The Historically Underutilized Business Zone (HUBZone) Empowerment Contracting program, which was enacted into law as part of the Small Business Reauthorization Act of 1997, provides federal contracting assistance and opportunities for qualified small businesses located in distressed historically underutilized business zones, known as "HUBZones." Among other things, it allows small firms located in many urban or rural areas to qualify for sole-source and other types of federal contract benefits. The underlying purpose of the program is to encourage economic development and increase employment opportunities.

The HUBZone program falls under the auspices of the Small Business Administration (SBA), which is responsible for implementing the program and determining which businesses are eligible to receive HUBZone contracts. SBA maintains a listing of qualified HUBZone small businesses that federal agencies can use to locate vendors and also adjudicates protests of eligibility to receive HUBZone contracts. In addition, SBA is responsible for reporting to Congress on the program's impact on employment and investment in HUBZone areas.

While the Small Business Reauthorization Act of 1997 increased the overall government-wide procurement goal for small business from 20 to 23 percent, the statute sets the goal for HUBZone contracts at 1½ percent for 2000, 2 percent for 2001, 2½ percent for 2002, and 3 percent for 2003 and each year thereafter.

Ten major agencies were included in the program for Fiscal Years 1999 and 2000:

1. Department of Defense (DOD)

2. Department of Agriculture (USDA)

3. Department of Health and Human Services (HHS)

4. Department of Transportation (DOT)

5. Department of Energy (DOE)

6. Department of Housing and Urban Development (HUD)

7. Environmental Protection Agency (EPA)

8. National Aeronautics and Space Administration (NASA)

9. General Services Administration (GSA)

10. Department of Veterans Affairs (VA)

On October 1, 2000, the HUBZone program became applicable to all federal departments and agencies.

Benefits of HUBZone Program

There are three types of contract benefits that a HUBZone certified business can qualify for:

- **A competitive HUBZone contract** can be awarded if the Contracting Officer has a reasonable expectation that at least two qualified HUBZone small businesses will submit offers and that the contract can be awarded at a fair market price.

- **A sole source HUBZone contract** can be awarded if the Contracting Officer does not have a reasonable expectation that two or more qualified HUBZone small businesses will submit offers, determines that the qualified HUBZone small business is responsible, and determines that the contract can be awarded at a fair price. The government estimate cannot exceed $5 million for manufacturing purchases or $3 million for all other requirements.

- **A full and open competition contract** can be awarded with a price evaluation preference. The offer of the HUBZone small business will be considered lower than the offer of a non-HUBZone/non-small business, providing that the offer of the HUBZone small business is not more than 10 percent higher than that of the non-HUBZone business.

In addition to the contract benefits, certified HUBZone firms can qualify for higher SBA-guaranteed surety bonds on construction and service contract bids. Firms in Empowerment Zones and Enterprise Communities (EZ/EC) can also benefit from employer tax credits, tax-free facility bonds, and investment tax deductions.

Eligibility and Certification

To qualify for the HUBZone program, a business must meet four requirements:

1. It must be a small business.

2. It must be owned and controlled *only* by U.S. citizens.

3. The principal office of the business must be located in a "historically underutilized business zone."

4. At least 35 percent of its employees must reside in a HUBZone. Existing businesses that choose to move to qualified areas are eligible. To fulfill the 35 percent requirement, employees must live in a primary residence within that area for at least 180 days or be a currently registered voter in that area.

Caution

If you are a one-person business and your office is located in a HUBZone, but you don't reside in the HUBZone, you do not qualify!

To be designated a "HUBZone," an area must also meet certain criteria. It must be located in one or more of the following three areas:

1. a qualified census tract (as defined in the Internal Revenue Code of 1986)

2. a qualified "non-metropolitan county" (as defined in the Internal Revenue Code of 1986) with a median household income of less than 80 percent of the State median household income or with an unemployment rate of not less than 140 percent of the statewide unemployment rate, based on U.S. Department of Labor recent data

3. a federally recognized Indian reservation.

The certification process is fully electronic, Internet-based, and integrated with PRO-*Net* (see Part II for details on PRO-*Net*). The SBA will verify eligibility and make sure that ownership, location, and employment percentage requirements are satisfied. The average time for processing is approximately 30 days, and SBA's decision will be in writing.

To apply, companies are encouraged to use the electronic application directly on the HUBZone web site at http://www.sba.gov/hubzone/. Applicants can also submit a paper copy to SBA headquarters in Washington, D.C. Applicants can download the paper version from the web site or obtain it from any local SBA district office.

Computer mapping software available on SBA's web site allows firms to search a database to determine whether or not they are located in a qualified HUBZone. The system allows searches by address, county or town and displays metropolitan areas, Indian reservations and areas that qualify by income, unemployment rate, or both.

For further information, you can e-mail the SBA at hubzone@sba.gov.

SDB, 8(a) and HUBZone Compared

The SBA administers three core certification programs for small businesses: the Small Disadvantaged Business Program (SDB), the 8(a) Business Development Program, and the HUBZone Program. All three are designed to help small businesses market themselves to both large business and government procurements. However, not every small business can participate in these programs. To participate, a business must meet specific criteria and must be certified by SBA that these criteria have been met.

Benefits Compared

There are some major differences in the benefits of the SDB, 8(a), and HUBZone programs. SDB and HUBZone are essentially contractor programs designed to expand economic opportunity for disadvantaged businesses. In contrast, 8(a) is a business development program that provides a broad scope of assistance to disadvantaged firms, including personalized business counseling. Under the program, each 8(a) certified company is assigned a Business Opportunity Specialist (BOS) who advises and coaches the company in business matters. There is no such benefit under the SDB and HUBZone Programs.

Only the HUBZone Program specifically promotes business opportunities in distressed communities. Small businesses not located within these areas may be eligible for certification in the SDB or 8(a) BD Programs.

Certification Requirements Compared

To be certified for the SDB, 8(a), or HUBZone programs, a business must demonstrate that it meets the basic requirements for admission. Although there are differences in the requirements for each, there is one universal requirement for all of these programs: the business must be classified as small.

For SDB and 8(a) certification, a business must generally show that it is unconditionally owned and controlled by one or more socially and economically disadvantaged individuals who are of good character and citizens of the United States. In addition, the net worth of the individual claiming economic disadvantage may not exceed the limit set by law. For SDB eligibility, net worth must be less than $750,000, excluding the value of the business and personal residence. For initial 8(a) eligibility, the net worth of an individual claiming disadvantage must be less than $250,000, excluding the value of the business and personal residence. For continued 8(a) eligibility after admission to the program, net worth must be less than $750,000. (Note that companies that are 8(a) firms automatically qualify for SDB certification.)

For HUBZone certification, your business must be located in a qualified HUBZone area. A pre-determined percentage of employees who work for the company must also live in a HUBZone.

Application Process Compared

You can apply to all three certification programs and, under the right circumstances, you could conceivably qualify for all three—for example, if you were an 8(a) eligible business located in an Historically Underutilized Business Zone.

Although you can apply to all three programs, there is no universal application. Each core program has its own application form and specific process for certification. However, all three certification programs require similar information along with your application, including such items as personal financial statements, previous tax returns, SBA forms, and IRS forms.

8(a) Mentor-Protégé Program

The SBA has recently implemented the Department of Defense Mentor-Protégé Program (MPP) to help starting 8(a) companies learn the ropes from experienced businesses. The new program is offered under SBA's 8(a) Business Development program serving disadvantaged firms.

The MPP seeks to encourage major DoD prime contractors (mentors) to help develop the technical and business capabilities of small disadvantaged businesses and other eligible protégés in order to enable the protégé to expand its business base within the Department of Defense. Through credit toward subcontracting goals or some direct reimbursement of costs, the MPP provides incentives for these mentors to establish and implement a developmental assistance plan that enables the protégé to compete more successfully for DoD prime contracts and subcontract awards.

The mentor firms represented in the MPP encompass a broad range of industries, including environmental remediation, manufacturing, telecommunications, and health care. Mentors provide technical and management assistance, financial assistance in the form of equity investments and/or loans, subcontract support, and assistance in performing prime contracts through joint venture arrangements with 8(a) firms.

Protégés have only one mentor at a time. Generally, a mentor will not have more than one protégé at a time without SBA authorization.

Protégé Requirements

To participate in the program, the protégé must be in good standing in the 8(a) program and must be current with all reporting requirements. In addition, the protégé must also meet *one* of the following requirements:

- It must be in the developmental stage of the 8(a) program.

- It must have never received an 8(a) contract.

- It must have a size of less than half the size standard for a small business based on its primary SIC code.

MPP Certification for Non-8(a) Firms

Beginning on October 1, 1999, any firm that is not an 8(a) certified firm but is seeking to be eligible as a Small Disadvantaged Business for participation as a Protégé under the DoD Mentor-Protégé Program must be certified as an SDB by the Small Business Administration. Self-certifications were no longer sufficient as of that date.

Contact the local SBA District Office (http://www.sba.gov) for an application package. Submit the completed application to SBA's Assistant Administrator for Small Disadvantaged Business Certification and Eligibility (AA/SDBCE) or to an approved private certifier, if directed by SBA. No firm will be recognized as an SDB without certification by the SBA for any of the purchasing programs that give an SDB preference for award.

Mentor Requirements

The mentor can be a business that has graduated from the 8(a) program, a firm in the transitional stage of the program, or a small or large business. A mentor must have the capability to assist the protégé and must make a commitment for at least a year. In addition, the mentor must meet *all* of the following requirements:

- It must be financially healthy and must have been profitable for at least the last two years.

- It must be a federal contractor in good standing.

- It must be able to provide support to a protégé through lessons learned and practical experience gained from the 8(a) program or through its general knowledge of government contracting.

Entering the Program

Mentor and protégé firms enter the program by entering into an SBA-approved written agreement outlining the protégé's needs and describing the assistance the mentor has committed to providing. The protégé's servicing district office evaluates the agreement according to the provisions contained in the regulations (13 CFR 124.520). SBA conducts annual reviews to determine the success of the mentor-protégé relationship.

For additional information on the program, contact your SBA District Office or:

> 8(a) BD—Mentor-Protégé Program
> U.S. Small Business Administration
> 409 Third Street, SW
> Washington, DC 20416
> Phone: (202) 205-6118

The SBA also provides details on the program at its web site (http://www.sba.gov).

Veterans Entrepreneurship Act

Enacted August 17, 1999, the Veterans Entrepreneurship and Small Business Development Act of 1999, also known as the "Veterans Act," is designed to provide assistance to veterans who are entrepreneurs and especially to service-disabled veteran entrepreneurs.

It is also designed to cushion the impact on small businesses when their owners or essential employees who are reservists are ordered to active duty during military conflicts by providing loans, loan payment deferrals, and technical and managerial assistance.

The law provides for technical, financial and procurement assistance to veteran-owned small businesses under the auspices of the SBA. However, at the time of publication of this book, there were no specifics as to the way the Act will be implemented in the acquisition area. There will be federal contracting and subcontracting goals required for participation of small businesses owned and controlled by service-disabled veterans. The exact level of these goals had not yet been set, but will likely be between 3-5 percent of the subcontract opportunities available. They may be graduated over a number of years, with gradual increases until a database of applicable companies is established.

The Act also revises some common definitions for purposes of taking advantage of the new benefits, including the terms "veteran," "service-disabled veteran," "small business concern owned and operated by service-disabled veterans" and "small business concern owned and operated by veterans."

You can check the status of this program by contacting SBA Office of Veterans Affairs at http://www.sba.gov/vets.

OTHER ASSISTANCE MEASURES

There is other assistance that is available to small businesses to help them in the acquisition process.

Certificate of Competency

This program, sometimes referred to as the "second bite of the apple," comes into play when a government buyer determines that a small business is "not responsible" for a specific contract award. In other words, the buyer has determined that the business does not show certain elements of responsibility, such as capability, competency, capacity, credit, integrity, perseverance, or tenacity, for the purposes of receiving and performing that specific government contract. In such a case, the Contracting Officer is required to withhold the contract and refer action to the Small Business Administration for a possible Certificate of Competency (COC).

Once the matter is referred to the SBA, the SBA must, within 15 days, inform the company of the Contracting Officer's decision and offer it an opportunity to apply to the SBA for a COC. After receiving an acceptable application, the SBA conducts an independent pre-award survey to determine the company's ability to perform on the specific contract. If the SBA determines that the company is able to perform, the COC program authorizes the SBA to issue a Certificate of Competency. The COC certifies to government Contracting Officers as to all elements of responsibility of the small business concern to receive and perform on the specific government contract.

If the small business decides that it has bid too low or a better job comes along, it may want to ignore the COC involvement. If the COC is refused, the government buyer can then make the award to the next low responsive and responsible bidder.

DoD Regional Councils

The DoD Regional Councils for Small Business Education and Advocacy are a nationwide network of small business specialists organized to promote national small business programs to include minority and disadvantaged small business concerns and minority universities and institutions.

Additional objectives include promoting the exchange of ideas and experiences and general information among small business specialists and the contracting community; developing closer relationships and better communication among government entities and the small business community; and staying abreast of statutes, policies, regulations, directives, trends and technology affecting the small business program.

There are eight councils in all: Northeast, Mid-Atlantic, District of Columbia, Southeastern, North Central, South Central, Pacific Northwest, and Western. They are sponsored by the DoD Office of Small and Disadvantaged Business Utilization (SADBU), but are governed by individual by-laws. Membership is open to small business advocates from the DoD and civilian agencies. The DoD Office of SADBU is an active participant and advisor to each Council; however, each Council establishes its own committee structure, meeting schedules and agendas.

Non-voting membership is extended to personnel representing small business interests such as Small Business Development Centers and Procurement Technical Assistance Centers. Some Councils invite the Small Business Liaison Officers representing prime contractors in an effort to promote small business subcontracting.

These councils offer small businesses a chance to "rub shoulders" with government and large contractors that may lead to contract opportunities.

DoD THRUST Program

The Department of Defense views small business as a critical part of the industrial base, especially in programs involving military readiness, economic security and advanced technology, and is committed to ensuring the participation of small disadvantaged business (SDB) in its procurement process.

In order to increase those efforts, DoD's Office of Small and Disadvantaged Business Utilization (OSADBU) has implemented the industry THRUST program, which concentrates on five areas of industry—environment, manufacturing, health care, telecommunications and management information including simulation—and seeks to provide small business concerns, SDBs, and women-owned business with increased awareness of DoD contracting and subcontracting opportunities available in those areas.

Under this program, OSADBU conducts conferences featuring a specific THRUST industry. Each conference is hosted by a designated military department or agency and features presentations and workshops conducted by industry experts from the contracting, technical and program offices and representatives from defense agencies. The conferences also offer sessions on procurement and acquisition policies and agendas.

Program materials are very helpful to the small companies interested in those areas.

For more information, check out the THRUST program web site at http://www.acq.osd.mil/sadbu/thrust.

Part V

Appendices

Abbreviations/Acronyms

Following are the abbreviations and acronyms that you will be using when doing business with the federal government. Although not an exhaustive listing, it does contain the most commonly used abbreviations and acronyms that occur in conversations with government buying offices and in documents related to the contracting process.

A

A-E: Architect-Engineer

ACMS: Advanced Cost Management Systems

ACO: Administrative Contracting Officer

ACRS: Accelerated Cost Recovery System

AF: Air Force

AFAA: Air Force Audit Agency

AICPA: American Institute of Certified Public Accountants

AID: Agency for International Development

AFLC: Air Force Logistics Command

AMC: Army Material Command

AMIS: Agency Management Information System (DCAA)

AMP: Annual Management Plan

AR: Army

ASBCA: Armed Services Board of Contract Appeals

ASPR: Armed Services Procurement Regulation (changed to the DAR, which in turn was replaced by the FAR)

B

B&P: Bid & Proposal

BCA: Board(s) of Contract Appeals

BDC: Business Development Center

BDE: Business Development Expense

BML: Bidder's Mailing List

BOA: Basic Ordering Agreement

BOPCR: Breakout Procurement Center Representative (SBA)

BOS: Business Opportunity Specialist

BPA: Blanket Purchase Agreement

C

CA: Commercial Activities

CAC: Contract Audit Coordinator (DCAA)

CACO: Corporate/Home Office ACO

CACS: Contract Audit Closing Statement(s) (DCAA)

CAD/CAM: Computer-Aided Design Manufacturing

CAGE: Commercial and Government Entity Code

CAIG: Cost Analysis Improvement Group (DoD)

CAM: Contract Audit Manual (DCAA)

CAO: Contract Administration Officer

CAS: Cost Accounting Standard(s)

CBD: Commerce Business Daily

CCDR: Contractor Cost Data Report(s)(-ing)

CDRL: Contracts Data Requirements List

CECSR: Contractor Employee Compensation System Review

CFSR: Contract Funds Status Report(s)(-ing)

CFY: Contractor Fiscal Year

CHOA: Corporate Home Office Auditor

CIPR: Contractor Insurance/Pension Review

CLIN: Contract Line Item Number

CMO: Contract Management Office

CMS: Contract Management Services

CO: Contracting Officer

COC: Certificate of Competency

COE: Corps of Engineers (Army)

CPA: Certified Public Accountant(s)

CPAF: Cost-Plus-Award-Fee (Contract)

CPFF: Cost-Plus-Fixed-Fee (Contract)

CPIF: Cost-Plus-Incentive-Fee (Contract)

CPR: Cost Performance Report(s)(-ing)

CPSR: Contractor Purchasing System Review

CPU: Central Processing Unit (EDP)

CRAG: Contractor Risk Assessment Guide

C/SCSC: Cost/Schedule Control System Criteria

CSRA: Civil Service Reform Act

CSSR: Cost/Schedule Status Report(s)(-ing)

CY: Calendar Year

D

DAC: Defense Acquisition Circular

DAR: Defense Acquisition Regulation (formerly the ASPR and now replaced by the FAR)

DCAA: Defense Contract Audit Agency

DCAAI: Defense Contract Audit Agency Instruction

DCAAM: Defense Contract Audit Agency Manual

DCAAP: Defense Contract Audit Agency Pamphlet

DCAAR: Defense Contract Audit Agency Regulation

DCAI: Defense Contract Audit Institute

DCMAO: Defense Contract Management Area Operations

DCMC: Defense Contract Management Command

DCMD: Defense Contract Management District

DCAA: Defense Contract Audit Agency

DD: Designation of Department of Defense Forms

DDAS: HQ, DLA Office of Small and Disadvantaged Business Utilization

DFARS: Defense Federal Acquisition Regulation Supplement

DFAS: Defense Finance & Accounting Service

DHHS: Department of Health & Human Services

DIIS: DCAA Integrated Information System

DL: General Counsel (DCAA HQ)

DLA: Defense Logistics Agency

DLAD: Defense Logistics Agency Acquisition Directive

DLAI: Defense Logistics Agency Instruction

DLAM: Defense Logistics Agency Manual

DLAR: Defense Logistics Acquisition Regulation

DLIS: Defense Logistics Information Service (formally DLSC)

DMS/DPS: Defense Materials System/Defense Priority System

DoC: Department of Commerce

DoD: Department of Defense

DoDD: Department of Defense Directive

DoDI: Department of Defense Instruction

DoDIG: Department of Defense Inspector General

DOE: Department of Energy

DOJ: Department of Justice

DoL: Department of Labor

DoT: Department of Transportation

DPRO: Defense Plant Representative Office

DSC: Defense Supply Center

DTIC: Defense Technical Information Center

DWG: Drawings

E

EAC: Estimate At Completion (Cost)

EC: Electronic Commerce

ECRC: Electronic Commerce Resource Center

EDI: Electronic Data Interchange

EDP: Electronic Data Processing (Computer[s])

EDPM: Executive Director of Procurement Management

EEO: Equal Employment Opportunity

EEOC: Equal Employment Opportunity Commission

8(a): Special Classification of Small Disadvantaged owned Business

EPA: Economic Price Adjustment or Environmental Protection Agency

ERISA: Employee Retirement Income Security Act (1974)

ESOP: Employee Stock Option Plan

ESS: Estimating System Survey

ETC: Estimate to Complete (Cost)

EVMS: Earned Value Measurement System

F

F/A: First Article

FAC: Federal Acquisition Circular

FAR: Federal Acquisition Regulation

FARA: Federal Acquisition Reform Act of 1996

FASA: Federal Acquisition Streamlining Act of 1994

FASB: Financial Accounting Standards Board

FCR: Federal Contracts Report (BNA)

FCRC: Federal Contract Research Center(s)

FED SPEC: Federal Specifications

FEMA: Federal Emergency Management Agency

FERC: Federal Energy Regulatory Commission

FFP: Firm Fixed Price

FFRDC: Federally Funded Research & Development Center(s)

FICA: Federal Insurance Contributions Act

FLRA: Federal Labor Relations Authority

FLSA: Fair Labor Standards Act

FMIS: Field Management Information System

FMP: Far Market Price

FMS: Foreign Military Sales

FOUO: For Official Use Only

FP: Fixed Price

FPC: Federal Procurement Conference

FPI: Federal Prison Industries or Fixed-Price Incentive (Contract)

FPR: Federal Procurement Regulation or Fixed-Price Redeterminable (Contract)

FPRA: Forward Pricing Rate Agreement(s)

FSC: Federal Supply Code

FSCM: Federal Supply Code for Manufacturers

FSN: Federal Stock Number

FUTA: Federal Unemployment Tax Act

FY: Fiscal Year

G

G&A: General & Administrative (Expense)

GAAP: Generally Accepted Accounting Principle(s)

GAAS: Generally Accepted Auditing Standard(s)

GAC: Group Audit Coordinator

GAGAS: Generally Accepted Government Auditing Standard(s) (GAO)

GAO: General Accounting Office

GASB: Governmental Accounting Standards Board

GBL: Government Bill of Lading

GFAE: Government-Furnished Aeronautical Equipment

GFE: Government Furnished Equipment

GFM: Government Furnished Material

GFP: Government Furnished Property

GOCO: Government-Owned, Contractor-Operated (Plant)

GPO: Government Printing Office

GSA: General Services Administration

H

HBCUs: Historically Black Colleges and Universities

HCA: Head of the Contracting Activity

HQ DLA: Headquarters, Defense Logistics Agency

I

IAW: In Accordance With

ICAPS: Internal Control Audit Planning Summary

ICQ: Internal Control Questionnaire

IFB: Invitation for Bid (the sealed bid process also known as Formal Advertising)

IG: Inspector General

IIA: Institute of Internal Auditors

IPE: Industrial Plant Equipment

IPT: Integrated Product Team

IRC: Internal Revenue Code

IRD: Independent Research & Development (Cost)

IRS: Internal Revenue Service

IS: Industrial Specialist

J

JWOD: Javits-Wagner-O'Day Act

JTR: Joint Travel Regulation

L

LSA: Labor Surplus Area

M

MAAR: Mandatory Annual Audit Requirement(s)

MBDA: Minority Business Development Agency

MICOM: U.S. Army Missile Command

MIL SPEC: Military Specification

MIs: Minority Institutions

MOD: Modification

MOU: Memorandum of Understanding

MRD: Memorandum for Regional Directors (DCAA)

MRP: Material Requirement Planning (Inventory Control System)

MSC: Major Subordinate Command (DLSC and DCMC)

MWS: Major Weapon System

N

NAV: Navy

NASA: National Aeronautics & Space Administration

NGB: National Guard Bureau (DoD)

NIB: National Industries for the Blind

NISH: formally, National Industries for the Severely Handicapped

NRC: Nuclear Regulatory Commission

NSN: National Stock Number. (The 13-digit stock number replacing the 11-digit federal stock number. It consists of the 4-digit federal supply classification code and the 9-digit national item identification number. The national item identification number consists of a 2-digit National Codification Bureau number designating the central cataloging office of the NATO or other friendly country that assigned the number, and a 7-digit (xxxxxxx) non-significant number. The number shall be arranged as follows: 9999-00-999-9999.)

NSP: Not Separately Priced

O

OAI: Manager, Defense Contract Audit Institute

OAL: Audit Liaison Division (DCAA HQs)

OFPP: Office of Federal Procurement Policy (OMB)

OIG: Office of the Inspector General

OMB: Office of Management & Budget

ONR: Office of Naval Research

OPSEC: DoD Operations Security Program

OTC: Manager, Technical Services Center (DCAA)

OUSD(A&T): Office of the Under Secretary of Defense (Acquisition and Technology)

OWD: Workload & Trends Analysis Division (DCAA HQs)

P

PAC: Accounting & Cost Principles Division (DCAA HQs)

PACO: Principal ACO

PAS: Pre-Award Survey

PASS: Procurement Automated Source System

PBIS: Performance Based Incentive System

PC: Purchase Order

PCO: Procuring Contracting Officer

PCR: Procurement Center Representative

PDR: Plant-wide Data Report

PFC: Pricing, Finance, & Claims Division (DCAA HQs)

PIC: Incurred Cost Division (DCAA HQs)

PL: Public Law

PLFA: Primary Level Field Activity

PHR: Procurement History Records

PMC: Procurement Method Code

P/N: Part Number

PNM: Price Negotiation Memorandum

PO: Purchase Order

PQA: Procurement Quality Assurance

PR: Purchase Request

PROCAS: Process Oriented Contract Administration Services

PS&C: Production Scheduling & Control

PSP: Special Projects Division (DCAA HQs)

PTAC: Procurement Technical Assistance Center

Q

QA: Quality Assurance

QAR: Quality Assurance Representative

QPL: Qualified Products List

R

R&D: Research & Development (Cost)

RAM: Regional Audit Manager (DCAA)

RCS: Report Control Symbol

RD: Regional Director (DCAA)

RFP: Request for Proposal (also known as Negotiated procurement)

REQ: Request for Quotation

S

SADBU: Small and Disadvantaged Business Utilization

SAS: Statement on Auditing Standards (AICPA)

SBA: Small Business Administration

SBIR: Small Business Innovation Research Program

SBLO: Small Business Liaison Officer

SBS: Small Business Specialist

SBSA: Small Business Set Aside

SBTA: Small Business Technical Advisor

SDB: Small Disadvantaged Business

SEC: Securities & Exchange Commission

SIC: Standard Industrial Classification Code

SF: Standard Form

T

T&M: Time & Material (Contract)

TBSR: Total Business System Review (ONR)

TCO: Termination (or Terminating) Contracting Officer

TEFRA: Tax Equity & Fiscal Responsibility Act

TRASOPs: Tax Reduction Act Stock Ownership Plans

TSC: Technical Services Center, Memphis (DCAA)

U

UNICOR: A Federal Prison Industry Business Entity

U.S.C.: United States Code

V

VAP: Vulnerability Assessment Procedure(s) (DCAA)

VLSI: Very Large Scale Integration

W

W/P: Working Papers

WBS: Work Breakdown Structure(s)

WOSB: Women Owned Small Business

Buying Offices

This Appendix gives you the identification of a number of government buying offices that should be contacted for opportunities. Many have their own web site, which include a lot of the information you will need. If you don't know their web address we suggest that you start at the federal jumpstation maintained by NASA for the government. (http://nais.nasa.gov/govproc.)

SPECIAL DEPARTMENT OF DEFENSE BUYING OFFICES

The first listing is for the Department of Defense and some locations that specialize in items or services that are not normally bought by the commands and base, camps and stations.

There are three categories of goods and services that are purchased by special purchasing offices; the categories are merchandise for defense commissary stores, resale merchandise for the military exchange services, and motion pictures and videotape production.

The Defense Commissary Agency (DeCA)

DeCA is a chain of supermarkets (commissaries) providing quality goods at the lowest possible cost to authorized patrons. We have three regional offices in the United States and one in Europe. For more information see web-site http://www.deca.mil/default.htm

DeCA is not associated with any other military resale or retail activity. Other entities operate and manage these activities known as club systems, ship stores, or exchanges. DeCA is also not associated with dining facilities (mess halls, dining halls, galleys, etc.). The dining facilities are operated by the individual Armed Services to provide prepared meals for their members.

What We Buy

Grocery Products-- Our resale products are those traditionally sold in commercial supermarkets. Commodities and products sold in the commissaries are restricted to those authorized by the U.S. Congress. (See the "Resale" section for more information.)

Operational Support-- Equipment, supplies and services required to support the operation of individual commissaries (stores).

Administrative Support - Supplies and services to support the overall operation of the Agency.

DeCA has a preference for commercial type products.

Resale Focus

Resale includes both brand name and non-brand name products. Brand name products are those that have identifiable customer recognition, and are marketed, merchandised and commercially available and sold based on that brand. We carry these products because the commissary patron prefers the brand name. Non-brand name products are products for which there is no customer preference and include meat, eggs, etc. and in-store resale operations (deli/bakery). They are procured competitively using commercial descriptions. (See the "Resale" section for more information.)

Other Than Resale Focus

Other than resale means operational and administrative support items as defined above. (See the "Operational and Administrative Support Items" section for more information.) These acquisitions account for less than 5 percent of DeCA's total contractual awards.

Your Market Key for Brand Name Items

The first step in selling us a brand name product is to make an item presentation to one of our buyers. The presentation is your opportunity to market your product and provide any unique information. Before selection, a brand name product must have a Universal Product Code (UPC) and be sold in commercial supermarkets. For more information regarding product UPC, you can contact Uniform Code Council Inc. at (937) 435-3870 or see web site http://www.uc-council.org. Details of your offer must be summarized on DeCA Form 40-33, Item Presentation Form, which may be obtained from a local commissary or from one of the points of contact under the "Getting Started" section.

For brand name resale items, your product's performance determines whether it remains in our stock assortment. We continuously analyze product sales information and if sales trends indicate your product is moving, then replenishment quantities are ordered, if not, your product will be removed from our shelves. Specific time frames for measuring product performance will be explained during your presentation.

Products for national distribution are normally presented at our corporate headquarters at Fort Lee, VA. Products with regional or local distribution may be presented at one of our region offices or an individual commissary. Our small business specialists, category managers, or region buyers can help you decide which location is best for your presentation.

Defense Commissary Agency
Acquisition Management
1300 E Avenue, Building 11200
Fort Lee, Virginia 23801-1800
(804) 734-8740

Points of Contact/DeCA Headquarters /Ft Lee

Location	Topic	Name	Telephone
Acquisition Management (AM)	Small Business	General Information	(804) 734-8740 Internet e-mail (smallbus@hqlee .deca.mil)
Contract Management Business Unit (CBU)	Operational Items	Small Business Specialist	(804) 734-8255
Information Management (IM)	Electronic Data Interchange (EDI)	Jeffrey Perry EDI Coordinator	(804) 734-8482 Internet E-mail (perryjc@hqlee.d eca.mil)
Marketing Business Unit (MBU)	Resale Items	Perishable Market Semi-Perishable Market Local/Regional Buying	(804) 734-9979 (804) 734-9980 (804) 734-9947

DeCA Region Locations and Points of Contact

REGION	LOCATION	AREA COVERED
Eastern Region	5151 Bonney Road, Suite 201 Virginia Beach, VA 23462-4314	
Northern Area Office	2257 Huber Rd Fort Meade, MD 20755-5220 Small Bus Specialist (301) 677-9893 Resale (301) 677-9265	Maine, New Hampshire, Vermont, Rhode Island Massachusetts, Connecticut, New York, New Jersey, Pennsylvania, Maryland, Delaware, Virginia, West Virginia, Kentucky, Missouri, Ohio, Washington DC
Southern Area Office	60 West Maxwell Blvd. Maxwell AFB, AL 36112-6307 Small Bus Spec* (334) 953-3136 Resale (334) 953-7795	Illinois, Indiana, Wisconsin, Minnesota, Michigan, Iowa, Arkansas, Tennessee, North Carolina, Louisiana, Mississippi, Alabama, Georgia, South Carolina, Florida, Caribbean and Central America
Midwest Region	300 AFCOMS Way Kelly AFB, TX 78241-6132 Small Bus Specialist (210) 925-5924 Resale (210) 925-6459	North Dakota, South Dakota, Wyoming, Kansas, Oklahoma, New Mexico, Texas, Colorado, Nebraska
Western/ Pacific Region	3401 Beech Street McClellan AFB, CA 95652-1164 Small Bus Specialist (916) 643-0222 Resale (916) 569-4827	Washington, Oregon, Idaho, Montana, California, Utah, Arizona, Alaska, Hawaii, Far East, Nevada
European Region	Gebaude 2780, Zimmer 109, Kapun AS, GE 67661 Resale Small Business Specialist 011-49-0631-3523-105	Germany, United Kingdom, Italy, Greece, Turkey, The Netherlands, Belgium, Spain, Azores, Saudi Arabia, Egypt Vogelweh/ Kaiserslautern

Military Exchange Services

The categories of merchandise and price limitations on goods sold by military exchange services in the continental United States are established by regulations approved by Congress. These limitations do not apply to overseas exchanges.

The buying offices and procedures for dealing with the exchanges are set forth below.

Army and Air Force Exchange Service

To sell to the Army and Air Force Exchange Service a firm must offer its product to the appropriate buyer at the Headquarters or the exchange region office. No merchandise is purchased by individual exchanges. The Headquarters buyers purchase all resale merchandise that is commonly stocked in post and base exchanges in the CONUS, and all resale merchandise of United States origin for overseas exchanges. Merchandise peculiar to single exchange regions is purchased by these four exchange regional offices, each of which has approximately 36 exchanges located in its geographical area.

Central Region
Army and Air Force Exchange Service
P. O. Box 650454
Dallas, TX 75265-0454
(972) 277-7203

Eastern Region
Army and Air Force Service
P. O. Box 650455
Dallas, TX 75265-0455
(972) 277-7103

Southern Region
Army and Air Force Exchange Service
P. O. Box 65044
Dallas, TX 75265-0447
(972) 277-7300

Western Region
Army and Air Force Exchange Service
P. O. Box 650429
Dallas, TX 75265-0429
(972) 277-7403

The Navy Exchange Program

The Navy Exchange Program is a Navy retailing operation that provides quality products and a variety of services to the men and women of the Armed Forces, with special emphasis on serving members of the U.S. Navy and their families. Navy Exchanges are located at U.S. Navy bases in the United States and in 19 countries around the world.

Navy Exchanges are self-supporting and do not receive tax dollars for their operation. Net profits generated by Navy Exchange sales are returned to Navy bases to help support local and Navy-wide recreation and morale programs. These include such on-base activities as physical fitness centers; swimming pools; child care centers; libraries; intramural sports programs; special entertainment events and other activities. Please note that additional information on the Navy and Marine Exchange program can be found by accessing the World Wide Web at: http://www.adm.rda.hq.navy.mil/.

Navy Exchanges

Navy Exchanges consist of retail and services departments and are operated in a similar manner to commercial retail enterprises, within imitations established by Congress and the Department of Defense. Exchanges provide basic staple merchandise and a selection of other items to meet the needs of authorized customers. There are 133 Navy Exchanges worldwide.

Services available to authorized Navy exchange customers include: automotive service centers; fast food outlets; snack bars; cafeterias, food arts, mobile canteens; laundry and dry cleaning; vending machines; optical shops; photo finishing, specialty stores; barber and beauty salons; flower shops; video and car rental; and other personalized services.

Contacting NEXCOM Buyers

The NEXCOM Command maintains an open door policy in meeting with all potential suppliers. Open Vendor Day is held the first Wednesday of each month for those vendors who are not currently doing business with the Navy Exchange System. Sales personnel are invited to call the appropriate buyer to schedule an appointment. Appointments are taken on a first-come, first-serve basis between 9:00 am - 3:00 p.m.

Inquiries and correspondence should be directed to a retail or services buyer at the address below:

Navy Exchange Service Command
3280 Virginia Beach Boulevard
Virginia Beach, VA 23452-5724
Phone: 757-631-6200

The Small Business Office provides information about how to go about doing business with the Navy Exchange System. The small business specialist can be contacted at 804-631-3582.

The locations of NEXCOMs and the Navy Exchanges that each supports is shown in the following list: (Numbers in parenthesis show the number of Navy exchanges in that particular area):

NEXCEN Norfolk
Eastern/Tidewater Area
Navy Exchange Service
Command
3280 Virginia Beach
Command Virginia
Beach, VA 23452-5724
Phone: 757-440-4500
Fax: 757-440-4526

NEXCEN Norfolk Exchanges
Lakehurst, NJ, Colts Neck, NJ,
Brunswick, ME, Cutler, ME, Newport,
RI, Winter Harbor, ME, Norfolk, VA
(3), Portsmouth, VA (2), Oceana, VA,
Chesapeake, VA, Yorktown, VA,
Dahlgren, VA, Dam Neck, VA, Little
Creek, VA, Patuxent River, MD,
Annapolis, MD, Indian Head, MD,
Bethesda, MD, Washington, DC, Sugar
Grove, WV, Philadelphia, PA (2),
Willow Grove, PA, Arlington, VA,
Bermuda, South Weymouth, MA,
Mechanicsburg, PA, Mitchel Field,
NY, Warminister, PA, Portsmouth,
NH, Scotia, NY, Keflavik, Iceland,
New London, CT, Cheltenham, MD

NEXCEN Jacksonville
Southern/Florida Area
Navy Exchange Service
Center
Box 13
Naval Air Station
Jacksonville, FL 32212
Phone: 904-777-7075
Fax: 904-777-7008

NEXCEN Jacksonville Exchanges
Jacksonville, FL, Key West, FL,
Mayport, FL, Cecil Field, FL, Orlando,
FL, Athens, GA, Kings Bay, GA,
Beaufort, SC, Charleston, SC, (2),
Antigua, Roosevelt Roads, PR,
Guantanamo Bay, Cuba, Sabana Seca,
PR

NEXCEN San Diego
California/Pacific
Northwest
Navy Exchange Service
Center Naval Station,
Box 368150
San Diego,
CA 92136-5150
Phone: 619-237-5601
Fax: 619-237-5609

NEXCEN San Diego Exchanges
Concord, CA, Coronado, CA, San
Diego, CA (4), Stockton, CA, San
Nicholas, CA, Treasure Island, CA,
Port Hueneme, CA, Hamilton-Novato,
CA, China Lake, CA, Alameda, CA (2),
El Centro, CA, Mare Island, CA,
Imperial Beach, CA, Oakland, CA (2),
Long Beach, CA, Ferndale, CA,
Miramar, CA, Lemoore, CA, North
Island, CA (2), Moffett Field, CA,
Point Mugu, CA, Monterey, CA,
Fallon, NV, Bangor, WA, Bremerton,
WA, Everett, WA, Smokey Point, WA,
Whidbey Island, WA

NEXCEN Pearl Harbor
Hawaii Area
Navy Exchange Service Center
Box 133
Pearl Harbor, HI 96860
Phone: 808-423-3201
Fax: 808-422-7897

NEXCEN Pearl Harbor Exchanges
Barbers Point, HI, Pearl Harbor, HI,
Kauai, HI, Wahiawa, HI, Laulualei, HI,
Christchurch, New Zealand

Independent Exchanges Domestic

Great Lakes, Illinois
Navy Exchange 2701
Sheridan Rd.,
Building 111
Naval Training Center
Great Lakes,
IL 60085-5129
Phone: 847-578-6103
Fax: 847-578-6301

Great Lakes Exchanges
Glenview, IL, Crane, IN, Great Lakes,
IL, (2)

Pensacola, Florida
Navy Exchange
Naval Air Station
250 Chamber Ave.
Pensacola,
FL 60085-5129
Phone: 904-578-6100

Pensacola Exchanges

Pensacola, FL, (2), Meridian, MS,
Panama City, FL, Gulfport, MS,
Whiting Field, FL, New Orlean, LA,
Pascagoula, MS

Dallas, Texas
Navy Exchange
Naval Air Station
Dallas, TX 75211-9501
Phone: 214-266-6411
Fax: 214-266-6414

Memphis, Tennessee
Navy Exchange
Naval Air Station, Memphis
7800 3rd Avenue
Millington, TN 38054-6024
Phone: 901-872-7716
Phone: 901-872-7716

Corpus Christi, Texas
Navy Exchange
Naval Air Station
651 Lexington Blvd.
Corpus Christi, TX 78419
Phone: 512-939-2033
Fax: 512-939-8529

Corpus Christi Exchanges
Corpus Christi, TX, Kingsville, TX,
Ingleside, TX

Independent Exchanges – Overseas

Guam Exchanges

U.S. Navy Exchange
Guam
PSC 455, Box 178
FPO AP 96540-1000
Phone: 011-671-339-3251
Fax: 011-671-564-3215

Agana, Guam (3), Singapore

Military Sealift Command (MSC) Exchanges

MSC Atlantic Area
Commander, Military
Sealift Command
Military Ocean Terminal
Building 42, Room 4.131
(code N43)
Bayonne, NJ 07002-5399
Phone: 201-823-7615 or
7479
Fax: 201-823-6573
(ATTN: Code N43)

MSC Pacific Area
Commander, Military Sealift
Command
Naval Supply Center
Building 310-1E (Code N43)
Oakland, CA 94625-5010
Phone: 510-302-6212 or 6214
Fax: 510-302-6940 (ATTN: Code N43)

Navy Uniform Program

As program manager for Navy Uniforms, the Navy Uniform Program is the only authorized source of certified Navy Uniforms. The Navy Uniform Program encompasses the management of government issue uniform items.

Information regarding Navy Uniform procurement procedures, inquiries and correspondence should be directed to Ms. Becky Adkins, Director of Navy Uniforms, at the address and numbers listed below:

Navy Uniforms
1545 Crossways Boulevard
Suite 100
Chesapeake, VA 23320
POC: Director, Ms. Becky Adkins
Phone: 757-420-9116
Fax: 757-420-4094

Ships Store Program

To meet the needs of the afloat sailor, ships stores carry basic toiletries and sundries, high demand items such as soft drinks and candy bars, and "nice to have" items which include consumer electronics merchandise. The limited cube and space on board each ship restricts selection to those items that are the most popular. However, sailors have the ability to special order almost any item a Navy Exchange carries. The Ship's Supply Officer or an appointed Ships Store Officer supervises and initiates the purchasing for the ships store based on the crew's needs and inventory limitations using the Ships Store Afloat Catalogs (SSAC), Contract Bulletins or by initiating a special purchase order. Inquiries and correspondence should be directed to Mr. Charles Vaughn, Director of Ship Stores Program, at the address and numbers listed below:

Ship Stores Program
3280 Virginia Beach Boulevard
Virginia Beach, VA 23452
POC: Director, Mr. Charles Vaughn (Code A)
Phone: 757-445-6899
Fax: 757-445-6920

The Marine Corps Exchange Program

Marine Corps Morale, Welfare and Recreation (MWR) is a diverse collection of activities, services, and programs which support the quality of life of the Marine Corps community, active duty, reserves and retired.

Marine Corps Market Points of Contact

MCLB Barstow, CA
MWR Director
Marine Corps Logistics Base
Building 44
Barstow, CA 92311-5018
Phone: 619-577-6733

HQMC, HQBN Arlington, Virginia
MWR Director
Headquarters Battalion
Henderson Hall
Arlington, VA 22214-5003
Phone: 703-979-0972 Ext. 324

MCAGCC Twentynine Palms, CA
MWR Director
Marine Corps Air Ground Combat Center
Box 788150
Twentynine Palms, CA 92278-8150
Phone: 619-830-6870

MCCDC Quantico, Virginia
MWR Director
Marine Corps Base
Building 2034
Quantico, VA 22134-5000
Phone: 703-784-3007

MCAS El Toro/Tustin, CA
MWR Director
Marine Corps Air Bases West
Building 75
Marine Corps Air Station El Toro
Santa Ana, CA 92709-5018
Phone: 714-726-2571

MCSFBN, Norfolk, Virginia
MWR Director
MCSFBN
1320 Piercy Street
Norfolk, VA 23511
Phone: 757-423-1187

MCB Camp Pendleton, CA
MWR Director
Marine Corps Base
P. O. Box 555020
Camp Pendleton, CA 92055-5020
Phone: 619-725-5551

MCRD San Diego, CA
MWR Director
Marine Corps Recruit
Depot/WRR
Building 10
San Diego, CA 92140-5196
Phone: 619-524-4433

MCAS Yuma, AZ
MWR Director
Marine Corps Air Station
Building 633
Yuma, AZ 85369-5000
Phone: 520-341-3531

MCAS Beaufort,
South Carolina
MWR Director
Marine Corps Air Station
Building 408
Beaufort, SC 29904-5003
Phone: 803-522-7572

MCRD Parris Island,
South Carolina
MWR Director
Marine Corps Recruit
Depot/ERR
Building 202
P. O. Box 5100
Parris Island, SC 29905-5003
Phone: 803-525-3301

MCAS Cherry Point, NC
MWR Director
PSC Box 8009
Marine Corps Air Station
Building 400
Cherry Point, NC 28533-809
Phone: 919-466-2430

MCB Camp Lejeune,
North Carolina
MWR Director
Marine Corps Base
Building 1
Camp Lejeune, NC 28542-5001
Phone: 910-451-2524

MCAS New River,
North Carolina
MWR Director
Marine Corps Air Station,
New River
Building 208
Jacksonville, NC 8545-5001

MCAS Iwakuni, Japan
MWR Director
Marine Corps Air Station,
Iwakuni
PSC 561, Box 1867
FPO AP 96310-1867
Fax: 011-81-827-21-4181

MCB Camp Butler, Okinawa,
Japan
MWR Director
Marine Corps Base Camp Butler
Unit 35023
FPO AP 96373-5023
Fax: 011-81-98-893-8329

MCLB Albany, Georgia
MWR Director
Marine Corps Logistics Base
814 Radford Boulevard
Building 7520
Albany, GA 31704-1128
Phone: 912-439-5267

MCAS Kansas City, Missouri
MWR Director
Richards-Gebaur
Marine Corps Support Activity
1500 East Bannister Road
Kansas City, MO 64197-0501
Phone: 816-843-3800

MCB Hawaii
MWR Director
Marine Corps Base Hawaii
Building 1404
Kaneohe Bay, HI 96863-5018
Phone: 808-254-7500

MCAS Guantanamo Bay, Cuba
MWR Director
Marine Barracks
U. S. Naval Base,
Guantanamo Bay, Cuba
Box 32
FPO AE 09596-0120
Fax: 011-53-99-3237

COMPUTER SYSTEMS

Activities Involved in Procurement of ADPE, Software, Maintenance
and Services for the military

Department of the Army

CECOM Acquisition Center
Navy Information System and
Acquisition Agency
Washington Operation Office
2461 Eisenhower Ave.
Alexandria, VA 22331-0700
Tel: (703) 325-5793
**Defense Supply Service-
Washington**
5200 Army Pentagon
Washington, DC 20310-5210
Tel: (703) 697-6024

Department of the Navy

Management Center
Code OOX1, Bldg. 176-4
Washington Navy Yard
Washington, DC 20374-5070
Tel: (202) 433-4337

**Naval Fleet and Industrial
Supply Center**
Long Beach Detachment
Code, PA, Bldg. 53, 2nd Floor
Long Beach, CA 90822-5074
Tel: (310) 901-3794

CECOM - Acquisition Center
ATTN: AMSEL-IE-SB
Fort Huachuca, AZ 85613-5000
Tel: (520) 538-7870

Department of Air Force
Electronic System Division
275 Randolph Road
Hanscom AFB, MA 01731-5000
Tel: (617) 377-4973

SSC/PK
375 Libby Street
Maxwell AFB
Gunter Annex, AL 36114-3207
Tel: (334) 416-5614

Defense Logistics Agency
Administrative Support Center
Office of Contracting
ATTN: Deputy for Small
Business
8725 John J. Kingman Road
Suite 0119, Room 1134
Fort Belvoir, VA 22206-6220
Tel: (703) 767-1161

Naval Fleet and Industrial
Supply Center
Washington Navy Yard,
Building 200
901 M Street S. E., Code OOA
Washington, DC 20374-2000
Tel: (202) 433-2957

Naval Fleet and Industrial
Supply Center
Code 09B
Philadelphia Detachment
Philadelphia, PA 19112-5083
Tel: (215) 697-9555

Defense Information System
Agency
701 South Courthouse Road
Arlington, VA 22204-2199
Tel: (703) 607-6920

Motion Picture And Videotape Productions

Motion picture and videotape productions are purchased only from qualified producers. To obtain an application form for acceptance on the qualified Film Producers List or the Qualified Videotape Producers List, contact the

Joint Visual Information Activity Office,
601 North Fairfax Street,
Room 334, Alexandria,
Virginia 22314-2007,
telephone (703) 428-0636

They serve as an executive agent for all Federal agencies, including the Department of Defense. To become qualified, producers submit sample films or videotapes to a review board. Ultimately, contracts are placed by authorized procurement offices of the Army, Navy and Air Force. In order for a producer to receive a contract from an authorized procurement office, the producer must first be approved for the appropriate qualified list.

Note that audiovisual services such as processing or graphics, and audiovisual equipment are purchased by the requiring post, camp, station, or installation.

Authorized Military Service procurement offices are:

Army

Joint Visual Information Activity
Washington - Contracting
601 N. Fairfax Street, Room 334
Alexandria, VA 22314-2007
703-428-1122

Joint Visual Information
Activity - Production
601 N. Fairfax Street, Room 334
Alexandria, VA 22314-2007
703-248-1118

Navy and Marine Corps

Navy Imaging Command
Anacostia Naval Station
Production Contracting Department
Building 168
Washington, DC 20374-1681
(202) 433-5775

DEPARTMENT OF VETERANS AFFAIRS

The following list is for the Veterans Affairs buying system. The abbreviations helps you understand some of the location identifications and size of office. Also, where special factors apply to help you market better notes have been included.

Department of Veterans Affairs Contracting Activities Abbreviations:

VAMC	VA Medical Center
VAM&ROC	VA Medical and Regional Office Center
VAD	VA Domiciliary
VISN	Veterans Integrated Service Network
VARO	VA Regional Office
VAOC	VA Outpatient Clinic
VARO&OC	VA Regional Office & Outpatient Clinic
AC	Automation Center

ILLINOIS
VAMC (Lakeside)
333 East Huron St.
Chicago 60611

Phone: (312) 943-600

VAMC (West Side)
820 South Damen Ave.
Chicago 60612
Phone: (312) 633-2152

VAMC
1900 East Main St.
Danville 61832
Phone: (217) 431-6535

VAMC
Hines 60141
Phone: (708) 343-7200

VAMC
2401 West Main St.
Marion 62959

Phone: (618) 997-5311

VAMC
3001 Greenbay Rd.
North Chicago 60064
Phone: (708) 688-1900

VASD
P. O. Box 27
Hines 60141
Phone: (708) 786-6230

INDIANA

VAMC Fort
2121 Lake Ave.
Wayne 46805
Phone: (219) 426-5431

VAMC
1481 West 10th St.
Indianapolis 46202
Phone: (317) 635-7401
IOWA

VAMC
3600 30th St.
Des Moines 50310
Phone: (515) 255-2173

VAMC
Highway 6 West
Iowa City 52240
Phone: (319) 338-0581

VAMC
1700 E. 38th St.
Marion 46952
Phone: (317) 674-3321

VAMC
1515 W. Pleasant
Knoxville 50138
Phone: (515) 842-3101

MICHIGAN

VAMC
Southfield & Outer Dr.
Allen Park 48101
Phone: (313) 563-6000

VAMC
2215 Fuller Rd.
Ann Arbor 48105
Phone: (313) 769-7100

VAMC
5600 Armstrong Rd.
Battle Creek 49015
Phone: (616) 966-5600

VAMC
325 East "H" St.
Iron Mountain 49801
Phone: (906) 774-3300

VAMC
1500 Weiss St.
Saginaw 48602
Phone: (517) 793-2340

MINNESOTA

VAMC
One Veterans Dr.
Minneapolis 55417
Phone: (612) 725-2175

VAMC
4801 8th St. North
St. Cloud 56303
Phone: (612) 252-1670

WISCONSIN

VAMC
2500 Overlook Ter.
Madison 53705

Phone: (608) 262-7609

VAMC
5000 West National Ave
Milwaukee 53295
Phone: (414) 384-2000

VAMC
500 E. Veterans St.
Tomah 54660
Phone: (608) 372-1703

DOING BUSINESS WITH AN INDIVIDUAL MEDICAL CENTER

The Department of Veterans Affairs (VA) operates a nationwide system of hospitals, clinics, Veterans Integrated Service Networks (VISN), data processing centers, and National Cemeteries which require a broad spectrum of goods and services. We purchase these goods and services on a national, regional, and local level. So no matter how large or small your business is, VA is a potential customer. Each facility is listed at the end of this document. Purchases a majority of its requirements for direct delivery through its local Acquisition and

Materiél Management office. You are encouraged to contact each facility for inclusion in its procurement process.

What do they buy?

Although there are certain priority sources identified by Federal regulations, each facility purchases a considerable amount of its requirements from both local and nationwide sources. Examples of items purchased are:

Pharmaceuticals and medical and surgical supplies
Perishable subsistence
Equipment, supplies, and materials for facility operation
Maintenance and repair of medical and scientific equipment
Building construction. maintenance and repair
Prosthetic and orthopedic aids
Medical gases

How do they buy?

Acquisitions are accomplished by the use of sealed bidding, negotiation, or simplified acquisition procedures. Each of these methods is designed to promote full and open competition to the maximum extent possible, which in turn allows all responsible bidders/offerors an opportunity to compete. The most suitable, efficient, and economical procedure will be used, taking into consideration the circumstances of each acquisition. Depending on the commodity (supplies, nonpersonal services, construction, etc.), most acquisitions at a medical center are of a definite-delivery/indefinite-quantity type. Much of the purchasing is accomplished through the use of mandatory sources such as Federal Supply Schedules and supply depots. A significant portion, however, will be acquired from sources obtained through the publication of solicitations in the Commerce Business Daily (CBD), solicitation mailing lists, commercial advertising, or any other accepted means that will provide the procuring activity with a sufficient number of responsible bidders/offerors to ensure full and open competition.

Full and Open Competition

VA medical centers strive to promote and provide full and open competition in the acquisition process. In so doing, specifications are designed to meet each medical center's minimum needs and also to be compatible with standard trade and prudent business practices. Potential bidders/offerors are encouraged to advise the procuring activity if they feel any language and /or requirement of a specification inadvertently restricts or limits competition or if, in their judgment, specifications do not comply with standard trade practices or impose an impractical or unreasonable procedural burden.

General Purchasing Information

Bonding and Sureties: Performance bonds and payment bonds for other than construction contracts will generally not be required. Performance bonds, may be required when it is determined that they are necessary to project the Government's interest in service acquisitions. Bid guarantees, performance bonds, and payment bonds are required for any construction contract exceeding $25,000 in accordance with the Miller Act (40 U.S.C. 270a-270f). Normally, the bid guarantee is 20 percent of the bid price; the performance bond is 100 percent of the contract price; and the payment bond is 50 percent of the contract price. A list of Federally approved sureties is available through the Department of Treasury, Surety Bond Branch, Financial Management Service, Washington, DC 20227, telephone number (202) 874-6850. Individual sureties will be considered on a case-by-case basis.

DOING BUSINESS WITH VA CENTRAL OFFICE

Most of our large purchases are made by the National Acquisition Center as described later in this document. However, offices listed below may be contacted for information:

The Deputy Assistant Secretary for Information Resources Management (045),
Department of Veterans Affairs
Washington, DC 20420, for:

Automatic data processing systems and equipment Communications systems and equipment

The Associate Chief Medical Director for Construction Management (08), Veterans Health Administration
Department of Veterans Affairs
Washington, DC 20420, for:

Medical center construction
Architect/Engineer services

The Director, National Cemetery System (40)
Department of Veterans Affairs
Washington, DC 20420, for:

Grave markers

The Director, Office of Marketing, Veterans Canteen Service (VCS)
Department of Veterans Affairs
1222 Spruce Street
St. Louis, MO 63103, for:

Retail store supplies
Restaurant supplies

The Deputy Assistant Secretary for Acquisition and Materiél
Management (90)
Department of Veterans Affairs
Washington, DC 20420, for:

ADP
Telecommunications
Consulting Services
Enhanced Use

DOING BUSINESS WITH THE VA NATIONAL ACQUISITION CENTER

Established in, 1951, the National Acquisition Center (NAC) in Hines, Illinois, is the largest combined contracting activity within the Department of Veterans Affairs. The NAC is responsible for supporting the health care delivery systems of the Department of Veterans Affairs and other Government agencies by providing and validating a centralized acquisition program for health care products in a cost-effective manner and for certain commodities under the Federal Supply Schedule (FSS) Program. The NAC is responsible for contract awards exceeding $1.5 billion annually. The NAC contracts for such items as medical, dental, and surgical supplies and equipment; pharmaceuticals and chemicals; semi-perishable foods; prosthetic and orthopedic aids; medical, radiological, and laundry equipment; medical wear; and flags.

Personal visits to the NAC are encouraged. The NAC is located in Buildings 17 and 37 on the Edward Hines Jr., VA Hospital complex in Hines, Illinois. The complex is located approximately 11 miles west of the Chicago Loop. The most direct route is via the Eisenhower Expressway (Interstate 290) to 1st Avenue. Go south on 1st Avenue to Roosevelt Road and proceed west on Roosevelt Road to 5th Avenue. Turn into the Hines complex. Coming from O'Hare Airport, take Interstate 294 south to the Eisenhower Expressway. Appointments are recommended, and may be made by telephoning (708) 786-5200.

One responsibility of the NAC is assuring contracts are in place to support the Department of Veterans Affairs Central Distribution System. Through the use of sealed bids and noncompetitive and competitive negotiations, the NAC awards high volume contracts for recurring items used throughout the Federal health care system. Purchases are made against these contracts, resulting in large quantity deliveries to the supply depots in New Jersey, Illinois, and California as the need arises, or for direct delivery to each VA medical center through an FSS contract.

The NAC is comprised of five divisions. Four of the divisions contract for items within assigned program responsibilities. The remaining division: Customer Service, ensures that the products under contract meet the needs of the NAC's customers. Examples of the commodities handled by each division are provided. For a complete definitive list contact the appropriate division.

The NAC maintains active solicitation mailing lists from prospective suppliers for the various items procured. If you are interested in having your firm placed on such lists, complete the Standard Form 129, Solicitation Mailing List Application, and information on Attachment A in the back of this publication and forward it to the National Acquisition Center.

If you have further questions, write to:
Director (904)
Department of Veterans Affairs National Acquisition Center
P.O. Box 76
Hines, IL 60141

The four NAC Divisions and their respective responsibilities follow:
Federal Supply Schedule Division
Telephone (708) 216-2481

The Federal Supply Schedule Division solicits, awards, and administers Federal Supply Schedule contracts, excluding pharmaceutical products and medical gases. All Federal Supply Schedule contracts are multiple or single award, requirements type, and national in scope for use by all Government agencies. The individual schedules assigned to this division by the General Services Administration are:

65 II B ... Medical and Veterinarian Supplies
65 II C ... Dental Equipment and Supplies
65 II D ... Medical Equipment and Supplies
65 II E ... Medical Equipment (Pacemakers)
65 II F ... Wheelchairs, Accessories. and Replacement Parts
65 V A ... Medical and Dental X-Ray Film
89 ... ... Cereals, Cookies, Crackers, Individual Condiments, and Granola Snacks
89 II ... ... Dietary Supplements, Therapeutic

Wholesale Distribution Division
Telephone (708) 216-2413

The Wholesale Distribution Division solicits, awards, and administers contracts for medical items and semi-perishable foods stocked in the Central Distribution System. Procurement of some of these items is made under Veterans Affairs/Department of Defense/Public Health Service (VA/DOD/PHS) shared procurement programs, or form mandatory sources, such as NISH, National Industries for the Blind

(NIB), and Federal Prison Industries (FPI). The Wholesale Distribution Division also contracts for direct delivery to VA users under the responsibility for VA membership contracts. In addition, this division solicits, awards, and administers numerous contracts for prosthetic items in support of the Denver Distribution Center. Orders against these contracts are placed by the Denver Distribution Center.

Examples of medical and semi-perishable food items stocked in the Central Distribution System are:

Applicators	Bandages, all types
Canned Fruits	Canned Juices
Canned Vegetables	Cannulas
Catheters	Coffee, Tea
Clinical Thermometers	Enema Sets
Examination Gloves	Flour Hypodermic
Needles	Interment Flags
Sugar	Surgical Adhesives
Surgical Drapes	Surgical Masks
Tongue Depressors	Wheelchairs

Examples of prosthetic contracts solicited, awarded, and administered in support of the Denver Distribution Center are:

Custom-In-The-Ear Hearing Aids	Flexible Orthoses
Hearing Aid Batteries	Hearing Aid Parts
Hearing Aid Repairs	Prosthetic Socks
Stock Hearing Aids	

Examples of some Decentralized Schedule Contracts for direct delivery to VA users are:

Artificial Limbs	Chinaware
Dedication	Graveliners
Plaques/Seals	

Examples of some VA Membership contracts are with the following organizations:

Joint Commission on Accreditation of Healthcare Organizations
College of American Pathologists
Pharmaceutical Products Division
Telephone (708) 786-4956

The Pharmaceutical Products Division solicits, awards, and administers contracts for pharmaceutical products and medical gases for items stocked in the Central Distribution System and Federal Supply Schedules as assigned. The Federal Supply Schedules assigned are:

65 I B ... Drugs and Pharmaceutical Products, Classes 6505, 6515, and 6810
65 I C ... Antiseptic Liquid Skin Cleansing Detergents and Soaps
65 VII ... Reagents, Diagnostics, and Test Kits and Sets
65 III A ... Medical Gases

Each of these schedule contracts are multiple or single award, requirements type, and national in scope for use by all Government agencies.

Examples of the items contracted for by the Pharmaceutical Products Division are:

Allergens	Analgesics	Antibacterials
Antibiotics	Antihypertensives	Antifungals
Anesthetics	Antipsychotics	Antiseptics
Antigens	Antituberculars	Barbituates
Chemicals	Decongestants	Diuretic
Enzymes	Intravenous Sets	Ointments
Stimulants	Serums	Vaccines
Vitamins		

Medical Equipment Division
Telephone (708) 216-2132

The Medical Equipment Division solicits, awards, and administers contracts for highly technical equipment and systems used in Federal Government medical facilities. Examples are:

Complete Diagnostic X-Ray Systems	Computerized Tomography Scanners
Diagnostic Ultrasound Systems	Laundry Equipment and Systems
Lithotripters Radiation	Magnetic Resonance Scanners
Nuclear Imaging Systems	Physiological Monitoring Systems
Therapy Equipment	

DOING BUSINESS WITH THE DENVER DISTRIBUTION CENTER

The Denver Distribution Center (DDC) is a national distribution center located in Denver, Colorado. The DDC procures, stocks, and distributes items directly to VA medical centers nationwide and to veterans throughout the world. Another major activity is a hearing aid repair service, conducted both in-house and with commercial contractors. Established in 1952, the DDC is the only facility of its kind within VA.

Items/services procured by the DDC

Custom-made, in-the-ear hearing aids (procurement only)

On-body, over-the-ear, and eyeglass hearing aids

Hearing aid accessories, e.g.. cords, tubing, ear hooks

Prosthetic socks in standard and specially made sizes, plies, and materials primarily tomeet the needs of amputee veterans

Items for the orthopedically impaired. e.g., corsets, binders, abdominal supports

Aids for the legally blind, e.g., canes, braille and low vision watches and clocks, TV audio radios, braille writers

Hearing aid repair parts

Equipment, supplies, and materials for local facility operation

The services of commercial contracts for hearing aid repair

How does DDC buy?

Federal and VA Acquisition Regulations and methods (sealed bidding, negotiation, simplified acquisition) are equally applicable to the DDC. The majority of items and services are ordered by the DDC from contracts established by the National Acquisition Center (see page 4). The DDC also uses the Commerce Business Daily (CBD), solicitation mailing lists, commercial advertising, or other acceptable means to ensure full and open competition.

General Purchasing Information

The same contract clauses and forms, warranty requirements, shipping and delivery procedures, bid evaluations, and prompt payment conditions in use throughout VA are applicable at the DDC.

Public Advertisement of Procurements

As required of all Federal agencies, the DDC advertises proposed contracts expected to exceed $25.000 in the CBD.

What must you do?

The DDC maintains solicitation mailing lists and supplier files. If you are interested in having your firm placed on such lists for the items/services listed, please complete a Standard Form 129, Solicitation Mailing List Application, and send to:

Chief, Acquisition and Materiel Management Division (905C)
Denver Distribution Center
P. O. Box 25166
Denver, CO 80225-0166

MILITARY R& D BUYING OFFICES

The DoD encourages participation by small concerns, including those owned by women and by disadvantaged persons, in its R&D programs. DoD seeks the most advanced scientific knowledge attainable and the best possible equipment and systems that can be devised and produced. It is the government's policy (FAR 35.008), in awarding an R&D contract, to select the organization ". . . that proposes the best ideas or concepts and has the highest competence in the specific field of science or technology involved." You should evaluate your firm critically before seeking a government R&D contract. Be sure that your firm is as well qualified as others who may want the same award. The telephone numbers in the lists which follow are for the small business specialists at the research organizations. Also, refer to Part 1 of this book, for information on the DoD Small Business Innovation Research (SBIR) program.

DEPARTMENT OF THE ARMY

U. S. Army Space & Missile Defense Command
PO Box 1500
Huntsville, AL 35807-3801
(205) 955-3412

Principal interests: Manages technology base research and development for Ballistic Missile Defense Organization and provides significant technical and program support to the Army Program Executive Office for Air and Missile Defense; supports Army space requirements; develops and demonstrates technologies required for kinetic energy weapons, directed energy weapons, structures, materials; conducts lethality and vulnerability analysis of various threat objects; conducts research in the areas of optics, radar and laser radar technology, high-performance electronics, sensor phenomenology, analysis, and measurement programs; develops theater and strategic missile targets for all of DoD; pursues innovative, high-risk, high-payoff research programs in acoustic-optical processing, laser satellite communications, radar range-doppler images, and threat destruction mechanisms.

U. S. Army Research Office
AMXRO-PR
PO 12211
Research Triangle Park, NC 27709-2211
(919) 549-4271

Principal interests: Research proposals on a competitive basis, from educational institutions, nonprofit organizations, and private industry in the fields of mathematics, physics, engineering, chemistry, electronics, materials, biology and geo-science.

U. S. Army Research Laboratory
AMSCL-SB
2800 Powder Mill Road
Adelphia, MD 20783-1197
(301) 394-3692

Principal interests: Research and technology development efforts provide scientific and technological innovation in ten fields of technical endeavor; lethality; survivability enhancement, assessment; sensors, signatures and signal processing, power resources; materials and structures; battlefield environmental effects; human factors; advanced computing and advanced electronics.

U. S. Army Aviation and Missile Command
ATTN: AMSAM-SB
Redstone Arsenal
Huntsville, AL 35898-5150
(205) 876-5441

Principal Interests: R&D of new helicopter systems, support of qualification testing of turbine engines, development and evaluation of prototype hardware for fueling and defueling equipment for use in combat areas and solving fuel contamination problems. Conducts research in both exploratory and advanced development in subsonic areas of application. R&D associated with free rockets, guided missiles, ballistic missiles, targets, air defense weapons systems, fire control coordination equipment, related special purpose and multisystem test equipment, missile launching and ground support equipment, metrology and calibration equipment, and other associated equipment.

Associated Installations:

Propulsion Directorate
NASA/Lewis Research Center
2100 Brookpart Road
Cleveland, OH 44135-3127
(216) 433-3703

Aviation Applied Technology
Directorate
Fort Eustis, VA 23604-5577
(804) 878-2208

Aerostructures Directorate
NASA/Langley Research Center
Hampton, VA 23665-5225
(804) 864-2447

U. S. Army Soldiers Systems
Command
ATTN: AMSS-C-SB
Kansas Street
Natick, MA 01760-5008
(508) 233-4995

Principal interests: R&D in the physical and biological sciences and engineering to meet military requirements in commodity areas of textiles, clothing, body armor, footwear, insecticides and fungicides, subsistence, containers, food service, equipment (as assigned) tentage and equipage, and air delivery equipment.

U. S. Army Communications-Electronics Command
ATTN: AMSEL-SB
Fort Monmouth, NJ 07703-5005
(908) 532-4511

Principal interests: R&D and acquisition, to include first production and initial fielding of communications, tactical data, and command and control systems. R&D programs related to communications, electronics intelligence, electronic warfare, reconnaissance surveillance, target acquisition, night vision, combat identification, position locations, tactical satellites, maneuver control, common hardware/software, sensors, power sources and other associated equipment.

U. S. Army Tank Automotive & Armaments Command
ATTN: AMSTA-CB
Warren, MI 48397-5000
(810) 574-5388

Principal interests: R&D associated with combat tactical and special purpose vehicles. R&D programs related to advanced concepts, development and engineering of combat and tactical vehicles, including automotive subsystems and components. Component programs involved engines, transmissions, suspensions, electrical and miscellaneous vehicular components.

U. S. Army Armament Research,
Development and Engineering Center
AMSTA-AR-SB
Picatinny Arsenal, NJ 07806-5000
(201) 724-4106

Principal interests: Product development/improvement of munitions, weaponry, and fire control systems; testing and analysis; and technical support for fielded armament systems.

U. S. Army Test & Evaluation Command
ATTN AMSTE-PR
Aberdeen Proving Ground, MD 21005-5005
(410) 278-1201

Associated installations:

U. S. Army Garrison
ATTN: STEAP-SB
Aberdeen Proving Ground, MD 21005-5001
(410) 278-1548

Principal Interests: R&D, production and post production testing of weapons, systems, ammunition, combat and support vehicles, and individual equipment.

U. S. Army Dugway Proving Ground
ATTN: STEDP-DBO-DOC
Dugway, UT 84022-5202
(801) 831-2102

Principal interests: Conducts field and laboratory tests to evaluate chemical and radiological weapons and defense systems and materiel, as well as defense research.

U. S. Army White Sands Missile Range
ATTN: STEWS-SBA
White Sands, NM 88002-5031
(505) 678-1401

Principal interests: Conducts testing and evaluation of Army missiles and rockets. Operates the United States only land based national range to support missile and other testing for the Army, Air Force, Navy, and National Aeronautics and Space Administration.

U. S. Army Yuma Proving Ground
ATTN: STEYP-CR
Yuma Proving Ground, AZ 85365-9102
(602) 328-6285

Principal interests: R&D, production and post production testing of weapons, systems, ammunition, and combat and support vehicles. Conducts environmental tests, air drop and air delivery tests, and participates in engineering testing of combat end support items.

U. S. Army Engineer Waterways Experiment Station
3909 Halls Ferry Road
Vicksburg, MS 39180-6199
(601) 634-2424

Principal interests: Research in support of the civil and military mission of the Chief of Engineers and other Federal agencies, through the operation of laboratories in the broad fields of hydraulics, soil mechanics, concrete, engineering geology, rock mechanics, pavements, expedient construction, nuclear and conventional weapons, protective structures, vehicle mobility, environmental relationships, aquatic weeds, water quality, dredge material and nuclear and chemical explosives excavation.

U. S. Army Cold Regions Research and Engineering Laboratory
72 Lyme Road
Hanover, NH 03755-1290
(603) 646-4324

Principal interests: Research pertaining to characteristics and events unique to cold regions, especially winter conditions, including design of facilities, structures, and equipment and methods for building, traveling, living, and working in cold environments.

U. S. Army Construction-Engineering Research Laboratory
2902 Newmark Drive
Campaign, IL 61826-1305
(217) 373-6748

Principal interests: Research in the materials, utilities, energy, and structures of all buildings except those specifically designed for cold regions. Conducts systems oriented R&D on the life-cycle requirements of military facilities and their management (the life cycle includes all the processes of planning, design, and construction through maintenance and disposition). Integrates technological developments into construction. Develops corrosion mitigation systems for structures utilizing improved organic coatings, cathodic protection methods, and alternative materials selection. Develops procedures and technology to protect and enhance environmental quality.

U. S. Army Topographic Engineering Center
7701 Telegraph Road, Building 2592
Fort Belvoir, Virginia 22301-3864
Web Site: http://www.tec.army.mil
(703) 428-6608

Principal interests: R&D in the topographic sciences including mapping, charting, geodesy, space research, remote sensing, spectral characterization and analysis, point positioning, surveying and land navigation, environmental support, computer image generation and 3-D battlefield visualizations, modeling and simulation, and distributed interactive simulations. Provides scientific and technical advisory services to support geographic intelligence and environmental resources requirements.

U. S. Army Medical Research & Materiel Command
U. S. Army Medical Research Acquisition Activity
MCMR-AAU
820 Chandler Street
Ft. Detrick, MD 21702-1014
(301) 619-2471

Principal interests: Basic and applied medical research and product development. Medical laboratory and logistical support services, supplies, equipment, and telecommunications.

Associated Activities:

U. S. Army Aeromedical
Research Laboratory
MCMR-UAC-E
Fort Rucker, AL 36362-5292
(334) 255-6908

U. S. Army Research Institute of
Environmental Medicine
MCMR-UE-RP
Natick, MA 01760-5007
(508) 651-4817

U. S. Army Institute of Surgical
Research
MCMR-USX
3400 Rayley E. Chambers
Avenue
Fort Sam Houston, TX 78234-6315
(210) 916-2250

U. S. Army Medical Research
Institute of Infectious Diseases
MCMR-UIZ-M
1425 Porter Street
Fort Detrick, MD 21702-5011
(301) 619-2775

U. S. Army Medical Materiel
Development Activity
MCMR-UMS-R
622 Neiman Street
Fort Detrick, MD 21702-5009
(301) 619-7584

Walter Reed Army Institute of
Research
MCMR-UWZ-C
Bldg 40, Walter Reed Army
Medical Center
Washington, D. C. 20307-5100
(202) 782-3061

U. S. Army Medical Research
Institute of Chemical Defense
MCMR-UV-RC
Aberdeen Proving Ground, MD
21010-5425
(410) 671-1834

Telemedicine Research
Laboratory
MCMR-AT
504 Scott Street
Fort Detrick, MD 21702-5012
(301) 619-7917

DEPARTMENT OF THE NAVY

Office of Naval Research
ONR 362 SBIR
800 North Quincy Street, Room 502
Arlington, VA 22217-5000
(703) 696-8528

Principal interests: Basic research and technology. Contracts are generally awarded in response to unsolicited proposals. The major areas of interest are: mathematical and physical sciences; environmental sciences; engineering sciences; life sciences; aviation and aerospace technology; undersea technology; integrated antisubmarine warfare; surface warfare and supporting technologies; manpower, personnel, and training technology; and advanced conformal submarine acoustic sensor.

Navy Personnel Research and Development Center
Code 022
San Diego, CA 92152-6800
(619) 553-7805

Principal interests: Research in manpower, personnel, education and raining, and human factors engineering in development and operation of Navy personnel systems.

National Naval Medical Center
Procurement Department
8901 Wisconsin Avenue, Bldg. 54
Bethesda, MD 20889-5000
(301) 295-0285

Principal interests: Research, development, test, and evaluation in the following technology areas: submarine medicine, aviation medicine, electromagnetic radiation, human performance, fleet health care, infectious diseases, oral and dental health.

Naval Air Systems Command
Code 02E, Room 424
1421 Jefferson Davis Highway
Arlington, VA 22243-2000
(703) 692-0935

Principal interests: Design, development, testing, and evaluation of airframes, aircraft engines, components, and fuels and lubricants; airborne electronic equipment, pyrotechnics, and mine countermeasures equipment; air launched weapons systems and underwater sound systems; aircraft drone and target systems; catapults, arresting gear, visual landing aids, meteorological equipment, ground handling equipment, parachutes, flight clothing, and survival equipment.

Space and Naval Warfare Systems Command
Code SPA-OOK
4301 Pacific Highway
San Diego, CA 92110-3127
(619) 524-7701

Principal interests: RDT&E for command, control and communications; undersea and space surveillance; electronic warfare; navigational aids; electronic test equipment; electronic materials, components and devices.

Naval Facilities Engineering Command
Code FAC-OOJ
200 Stovall Street, Room 11N59
Alexandria, VA 22332-5000
(703) 325-8549

Principal interests: R&D for new or improved materials, equipment, or engineering techniques to resolve specific engineering problems pertaining to design, construction, operation, and maintenance of shore facilities.

Naval Sea Systems Command
Code SEA-02K
2531 Jefferson Davis Highway
Arlington, VA 22242-5160
(703) 602-1964

Principal interests: R&D, procurement, and logistics support and other material functions for all ships and craft, shipboard weapon systems and ordnance, air launched mines and torpedoes, shipboard components such as propulsion sonar search radar and auxiliary equipment; procurement, technical guidance, and supervision of operations related to salvage of stranded or sunk ships and craft.

Naval Supply Systems Command
Building 9
P.O. Box 2050
Mechanicsburg, PA 17055-0791
(717)790-3575

Principal interests: R&D in supply systems management techniques, including mathematical and statistical analyses, materials handling, clothing and textiles, transportation, and logistics data processing systems.

Naval Research Laboratory
Contracts Division, Code 3204, Bldg. 57
4555 Overlook Avenue, SW
Washington, DC 20375-5326
(202) 767-6263

Principal interests: Scientific research and advanced technology development for new and improved materials, equipment, techniques, systems and related operational procedures for the Navy. Fields of interest include space science and systems; environmental sciences; plasma physics; acoustics; radar; electronic warfare; marine technology; chemistry; materials; optical and radiation sciences; electronics and information technology.

Naval Construction Battalion Center
Code 10G/27G, Bldg 41
1000 23rd Avenue
Port Hueneme, CA 93043-4301
(805) 982-5066

Principal interests: RDT&E center for shore and seafloor facilities and for the support of Navy and Marine Corps construction forces.

Naval Underwater Warfare Center
Code OOSB Ext. 270
1176 Howell Street, Bldg. 11
Newport, RI 02840
(401) 841-2442

Principal interests: Submarine warfare analysis, combat systems engineering and integration, acoustic reconnaissance and search systems, electronic warfare systems, command and control systems, combat control systems, submarine unique communications systems, submarine launchers, submarine-launched torpedoes, submarine unique antisubmarine warfare tactical missile systems, underwater acoustics for system performance prediction, subsurface target simulators, and undersea range development and operation.

Naval Air Warfare Center
Aircraft Division, Code 20C00W
Contracts Building 588, Suite 2
22347 Cedar Point Road, Unit 6
Patuxent River, MD 20670-1161
(301) 342-7567 Ext. 103

Principal interests: RDT&E of aircraft weapons systems, command and control systems, subsystems and components, external stores ordnance and explosive devices for aircraft, electrical and electronics both air and ship systems, instrumentation, data management and analyses, reliability and maintainability (R&M), integrated logistics support (ILS), systems safety, simulation planning and analysis, flight services and program operation, flight services and program operation, program training management, computer programming and operations, software/hardware integration and analysis, electronic, computer, and communication laboratory operational support, software/hardware risk management.

Naval Air Warfare Center
Weapons Division, Code 00K000D
One Administration Circle
China Lake, CA 93555-6001
(760) 939-2712

Principal interests: RDT&E center for air warfare systems (except antisubmarine warfare systems) and missile weapons systems including missile propulsion, warheads, fuses, avionics and fire control, missile guidance, and the national range/facility for parachute test and evaluation.

Naval Air Warfare Center
Training Systems Division
Code 86D1/27B
12350 Research Parkway
Orlando, FL 32826-3224
(407) 380-8253

Principal interests: Research investigations and exploratory development in simulation technology and techniques, investigations and studies in the fields of training psychology, human factors and human engineering, design and engineering development of training devices, weapons system trainers and simulators, and technical data and related ancillary support materials and services.

Naval Surface Warfare Center
Carderock Division
Building 30, Code 303
9500 McArthur Blvd, Room 1
West Bethesda, MD 20817-5700
(301) 227-2871

Principal interests: New vehicle concepts, ship and aircraft compatibility, ship trials and the development of vehicle technology. Areas addressed include hull form; structures; systems development and analysis; Marine Corps systems; fleet support; survivability, vulnerability, protection and weapons effects; propulsion; silencing;

maneuvering and control auxiliary machinery; structural, propulsion and machinery materials; environmental effects, pollution abatement, alternate energy sources (non nuclear); logistics research and information systems; engineering development and design of specialized testing equipment; computer techniques and software for analysis, design and manufacturing, and numerical mechanics. Provides RDT&E support to the U.S. Maritime Administration and the maritime industry.

Naval Air Warfare Center
Aircraft Division
P.O. Box 7176, Code SUA
1440 Parkway Avenue
Trenton, NJ 08628-0176
(609) 538-6640

Principal interests: RDT&E of aircraft propulsion systems and components and accessories and fuels and lubricants.

Naval Surface Warfare Center
Crane Division
Code SB
300 Highway 121, Building 221A
Crane, IN 47522-5001
(812) 854-1542

Principal interests: Design, engineering, evaluation, and analysis programs required in providing support for ships and crafts, shipboard weapons systems, and expendable and non expendable ordnance items.

Naval Surface Warfare Center
Indian Head Division
Code SB
101 Strauss Avenue
Indian Head, MD 20640-5035
(301) 743-6604

Principal interests: Research, development, pilot manufacture, test, and evaluation and fleet support of gun propellants, cartridges, cartridge actuated devices, and weapon system simulators. Provides process development, pilot manufacture and engineering in the transition of rocket engines and warheads from development to production. Provides design support, in-service engineering and acquisition engineering support for Navy rocket engines.

Naval Weapons Station
Supply Department, Code 113
P.O. Box 140
Yorktown, VA 23691-0140
(804) 887-4644

Principal interests: Development of weapons and explosive loading equipment.

Naval Oceanographic Office
Contracts Office, Code N4212, Bldg. 9134
Stennis Space Center, MS 39522-5001
(601) 689-8369

Principal interests: R&D in oceanographic, hydrographic, and geodetic equipment, techniques, and systems.

Naval Surface Warfare Center
Dahlgren Division, Code C6
Dahlgren, VA 22448-5000
(703) 663-4806

Principal interests: Provide RDT&E, engineering and fleet support for surface warfare systems, surface ship combat systems, ordnance, mines, amphibious warfare systems, mine countermeasures special warfare systems, and strategic systems.

Naval Surface Warfare Center
Dahlgren Division
Coastal Systems Station, Code 20D
6703 West Highway 98
Panama City, FL 32407-5000
(904) 234-4347

Principal interests: Provide RDT&E for mines and countermeasures, special warfare, amphibious warfare, diving and other naval missions that take place primarily in the coastal region.

Naval Air Warfare Center
Weapons Division, Code P65
Point Mugu, CA 93041-5000
(805) 989-8914

Principal interests: Performs test and evaluation, development and follow-on engineering; provides logistics and training support for naval weapons, weapon systems, and related devices; and provides major range, technical, and base support for fleet users and other DoD and government agencies. Functions relate to guided missiles, rockets, free-fall weapons, fire control and radar systems, drones and target drones, computers, electronic warfare devices and countermeasures equipment, range services and instrumentation, test planning simulations, and data collection.

Space and Navy Warfare System Center
RDT&E Division, Code 02202
53570 Silvergate Avenue
San Diego, CA 92152-5113
(619) 553-4326

Principal interests: RDT&E for command control, communications, ocean surveillance, surface and air-launched undersea weapon systems, submarine arctic warfare, and supporting techniques.

DEPARTMENT OF THE AIR FORCE

Space and Missile System Center (SMC/BC)
155 Discoverer Blvd., Ste 2017
Los Angeles AFB CA 90245-4692
(310) 363-2855

Principle interests: The mission of SMC is to plan, program, and manage AFMC programs to acquire space systems, subsystems, support equipment, and related hardware and software; provide for the maintenance, construction, alteration, and security of launch, tracking, and support facilities; conduct research, exploratory development, and advanced development programs to support future space missions; provide for and conduct launch and flight test and evaluation support of major DoD programs and programs of other federal agencies; perform the functions of launch, launch control, deployment checkout prior to turnover, and sustaining engineering; perform on-orbit test and evaluation of systems, subsystems and components, discharge AF responsibilities for designated AF, DoD, and international space programs; plan, program, and acquire test facilities and other test investments required by AFMC programs at all locations (test centers ands contractor facilities); plan and provide for security on all systems and information requiring safeguards consistent with AF and DoD security directives; provide management oversight for commercial expendable Launch Vehicle Activity; conduct launch agreement negotiations with commercial space launch operators; provide system engineering management support for selected space systems, subsystems, facilities, support equipment, and related hardware and software; support other product divisions and federal agencies with technologies derived from its subordinate laboratories.

While there are no AF aircraft assigned to Los Angeles AFB, the operational contracting directorate does contract for all other work necessary for the operation and maintenance of the base.

HQ Air Force Space Command (HQ AFSPC/LGCM)
150 Vandenberg St, Ste 1105
Peterson AFB, CO 80914-4350
(719) 554-5324

Principle interests: HQ AFSPC awards and administers contracts for AF Space Command services and associated supply requirements to support major operational defense systems, space launch operations and maintenance, satellite control, and satellite operations. This includes associated engineering and technical support services, as well as local purchase requirements for the following bases:

Buckley ANGB, Colorado
Falcon AFB, Colorado
FE Warren AFB, Wyoming
Malmstrom AFB, Montana
Onizuka AFB, California
Patrick AFB, Florida
Peterson AFB, Colorado
Vandenberg AFB, California

Human Systems Center/BC (AFMC) (210)536-4348
8106 Chennault Rd, Bldg 1160
Brooks AFB, TX 78235-5318

Principle interests: The Human Systems Center has the role of integrating and maintaining people in AF systems and operations. People are the enabling factor in AF operations. Recognizing this, the center was established as the AF agent for human-centered research, development, acquisition, and specialized operational support. * (Also cover AF-wide environmental restoration and base closure efforts.)

The center prepares, maintains, protects, and enhances human capabilities and human-system performance, from the scope of the individual to the entire forces. The center works in four functional areas to meet current and future human-centered operational requirements:

Crew-system integration
Crew protection
Environmental protection
Force readiness (human resources and aerospace medicine)

The Armstrong Laboratory, Human Systems Program Office, the USAF School of Aerospace Medicine and an air base group are major units of the center.

HSC/BC also provides contract support to the AF Center for Environmental Excellence (AFCEE) which provides a full range of technical services in environmental areas, including contracting for full service remediation/remedial action, worldwide environmental services, preliminary assessment/site inspections, tank removals, environmental support, community relations, general systems engineering and integration (GSE&I), information clearing house, and Installation Restoration Program Information Management System (IRPIMS).

The Operational Contracting Division acquires supplies, equipment, services, construction, and utilities in support of Brooks AFB and tenant organizations.

Armstrong Laboratory
c/o Human Systems Center/BC
Brooks AFB, TX 78235-5320
(210) 536-4348

Principle interests: Ensuring that the AF's weapon systems and the people operating them are compatible. The laboratory researches and develops technology for maintaining, protecting, and enhancing human capabilities during AF operations. The seven major components of the Armstrong Laboratory and its related technical concerns are:

Aerospace Medical Research Laboratory Directorate, Wright-Patterson AFB, OH, conducts and directs R&D in aerospace biotechnology. Activities are directed toward advancing technology in man-machine integration, physiological tolerances, protection requirements, toxic hazards, and the influence of noise, vibration, and acceleration.

School of Aerospace Medicine (SAM) plans and conducts R&D on work dealing with applied aeromedical research including medical education and training, clinical evaluation/consultations, and special support activities.

Human Resources Directorate conducts exploratory and advanced development programs for manpower and personnel, operational and technical training, simulation, and logistics systems in four research divisions. Their goal is to assist the AF in achieving the best methods for acquiring enlisted and officer members; training and maintaining this force at peak readiness.

Occupational and Environmental Health Directorate provides professional consultation, specialized laboratory services, and operational field support to assist the AF in meeting its worldwide responsibilities in the management of occupational, radiological, and environmental health problems. It is a technical center for the AF's Installation Restoration Program and host for the AF Radiation Assessment Team.

Human Systems Program Directorate conducts advanced and full-scale development and acquisition programs in crew-system integration, personnel protection, air base support, computer based training systems, and clothing design in response to Air Force needs. This office is also responsible for aeromedical casualty, manpower, and personnel programs; advanced anti-G system for fighter aircraft, life support/survival equipment, chemical defense, hazardous waste cleanup, integrated aircrew protection, space crew enhancement technology, cockpit design, helmet mounted systems (night vision, etc.), crew escape technology, and noise (sonic boom impact) technology.

Science, Technology and Operational Aeromedical Support Program Office develops technology for future warfighting capabilities by generating the strategy to produce the enabling human centered technology options.

Drug Testing Directorate implements the AF drug abuse program, conducts testing for known drugs of abuse, such as cocaine, amphetamines, barbiturates and marijuana for CONUS AF members and Army personnel in the South Central US, as well as research and testing on other drugs to ensure drug users are deterred from switching to substances not currently being analyzed.

Phillips Laboratory (PL/BC)
2000 Wyoming Blvd SE, Bldg 2064
Kirtland AFB, NM 87117-5060
(505)846-8515

The Phillips Laboratory provides contracting support to its own activities which include the following Laboratories:

PL/GP Geophysics PL/WS Adv Weapons and Surveillance
PL/RK Propulsion PL/SX Space Experiments
PL/VT Space and Missiles Technology
PL/LI Lasers and Imaging

In addition, support is provided for acquisition of research and development projects and major support contracts to other Government agencies such as: The Air Force Operational Test and Evaluation Center (AFOTEC), Defense Advanced Research Agency(DARPA), Theater Air Command Computer Simulation Facility (TACCSF), AirBorne Laser Program Office (ABL), Space and Missile Systems Center's Space and Missile Test and Evaluation Directorate (SMC/TE), San Antonio Air Logistics Center's Nuclear Weapons Integration Facility (SA-ALC/NWI), and the U.S. Army's BIG CROW Program Office.

The Phillips Laboratory establishes and maintains comprehensive in-house resources for research, development, testing, and evaluation; manages activities of the various

Phillips Laboratory centers; integrates technology products and conducts configuration research; develops and tests experimental space systems and subsystems, nonconventional and advanced weapons, and rocket propulsion systems to acquire design data and demonstrate new and integrated technology; acts as focal point or lead organization for designated programs or activities involving two or more AF or DoD organizations, or DoD and NASA organizations; acts in coordination with space test programs; advocates and sponsors space experimentation and test of assigned technologies in space.

The operational contracting division contracts for supplies, equipment, and work necessary for the operation and maintenance of Phillips Laboratory and Kirtland AFB.

Wright Laboratory
Directorate of R&D Contracting
c/o Aeronautical Systems Center (ASC/BC)
2196 D St.
Wright-Patterson AFB OH 45433-7201
(937) 255-5422

Principle interests: This directorate provides business and contracting support for Wright Laboratory (WL). Contracts are written for requirements of the following directorates:

Aero Propulsion and Power Directorate is responsible for development of air breathing propulsion and aerospace power technology needed for future AF systems, as well as providing assistance to the "product divisions" of AFMC in acquiring new systems and in helping to resolve developmental and operation problems.

Avionics Directorate conducts R&D programs for aerospace reconnaissance, weapons delivery, electronic warfare systems, navigation, communication and avionics integration.

Solid State Electronics Directorate is responsible for electronic device R&D for future AF systems needs in the areas of microelectronics, microwaves, and electro-optics. Research extends from fundamental semiconductor layer growth and device fabrication through analog and digital integrated circuits; also included is the computer-aided design software and work stations needed to pursue sample hybrid and monolithic integrated circuits.

Flight Dynamics Directorate pursues AF flight vehicle technologies to support aircraft, missiles and space systems in the technical areas of structures, vehicle subsystems, flight control, aeromechanics and experimental flight vehicle test beds. Materials Directorate explores new materials and processes for advanced aerospace applications. Its current focus is on thermal protection materials, metallic and nonmetallic structural materials, aerospace propulsion materials, fluids and lubricants, electromagnetic and electronic materials and laser hardened materials.

Manufacturing Technology Directorate focuses on process technologies and integrated manufacturing. This directorate is responsible for a new initiative which integrates design and manufacturing technologies to stimulate a new focus on design for producibility, design for quality, and design for life cycle costs. Key elements of this concurrent engineering involve development of advanced tools in computer aided design and computer aided manufacturing for analyses of design for weapon performance and low cost manufacturing.

Plans and Programs Directorate is made up of cockpit integration, which involves research to advance the state of the art crew systems technologies for all classes of aerospace vehicles; and signature technology, which includes planning, formulating, and executing USAF exploratory and advanced development programs for vehicle signature reduction technology and counter low observable technology.

Armament Directorate develops conventional armament technology and integrates these technologies into air vehicle platforms and other delivery platforms. The directorate provides conventional armament technology for four major thrusts that include advanced guidance, weapon flight mechanics, ordnance, and conventional strategic defense.

AF Flight Test Center (AFFTC/BC)
5 South Wolfe Ave, Bldg 2800
Edwards AFB, CA 93524-1185
(805)277-3900 x2275

Principles interests: Test and evaluation of new and research aircraft. The center's contracting activity provides the contracting support necessary to accomplish the test mission and to provide operational support for base personnel/facilities, including the USAF Test Pilot School. Test mission procurements include telemetry equipment; flight test instrumentation; computer hardware and software; engineering, scientific and technical services, including management of the Edwards AFB Range; precision milling machines; aircraft maintenance; and radar components. Support to the test pilot school includes contracting for simulator training, glider training, and flight training/lectures. In addition, the AFFTC Contracting Center provides contracting support to the Propulsion Directorate of the Phillips Laboratory, a major tenant organization. Propulsion Directorate requirements include basic research, exploratory development and advanced development for strategic, tactical and space system propulsion.

The directorate also contracts for multiple space vehicle technologies including structures, structure dynamics, controls and power systems and is heavily involved in the Space Defense Initiative (SDI) program. The operational contracting division contracts for supplies, equipment, and work necessary for the operation and maintenance of Edwards AFB.

Electronic Systems Center (ESC/BC) (617) 377-4973
275 Randolph Rd
Hanscom AFB, MA 01731-2818

Principle interests: Plans and manages the acquisition and related engineering development of command, control, communications, and intelligence systems, subsystems and equipment including surveillance systems, navigation systems, air traffic control and landing systems, intelligence systems, electronic physical security surveillance and intrusion detection systems and weather systems, information and management systems until transfer of responsibility to the using command or agency. Evaluates using command requirements against available technology and potential costs and recommends necessary revisions. R&D contracts are also initiated by the Geophysics Division of the AF Laboratory in the environmental, physical and engineering sciences. The Geophysics Division performs research and exploratory and advanced Development in geophysics that is essential to the enhancement of AF operational capabilities. The work pursued may be categorized generally as falling within the following functional areas: Space Physics, Ionospheric Physics, Terrestrial Science, Upper Atmospheric and Stratospheric operations, Optical/IR Backgrounds and Targets, Weather Specification and prediction. Close liaison is maintained with AF operational elements, system development activities, and other AF laboratories, to identify research and technology needs and to accelerate the integration of scientific advances into AF technology. Geophysics Division carries out its assigned R&D mission responsibilities with in-house as well as contractual support.

While there are no AF aircraft assigned to Hanscom AFB, the operational contracting directorate does contract for all other work necessary for the operation and maintenance of the base.

Rome Laboratory (RL/BC)
26 Electronic Parkway
Griffis AFB, NY 13441-4514
(315) 330-3311

Principle interests: AFMC laboratory specializing in the development of technologies for command, control, communications and intelligence systems. The laboratory's focus is to develop AF command and control systems, advanced computers and microchips, communication devices and techniques, software engineering, intelligence gathering and processing devices, surveillance systems, advanced radar, super conductivity, infrared sensors, cryogenics, artificial intelligence applications, and related technologies. It is the AF Center of Excellence in photonics research and the DoD focal point for reliability and compatibility.

AF Development Test Center (AFDTC/BC)
205 West D Ave., Ste 449
Eglin AFB, FL 32542-6863
(904) 882-2843

Principles interests: Plans, directs, and conducts the test and evaluation of nonnuclear munitions, electronic combat, and navigation/ guidance systems. Related ASC System Program Offices (SPOs) are also located here and supported by AFDTC/BC. To accomplish this mission, AFDTC manages the large land test ranges that are located on the 724 square mile Eglin complex as well as the 86,500 square miles of water ranges located in the adjacent Gulf of Mexico. Major tests on or above AFDTC's ranges cover aircraft systems, subsystems, missiles, guns, rockets, targets and drones, high-powered radars, and electronic countermeasures equipment. AFDTC's unique assets include the Guided Weapons Evaluation Facility (GWEF), the Preflight Integration of Munitions and Electronic Systems (PRIMES),and the McKinley Climatic Laboratory, a facility capable of testing military hardware as large as aircraft in environments ranging from minus 65 to plus 165 degrees Fahrenheit with 100 mph winds,icing clouds, rain, and snow. AFDTC also is responsible for the 46th Test Group at Holloman AFB NM, with its high speed test track, two radar target scatter measurement facilities, and the Central Inertial Guidance Test Facility (CIGTF).

The operational contracting division contracts for supplies, equipment, and work necessary for the operation and maintenance of Eglin AFB.

Arnold Engineering Development Center (AEDC/BC)
100 Kindel Dr., Ste A332
Arnold AFB, TN 37389-1332
(615) 454-7841

Principle interests: Provides aerodynamics R&D of power plants related to operation and test of air breathing propulsion systems (turbojet, ramjet, and turboprop); simulation of conditions of atmospheric, ballistic, orbital, and space flight; problems associated with high temperature materials; unique mechanical, electrical, and thermodynamic problems related to the construction of wind tunnels; high altitude propulsion test cells; space simulation chambers; impact and ballistic ranges and research units. Procurements include pumps and compressors (axial); compressors (centrifugal), rotors, and diffusers; high pressure airducting; wind tunnel accessories; test instrumentation; electromagnetic generators; test facility construction and modernization; high speed cameras; high temperature materials, cores, and bricks; architectural engineering services; ADP equipment; laboratory equipment; shop machinery.

Air Force Civil Engineering Center
Support Agency
Tyndall AFB, FL 32401
(904) 882-2843

Principal interests: Contracts for the Air Force Engineering Service Center (AFESC). AFESC conducts planning, engineering development, investigative/applications engineering, and specialized civil engineering functions to enhance the technology and capabilities of AF civil engineering. The Center's capability complements the integral capabilities of major air commands, base level civil engineering organizations, and the civil engineering R&D community. The Center manages applied technology programs and introduces new technology into civil engineering operations through translation of state of the art research into usable systems, hardware, and techniques. Specific programs and areas of interest are mobility shelters; pre-engineered and relocatible facilities; modular facilities; snow and ice removal equipment and materials; corrosion abatement techniques and materials; fire/crash rescue equipment and materials; and other facilities, equipment materials, and techniques with potential application to the overall AF civil engineering area.

AF Office of Scientific Research (AFOSR/PK)
110 Duncan Ave., Ste B115
Bolling AFB, DC 20332-8050
(202) 767-4946

Principle interests: Encourages and supports fundamental research designed to increase the understanding of the natural sciences and to stimulate the recognition of new scientific concepts. Particularly desired are original and unique scientific approaches likely to clarify or extend understanding of the sciences which are of interest to the principal technical directorates of AFOSR. The AFOSR scientific directorates and areas of interest are:

Directorate Of Aerospace And Material Sciences (NA)
(202) 767-4987
Structural mechanics; mechanics of materials; particulate mechanics; external aerodynamics and hypersonics; turbulence and internal flows; airbreathing combustion; space power and propulsion; metallic structural materials; ceramics and nonmetallic structural materials; organic matrix composites.

Directorate Of Physics And Electronics (NE)
(202) 767-4985
Electromagnetic devices; novel electronic components, opto-electronic information processing: devices and systems; quantum electronic solids; emi conductor materials; electromagnetic materials; photonic physics; optics; atomic and molecular physics; plasma physics; imaging physics.

Directorate Of Chemistry And Life Sciences (NL)
(202)767-5021
Chemical reactivity and synthesis; polymer chemistry; surface science; theoretical-chemistry molecular dynamics; chronobiology and neural adaptation; perception and cognition; sensory systems; bioenvironmental sciences.

Directorate Of Mathematics And Geosciences (NM)
(202) 767-5025
Dynamics and controls; physical mathematics and applied analysis; computational mathematics; optimization and discrete mathematics; signal processing, probability, and statistics; software and systems; artificial intelligence; electromagnetic; meteorology; atmospheric sciences; space sciences.

Directorate Of Academic And International Affairs (NI)
(202) 767-8073
Sponsors researcher assistance programs that stimulate scientific and engineering education and increase the interaction between the broader research community and the Air Force laboratories.

The directorate is also responsible for managing the Small Business innovative Research (SBIR) and the Small Business Technology Transfer (STTR) programs for AFOSR. Specific research topics are selected for each solicitation. Industrial concerns and nonprofit organization having research capabilities in major scientific fields, and those whose personnel include competent scientific investigators, may submit basic research proposals. General questions about the Department of Defense SBIR/STTR programs should be referred to the SBIR/STTR Help Desk at (800) 382-4634. AFOSR specific questions should be referred to the SBIR/STTR program manager in AFOSR/NI, (202) 767-6962.

New World Vistas
AFOSR is specifically, but not exclusively, interested in sponsoring basic research that supports the science and technology areas identified in the Air Force Scientific Advisory board's New World Vistas report. The New World Vistas report identifies science and technology needed to support six future Air Force capability areas. The Air Force intends to invest in basic research that supports some or all of these subareas in the near future.

Global Awareness
(202) 767-7899
Network data fusion for global awareness; lightweight antenna structures; low-cost, lightweight membrane structures; in situ sensors; global awareness virtual testbed; low noise/high-uniformity broadband sensors.

Dynamic Planning and Execution Control
(202) 767-7899
Planning and scheduling; communications; knowledge bases; intelligent agents for Air Force battlefield and enterprise information assistants; information warfare; new models of computation; domain-specific component-based software development.

Global Mobility In War And Peace
(202) 767-0467
Precision air delivery; composite materials and structures; low-specific-fuel-consumption propulsion; aerodynamics and controls subsystems integration/power; advanced landing gear; microelectromechanical systems; active defense systems; battlefield awareness/weather predictions; human systems interface and training.

Projection Of Lethal And Sublethal Power
(202) 767-0467
Uninhabited aerial vehicles; hypersonics; lethal andsublethal directed-energy weapons; energy-coupling modeling and simulation.

Space Operations
(202)767-4984
Microsatellites; distributed functionality; precision deployable large antennas/optics; high efficiency electrical laser sources; space object identification and orbit prediction; high-energy-density propellants; jam-proof, area-deniable propagation; nanosecond global clock accuracy; hypervelocity dynamics; low-cost, lightweight structures and materials; power generation and storage.

People
(202) 767-4278
Human-machine interface; team decision making; cognitive engineering.

ADVANCED RESEARCH PROJECTS AGENCY

The Advanced Research Projects Agency (ARPA) is the central research and development organization for the Department of Defense (DoD). It manages and directs selected basic and applied research and development projects for DoD, and pursues research and technology where risk and payoff are both very high and where success may provide dramatic advances for traditional military roles and missions and dual-use applications.

ARPA's primary responsibility is to help maintain U.S. technological superiority and guard against unforeseen technological advances by potential adversaries. Consequently, the ARPA mission is to develop imaginative, innovative, and often high risk research ideas offering a significant technological impact that will go well beyond the normal evolutionary developmental approaches; and to pursue these ideas from the demonstration of technical feasibility through the development of prototype systems.

The challenge of the ARPA mission is met by a small group of technical program managers with flexibility for quick implementation of R&D initiatives. The current ARPA Technical Program has been organized around the following major thrusts, selected because of their importance to national defense and dual-use applications.

Technology Reinvestment Project
Joint Biomedical Technology Program
High Performance Computing
Acoustic Warfare and Submarine Stealth
Advanced Simulation
Smart Weapons
Software and Intelligent Systems
Microelectronics Production Technology
Advanced Satellite Technology
Special Materials

Entities seeking R&D support from ARPA should explore the Agency's interests in research by reviewing sources such as the Commerce Business Daily (CBD), open literature, published testimony before Congressional committees, and the Department of Defense Small Business Innovation Research (SBIR) Program Solicitation. Inquiries regarding ARPA technologies may be addressed to:

Director
Advanced Research Projects Agency
3701 North Fairfax Drive
ATTN: OASB
Arlington, VA 22203-1714
(703) 696-2448

Defense Technical Information Center
ATTN: DTIC, Suite 0944
8725 John J. Kingman Road
Fort Belvoir, VA 22060-6218 1
(703) 767-8226
Toll-free: (outside DC area) (800) DOD SBIR

DoD's central facility for the distribution of scientific and technical reports generated by defense-funded efforts in virtually all areas of

R&D; operates computer-based data bank of management and technical information and is responsible for the development of information storage and retrieval systems. Data banks cover the past, present, and future defense R&D programs. The services offered are available to defense and other federal activities and to all their contractors, subcontractors, and grantees.

GUIDE FOR PREPARING UNSOLICITED PROPOSALS

An unsolicited proposal is a written proposal independently originated and developed by the offeror and submitted to DoD for the purpose of obtaining a contract. To be considered for acceptance, an unsolicited proposal must be innovative and unique and in sufficient detail to allow a determination that DoD support would benefit the agency's mission responsibilities. An unsolicited proposal is not a response to an agency request or an advance proposal for an agency requirement that could be met by competitive methods.

There is no particular format to be followed in preparation of unsolicited proposals. Elaborate proposals are discouraged. The proposal should contain the following information to permit consideration in an objective and timely manner:

Basic Information. Offeror's name, address, and type of organization; e.g., profit, nonprofit, educational, small business, minority business, women-owned business.

Names and telephone numbers of technical and business personnel to be contacted for evaluation or negotiation purposes.

Names of other Federal, State, and local agencies, or other parties, if any, receiving the proposal or funding the proposed effort.

Date of submission and signature of a person authorized to represent and contractually obligate the offeror.

Technical Information

A concise, descriptive title and an abstract (200-300 words) stating the basic purpose, summary of work, and expected end result of the proposed effort.

A reasonably complete narrative in which the relevance of the proposed work to the DoD mission is discussed. State the problems to be addressed; the specific objectives of the research, and the expected consequences of successful completion of the research, including potential economic and other benefits.

Provide a full and complete description of the work to be performed, the method of approach, and the extent of effort to be employed.

Indicate an estimated period of time in which to accomplish the objectives, and criteria by which success of the project can be evaluated.

Names and biographical information on the key personnel who would be involved in the project.

Any support needed from the agency; e.g., facilities, equipment, material.

Supporting Information

A breakdown of the proposed cost or price in sufficient detail for meaningful evaluation. Show the estimated cost of materials and how you established it. Show the estimated costs of labor by category (engineering, manufacturing, test, etc.) and show the salary rates for each category. Show the indirect expense rates (manufacturing and engineering overheads, general and administrative expenses) to be applied. Explain the basis for the labor and indirect expense rates included in your cost breakdown (e.g., current experienced rates, projected from current experience, budgetary, etc.). Identify and explain the basis for any other cost elements included in your proposal.

A statement as to the proposed duration of the effort, the type of contract preferred, and the length of time for which the proposal is valid (a 6 month minimum is suggested).

A brief description of any previous or ongoing R&D work performed in the field or in related fields. Describe briefly the facilities and any special equipment available to perform the proposed effort.

Unsolicited proposals may include proprietary data which the offeror does not want disclosed to the public or used by the Government for any purpose other than proposal evaluation. DoD cannot assume responsibility for use of such data unless it is specifically and clearly marked with the following legend on the title page:

Use and Disclosure of Data

The data in this proposal shall not be disclosed outside the Government and shall not be duplicated, used, or disclosed in whole or in part for any purpose other than to evaluate the proposal; provided that if a contract is awarded to the offeror as a result of or in connection with the submission of these data, the Government shall have the right to duplicate, use, or disclose the data to the extent provided in the contract. This restriction does not limit the Government's right to use information contained in the ata if it is obtainable from another source without restriction. The data subject to this restriction are contained in Sheets _____. Each restricted sheet should be marked with the following legend: "Use or disclosure of proposal data is subject to the restriction on the title page of this proposal."

MILITARY BUYING OFFICES BY DoD COMPONENT

Major Army Buying Offices

U. S. Army Industrial Operations Command
ATTN: AMSIO-SB
Rock Island, IL 61299-6000
(309) 782-7302
Principal interests: Ammunition, fuses, projectile assemblies, mortars; ammunition destruction; nuclear and nonnuclear munitions; rocket and missile warhead sections; demolition munitions; mines, bombs, grenades; and pyrotechnic boosters.

U. S. Army Chemical Biological Defense Command
AMSCB-SBA(A)
Aberdeen Proving Ground, MD 21010-5423
(410) 671-3136
Principal Interests: Research, concept exploration, demonstration and validation, engineering manufacturing development and internal production of chemical defense system, obscuring smoke and aerosol systems and flame weapons, chemical material destruction (stockpile/nonstockpile)

U. S. Army Aviation and Missile Command
AMSAM-SB
Redstone Arsenal, AL 35898-5150
(205) 876-5441
Principal Interests: Army aircraft, equipment, and supplies; development of turbine engines and new helicopter systems. Free rockets, guided missiles, ballistic missiles, targets, air defense, fire control coordination equipment, related special-purpose and multisystem test equipment, missile launching and ground support equipment, and metrology and calibration equipment.

U. S. Army Communications and Electronics Command
AMSEL-SB
Fort Monmouth, NJ 07703-5005
(908) 532-4511
Principal interests: Communications-electronics systems and subsystems and related equipment for command, control and communications; countermine and tactical sensor equipment.

Subordinate Activities:

U. S. Army Communications and Electronics Command
Acquisition Center-Combat Support Center
AMSEL-CB
Fort Huachuca, AZ 85613-5300
(520) 538-7870
Principal Interests: Equipment and systems to support the Army's
total information needs, including communications, data processing,
and multi-command management information systems.

U. S. Army Communications and Electronics Command
Acquisition Center-Washington Operations Office
2461 Eisenhower Avenue, Hoffman 1 Building
Alexandria, Virginia 22331-0700
(703) 325-5793
Principal interests: Automated information hardware, software,
services, maintenance, and systems.

U. S. Army Research Laboratory
ATTN: AMSRL-SB
2800 Powder Mill Road
Adelphia, MD 20783-1197
(301) 394-3692
Principal Interests: Nuclear survivability, lethality, radar, signal sensors,
signatures, information processing; electronic surveillance systems;
high-power microwave and acoustic technology, materials, digitization
of battlefield, MANTECH, advanced computing.

U. S. Army Tank-automotive and Armaments Command
AMSTA-CS-CB
Warren, MI 48397-5000
(810) 574-5388
Principal interests: Ground vehicles (tanks, infantry fighting vehicles,
trucks and trailers, construction and material handling vehicles); vehicle
components and supplies (e.g., power train components, electronic
assemblies, armor, tires, special purpose kits); combat engineering
equipment (e.g., bridges); railway cars; watercraft; fuel and water tanks;
and research and development services (product development/
improvement, testing and analysis, technical support for fielded systems).

Subordinate Installations:

U. S. Army Armament and Chemical Acquisition and Logistics
Activity
AMSTA-AC-SB
Rock Island, IL 61299-7630
(309) 782-6709

Principal Interests: Armament systems (artillery, small arms, fire control equipment); armament components and supplies (e.g., optical equipment, electronic assemblies); and chemical, nuclear and biological protection equipment.

U. S. Army Armament Research,
Development and Engineering Center
AMSTA-AR-SB
Picatinny Arsenal, NJ 07806-5000
(201) 724-4106
Principal interests: Product development/improvement of munitions, weaponry, and fire control systems; testing and analysis; and technical support for fielded armament systems.

Department of the Army
Defense Supply Service-Washington
5200 Army Pentagon
Washington, D. C. 20310-5200
(703) 697-6024
Principal interests: Supplies, materials, and equipment; research; contractual services; studies and analytical support services; machine rental, repair, and maintenance services; and other related services for DoD agencies located in or near Washington, D. C.

Military Traffic Management Command
5611 Columbia Pike, ATTN: MTAQ-S
Falls Church, VA 22041-5050
(703) 681-3515
Principal interests: Stevedoring and related terminal services; transportation and storage of personal property, including household goods; commercial travel services; federal information processing services, and transportation of personnel.

Associated installations:

Military Traffic Management Command,
Eastern Area Acquisition Office
ATTN: MTELO-CO, Building 42
Bayonne Military Ocean Terminal, Room 705A
Bayonne, NJ 07002-5302
(201) 823-6509
Principal interests: Repair and maintenance services for the Defense Freight Railway Interchange Fleet; processing privately-owned vehicles; terminal support supplies and services, and other services such as guard, trucking, towing, janitorial, refuse collection, and minor construction and repair.

Military Traffic Management Command
Western Area Acquisition Office
MTWLO-CO, Oakland Army Base
Oakland, CA 94626-5000
(510) 466-2703
Principal interests: Container freight stuffing and unstuffing, processing privately-owned vehicles; reefer cargo services, base maintenance services, and minor construction and repair.

U. S. Army Medical Research & Materiel Command
MCMR-AAA
820 Chandler Street
Fort Detrick, MD 21702-5014
(301) 619-2471
Principal interests: Basic and applies medical research and product development. Medical laboratory and logistical support services, supplies, equipment, and telecommunications.

U. S. Army Medical Commands

Principal interests: Medical supplies and equipment, direct health care professionals.

Fitzsimons Army Medical
Center
MCHG-DC
Aurora, CO 80045-5000
(303) 361-8488

Brooke Army Medical Center
MCAA-C
Fort Sam Houston,
TX 78234-6039
(210) 221-9088

Walter Reed Army Medical
Center
MCHL-Z
Washington, D. C. 20307-5000
(202) 782-1255

William Beaumont Army
Medical Center
MCAA-SW
El Paso, TX 79920-5001
(915) 569-2815

Dwight D. Eisenhower Army
Medical Center
MCAA-SE
Fort Gordon, GA 30905-5650
(706) 787-6793

Madigan Army Medical Center
MCAA-NW
Tacoma, WA 94831-5021
(206) 698-4914

Tripler Army Medical Center
MCAA-PC
Honolulu, HI 96819
(808) 433-3503

U. S. Army Depots

Principal interests: Overhaul, rebuild, and modify munitions, weapon systems, helicopters, and communication equipment.

Anniston Army Depot
SIOAN-DOC
Anniston, AL 36201-5003
(205) 235-4258

Red River Army Depot
SIORR-P
Texarkana, TX 75507-5000
(903) 334-3989

Bluegrass Army Depot
SIOBG-PO
Richmond, KY 40475-5115
(606) 625-6866

Sierra Army Depot
SIOSI-CONT
Herlong, CA 96113-5009
(916) 827-4836

Corpus Christi Army Depot
SIOCC-C
Corpus Christi, TX 78419-6170
(512) 939-3913

Tobyhanna Army Depot
SIOTY-K
Tobyhanna, PA 18466-5045
(717) 895-7232

Letterkenny Army Depot
SIOLE-P
Chambersburg, PA 17201-4150
(717) 267-9007

Tooele Army Depot
SIOTE-CO
Tooele, UT 84074-5020
(801) 833-2616

U. S. Army Corps of Engineers
20 Massachusetts Avenue, N. W.
Washington, D. C. 20314-1000
(202) 761-0725

Interested businesses should contact the Corps division and district offices which are included in the geographical listing of the booklet entitled "Small Business Specialists."

Principal interests: Designs and manages the construction of military facilities for the Army and Air Force. Provides design and construction management support for other DOD and Federal agencies. Plans, designs, builds and operates water resources and other civil works projects. Provides research and development services for both military and civil works projects and for other agencies on a reimbursable basis.

Other Army Commands

Installation contracting offices for the commands listed below are included in the geographical listing of the booklet "Small Business Specialists that can be reviewed at http://www.acq.osd.mil/sadbu then click on publications."

Principal interests: Supplies and services in support of each installation such as: office supplies/services, grounds maintenance, ADP maintenance and repair, laundry services, refuse collection, food services, printing, education and training services, minor construction, building maintenance and repair, and automotive spare parts.

U. S. Army Training & Doctrine Command
ATCS-B
Fort Monroe, VA 23651-5000
(757) 727-3291

National Guard Bureau
NGB-SADBU
Falls Church, VA 22041-3201
(703) 681-0655

US Army Forces Command
AFCS-SB
Fort McPherson, GA 30330-6000
(404) 464-6223

US Army Military District of Washington
ANPC-SB
Fort Leslie J. McNair
Washington, D. C. 20319-5058
(202) 685-1990

US Army, Pacific
APAM
Fort Shafter, HI 96858-5100
(808) 438-6530

Major Navy Buying Offices

Headquarters U.S. Marine Corp
Code L-2
2 Navy Annex
Washington, DC 20380-1775
(703) 696-1022
Principal interests: Electronics equipment, specialized vehicles, and equipment peculiar to the Marine Corps.

Marine Corps Systems Command
Code SBS ext. 236
2033 Barnett Avenue, Suite 315
Quantico, VA 22134-5010
(703) 784-5822
Principal interest: Research, development and acquisition of equipment, information systems, training systems and weapon systems to satisfy approved material requirements of the Marine Corps.

Military Sealift Command
Washington Navy Yard, Bldg-210,
Code NOOB, Room 419
901 M. Street, SE
Washington, DC 20398-5100
(202) 685-5025
Principal interests: Ocean shipping services to maintain strategic

sealift, support of fleet units worldwide, and meeting special transportation needs of DoD sponsors for research, cable laying and repair, and special missions; movement of material, petroleum, oil, and lubricants, and personnel using U.S.-flag vessels; repair of oceangoing noncombatant ships.

Office of Naval Research
Code 00SB
800 North Quincy Street, Rm 704
Arlington, VA 22217-5660
(703) 696-4605
Principal interests: Studies in the areas of mathematical and physical sciences, environmental sciences, engineering sciences, life sciences, and technology projects.

Naval Research Laboratory
Code 3204
Building 222, Room 115
4555 Overlook Ave., SW
Washington, D.C. 20375-5326
(202) 767-6263
Principal interests: Scientific research and advanced technology development for new and improved materials, equipment, techniques, systems and related operational procedures for the Navy. Fields of interest include space science and systems; environmental sciences; plasma physics; acoustics; radar; electronic warfare; marine technology; chemistry; materials; optical and radiation sciences; electronics and information technology.

Strategic Systems Program
Code, SP-01G1
1931 Jefferson Davis Highway
Arlington, VA 22241-5362
(703) 607-0217
Principal interests: Fleet ballistic missiles.

Naval Air Systems Command
Building 441
21983 Bundy Road, Unit 8
Patuxent River, MD 20670
(301) 757-9044
Principal interests: Navy and Marine Corps aircraft systems; air-launched weapons systems and subsystems; airborne electronics systems; air-launched underwater sound systems; airborne pyrotechnics; astronautics and spacecraft systems; airborne mine countermeasures equipment (except for explosives, explosive components, and fusing); aeronautical drones and towed target systems, including related ground control equipment and launch and

control aircraft; meteorological equipment; overhaul and modification of all Naval aircraft/engines; operation and maintenance of weapons training ranges.

Naval Air Warfare Center
Aircraft Division
Code 29.S South, Building 129
Lakehurst, NJ 08053-5082
(908) 323-2812
Principal interests: Launching, guidance, and recovery of Navy and Marine Corps aircraft in connection with test and evaluation; test design; stress analysis; structures; environmental simulation; design evaluation; aeronautical design; hydraulics; computer sciences; metallurgy; synthetic materials; electrical systems; mechanical systems and electronics; industrial engineering; optics; propulsion systems; acoustics; corrosion control; cryogenics; and control techniques. Procurements also include ground support equipment such as handling and servicing; armament support; avionics, propulsion, and mechanical devices; and medium and heavy machine shop assemblies and components.

Naval Air Warfare Center
Aircraft Division, Code 20C00W
Contracts Building 588, Suite 2
22347 Cedar Point Road, Unit 6
Patuxent River, MD 20670-1161
(301) 342-7567 Ext. 103
Principal interests: Development of aircraft systems and their components; also antisubmarine warfare command systems and related equipment.

Naval Air Warfare Center
Weapons Division, Code 00K000D
One Administration Circle
China Lake, CA 93555-6001
(760) 939-2712
Principal interests: Air warfare systems (except antisubmarine warfare systems) and missile weapons systems including propulsion, warheads, fuses, avionics and fire control, and guidance; and the national range/facility for parachute test and evaluation.

Naval Air Warfare Center
Training Systems Division
Code 86D1/27B
12350 Research Parkway
Orlando, FL 32826-3224
(407) 380-8253
Principal interests: Training aids, devices, equipment, and material for the Navy, Marine Corps, and other DoD activities.

Space and Naval Warfare Systems Command
Code SPA-OOK
4301 Pacific Highway
San Diego, CA 92110-3127
(619) 524-7701
Principal interests: Shore (ground) electronics; shipboard communications IFF, ECM, radio-navigation; fixed underwater surveillance systems; navigation aids; landing aids and air traffic control aids, except airborne communications via satellite and space surveillance systems; shore-based strategic data systems; communication data-link systems; radial equipment; special communications for fleet ballistic missile systems; standardized telemetry equipment and components; cryptographic equipment; expeditionary and amphibious electronic equipment; multi-platform electronic systems not otherwise assigned; antenna design and integration.

Space and Navy Warfare System Center
RDT&E Division, Code 02202
53570 Silvergate Avenue
San Diego, CA 92152-5113
(619) 553-4326
Principal interests: New developments in command, control, and communications, electronic warfare, ocean surveillance, antisubmarine warfare weapon systems, submarine arctic warfare, ocean science, ocean engineering, biosystems research, and related technologies. Purchases include computer software and systems engineering services, computer equipment, electronic test instruments, and miscellaneous support equipment and services.

Space and Navy Warfare System Center
Code OAL
P.O. Box
North Charleston, SC 29419-9022
(803) 974-5115
Principal interests: Sensors, video teleconferencing, image processing, air traffic control, meteorology, navigation, physical and computer security, command and control, communications, and cryptologic and intelligence.

Naval Facilities Engineering Command
Code FAC-OOJ
200 Stovall Street, Room 11N59
Alexandria, VA 22332-5000
(703) 325-8549
Principal interests: Cranes; power plants; floating pile drivers; major boiler plants and electrical generators; and permanent facilities

(including acquisition and disposal of real estate); design and construction projects as well as station maintenance and repair, including public utilities services.

Navy Construction

Principal interests: A&E services, construction, and major maintenance and repair of naval facilities.

Northern Division
Naval Facilities Engineering
Command
Code 09J
10 Industrial Highway, M/S 82
Lester, PA 19113-2090
(610) 595-0637

Southern Division
Naval Facilities Engineering
Command
Code 09J, P. O. , Box 190010
2155 Eagle Drive
North Charleston,
SC 29419-9010
(803) 820-5935

Atlantic Division
Naval Facilities Engineering
Command
Code 09W
1510 Gilbert Street
Norfolk, VA 23511-2699
(757) 322-8222

Southwest Division
Naval Facilities Engineering
Command
Code 09J
1220 Pacific Highway
San Diego, CA 92132-5190
(619) 532-3003

Pacific Division
Naval Facilities Engineering
Command
Code 09J
4262 Radford Drive
Honolulu, HI 96818
(808) 471-4577

Engineering Field Activity,
Chesapeake
Naval Facilities Engineering
Command
Code O9J, Building 212
Washington Navy Yard
901 M Street, SE
Washington, DC 20374-2121
(202) 685-0088

Engineering Field Activity,
Northwest
Naval Facilities Engineering
Command
Code 09J
19917 Seventh Avenue, NE
Poulsbo, WA 98370-7570
(360) 396-0038

Engineering Field Activity,
Midwest
Naval Facilities Engineering
Command Ext 105
Code 09J, Building 1A, Suite 120
2703 Sheridan Road
Great Lakes, IL 60088-5600
(847) 688-2600

Engineering Field Activity, West
Naval Facilities Engineering
Command
Code 09J
900 Commodore Drive
San Bruno, CA 94066-5006
(650) 244-2305

Navy Public Works Center
Acquisition Support Office
Code 40H
9742 Maryland Avenue
Norfolk, VA 23511-3095
(757) 444-8065 Ext. 3052

Navy Public Works Center
Code 200D, Suite 1,
Box 368113
2730 McKean Street
San Diego, CA 92136-5294
(619) 556-6352

Navy Public Works Center
Contracting Department
Code 200
Pearl Harbor, HI 96860-5470
(808) 471-9997

Naval Construction Battalion
Center
Code 10G/27G, Bldg 41
1000 23rd Avenue
Port Hueneme, CA 93043-4301
(805) 982-5066

Naval Sea Systems Command
Code SEA-00K
2531 Jefferson Davis Highway
Arlington, VA 22242-5160
(703) 602-1964

Principal interests: Shipboard weapons systems and components, explosives and propellants, and related actuating technology. Ship systems design and integration including construction, overhaul, modernization, and conversion; propulsion; auxiliary power generating and distribution; navigational equipment; habitability and environment control features; rescue and salvage systems; ship maintenance and support; degaussing; and shipboard minesweeping equipment, including R&D needs for these items.

Naval Surface Warfare Center
Crane Division
Code SB
300 Highway 121, Building 221A
Crane, IN 47522-5001
(812) 854-1542

Principal interests: Shipboard weapons systems and assigned ordnance items.

Naval Surface Warfare Center
Indian Head Division
Code SB
101 Strauss Avenue
Indian Head, MD 20640-5035
(301) 743-6604
Principal interests: Chemicals, igniters, metal parts, and components for rocket engines; electronic weapon system simulators and components; and cartridges, cartridge-actuated devices, and propulsive components for aircrew escape systems. Includes all related engineering tasks for fleet support and test.

Naval Surface Warfare Center
Port Hueneme Division
Code 00B, Building 5
4363 Missile Way
Port Hueneme, CA 93043-5007
(805) 982-0372
Principal Interests: Test and evaluation, in-service engineering, and integrated logistic support for Nay surface fleet surface and mine warfare combat systems, command and control systems F-I System interface, weapons systems and subsystems and related expendable ordnance. Engineering, production and logistic support for cruiser, destroyer, battleship and frigate combatants for the following software requirements: combat direction systems operational programs, inter-computer communications for integrated systems, Navy standard program generation system computer programs, and shore establishment computer programs.

Naval Surface Warfare Center
Dahlgren Division, Code CD2K
17320 Dahlgren Road
Dahlgren, VA 22448-5100
(540) 653-4806
Principal interests: Advanced technology developments in radar, communications, electronics, optics, chemistry, materials, plasma physics, space systems, and countermeasures.

Naval Surface Warfare Center
Carderock Division
Building 30, Code 303
9500 McArthur Blvd., Room 1
West Bethesda, MD 20817-5700
(301) 227-2871
Principal interests: Development and evaluation of systems, subsystems, and components.

Naval Undersea Warfare Center
Code 00SB Ext. 270
1176 Howell Street, Building 11
Newport, RI 02840
(401) 841-2442
Principal interests: Submarine and other underwater combat systems.

Navy Exchange Service Command
3280 Virginia Beach Boulevard
Virginia Beach, VA 23452-5724
(757) 631-3582
Principal interests: Supplies for Navy exchanges, commissary stores, lodges, ships stores, and military sealift exchanges, including retail merchandise of various types; food; vending machine items; service station supplies; air conditioners; vehicles; hotel furnishings; store fixtures; and other supplies and equipment.

Supply Centers

Principal interests: Ship and marine equipment, parts, accessories, and components, and a wide array of services. Support for naval activities in the region.

Naval Supply System Command
Building 9
P.O. Box 2050
Mechanicsburg, PA 17055-0791
(717) 790-3575

Naval Inventory Control Point
Code 0062
P.O. Box 2020
5450 Carlisle Pike
Mechanicsburg, PA 17055-0788
(717) 790-6625

Naval Inventory Control Point
Code P0061, Room 2213A
700 Robbins Avenue
Philadelphia, PA 19111-4098
(215) 697-2806

Fleet and Industrial Supply
Center
Code 04, Bldg W-143, Suite 600
1968 Gilbert Street
Norfolk, VA 23511-3392
(757) 443-1435

Fleet and Industrial Supply
Center Norfolk
Detachment Washington
Code 0200SB, Building 200
Washington Navy Yard
901 M Street, SE
Washington, DC 20374-5014
(202) 433-2957

Fleet and Industrial Supply
Center Norfolk
Detachment Philadelphia
Code 09B, Bldg 2B
700 Robbins Avenue
Philadelphia, PA 19111-5083
(215) 697-9555

Fleet and Industrial Supply
Center
Code COA
937 N. Harbor Drive
San Diego, CA 92132 -5075
(619) 532-3439

Fleet and Industrial Supply
Center
Puget Sound
Code 04
467 W. Street
Bremerton, WA 98314-5104
(360) 476-2812

Major Air Force Buying Offices

Oklahoma City Air Logistics Center
3001 Staff Dr., Ste 1AJ84A
Tinker AFB, OK 73145-3009
(405)739-2601

Principal interests: This center repairs, maintains, and modifies the
following aircraft, missiles, and engines:

Aircraft - B-1B, B-2, B-52, C/EC/RC-135, KC/NKC/WC-135, E-3

Engines - J-33 Allison, J-57 Pratt & Whitney, J-75 Pratt & Whitney, J-79 General Electric, TF-30 Pratt & Whitney, TF-33 Pratt & Whitney,
TF-41 Allison/Rolls-Royce, T-58 General Electric, T-64, General
Electric, F-101 General Electric, F-107 Williams,F-108 General
Electric, CFM-56 General Electric/Snecma, F-110 General Electric,
F-112 Williams, F-118 General Electric

Missiles - AGM-69A, AGM-84, AGM-86B/C, AGM-129A

The operational contracting division contracts for supplies,
equipment, and work necessary for the operation and maintenance of
Tinker AFB.

Ogden Air Logistics Center
5975 Arsenal Road
Hill AFB, UT 84056-5802
(801) 777-4143

Principles interests: This center manages, repairs or purchases 350,000
items used by a variety of weapons systems in the AF.

The following lists show the assigned systems and commodities that
Ogden ALC supports as a System Program Manager and Tech Repair
Center.

MANAGEMENT SYSTEMS:
F/RF-4 Phantom
F-16 Fighting Falcon
LGM-30 Minuteman
MGM-118A Peacekeeper

COMMODITIES:
Landing Gear
Wheels and Brakes
Photographic Equipment
Ammunition and

AGM-65 Maverick
GBU-15 Laser Guided

Explosives

AIRCRAFT:
F-16 Fighting Falcon
C-130 Hercules

MISSILES:
AGM-65 Maverick
ALCM-86B Cruise Missile
AGM-69A SRAM
LGM-118A Peacekeeper
LGM-30 Minuteman

OTHER:

Airmunitions
Avionics (F-4 and F-16)
Hydraulics/Pneudraulics
Simulators and Training Devices
Instruments
Landing Gear

Photographic Equipment
Rocket Motors
Wheels and Brakes
External Fuel Tanks and Pylons

The operational contracting division contracts for supplies,
equipment, and work necessary for the operation and maintenance of
Hill AFB.

Sacramento Air Logistics Center
5033 Roberts Ave., Ste 1
McClellan AFB, CA 95652-1326
(916)643-5209

Principles interests: This center repairs, maintains, and modifies the
following aircraft, missiles, and systems:

AIRCRAFT: A-10, EF-111, F-117, and F-22
SYSTEM CODE PROGRAM
404L ATCALS
407L GTACS
414L/968H Atmospheric Early Warning
428L MEECN/GWEN
433L Weather
465L SACCS
478T TRI-TAC
484L/802L Scope Command
485L GTACSI
487L MEECN
492L/493L Radio & TV
494L Telecommunications
495L AMCC2IPS
497L Ground Based Sensor
498L MILSTAR

500L Comm PG
542N Shelters
745C MILSATCOM
806L/846L/9952 Range Threat System
SRER/SRWR Space Lift Range

GROUND GENERATORS AND GENERATOR SETS:
60KW AND 72KW Aircraft Startcarts 5, 10, 15, 30, 60, 100, 200, and
750 KW Generators 50KW and 100KW Frequency Converters
Uninterruptable Power Systems
Power Conditioning and Continuation Interface Equipment
The operational contracting division contracts for supplies,
equipment, and work necessary for the operation and maintenance of
McClellan AFB.

San Antonio Air Logistics Center
303 S Crickett Dr, Ste 4
Kelly AFB, TX 78241-6025
(210)925-6918

Principle interests: The following are weapon systems managed by the
center. The older systems that are not in the current inventory are
listed because of continuing support requirements under inter-service
agreements or to foreign countries under the security assistance and
FMS agreements.

AIRCRAFT AND COMPONENTS:
A-37 C-119 F-20 OV-10
B-57 C-123 F-84 PC-7
C-5 C-131 F-86 T-28
C-7 C-140 F-104 T-33
C-17 CASA 212 F-106 T-37
C-46 CESSNA 152 H-43 T-38
C-47 CESSNA 172 HU-16 412A
C-54 CESSNA 206 O-1 627A
C-118 F-5 O-2

ENGINES AND COMPONENTS:
F100 T53 TFE731 R4360
F103 T55 TPE33 O-300
F117 T56 TR160 IO-360
J60 T76 R1340 O-470
J65 T400 R1830 TCAE-373
J69 T700 R2000 PT6
J85 TF34 R2800
J100 TF39 R3350

AIRBORNE AUXILIARY POWER PLANTS AND GROUND
GAS TURBINES

T62 T300 GTCP30 GTCP70 GTCP105 T41 GTC85 GTCP36 GTCP85 GTCP165

The operational contracting division contracts and supplies, equipment and work necessary for the operation and maintenance of Kelly AFB.

Warner Robins Air Logistics Center
180 Page Rd
Robins AFB, GA 31098-1600
(912)926-5873

Principle interests: This center repairs, maintains, and modifies the following aircraft and missiles:

AIRCRAFT/MISSILES/DRONES DIRECTORATE
C-130 Hercules C-130
C-141 Starlifter C-141
F-15 Eagle F-15
U-2 Dragon Lady U-2 Specialized Management
H-1 Helicopter (All Models) Special Operations Forces
H-53 Helicopter (All Models) Special Operations Forces
H-60 Helicopter (All Models) Special Operations Forces
C-130 (All Special Operations Forces Configutred AC)

SPECIAL OPERATIONS FORCES
97C-141B (SOLL) Special Operations Forces
AGM-45 SHRIKE Space & Special Systems
AGM-88 HARM Space & Special Systems
AIM-7 SPARROW Space & Special Systems
AIM-9 SIDEWINDER Space & Special Systems
AIM-120 AMRAAM Space & Special Systems
BQM-34A FIREBEE Space & Special Systems
FIM-92A STINGER Space & Special Systems
MQM-107 TARGET DRONE Space & Special Systems
E-8C JOINT STARS Space & Special Systems
NAVSTAR GPS Space & Special Systems

GPS RANGE APPLICATION PROGRAM Space & Special Systems
LANTRN NAVIGATION & TARGET SET Avionics
The operational contracting division contracts for supplies, equipment, and work necessary for the operation and maintenance of Robins AFB.

Space and Missile Systems Center (SMC/BC)
155 Discoverer Blvd, Ste 2017
Los Angeles AFB CA 90245-4692
(310)363-2855

Principle interests: The mission of SMC is to plan, program, and manage AFMC programs to acquire space systems, subsystems, support equipment, and related hardware and software; provide for the maintenance, construction, alteration, and security of launch, tracking, and support facilities; conduct research, exploratory development, and advanced development programs to support future space missions; provide for and conduct launch and flight test and evaluation support of major DoD programs and programs of other federal agencies; perform the functions of launch, launch control, deployment checkout prior to turnover, and sustaining engineering; perform on-orbit test and evaluation of systems, subsystems and components, discharge AF responsibilities for designated AF, DoD, and international space programs; plan, program, and acquire test facilities and other test investments required by AFMC programs at all locations (test centers and contractor facilities); plan and provide for security on all systems and information requiring safeguards consistent with AF and DoD security directives; provide management oversight for commercial expendable Launch Vehicle Activity; conduct launch agreement negotiations with commercial space launch operators; provide system engineering management support for selected space systems, subsystems, facilities, support equipment, and related hardware and software; support other product divisions and federal agencies with technologies derived from its subordinate laboratories.

While there are no Air Force aircraft assigned to Los Angeles AFB, the operational contracting directorate does contract for all other work necessary for the operation and maintenance of the base.

11th Contracting Squadron (11CONS/LGC)
500 Duncan Ave.
Bolling AFB
Washington, DC 20332-0305
(202) 767-8086

Principle interests: The mission of the 11th Contracting Squadron is to provide contracting support for supplies and services necessary to the operation of approximately 300 requiring activities in the National Capital Region. The 11th Contracting Squadron (11CONS) provides support to the Office of the Secretary of Defense, Office of the Secretary of the Air Force, HQ 11th Wing and other AF agencies within the National Capitol Region. The 11 CONS operational contracting functions are responsible for purchasing base supplies, services, construction and specialized services for ADP and studies and analysis.

Typical Item Acquisitions: ADPE, Software, Hardware, Maintenance, AF Plaques, Base Supply Support, Base Wide Grounds Maintenance, Construction and AE Services, Contractor Technical Support to AF Pentagon Elements, Historical, Personnel and Research Studies, Laundry, Dry Cleaning, Maintenance, Food and Custodial Services,

Logistic Systems Research and Analysis, Military Family Housing Maintenance, O&M of Computer Modeling Systems and

Base Contracting Activities: Contracting responsibility for support of a command's mission generally is assigned to a particular base or bases within the command. Contracts awarded by the other bases assigned to the command generally are limited to the supplies and services required for the daily operation of the base. The following lists are typical of the services and items bought by all base contracting offices.

Representative Service Acquisitions: Air Conditioning, General Construction, Appliance Repair, Grounds Maintenance, Architect Engineer, Laundry and Dry Cleaning, Audio Visual, Military Family Housing Maintenance, Boiler Repairs, Refuse Collection, Custodial, Road Maintenance, Education, Roofing, Environmental Detection, Steam Line Installation & Disposal/Prevention, Swimming Pool Maintenance, Environmental Restoration, Transient Aircraft Services, Equipment Maintenance, Transportation Services, Equipment Rental, Utility Services, Equipment Repair, Various Maintenance of ADP, Food Services, Vehicles Operation & Maintenance.

Electronic Systems Center (ESC/BC)
275 Randolph Rd.
Hanscom AFB, MA 01731-2818
(617) 377-4973

Principle interests: ESC plans and manages the acquisition and related engineering development of command, control, communications, and intelligence systems, subsystems and equipment including surveillance systems, navigation systems, air traffic control and landing systems, intelligence systems, electronic physical security surveillance and intrusion detection systems and weather systems, information and management systems until transfer of responsibility to the using command or agency. Evaluates using command requirements against available technology and potential costs and recommends necessary revisions. R&D contracts are also initiated by the Geophysics Division of the AF Laboratory in the environmental, physical and engineering sciences. The Geophysics Division performs research and exploratory and advanced Development in geophysics that is essential to the enhancement of AF operational capabilities. The work pursued may be categorized generally as falling within the following functional areas: Space Physics, Ionospheric Physics, Terrestrial Science, Upper Atmospheric and Stratospheric operations, Optical/IR Backgrounds and Targets, Weather Specification and Prediction. Close liaison is maintained with AF operational elements, system development activities, and other AF laboratories, to identify research and technology needs and to accelerate the integration of scientific advances into AF technology. Geophysics Division carries out its assigned R&D mission responsibilities with in-house as well as contractual support.

While there are no AF aircraft assigned to Hanscom AFB, the operational contracting directorate does contract for all other work necessary for the operation and maintenance of the base.

Aeronautical Systems Center (ASC/BC)
2196 D Street
Wright-Patterson AFB, OH 45433-7201
(937)255-5422

Principle interests: ASC's responsibilities include design, development, and acquisition programs for aeronautical systems, cruise missiles, their components, and related government-furnished aerospace equipment including aircraft engines, airborne communication systems, aircraft navigation systems, aircraft instruments; management of engineering development and initial procurement of aeronautical reconnaissance systems, aeronautical electronic warfare systems, life support systems, chemical/biological defense systems, and simulators, including armament, operational, and communication training devices.

ASC has central contracting responsibility for a number of specialized programs including the following:

Specialized Programs and Aircraft and Reconnaissance
Contractor Engineering and Technical Services
Mechanized Material Handling Systems
AF Packaging Evaluation Agency Requirements
Automatic Data Processing Studies, Software, and Equipment
Chaplain Supplies and Equipment
Educational Services Contractual Support
Library Books and Publications

ASC provides contracting support for the National Aerospace Intelligence Center which acquires, collects, analyzes, produces, and disseminates foreign aerospace scientific and technical (S&T) intelligence and intelligence information; conducts an integrated analysis program; operates an S&T intelligence data handling system; collaborates with other organizations to improve the collection, acquisition, and utilization of foreign technology and intelligence; and develops and maintains the highest attainable level of knowledge concerning foreign aerospace technology, capabilities, and limitations.

ASC Small Business Office provides contracting support for the Joint Logistics Systems Center (JLSC) which is located at Wright-Patterson AFB. JLSC is involved in the development, operation, and enhancement of the management information systems for logistics management systems for the military services and Defense Logistics Agency.

ASC Operational Contracting organization contracts for supplies, equipment, and work necessary for the operation and maintenance of Wright-Patterson AFB.

Wright Laboratory
Directorate of R&D Contracting
c/o Aeronautical Systems Center (ASC/BC)
2196 D Street
Wright-Patterson AFB OH 45433-7201
(937)255-5422

Principle interests: This directorate provides business and contracting support for Wright Laboratory (WL). Contracts are written for requirements of the following directorates: Aero Propulsion and Power Directorate is responsible for development of airbreathing propulsion and aerospace power technology needed for future AF systems, as well as providing assistance to the "product divisions" of AFMC in acquiring new systems and in helping to resolve developmental and operation problems. Avionics Directorate conducts R&D programs for aerospace reconnaissance, weapons delivery, electronic warfare systems, navigation, communication and avionics integration. Solid State Electronics Directorate is responsible for electronic device R&D for future AF systems needs in the areas of microelectronics, microwaves, and electro-optics. Research extends from fundamental semiconductor layer growth and device fabrication through analog and digital integrated circuits; also included is the computer-aided design software and work stations needed to pursue sample hybrid and monolithic integrated circuits. Flight Dynamics Directorate pursues AF flight vehicle technologies to support aircraft, missiles and space systems in the technical areas of structures, vehicle subsystems, flight control, aeromechanics and experimental flight vehicle test-beds.

Materials Directorate explores new materials and processes for advanced aerospace applications. Its current focus is on thermal protection materials, metallic and nonmetallic structural materials, aerospace propulsion materials, fluids and lubricants, electromagnetic and electronic materials and laser hardened materials. Manufacturing Technology Directorate focuses on process technologies and integrated manufacturing. This directorate is responsible for a new initiative which integrates design and manufacturing technologies to stimulate a new focus on design for producibility, design for quality, and design for life cycle costs. Key elements of this concurrent engineering involve development of advanced tools in computer aided design and computer aided manufacturing for analyses of design for weapon performance and low cost manufacturing. Plans and Programs Directorate is made up of cockpit integration, which involves research to advance the state of the art crew systems technologies for all classes of aerospace vehicles; and signature technology, which includes planning, formulating, and executing USAF exploratory and advanced development programs for vehicle signature reduction technology and counter low observable technology. Armament Directorate develops conventional armament technology and integrates these technologies into air vehicle platforms and other delivery platforms. The directorate provides conventional armament technology for four major thrusts that include advanced guidance, weapon flight mechanics, ordnance, and conventional strategic defense.

AF Development Test Center (AFDTC/BC)
205 West D Ave, Stuite 449
Eglin AFB, FL 32542-6863
(904)882-2843

AFDTC plans, directs, and conducts the test and evaluation of nonnuclear munitions, electronic combat, and navigation/guidance systems. Related ASC System Program Offices (SPOs) are also located here and supported by AFDTC/BC. To accomplish this mission, AFDTC manages the large land test ranges that are located on the 724 square mile Eglin complex as well as the 86,500 square miles of water ranges located in the adjacent Gulf of Mexico. Major tests on or above AFDTC's ranges cover aircraft systems, subsystems, missiles, guns, rockets, targets and drones, high-powered radar, and electronic countermeasures equipment.

AFDTC's unique assets include the Guided Weapons Evaluation Facility (GWEF), the Preflight Integration of Munitions and Electronic Systems (PRIMES),and the McKinley Climatic Laboratory, a facility capable of testing military hardware as large as aircraft in environments ranging from minus 65 to plus 165 degrees Fahrenheit with 100 mph winds, icing clouds, rain, and snow. AFDTC also is responsible for the 46th Test Group at Holloman AFB NM, with its high speed test track, two radar target scatter measurement facilities, and the Central Inertial Guidance Test Facility (CIGTF). The operational contracting division contracts for supplies, equipment, and work necessary for the operation and maintenance of Eglin AFB.

Other Major Commands

Principal interests: Base contracting support, including major data major data processing, construction, and command wide acquisition of mission-related supplies and services.

3 CONS/CC
6920 12th Street, Suite 301
Elmendorf AFB, Anchorage, AK
99506-2570
(907)552-4338

Headquarters Air Education
and Training Command (16
Bases)
550 D Street East, Rm 131
Randolph AFB,
TX 78150-4425
(210)652-4840

Air Military Command (12 Bases)
402 Scott Drive, Unit 2A2
Scott AFB, IL 62225-5308
(618)256-8725

Air Combat Command (20
Bases)
130 Douglas Street, Suite 210
Langley AFB, VA 23665-2791
(757)764-5371

10th Air Base Wing (10
ABW/LGCP)
8110 Industrial Drive, Suite 103
USAF Academy, CO 80840-2315
(719)333-6642

Air Intelligence Agency
102 Hall Blvd., Suite 258
San Antonio, TX 78243-7030
(210)977-2453

Air Force Space Command
(7 Bases)
150 Vandenburg Street, Suite 1105
Peterson AFB, CO 80914-4350
(719)554-5324

15 CONS/CC (4 Bases)
90 G Street Ext. 103
Hickam AFB, HI 96853-5320
(808)449-6860

Air Force Reserve
155 2nd Street
Robbins AFB, GA 31098-1635
(912)327-1611

Major Defense Logistics Agency Buying Offices

Defense Supply Center Columbus
3990 East Broad St.
Columbus, OH 43216-5000
(614) 692-3541
Toll-free:1(800) 262-3272

Principal interests: Guns, mechanisms and components; aircraft landing gear components; aircraft launching, landing, and ground handling equipment; aircraft wheel and brake systems; right-of-way construction and maintenance equipment, railroad; track materials, tractors; vehicular cab, body, and frame structural components; vehicular power transmission components; vehicular brake, steering, axle, wheel and track components; vehicular furniture and accessories; miscellaneous vehicular components; gasoline reciprocating engines and components; diesel engines and components; steam turbines and components; water turbines and water wheels and components; gasoline rotary engines and components; steam engines, reciprocating; non-aircraft engine fuel system, electrical system, and engine cooling system, engine and oil filters; miscellaneous engine accessories, non-aircraft; torque converters and speed changers; gears, pulleys, sprockets, and transmission chain; belting, drive belts, V-belts, and accessories, ship and boat propulsion equipment.

Farm equipment; pest, disease, and frost control equipment; saddlery; earth moving and excavating equipment; earth boring and related equipment; road clearing and cleaning equipment; miscellaneous construction equipment; fire fighting equipment.

Marine lifesaving and diving equipment; compressors and vacuum pumps; power and hand pumps; centrifugal; separators and pressure and vacuum filters; industrial boilers; heat exchangers and steam condensers; industrial furnaces; air and water purification equipment; space heating equipment; fuel burning equipment units; miscellaneous plumbing, heating, and sanitation equipment; piping and tubing; noses and fittings, valves, powered; valves, non-powered; motor vehicle maintenance and repair shop equipment; prefabricated and portable buildings; storage tanks; scaffolding equipment and concrete forms; prefabricated tower structures; and miscellaneous construction equipment.

Defense Energy Support Center
8725 John J. Kingman Road
Suite 4950, Room 4950
Fort Belvoir, VA 22060-6222
(703) 767-9400
1-(800) 523-2601

Principal interests: Petroleum products and petroleum related services for the U.S. military and U.S. Government agencies worldwide. Products include jet fuels, aviation gasoline, motor gasoline, gasohol, distillates, residuals, bulk lubricating oil, coal, crude oil for strategic petroleum reserve, natural gas and synfuels. Services include aircraft refueling, into-plane, bunkers, storage terminals, laboratory testing, and environmental assessment and remediation for Defense Fuel Supply Points.

Defense Supply Center Richmond
8000 Jefferson Davis
Richmond, VA 23297-5124
(804) 279-3617
1(800) 544-5634 (VA)

Principal interests: Laundry and dry cleaning equipment; shoe repairing equipment; industrial sewing machines and mobile textile repair shops; electric arc-welding equipment; woodworking machinery and equipment; printing; duplicating and bookbinding equipment; gas generating equipment; nonself-propelled materials-handling equipment; pallets, skids, load binder, and support sets: refrigeration equipment, fans, and air circulators; lugs, terminals, and terminal strips; electrical hardware and supplies; electrical insulators and insulating materials; contact brushes and electrodes; cable, cord, and wire assemblies for communication equipment: electrical motors and electrical control equipment; electrical generators and generator sets; distribution and power station transformers; miscellaneous electric power and distribution equipment; secondary batteries, miscellaneous alarm and signal systems; lighting fixtures and lamps; photographic supplies; chemicals and chemical specialties; pest control agents and disinfectants; food cooking, baking, and warming equipment; food preparation and serving sets, kits, and outfits; books and pamphlets, sheet and book music, and miscellaneous printed matter; drums and cans; commercial and industrial gas cylinders; bottles and jars; rubber, plastic, and glass fabricated materials; refractories and fire surfacing materials, asbestos, clay, cork, and other vegetable and mineral materials; ecclesiastical equipment, furnishings, and supplies; mortuary supplies; physical properties testing equipment; geophysical and astronomical instruments; scales and balances; drafting, surveying, and mapping instruments; and liquid and gas flow, liquid level, and mechanical motion measuring instruments, packaged petroleum products, cutting tools, industrial plant equipment. tackle blocks; shackles and slings; airframe structural components; parachutes; aerial pickup, delivery, and recovery systems; cargo tie-down equipment; cargo nets; aircraft accessories and components; rigging and rigging gear; deck machinery; marine hardware and hull items.

Defense Industrial Supply Center
700 Robbins Avenue
Philadelphia, PA 19111-5096
(215) 697-2747
Toll-free: 1(800) 831-1110

Principal interests: Bearings; chain and wire rope; fiber rope, cordage and twine; rope, cable, and chain fittings; ores and minerals; ferrous and nonferrous scrap; ferrous and nonferrous bars, sheets, and shapes; electrical wire and cable; screws, bolts, and studs; nuts and washers; nails, keys, and pins; rivets; fastening devices; packing and gasket materials; metal screening; coil, flat, and wire springs; rings; shims; spacers; miscellaneous hardware; plumbing fixtures and accessories; knobs and pointers; construction materials; film; kitchen equipment and appliances; lumber; photographic equipment and supplies.

Defense Supply Support Center
2800 South 20th St.
Philadelphia, PA 19101-8419
(215) 737-2321
Toll-free: 1(800) 523-0705

Principal interests: Men's and women's military clothing, dress and work; textile fabrics; wool tops; artificial leather; tents and tarpaulins; flags and pennants; leather and rubber footwear; hats and caps; canvas products; special-purpose clothing; underwear; hosiery; gloves; badges and insignia; luggage; individual equipment; body armor; specialized flight clothing; helmets. Drugs and biological; surgical dressing materials; surgical, dental, and optical instruments, equipment and supplies; X-ray equipment and supplies; hospital furniture, equipment, utensils, and supplies; medical sets, kits, and outfits; chemical analysis instruments; laboratory equipment and supplies; medicinal chemicals; hospital and surgical clothing. Perishable and nonperishable foods are purchased for distribution in the United States and overseas. Such purchases include meats and meat products, fresh fruits and vegetables, dehydrated items, seafood or water foods, cereals, dairy products, poultry, and other related food items. Canned, packaged, fresh, and frozen items are purchased in car-lots or less. Retort pouched foods are bought in large quantities as ration components.

DLA Administrative Support Center
Office of Contracting
8725 John J. Kingman Road
Suite 0119, Room 1134
Fort Belvoir, VA 22060-6220
(703) 767-1161

Principle Interests: Centralized contracting of Federal Information Processing (FIP) Resources (ADP, Computer and Telecommunications products and services) at DLA HQ for all DLA activities, including large and small purchases, and GSA schedule purchases. Responsible for managing the life cycle contracting process in support of the DLA mission, and providing the highest quality contracting and customer service. DLA field activities may purchase similar items at the small purchase level and, under competitive circumstances, up to a threshold of $250,000.

In addition, provides general contracting in support of the DLA HQ COMPLEX, Fort Belvoir, VA and other DASC supported customers. All contracting on a Fee-For-Service basis.

Defense National Stockpile Center
8725 John J. Kingman Road
Suite 4616
Fort Belvoir, VA 22060-6223
(703) 767-5505

Principal interests: Manages the nation's reserves of strategic and critical materials for times of national emergency. Procures and sells aluminum, beryllium, cobalt, germanium, lead, manganese, mercury, mica, and rubber.

Television-Audio Support Activity
3116 Peacekeeper Way
McClellan AFB, CA 95652-1068
(916) 364-4223

Principal interests: A wide variety of Radio and Television Broadcast Equipment for all DoD activities worldwide. Procures video camcorders (all formats), broadcast TV equipment, recorders/reproducers, transmitters, switchers, monitors, cameras, color laser copiers, graphics systems, and test equipment that is used to support the Broadcast and Audio/Video Equipment.

General Services Administration FSS Acquisition Centers

To streamline operations, FSS has organized its supply support functions into Acquisition Centers. Products and services are assigned to specific GSA Acquisition Centers for procurement and related supply functions including inventory management, engineering, and requisition processing functions. Please direct inquiries to the appropriate Acquisition Center.

IT Acquisition Center (FCI)
Washington, DC 20406
Phone: (703) 305-3038
e-mail: Darlena.Bitkowski@gsa.gov

Commodities: Automatic Data Processing and communication equipment - hardware, software, supplies, components, and related services.

Automotive Division (FFA)
Washington, DC 20406
Nancy Tyrrell or Mike Harris
Phone: (703) 308-CARS(2277)
FAX: (703) 305-3034
Internet: Nancy.Tyrrell@gsa.gov or Mike.Harris@gsa.gov

Commodities: The acquisition of automotive commodities has MOVED to a larger organization that provides one stop shopping for both your vehicle purchase and leasing needs. Check it out!

General Products Commodity Center (7FX)
819 Taylor Street
Ft. Worth, TX 76102

Genni Brown
Phone: (817) 978-4545
FAX: (817) 978-2605
Internet: Genni.Brown@gsa.gov

Commodities: Law Enforcement Equipment and Supplies; Food Service Equipment and Supplies; Janitorial and Cleaning Equipment and Supplies; Boats; Athletic Equipment and Supplies; Park and Outdoor Recreational Equipment and Supplies; Firefighting and Rescue Equipment and Supplies; Prefab Structures, Warehouses; Above Ground Storage Tanks; Power Distribution Equipment, Generators, and Batteries; Energy Saving Lighting Products; Alarm and Signal Systems; Water Treatment and Purification Chemicals; Deodorants and Disinfectants; Dishwashing and Laundry detergents; Recycling Collection Containers and Specialty Waste Receptacles; Musical Instruments; Etc.

National Furniture Center (3FN-CO)
Washington, DC 20406
Rick Walton
Phone: (703) 305-7003
FAX: (703) 305-6032
Internet: Rick.Walton@gsa.gov

Commodities: Office furniture, systems and automated data processing furniture, dormitory and quarters furnishings targeted at the Department of Defense Quality of Life Program, hospital furniture, carpeting, etc.

Office Supplies and Paper Products Commodity Center (2FY)
26 Federal Plaza
New York, NY 10278
Alexandra Sabbers
Phone: (212) 264-0479
FAX: (212) 264-1780
Internet: Alexandra.Sabbers@gsa.gov

Commodities: Xerographic paper, pens/pencils, diskettes, video and recording tapes, envelopes, boxes and cartons, folders, etc.

Office and Scientific Equipment Center (FCG)
1941 Jefferson Davis Highway
CM#4, Room 503
Arlington, VA 22202
Janese Gadsden
Phone: (703) 305-7597
FAX: (703) 305-7135
E-Mail: Janese.Gadsden@gsa.gov

Commodities: Document Management Products and Services, Document

Conversion, Multifunctional Copiers, Digital Cameras, Photo ID Equipment, Full Film Processing Services, Website Photo Storage, Shredders, Calculators, Typewriters, Filing and Storage Equipment, Avionics Test Equipment, Flight Data Recorders, Unmanned Aerial Vehicles (UAV), Geophysical and Environmental Analysis Equipment and Services, Laboratory Furniture, Laboratory Services, Instruments and Laboratory Equipment, etc.

Management Services Center (10FT)
400 15th Street, SW
Auburn, WA 98001
Joan Rodgers
Phone: (253) 931-7900
FAX: (253) 931-7544
Internet: joan.rodgers@gsa.gov

Commodities: MOBIS, Environmental, and Mail Management

Services Acquisition Center
1941 Jefferson Davis Highway
CM#4, Rm. 507
Arlington, VA 22202
Amanda Fredriksen
Phone: (703) 305-6885
FAX: (703) 305-5094
Internet: Amanda.Fredriksen@gsa.gov

Services: We establish Service Contracts to assist Federal Agencies including the Military in meeting their missions. We have Financial services such as Auditing and Financial Management, Financial Asset Services, Business Information Services, and GSA SmartPay: The Next Generation of Fleet, Travel, and Purchase Payment Systems. We also provide Organizational services such as Temporary Clerical and Professional Services, Marketing and Media Services, EEO Services, Human Resource Services, and Engineering Services. In addition, we provide Travel Services such as the Air Transportation Services, Government Employee Relocation Services, and Express Small Package Delivery Services.

Hardware and Appliances Center (6FE)
1500 E. Bannister Road
Kansas City, MO 64131
Bob Koczanowski
Phone: (816) 926-6760
FAX: (816) 926-1271
DSN: 465-6760
Internet: Bob.Koczanowski@gsa.gov

Commodities: Wrenches, sockets, screwdrivers, hammers, tool kits, refrigeration equipment, air conditioning equipment, fans, etc.

Web Sites

Following is a consolidated listing of web sites related to the government procurement process that, in our opinion, are most valuable and interesting from a small business owner's perspective. Although we made every attempt to assure that all of these sites were "live" when this book went to press, we all know that the Internet is a dynamic environment and changes constantly.

To help you understand the variety of locations using the Internet, the following information is provided for the last part of the URL address:

.com = commercial entity	.mil = military entity
.edu = educational entity	.net = network entity
.gov = government entity	.org = an organization

Two tips about using these web sites: First, don't forget to "bookmark" the address once you have gotten to a location that interests you. Second, if you try an address that does not respond, try backing up the address. In other words, eliminate the part of the address after the last "/" and keep doing this until you get a hit. Then look around that location for a way to the specific area in which you are interested.

Web Site	URL
American Bar Association	http://www.abanet.org
ECRC	http://www.ecrc.ctc.com/necrcc/ecrcpr.htm
ECRC (National)	http://www.ecrc.etc.corn
ECRC (San Antonio)	http://www.saecrc.org
Electronic Commerce 'World	http://pwr.com/ediworld
FedCenter	http://www.fedcenter.com
The Federal Marketplace	http://www.fedmarket.com
FedMart	http://www.fedmart.com
Govcon	http://www.govcon.com
ISBC	http://www.isbc.com
NCMA	http://www.ncmahq.org
AGMAS	http://www.agmas.org

Web Sites

Government Sites

abm online	http://www.abm.rda.hq.navy.mil
ARNet	http://www.arnet.gov
CCR	http://ccr2000.com
Commerce Business Daily	http://cbdnet.gpo.gov
Defense Finance and Accounting Service	
	http://www.dfas.mil
Department of the Treasury--Electronic Funds Transfer Notice of Proposed Rulemaking	http://www.fms.treas.gov/eft/
Department of the Treasury Financial Management Service	
	http://www.fms.treas.gov
DITCO headquarters	http://www.ditco.disa.mil
DOD's SBIR & STIR Programs	http://www.acq.osd.mil/sadbu/sbir/homepg.htm
DOD's Small and Disadvantaged Business Utilization Office	
	http://www.acq.osd.mil/sadbu
Electronic Commerce Office	http://www.acq.osd.mil/ec
FAA Acquisition Toolset	http://fast.faa.gov
FAR	http://farsite.hill.af.mil/far1.htm
Federal Procurement Data System	
	http://fdps.gsa.gov/fdps/fdps.htm
GSA Advantage! Program	http://www.fss.gsa.gov
GSA Regional Customer Supply Centers	
	http://pub.fss.gsa.gov/c-assist/location.htm
GPO	http://www.access.gpo.gov
NAIS	http://procurement.nasa.gov
NASA	http://www.nasa.gov
NASA Electronic Handbooks	http://lincoln.gsfc.nasa.gov/ehbs.html
NASA EPS Demonstration Page	
	http://aim5msfc.msfc.nasa.gov/nais.html
NASA's Office of Small and Disadvantaged Business Utilization	
	http://www.hq.nasa.gov/office/codek
NASA's Procurement at a Glance	
	http://www.hq.nasa.gov/office/procurement/comm.html
SBA Gopher	http://www.sbaonline.sba.gov/gopher/Ecedi/Facts (case sensitive)
SBA Gopher--Fact Sheet: Planning for EDI Implementation	
	http://www.sbaonline.sba.gov/gopher/Ecedi/Facts/factl.txt (case sensitive)
SBA's Office of Women's Business Ownership	
	http://www.sba.gov/womeninbusiness
SBA's PRO-Net	http://pro-net.sba.gov
SBA's Web site	http://www.sba.gov
SSA's Office of Acquisition and Grants' Acquisition Information Page	
	http://www.ssa.gov/oag/oag2.htm
Standard Procurement System Program Management Office	
	http://www.sps.hq.dla.mil
UNICOR Catalog	http://www.unicor.gov
USAF Office of Small and Disadvantaged Business Utilization	
	http://www.safsb.hq.af.mil
White House home page	http://www.whitehouse.gov

NASA Procurement Addresses

Ames Research Center	http://procure.arc.nasa.gov/acq/acq.html
Doing Business with NASA	http://www.hq.nasa.gov/office/codek/Index.html
Dryden Flight Research Center	http://www.dfrc.nasa.gov/Procure
Goddard Space Flight Center	http://genesis.gsfc.nasa.gov/procure.htm
Jet Propulsion Lab (JPL)	http://procure.msfc.nasa.gov/jpl_link.html
Johnson Space Center	http://www.jsc.nasa.gov/bd2/
Kennedy Space Center	http://www.ksc.nasa.gov/procurement/ procurement.html
Langley Research Center	http://db-www.larc.nasa.gov/procurement/ home-page.html
Lewis Research Center	http://www.lerc.nasa.gov/Other_Groups/ Procure/home.htm
NASA Acquisition Forecast	http://procure.msfc.nasa.gov/forecast/index.html
Marshall Space Flight Center	http://procure.msfc.nasa.gov/home.html

NASA Acquisition Internet Service (NAIS) E-mail Notification Service
http://procurement.nasa.gov/maillist.html

NASA Commercial Technology Network
http://nctn.hq.nasa.gov/

NASA Financial and Contractual Status (FACS) Home Page
http://procurement.nasa.gov/facs/html/

NASA Headquarters	http://www.hq.nasa.gov/office/procurement/ acquisition/

NASA Management Office Jet Propulsion Lab (JPL)
http://procure.msfc.nasa.gov/nmo/nmohome.html

NASA Office of Procurement	http://www.hq.nasa.gov/office/procurement/

NASA Office of Small and Disadvantaged Business Utilization
http://www.hq.nasa.gov/office/codek/

NASA Procurement Synopsis Search
http://procurement.nasa.gov/NPSE

Stennis Space Center	http://www.ssc.nasa.gov/~procure/

Contract Activities

Acquisition Program Integration
http://www.acq.osd.mil/api/

Acquisition Reform--Air Force	http://www.safaq.hq.af.mil/acq_ref/
Acquisition Reform--Army	http://acqnet.sarda.army.miI/acqref/default.htm

Acquisition Reform Net Electronic Forum
http://www.arnet.gov/Discussions/Water-Cooler/

Acquisition Reform Net of NPR	http://www.arnet.gov/

Acquisition Systems Management
http://www.acq.osd.mil/api/asm/

Acquisition Web Index	http://www.acq.osd.mil/acqweb/topindex.html

Air Force Acquisition Home Page
http://www.hq.af.mil/SAFAQ/
http://www.safaq.hq.af.mil/
http://www.safaq.hq.af.mil/contracting/

Army Acquisition Corps	http://dacm.sarda.army.mil/
Army Acquisition Logistics	http://www.logistics.army.mil/acq.html
Army Acquisition Web site	http://acqnet.sarda.army.mil/

Army, AMC, TACOM-ARDEC Acquisition Ctr.
http://procnet.pica.army.mil/

Bureau of Engraving & Printing Office of Procurement
http://www.ustreas.gov/treasury/bureaus/bep/proc/

Bureau of Land Management http://www.ios.doi.gov/pam/acqsites.html

Coast Guard   http://www.dot.gov/dotinfo/uscg/welcome/

Defense Acquisition Information
http://www.dtic.dla.mil/hovlane/

Defense Advanced Research Projects
http://www.arpa.mil/cmo/

Defense Contract Management Command
http://www.dcmc.dcrb.dla.mil/

Defense Fuel Supply Center   http://www.dfsc.dla.mil/

Defense Industrial Supply Center
http://www.disc.dla.mil/

Defense Information Systems Agency
http://www.disa.mil/line/ncrco.html

Defense Logistics Agency   http://www.dla.mil/

Defense Logistics Service Center
http://www.dlsc.dla.mil/
http://www.dlsc.dla.mil/cprdproc.htp

Defense Mapping Agency   http://www.dma.gov/business/contracts/
contracts.htm

Defense Personnel Support Center
http://www.dpsc.dla.mil/

Defense Procurement Homepage
http://www.acq.osd.mil/dp/

Defense Supply Center Columbus
http://www.dscc.dla.mil/Procurement.html

Defense Supply Center Richmond
http://www.dscr.dla.mil/procurement/procurement.htm

Defense Technical Information Center
http://www.dtic.dla.mil/hovlane/

Department of Ag.--Rural Bus.-Coop. Service
http://www.rurdev.usda.gov/agency/rbcds/html/
rbcdhome.html

Department of Agriculture   http://www.usda.gov/da/procure.html

Department of Agriculture--Food and Consumer Service
http://www.usda.gov/fcs/contract.htm

Department of Agriculture--Ag: Res. Service
http://www.usda.gov/da/procure/pocars.htm

Department ofAgriculture-Animal and Plant Health Inspection Service (APHIS)
http://www.usda.gov/da/procure/pocmrp.htm

Department of Agriculture--Farm Service Agency
http://www.fsa.usda.gov/amb/

Department of Commerce   http://netsite.esa.doc.gov/oam/

Department of Education   http://gcs.ed.gov/

Department of Energy   http://www.doe.gov/html/procure/prpages.html

Department of Health & Human Serv.-Grants
http://www.os.dhhs.gov:80/progorg/grantsnet/

Department of Health and Human Services
>http://www.os.dhhs.gov:80/progorg/oam/
>gopher://gopher.os.dhhs.gov:70/i/Topics/grantsnet

Department of Housing and Urban Development
>http://www.hud.gov/business.html

Department of Interior   http://www.ios.doi.gov/pam/pamhome.html

Department of Interior--Electronic Commerce
>http://ns.ios.doi.gov/osdbu/elec.html

Department of Justice   http://www.usdoj.gov/jmd/pss/acquistn.htm

Department of Labor   http://dol.gov/cgi-bin/consolid.pl?grants

Department of State   http://www.statebuy.Inter.net/home.htm
>http://www.statebuy.Inter.net/

Department of Transportation http://www.dot.gov/dotinfo/ost/m6O/index.html

Department of Treasury http://www.ustreas.gov/treasury/bureaus/sba/
>sba.html

Department of Veterans Affairs http:/www.va.gov/gils/files/HTM18.HTM

Dept. of Defense Acquisition Reform
>http://www.acq.osd.mil/ar/

Dept. of Defense Acquisition Web (AC QWEB)
>http://www.acq.osd.mil

Dept. of Defense Ballistic Missile Defense Organization Acquisition
>http://www.acq.osd.mil/bmdo/barbb/barbb.htm

Dept. of Defense Commercial Advocates Forum
>http://www.Imi.org/comm_adv/cadv.htm

Dept. of Defense Environmental Restoration
>http://www.dtic.mil/envirodod

Dept. of Defense Health Affairs http:/www.ha.osd.mil/hpaq2.html#Start

Dept. of Energy Procurement and Assistance Mgt.
>http://www.pr.doe.go

Dept. of Housing and Urban Development
>http://www.hud.gov/cts/ctshome.html

Environmental Protection Agency
>http://www.cpa.gov/oam/
>http://www.epa.gov/OER/
>http://www.epa.gov/epahome/finance.htm

FAA Acquisition Reform Information Center
>http://www.faa.gov/asu/asu100/acq-reform/
>acq_home.htm

Federal Acquisition Institute http://www.gsa.gov/staff/v/training.htm

Federal Acquisition Jumpstation
>http://procure.msfc.nasa.gov/fedproc/home.html

Federal Aviation Administration gopher://gopher.faa.gov/

Federal Prison Industry--Unicor http://www.unicor.gov/

General Servces Administration http://www.gsa.gov

Government Printing Office httg://www.access.gpo.gov/procurement/index.html

Government Printing Office-Procurement Information on the Internet
>http://www.access.gpo.gov/procurement/
>info-net.html

Interior Department Electronic Acquisition Sys.
>http://www.ios.doi.gov/pam/ideahome.html

NASA Acquisition Internet Service
> http://procurement.nasa.gov

NASA Acquisition Internet Service Survey
> http://procurement.nasa.gov/cgi-bin/nais_survey.cgi

National Aeronautics and Space Admin. (NASA)
> http://www.hq.nasa.gov/office/procurement/

National Coordination Office for High Performance Computing and Communications
> http://www.hpcc.gov/grants-contracts/index.html

National Imagery and Mapping Agency
> http://164.214.2.59/poc/contracts/pchome.htm

National Institute of Standards and Technology
> http://www.nist.gov/admin/od/contract/contract.htm

National Institutes of Health   gopher://gopher.nih.gov:70/1i/res

National Oceanic and Atmospheric Admin.
> http://www.sao.noaa.gov/procure.html

National Oceanic and Atmospheric Admin.--Western Administrative Support Center
> http://www.wasc.noaa.gov/wasc/proc.htm

National Science Foundation   http://www.nsf.gov:80/nsf/homepage/grants.htm

National Telecommunications and Info. Admin.
> http://www.ntia.dec.gov/otiahome/otiaact.html

Navy Acquisition & Business Management
> http://www.abm.rda.hq.navy.mil/

Navy Acquisition Reform Home Page
> http://www.acq-ref.navy.mil

Navy Acquisition Reform Office
> http://www.acq-ref.navy.mil/

Office of Economic Conversion Information
> http://netsite.esa.doc.gov/oeci/

Office of Federal Procurement Policy
> http://www.arnet.gov/OFPP.html

Office of Secretary of the Army for Research, Development, and Acquisition
> http://www.sarda.army.mil/

Office of the Under Secretary of Defense for Acquisition and Technology
> http://www.acq.osd.mil/

Securities and Exchange Commission
> http://www.sec.gov/

Small Business Administration   http://www.sbaonline.sba.gov

Social Security Administration   http://www.ssa.gov/oag/oag1.htm

State of California Contracts Register
> http://www.dgs.ca.gov

State of Illinois Department of Commerce & Community Affairs
> http://accessil.com/dcca

State, Provincial & Pacific Rim Purchasing/Contracting Offices
> http://www.primaryaccess.com/

Tri-Service Contract Solicitation Network
> http://tsn.wes.army.mil/

U.S. Agency for International Development
> gopher://gaia.info.usaid.gov:70/1l/procurement_bus_opp

U.S. Govt. Printing Office Procurement Services
> http://www.access.gpo.gov/procurement/index.html

U.S. Patent and Trademark Office Acquisitions
               http://www.uspto.gov/web/offices/ac/comp/ proc/acquisitions/

U.S. Postal Service   http://www.usps.gov/business/

United States Geological Survey http://www.usgs.gov/contracts/index.html

Small Business Resources

Accelerate Technology Small Business Development Center
               http://www.accelerate.uci.edu/

American Institute of Small Business
               http://www.accessil.com/aisb/home.htm

Business and Economic Development Program Bureau of Land Mgt.
               http://www.blm.gov:80/natacq/proc6.html

Business Owner's Toolkit   http://www.toolkit.cch.com/

California Trade and Commerce Agency
               http://commerce.ca.gov/index.html

Center for Innovation   http://www.und.nodak.edu/dept/cibd/default.htm

Defense Technical Information Center-Small Business Program
               http://www.dtic.mil/dtic/sbir/

Dept. of Energy-Small Business Information
               http://www.pr.doe.gov/small.html

Dept. of Energy Field and Contractor Home Pages and Doing Business Pages
               http://www.pr.doe.gov/prpages.html

Dept. of Labor Office of Small Business Program
               http://gatekeeper.dol.gov/dol/osbp/

EntreWorld-Entrepreneurial Leadership
               http://www.entreworld.org/

Home Business   http://www.gohome.com/

Mentor-Protege Program-NASA
               http://www.hq.nasa.gov/office/procurement /sdbfed .html

Minority Business Development Agency
               http://www.doc.gov/agencies/mbda/index.html

Minority Telecommunications Develop. Program--National Telecom. and Info. Admin.
               http://www.ntia.dec.gov/opadhome/mtdpweb /outline.htm

Office of Economic Conversion Information
               http://netsite.esa.dec.gov/oeci/

Office of Small and Disadvantaged Business Utilization -Air Force
               http://www.safsb.hq.af.mil/

Office of Small and Disadvantaged Business Utilization Bureau of Land Management
               http://ns.ios.doi.gov/osdbu/index.html

Office of Small and Disadvantaged Business Utilization-Department of Agriculture
               http://www.usda.gov/da/smallbus.html
               http://www.usda.gov/da/smallbus/sbonline.htm

Office of Small and Disadvantaged Business Utilization-Department of Commerce
               http://www.osec.doc.gov/osdbu/

Office of Small and Disadvantaged Business Utilization-Department of Interior
               http://ns.ios.doi.gov/osdbu/index.html

Office of Small and Disadvantaged Business Utilization-Department of Justice
               http://www.usdoj.gov/jmd/pss/home_osd.htm

Office of Small and Disadvantaged Business Utilization-Department of Labor
http://gatekeeper.dol.gov/dol/osbp/public
/contacts/main.htm

Office of Small and Disadvantaged Business Utilization-Department of Transportation
http://www.dot.gov/dotinfo/ost/osdbu/

Office of Small and Disadvantaged Business Utilization-Department of State
http://www.statebuy.Inter.net/osdbul.htm

Office of Small and Disadvantaged Business Utilization-Department of Treasury
http://www.ustreas.gov/treasury/bureaus/sba/sba.html

Office of Small and Disadvantaged Business Utilization-DOD
http://www.acq.osd.mil/sadbu

Office of Small and Disadvantaged Business Utilization-Government Printing Office
http://www.access.gpo.gov/procurement/nb005.html

Office of Small and Disadvantaged Business Utilization-Housing and Urban Develop.
http://www.hud.gov/pop.html

Office of Small and Disadvantaged Business Utilization-NASA
http://www.hq.nasa.gov/office/codek

Offices of Small and Disadvantaged Business Utilization with their 'Women-Owned Business Representatives (WOBREP)
http://www.osec.doc.gov/osdbu/sources/contacts
/osdbu1.htm

Procurement Points of Contact GPO
http://www.access.gpo.gov/procurement/pp002.html

Procurement Technical Assistance Centers
http://www.fedmarket.com/ptac.htm

SBA--Women Business-Ownership Homepage
http://www.sbaonline.sba.gov/womeninbusiness

SBA's Office of Women's Business Ownership
http://www.sbaonline.sba.gov/womeninbusiness
/hotlist/

SBIR Commercialization Matching System
http://www.sbaonline.sba.gov/cgi-bin/print_hit_bold.pl
/Research_And_Development/cms.html?SBIR#first_hit

Securities and Exchange Commission: Small Business Information
http://www.sec.gov/smbusl.htm

Service Corps of Retired Executives (SCORE) -Free Business Counseling
http://www.scn.org/civic/score-online/

Small Business Administration   http://www.sbaonline.sba.gov

Small Business Advancement National Center
http://www.sbaer.uca.edu/

Small Business Development Centers
http://www.sbaonline.sba.gov/SBDC/

Small Business Development Ctrs. National List
http://www.businessfinance.com/sbdc. htm

Small Business Development Ctrs. on the Internet
http://www.smallbiz.sunycentral.edu/sbdcnet.htm

Small Business Innovative Research
http://www.sbaonline.sba.gov/Research_And
_Development/sbir.html

Small Business Innovative Research-National Conference Center
http://www.zyn.com/sbir/

Small Business Innovative Research and Small Business Technology Transfer
Solicitations http://www.sbaonline.sba.gov/Research_And
_Development/otagency.html
Small Business Innovative Research: Defense Technical Information Center
http://www.dtic.mil/dtic/sbir/
Small Business Innovative Research: NASA
http://nctn.oact.hq.nasa.gov/SBIR/SBIR.html
http://sbir.hql.nasa.gov/
http://change.oact.hq.nasa.gov/SBIR/SBIR.html
Small Business Innovative Research: NASA Participation Guide
http://nctn.hq.nasa.gov/SBIR/partintro.htm
Small Business Office Directors- U. S. Govt.
http://www.usda.gov/da/smallbus/sbdirect.htm
Small Business Personnel Bureau of Land Mgt.
http://www.blm.gov:80/natacq/proc6.html
http://www.blm.gov/natacq/proc3.html
Small Business Personnel Bureau of Land Mgt. Bus. Utilization & Developmt.
Specialists (BUDS) http://www.blm.gov:80/natacq/proc6.html
Small Business Personnel--Dept. of Agriculture
http://www.usda.gov/da/smallbus/sbcoord.htm
Small Business Personnel--Dept. of Energy
http://www.hr.doe.gov/ed/list.htm
Small Business Personnel--Dept. of Interior
http://ns.ios.doi.gov/osdbu/budlist.html
Small Business Personnel--Dept. of Justice
http://www.usdoj.gov/jmd/pss/forcst97.htm#7
Small Business Personnel--Dept. of Labor
http://gatekeeper.dol.gov/dol/osbp/public/
contacts/main.htm
Small Business Personnel—DOD
http://www.acq.osd.mil/sadbu/sbs.html
Small Business Personnel—HUD
http://www.hud.gov/cts/ctsbspec.htm
Small Business Personnel—NASA
http://www/Procure/sm_personnel.html
Small Business Personnel National Institute of Standards and Technology
http://www.nist.gov/admin/od/contract/smallbus.htm
Small Business Regulatory Compliance Assistance
http://www.dol.gov/dol/osbp/public/sbrefa/main.htm
Small Business Regulatory Enforcement Fairness Act of 1996
http://www.dol.gov/dol/osbp/public/programs/
sbrefa.htm#IMPROVING
Small Disadvantaged Business Program--U. S. Govt. Printing Office
http://www.access.gpo.gov/procurement/nb005.html
SmallbizNet http:www.lowe.org/smbiznet/index.htm
State of California, Office of Sm. & Minority Bus.
http://www.dgs.ca.osmb
Women-Owned Business Resources Am. Society of Women Entrepreneurs (ASWE)
http://www.membership.com/aswe/
BizWomen http://www.bizwomen.com/
Business Owner's Toolkit http://www.toolkit.cch.com/

Defense Contracting Regulations: A Guide for Small Business, Small Disadvantaged Business, and Women-Owned Business
                        http://www.dtic.mil/envirodod/smbustoc.html

Dept. of Labor--Women Bureau http://www.dol.gov/dol/wb/

Entrepreneurial Edge Online   http://www.edgeonline.com/

Entrepreneurs and Small Business Information
                        http://www.lowe.org/

EntreWorld-Entrepreneurial Leadership
                        http://www.entreworld.org/

Guide for Minority, Women Owned, and Small Businesses--Housing and Urban Development   http://www.hud.gov/cntrt.html

Home Business   http://www.gohome.com/

Home Office Association ofAmerica (HOAA)
                        http://www.hoaa.com/

Inc Online   http://www.inc.com/

Minority Business Entrepreneur (MBE) Magazine
                        http://www.mbemag.com/

National Association for Female Executives
                        http://www.nafe.com/

National Foundation for Women Business Owners
                        http://www.nfwbo.org/

Offices of Small and Disadvantaged Business Utilization with their Women Owned Business Representatives (WOBREP)
                        http://www.osec.doc.gov/osdbu/sources/contacts
                        /osdbul.htm

SBA--Women Business-Ownership Homepage
                        http://www.sbaonline.sba.gov/womeninbusiness

SBA's Office of Women's Business Ownership
                        http://www.sbaonline.sba.gov/womeninbusiness
                        /hotlist/

Service Corps of Retired Executives (SCORE)-- Free Business Counseling
                        http://www.scn.org/civic/score-online/

Women Business Owners Corporation
                        http://www.wboc.org/

Women In Technology International
                        http://www.witi.com/

Women Organization Directory http://www.feminist.org/gateway/womenorg.html

Women's Enterprise   http://www2.womens-enterprise.com/we/

WomenBiz   http://www.frsa.com/womenbiz/

Women's Business Exclusive (MrgE)
                        http://www.mbemag.com/html/WBEwelcome.html

How to Do Business Resources

Contracting Opportunities with GSA
                        http://www.gsa.gov/pubs/ctropgsa/ctropgsa.htm

Defense Contracting Regulations: A Guide for Small Business, Small Disadvantaged Business, and WomenOwned Business
                        http://www.dtic.mil/envirodod/smbustoc.html

Dept. of Energy--Small Business Information
                        http://www.pr.doe.gov/small.html

Doing Business with Dept. of Energy Field and Contractor Offices
    http://www.pr.doe.gov/prpages.html
Doing Business with Bureau of Land Mgt.
    http://www.blm.gov:8O/natacq/
    http://www.blm.gov:80/natacq/proc6.html
Doing Business with Dept. of Energy
    http://www.pr.doe.gov/prbus.html
    http://www.pr.doe.gov/prhow.html
Doing Business with Dept. of Energy Field and Contractor Offices
    http://www.pr.doe.gov/prpages.html
Doing Business with Dept. of Interior
    http://ns.ios.doi.gov/osdbu/index.html
Doing Business with Dept. of Justice
    http://www.usdoj.gov/jmd/pss/doin_bus.htm
Doing Business with Dept. of Veterans Affairs
    http://www.va.gov/oa&mm/busopp/dbwva1.htm
Doing Business with Environ. Protection Agency
    http://www.epa.gov/oam/
Doing Business with General Services Admin.
    http://www.gsa.gov/pubs/dbgsa/dbgsa.htm
Doing Business with Government
    http://www.business.gov/DoingBusiness.html#WSG
Doing Business with NASA http://www.hq.nasa.gov/office/codek/Index.html
Doing Business with Navy http://www.abm.rda.hq.navy.mil/doing.html
Doing Business with Small Business Admin.
    http://www.sba.gov/SBDC/13cfr130.html
Guide for Minority, Women Owned, and Small Businesses--Housing and Urban
Development   http://www.hud.gov/cntrt.html
How to Do Business with Dept. of Energy
    http://www.pr.doe.gov/prhow.html
How to Do Business w/ Govt. Printing Office
    http://www.access.gpo.gov/procurement/pub1050.pdf
How to Sell to Department of Commerce
    http://www.osec.doc.gov/osdbu/sources/selling/
Let's Do Business with U. S. Postal Service
    http://www.usps.gov/business/ldb.htm
Marketing to the Navy http://38.242.41.5:8O/marketing/
Marketing Your Capability--Dept. of Interior
    http://ns.ios.doi.gov/osdbu/market.html
Quick Guide to HUD Contracting
    http://www.hud.gov/cts/ctsguide.html
Selling to the Dept. of Agriculture
    http://www.usda.gov/da/procure
    /poc.htm#SellingtoUSDA
Selling to the Military http://www.dtic.mil/envirodod/sell4toc.html
Small Business Information-Securities and Exchange Commission
    http://www.sec.gov/smbusl.htm
What the Dept. of Labor Buys
    http://gatekeeper.dol.gov/dol/osbp/public/pubs
    /doIbuys/main.htm

Business Opportunities Resources

Acquisition Forecast--Bureau of Land Mgt.
http://www.blm.gov:80/natacq/proc7.html

Acquisition Forecast--Dept. of Agriculture
http://www.uscia.gov/da/smalIbus/forecast.htm

Acquisition Forecast--Dept. of Agriculture--Agricultural Marketing Service
http://www.usda.gov/da/smallbus/97ams.htm

Acquisition Forecast-Dept. of Agriculture--Farm Service Agency
http://www.usda.gov/da/smallbus/97fsa.htm

Acquisition Forecast-Dept. of Agriculture--Food & Consumer Service
http://www.usda.gov/da/smalIbus/97fcs.htm

Acquisition Forecast-Dept. of Agriculture--Food Safety and Inspection Service
http://www.usda.gov/da/smalIbus/97fsis.htm

Acquisition Forecast--Dept. of Agriculture-- Forest Service
http://www.usda.gov/da/smallbus/97fs.htm

Acquisition Forecast--Dept. of Agriculture--Marketing and Regulatory Programs
http://www.usda.gov/da/smallbus/97mrp.htm

Acquisition Forecast-Dept. of Agriculture--Natural Resources Conservation
Service   http://www.usda.gov/da/smallbus/97nrcs.htm

Acquisition Forecast--Dept. of Agriculture--Office of the Inspector General
http://www.usda.gov/da/smallbus/97oig.htm

Acquisition Forecast--Dept. of Agriculture--Office of Operations
http://www.usda.gov/da/smallbus/97oo.htm

Acquisition Forecast-Dept. of Agriculture--Research, Education and Economics
http://www.usda.gov/da/smallbus/97ree.htm

Acquisition Forecast--Dept. of Agriculture--Rural Development
http://www.usda.gov/da/smallbus/97rd.htm

Acquisition Forecast--Dept. of Commerce
http://www.osec.doc.gov/osdbu/sources/ops/

Acquisition Forecast--Dept. of Energy
http://www.pr.doe.gov/96sbl.html
http://www.hr.doe.gov/ed/ftoc1.htm
http://www.hr.doe.gov/ed/confldl.htm

Acquisition Forecast--Dept. of Interior
http://ns.ios.doi.gov/osdbu/welcome.html

Acquisition Forecast-Dept. of Justice
http://www.usdoj.gov/jmd/pss/forcst97.htm

Acquisition Forecast--Dept. of Labor
http://gatekeeper.dol.gov/dol/osbp/public/nonregs
/aapp/main.htm
http://gatekeeper.dol.gov/dol/osbp/public/pubs
/nopup.htm

Acquisition Forecast -HUD   http://www.hud.gov/cts/cts4cast.html

Acquisition Forecast-NASA   http://procure.msfc.nasa.gov/forecast/index.html

Acquisition Forecast--Navy   http://lrae.abm.rda.hq.navy.mil/

Acquisition Forecast--Social Security Admin.
http://www.ssa.gov/oag/oagl.htm

Bid Information-Government Printing Office
http://www.access.gpo.gov/procurement/nb001.html

Business Leads and Procurement Opportunities
http://www.stat-usa.gov/BEN/subject/procure.html

Business Opportunities--Air Force
                    http://www.safaq.hq.af.mil/contracting/biz_opty.html
Business Opportunities--Army
                    http://acqnet.sarda.army.mil/busopp/default.htm
                    http://acqnet.sarda.army.mil/acqref/default.htm
Business Opportunities-Bureau of Land Mgt.
                    http://www.bim.gov:80/natacq/sol.html
                    http://www.blm.gov/natacq/sol.html
Business Opportunities-Defense Advanced Research Projects Agency
                    http://www.arpa.mil/baa/
Business Opportunities-Defense Info. Sys. Ag.
                    http://www.disa.mil/line/ciaop.html
Business Opportunities-Defense Mapping Ag.
                    http://www.dma.gov/business/contracts/solicit.htm
Business Opportunities--Dept. of Agriculture
                    http://www.usda.gov/da/procure/busopps.htm
Business Opportunities--Dept. of Agriculture
                    http://www.usda.gov/da/smallbus.html
Business Opportunities--Dept. of Agriculture--Farm Service Agency
                    http://www.fsa.usda.gov/amb/solic.htm
Business Opportunities--Dept. of Agriculture--Farm Service Agency-Food &
Consumer Service   http:/www.usda.gov/fcs/contract.htm
Business Opportunities--Dept. of Agriculture--Set-Asides
                    http://www.usda.gov/da/smallbus/procopps.htm
Business Opportunities--Dept. of Commerce
                    http://netsite.esa.doc.gov/oam/lf2.html
Business Opportunities--Dept. of Energy
                    http://www.pr.doe.gov/propp.html
                    http://www.pr.doe.gov/solicit.html
Business Opportunities--Dept. of Health & Human Services
                    http://www.os.dhhs.gov:80/progorg/oam/contrct/
                    http://www.os.dhhs.gov:80/progorg/oam/cbd/
Business Opportunities--Dept. of Justice
                    http://www.usdoj.gov/jmd/pss/proposal.htm
Business Opportunities--Dept. of State
                    http://www.statebuy.Inter.net/busops.htm
Business Opportunities--Dept. of Transportation
                    http://www.dot.gov/dotinfo/ost/m60/dotrfp.html
Business Opportunities--Dept. of Veterans Affairs
                    http://www.va.gov/oa&mm/busopp.htm
Business Opportunities--Dept. of Veterans Affairs CDB Announcements
                    http://www.va.gov/oa&mm/busopp/cbdaug.htm
Business Opportunities--Dept. of Veterans Affairs Solicitations
                    http://www.va.gov/oa&mm/busopp/sols.htm
Business Opportunities--DOD Ballistic Missile Defense Organization
                    http://www.acq.osd.mil/bmdo/barbb/forecast
                    /current.htm
Business Opportunities--DOD Health Affairs
                    http://www.ha.osd.mil/rmo/solinote.html
Business Opportunities--EPA   http://www.epa.gov/oam/#Business Opportunities

Business Opportunities-Federal Communications Commission
        http://www.fcc.gov/Bureaus/OCBO/ocbo.html

Business Opportunities-General Services Admin.
        http://www.gsa.gov/pubs/ctropgsa/ctropgs

Business Opportunities--Govt. Printing Office
        http://www.access.gpo.gov/procurement/bids
        /synopsis.shtml

Business Opportunities--HUD   http://www.hud.gov/cts/ctsoprty.html

Business Opportunities--NASA
        http://procure.msfc.nasa.gov/midrange/link_syp.html

Business Opportunities-National Imagery and Mapping Agency
        http://164.214.2.59/poc/contracts/solici.htm

Business Opportunities-National Institute of Standards and Technology
        http://www.nist.gov/admin/od/contract/business.htm

Business Opportunities-National Oceanic & Atmospheric Admin.
        http://www.sao.noaa.gov/solicit.html

Business Opportunities--Navy Solicitations
        http://www.abm.rda.hq.navy.mil/solicit.html

Business Opportunities--NOAA, Western Administrative Support Center
        http://www.wasc.noaa.gov/wasc/curtoppr.htm

Business Opportunities-Personal Communications Services
        http://www.ntia.dec.gov/opadhome/mtdpweb
        /pbusopp.htm

Business Opportunities-Social Security Admin.
        http://www.ssa.gov/oag/acq/toc.htm

Business Opportunities-Tri-Service Contract Solicitation Network
        http://cadlib.wes.army.mil/contract/

Business Opportunities--U. S. Postal Service
        http://www.usps.gov/business/wantad.htm

Business, Economic, and Govt. Information
        http://www.stat-usa.gov/BEN/Services/globus.html

Commerce Business Daily   http://cbdnet.gpo.gov/
        http://cbdnet.access.gpo.gov/
        http://www.safsb.hq.af.mil/cbd.html
        http://www.govcon.com/
        http://www.ld.com/
        http://www.bidcast.com/
        http://cos.gdb.org/repos/cbd/cbd-dom.html
        http://www.stat-usa.gov/BEN/subject/procure.html

CommerceNet   http://www.commerce.net/

Dept. of Treasury E-mail Notification
        http://www.fms.treas.gov/subscrib.html

FACNET: Bidding Opportunities Under $100,000
        http://www.govcon.com/

Federal Acquisition & Procurement Opportunities
        http://www-far.npr.gov/AcqOpp/AcqOpp.htm

Major Defense Acquisition Programs
        http://www.acq.osd.mil/api/asm/mdaplist.html

NASA Acq. Internet Service E-mail Notification
        http://procurement.nasa.gov/maillist.html

NASA Procurement Synopsis Search
        http://procurement.nasa.gov/NPSE/

Subcontracting Opportunities With DOD Major Prime Contractors
http://www.dtic.mil/envirodod/dodsubs.html

Financial/Venture Capital Resources

America's Business Funding Directory
http://www.businessfinance.com/

Angel Capital Electronic Network (ACE-Net)
http://ace-net.sr.unh.edu/

Ben Franklin Franklin Technology Center
http://www.benfranklin.org/

Business Owner's Toolkit   http://www.toolkit.cch.com/

Center for Innovation
http://www.und.nodak.edu/dept/cibd/default.htm

ConnectNet   http://darwinl.ucsd.edu:8000/connect/

Creative Investment Research   http://www2.ari.net/cirm/

Defense Loan and Technical Assistance Program
http://www.sbaonline.sba.gov/business_finances/delta/

Home Business   http://www.gohome.com/

Home Office Association of America (HOAA)
http://www.hoaa.com/

Kansas Technology EnterpriseCorporation (KTEC)
http://www.ktec.com/

MIT Entrepreneurs Club   http://www.mit.edu:800l/activities/e-club
/e-club-home.html

MoneyHunter   http://www.moneyhunter.com/

Pacific Venture Capital Network
http://www.accelerate.uci.edu/pacnet.html

SBA Financing Your Business
http://www.sbaonline.sba.gov/business_finances
/FinancingYourBusiness.html

SBA's Export Working Capital Program Loans
http://www.sbaonline.sba.gov/business_finances/export

SBA's International Loan Program
http://www.sbaonline.sba.gov/business_finances/inter

SBA's Minority and Women's Prequalification Pilot Loan Program
http://www.sbaonline.sba.gov/business_finances
/prequal

SBA's Qualified Employee Trusts Loans
http://www.sbaonline.sba.gov/business_finances/qet/

SBA's Surety Bond Program   http://www.sbaonline.sba.gov/business_finances
/surety.html

SBA's Veterans Loan Program   http://www.sbaonline.sba.gov/business_finances
/vets/

SBA's 7(a) Loan Guaranty Program SBA's Certified and Preferred
http://www.sbaonline.sba.gov/business_finances
/7aloan.html

Lenders Program   http://www.sbaonline.sba.gov/business_finances
/lender.html

SBA's Certified Development Company (504 Loan) Program
http://www.sbaonline.sba.gov/business_finances
/cert.html

SBA's Secondnrv Market Program
> http://www.sbaonline.sba.gov/business_finances/second.html

Shareware Programs for Financing a Business
> http://www.sbaonline.sba.gov/shareware/finfile.html

Small Business Innovative Research
> http://www.sbaonline.sba.gov/Research_And_Development/sbir.html

Small Business Innovative Research and Small Business Technology Transfer Solicitations
> http://www.sbaonline.sba.gov/Research_And_Development/otagency.html

Small Business Investment Companies
> http://www.sbaonline.sba.gov/INV/

The Capital Network http://www.thecapitaInetwork.com/

Venture Capital Clubs Nationwide
> http://www.businessfinance. com/vcclubs.htm

General Contracting Resources

Bid Protest–GAG Decisions http://www.gao.gov/decisions/bidpro/bidpro.htm

Bureau of Economic Analysis http://www.bea.doc.gov/

Bureau of Export Administration
> http://www.bxa.doc.gov/
> http://www.doc.gov/agencies/bxa/index.html

Business Background Report http://ww.dbisna.com/dbis/promo/051796a1.htm

Business, Economic, and Govt. Information
> http://www.stat-usa.gov/BEN/Services/globus.html

Commercial Advocates Forum http://www.acq.osd.mil/ar/cadv.htm

Comptroller General Decisions http://www.gao.gov/decisions/decision.htm

Congressional Legislation/Bills http://thomas.loc.gov/

Congressional Record http://thomas.loc.gov/

Consolidated Acquisition Reporting Sys. (CARS)
> http://www.acq.osd.mil/cars/

Davis-Bacon Wage Determination Database
> http://kirk.fedworld.gov/dbhome.htm

Debarred List of Parties Excluded from Federal Procurement and Nonprocurement Programs http://www.arnet.gov/epls/
> http://www.dlsc.dla.mil/~Debarred/debar.htp

Defense Acquisition Deskbook http://deskbook.osd.mil/deskbook.html

Defense Acquisition University http://www.acq.osd.mil/dau/

Defense Investigative Service http://www.dis.mil/

Defense Systems Management College
> http://www.dsmc.dsm.mil/

Defense Technical Information Center
> http://www.dtic.mil/dtic/

Dept. of Defense Electronic Commerce Office
> http://www.acq.osd.mil/ec/

Dept. of Treasury E-mail Notification
> http://www.fms.treas.gov/subscrib.html

Dept. of Treasury's Listing of Approved Sureties
> http://www.fms.treas.gov/c570.html

Economic Development Administration
                http://www.doc.gov/eda/

Electronic Commerce-Department. of Defense
                http://www.acq.osd.mil/ec/

Electronic Commerce Resource Centers
                http://www.ecrc.gmu.edu/fecrc/location.html
                http://www.oakland.ecrc.org/ecrcres.html

Electronic Systems Center: Technology Transfer
                http://www.hanscom.af.mil1/0rgs/0_0rgs/XR
                /TechX/

E-Mail Directory Search Engine http://www.hq.nasa.gov/x.500.html
                http://fourll.com/

Federal Acquisition Computer Net (FACNET)
                http://www.acq.osd.mil/ec/facnet.htm

Federal Acquisition Institute   http:/www.gsa gov/staff/v/training.htm

Federal Acquisition Jumpstation http://procure.msfc.nasa.gov/fedproc/home.html

Federal Community   http://www.usgov.digital.com/info/dircomm.htm

Federal Depository Libraries by State/Area Code
                http://www.access.gpo.gov/su_docs/dpos
                /adpos004.html

Federal Depository Library Gateway
                http://www.access.gpo.gov/su_docs/aces
                /aaces004.html

Federal Discount Lodging Directory
                http://www.usgov.digital.com/info/dirlodg.htm

Federal Information Center   http://fic.info.gov/

Federal Procurement Data System (FPDS) Contract Data Information
                http://www.gsa.gov/staff/oppe/fpds/fpds.htm

Federal Register   http://law.house.gov/7.htm
                http://www.access.gpo.gov/su_docs/aces/acesl40.html
                http://www.access.gpo.gov/su_docs/aces/aaces002.html
                http://cos.gdb.org/repos/fr/fr-intro.html
                http://www2.infoseek.com/Titles?qt=federal+register

Federal Supply Schedule   http://pub.fss.gsa.gov/

FedWorld Information Network (NTIS)
                http://www.fedworld.gov

General Accounting Office Decisions
                http://www.gao.gov/
                http://www.access.gpo.gov/su_docs/aces/aaces002.html

General Accounting Office Decisions (Searchable)
                http://www.access.gpo.gov/su_docs/aces
                /aces170.shtml

GLOBUS- International Procure. Marketplace
                http://www.stat-usa.gov/BEN/Services/globus.html

Government Information Xchange
                http://www.info.gov/

Government Printing Office (GPO) Access
                http://www.access.gpo.gov/

Government Printing Office Access
                http://www.access.gpo.gov/su_docs/aces
                /aaces002.html

GSA Advantage	https://www.fss.gsa.gov/cgi-bins/advwel
International Trade Administration	
	http://www.ita.dec.gov/
Labor Surplus Areas	http://purchl.lbl.gov/lsa.txt
Legislative Information on the Internet	
	http://thomas.loc.gov
National Technology Transfer Center (NTTC)	
	http://www.nttc.edu/
NASA Acq. Internet Service E-mail Notification	
	http://procurement.nasa.gov/maillist.html
NASA Financial and Contractual Status (FACS)	
	http://procurement.nasa.gov/facs/html/
NASA Procurement Synopsis Search	
	http://procurement.nasa.gov/NPSE/
NASA Technology Transfer Center	
	http://www.nttc.edu/
Office of Air & Space Commercialization	
	http://cher.eda.dec.gov/oasc.html
Standard Industrial Class. Codes Construction	
	http://www.opsafesite.com/mw3/siccod~1.htm
Standard Industrial Classifications Codes	
	http://www.sba.gov/regulations/siccodes
	http://purchl.lbl.gov/sic.txt
	http://weber.u.washington.edu/~dev/sic.html
Standard Industrial Classifications Codes Search	
	http://www.osha.gov/oshstats/sicser.html
Supreme Court Decisions	http://www.law.cornell.edu/supct/supct.table.html
Trade Adjustment Assistance Program	
	http://www.tradeassistance.com/
U. S. Govt. Information Sources (Virtual Library)	
	http://www.nttc.edu/gov_res.html
U. S. Business Advisor Home Page	
	http://www.business.gov
U. S. Federal Court Opinions/Decisions	
	http://www.ll.georgetown.edu/Fed-Ct/
U. S. Patent and Trademark Office	
	http://www.uspto.gov/
U. S. Statistics Database	http://www.stat-usa.gov/
U. S. Trade Representative	http://www.ustr.gov/index.html
Value Added Network (VAN) Providers	
	http://www.acq.osd.mil/ec/van_list.htm
	http://www.oakland.ecrc.org/resources11.html
WWW Servers (U.S. Federal Government)	
	http://www.fie.com/www/us_gov.htm

Laws, Regulations, and Other Related Procurement Documents

Air Force Alternative FAR Site	http://FARSITE/HILL.AF.MIL/
Air Force FAR Supplement	http://www.hq.af.mil/SAFAQ/contracting/far/affars.html
Army Acquisition Circulars	http://acqnet.sarda.army.mil/library/afar/aac/aactoc.html

Army FAR Supplement http://acqnet.sarda.army.mil/library/zpafar.htm

Army Publications and Printing Command
 http://www-usappc.hoffman.army.mil/

Bid Protest: GAO Administrative Practice & Procedure, Regulations, and Govt.
Contracts http://www.gao.gov/decisions/bidpro/new.reg
 /regulation.htm

Code of Federal Regulations http://law.house.gov/cfr.htm
 http://law.house.gov/4.htm
 http://www.access.gpo.gov/nara/cfr/
 http://www.access.gpo.gov/su_docs/aces
 /aaces002.html
 http://www.law.cornell.edu/regs.html

Congressional Legislation/Bills http://thomas.loc.gov/

Defense Acquisition Circulars http://www.dtic.mil/contracts/dacs.html

Defense Acquisition Information http://www.dtic.dla.mil/hovlane/

Defense FAR Supplement http://www.dtic.mil/dfars/

Defense Printing Service Documents
 http://www.dtic.dla.mil/dps-phila/index.html

Defense Technical Information Center
 http://www.dtic.dia.mil:80/dtiwltoc_acq.q.html
 http://www.dtic.dia.mil.80/dtwl/hovlane
 http://www.dtic.dia.mil/acqad2.acqed.html

Dept. of Ag. Procure. Regulations & Notices
 http://www.usda.gov/da/procure/procdrdn.htm

Dept. of Ag. Procurement Regulatory Info.
 http://www.usda.gov/da/procure/procreg.htm

Dept. of Ag. Acquisition Pegs. Advisories
 http://www.usda.gov/da/procure/agaradv.htm

Dept. of Agriculture Acquisition Regulations
 http://www.usda.gov/da/procure/agar.htm

Dept. of Commerce Policy and Guidance
 http://netsite.esa.doc.gov/oam/lc2.html

Dept. of Defense Contracting Regulations
 http://www.dtic.mil/contracts/

Dept. of Defense Defense Acquisition Deskbook
 http://deskbook.osd.mil/deskbook.html

Dept. of Energy Acquisition Regulations
 http://www.doe.gov/html/procure/pr6.html

Dept. of Energy Procurement and Property Regs.
 http://apollo.osti.gov/procure/pr6.html

Dept. of Health and Human Services Acq. Regs.
 gopher://gopher.os.dhhs.gov:70/1l/Topics
 /grantsnet/laws-reg

Dept. of Interior Acquisition Policy Releases
 http://www.ios.doi.gov/pam/diapr.html

Dept. of Interior Acquisition Regulations
 http://www.ios.doi.gov/pam/aindex.html
 http://www.usdoj.gov/not_aval.htm

Dept. of Interior Policy and Regulation
 http://www.ios.doi.gov/pam/pamareg.html

Dept. of State Acquisition Policy and Tools
 http://www.statebuy.Inter.net/acpolicy.htm

Dept. of State Acquisition Regulations
http://patriot.net/~roblloyd/dosartoc.htm
http://adams.patriot.net/~roblloyd/dosartoc.htm

Dept. of Transportation Acq. Manuals & Regs.
http://www.dot.gov/dotinfo/ost/m60/tamtar/

DOD and Navy Instructions, Manuals, Standards, Flowcharts and Guidebooks
http://www.spawar.navy.mil:80/~wrynns/

DOD Contracting Regulations   http://www.dtic.mil/contracts/

DOD Directives and Instructions
http://web7.whs.osd.mil/corres.htm

DOD FAR Supplement   http://www.dtic.mil/dfars/

DOD Single Stock Point for Specs. & Standards
http://www.dodssp.daps.mil/

Executive Orders   http://library.whitehouse.gov
/?request=ExecutiveOrder

Exec. Orders and Procurement Policy Letters
http://www-ar.npr.gov/References/Policy_Letters/

Federal Acquisition Circulars   http://www.gsa.gov/far/FAC/FACs.html
http://www.gsa.gov:80/far/FAC/FACs.html

Federal Acquisition Regulations   http://www.gsa.gov/far/
http://www.govcon.com/
http://www.fedmarket.com/far_indx.html

Federal Acquisition Regulations and NASA FAR Supplement (Searchable)
http://procurement.nasa.gov/FAR/

Federal Acquisition Regulations(Searchable)
http://www-far.npr.gov/References/References.html

Federal Acquisition Streamlining Act
http://www.saecrc.org/dodedi/dodedi02.html

Fed'l Information Resources Management Reg.
http://www.itpolicy.gsa.gov/firmr/firmrtoc.htm

FedWorld Information Network (NTIS)
http://www.fedworld.gov

Forms: Standard Forms Index   http://msfcinfo.msfc.nasa.gov/forms/forms.html

Freedom of Information Act (FOIA): A Citizen's Guide on Using the FOIA and the Privacy Act of 1974 to Request Government Records
http://foia.larc.nasa.gov/citizens_guide_to_foia_93.txt

FOIA: NASA Information   http://www.hq.nasa.gov/office/pao/FOIA
/general.html

GSA Procurement Regulations   http://www.gsa.gov

Information Technology Issues   http://www.itpolicy.gsa.gov/

Information Technology Standards Dec. Library
http://www.itsi.disa.mil/cfs/itsi_lib.html

Javits-Wagner-O'Day (JWOD) Act Proc. List
http://www.usda.gov/da/procure/jwod.htm

Labor Laws and Executive Orders
http://www.dol.gov/cgi-bin
/consolid.pl?regs+statutes

Labor Laws and Regulations [DOL]
http://www.doleta.gov/regs/regstats.htm

Legislative Information on the Internet
http://thomas.loc.gov/

NASA Center's Unique Clauses   http://www.ksc.nasa.gov/procurement/uniq_cls.htm

NASA Grant and Cooperative Agmt. Handbook
http://procure.msfc.nasa.gov/grcover.htm

NASA Management Directives
http://Lincoln.GSFC.nasa.gov/rnd/Welcome.html

NASA Midrange Procurement Procedures
http://msfcinfo.msfc.nasa.gov/midrange/otherdoc
/procedur.html

NASA Procurement Library   http://msfcinfo.msfc.nasa.gov/library/library.html

NASA Regs., Documents, and Handbooks
http://procure.msfc.nasa.gov/nasa_ref.html

NASA SBIR Participation Guide
http://nctn.hq.nasa.gov/SBIR/partintro.htm

NASA Submission of Unsolicited Proposal
http://msfcinfo.msfc.nasa.gov/nasahdbk.html

National Industrial Security Program Operating Manual (NISPOM)
http://www.tscm.com/Nispom.html

National Institute of Standards and Technology
http://www.nist.gov/

Navy Acquisition Procedures Supplement
http://www.abm.rda.hq.navy.mil/branch14.html

Navy Contract Writing Guide   http://www.abm.rda.hq.navy.mil/toolkit.html

Occupational Safety and Health Administration (OSHA) Regulations
http://gabby.osha-slc.gov/OshStd_toc
/OSHA_Std_toc.html

Office of Mgt. and Budget (OMB) Circulars
http://www.ucop.edu:80/raohome/circulars
/circtc.html

gopher://pula.financenet.gov:70/1l/docs/central/omb

OMB Circulars (Searchable)   http://www.ucop.edu/cgi-bin/cgcircular.pl

OSHA Computerized Information System
http://gabby.osha-slc.gov
http://gabby.osha-slc.gov:80/

OSHA Notices, Pegs., and Rules (Searchable)
http://gabby.osha-slc.gov:80/0CIS/toc_fed_reg.html

Regulatory Information Service Center
http://www.gsa.gov/staff/c/cr/risc.htm

Social Security Handlbook   http://www.ssa.gov/handbooldssa-hbk.htm

U.S. House of Representatives Law Library
http://law.house.gov/l.htm

Uniform Commercial Code   http://www.law.cornell.edu/topics/contract.html

United States Code   http://www.law.cornell.edu/uscode

United States Code (Searchable)   http://law.house.gov/usc.htm

US Postal Service Procurement Manual
http://www.usps.gov/business/pub4l.htm

USAID Procurement Regulations (Handbooks)
gopher://gaia.info.usaid.gov:70/11/procurement_
bus_opp/handbook

World Wide Web Home Page Guidelines and Best Practices
http://www.dtic.mil/staff/cthomps/guidelines/

Zip Codes	http://www.usps.gov/ncsc/lookups /lookup_zip+4.html http://mcia.com/~jswift/search/srchtele.htm

Employment and Labor Resources

America's Job Bank	http://www.AJB.dni.us/
America's Labor Market Information System	
	http://ecuvax.cis.ecu.edu/~lmi/lmi.html
Career Path	http://www.careerpath.com/
Dept. of Labor--Compliance Assistance Info.	
	http://www.dol.gov/cgi-bin /consolid.pl?regs+compliance
Dept. of Labor--Employment & Training Admin.	
	http://www.doleta.gov/
Dept. of Labor--Women Bureau	http://www.dol.gov/dol/wb/
Dept. of Labor Posters	http://www.dol.gov/dol/osbp/public/sbrefa /poster.htm
Employment Opportunities	http://www.whitehouse.gov/WH/pointers/html/ employment.html
Family Medical and Leave Act	http://www.dol.gov/dol/esa/fmla.htm
Federal Job Finder	http://www.usgov.digital.com/info/dircomm.htm
Federal Jobs	http://www.cybercomm.net/~digibook/
Federal Jobs Search	http://www.fedworld.gov/jobs/jobsearch.html
Federal Jobs--USA Jobs	http://www.usajobs.opm.gov/
Federal Labor Relations Authority	
	http://www.access.gpo.gov/flra/index.html
Federal Work-Study Program	http://www.ed.gov/prog_info/SFA/StudentGuide /1996-7/fws.html
Finance Net Jobs	http://www.usgov.digital.com/info/dircomm.htm
Heart---Career Connections	http://www.career.com/
Internet Job Source	http://www.usgov.digital.com/info/dircom
Job Bank America	http://www.jobbankusa.com/
Job Hunt	http://www.job-hunt.org/
Job Net	http://www.westga.edu/~coop/
Job Trak	http://www.jobtrak.com/
Job Web-Nat. Assoc. of Colleges & Employers	
	http://www.jobweb.org//
Jobs Career Mosaic	http://www.careermosaic.com/
Jobs Library	ftp://ftp.fedworld.gov/pub/jobs/jobs.htm
Labor Laws and Executive Orders	
	http://www.dol.gov/cgi-bin /consolid.pl?regs+statutes
Labor Laws and Regulations [DOL]	
	http://www.doleta.gov/regs/regstats.htm
National Recruiters	http://www.natrec.com/
Occupational Safety and Health Admin. (OSHA)	
	http://www.osha.gov/index.html
Office of Federal Contract Compliance Programs	
	http://www.dol.gov/dol/esa/public/ofcp_org.htm

Office of Labor-Management Standards (OLMS)
http://www.dol.gov/dol/esa/public/olms_org.htm

Office of Workers' Compensation Programs
http://www.dol.gov/dol/esa/public/owcp_org.htm

Skill Search http://www.internet-is.com/skillsearch/

Small Business Regulatory Compliance Assistance
http://www.dol.gov/dol/osbp/public/sbrefa
/main.htm

Standard Occupational Class. (SOC) Codes
http://weber.u.washington.edu/%7Edev/soc.html

U. S. Census Bureau http://www.census.gov/

U. S. Census Bureau Business Statistics
http://www.census.gov/econ/www/

U. S. Department of Labor http://www.dol.gov/dol/welcome.htm

U. S. Dept. of Interior Vacancy Announcements
http://www.usgs.gov/doi/avads/index.html

U. S. National Labor Relations Board
http://www.nlrb.gov/index.html

U. S. Office of Compliance http://www.compliance.gov/index.html

U. S. Office of Government Ethics
http://www.access.gpo.gov/usoge/index.html

U. S. Office of Special Counsel for Prohibited Personnel Practices
http://www.access.gpo.gov/osc/index.html

U.S. Commission on Civil Rights
http://www.useer.gov/index.html

U.S. Equal Employment Opportunity Commission
http://www.eeoc.gov/

U.S. Merit Systems Protection Board
http://www.access.gpo.gov/mspb/index.html

Wage and Hour Division http://www.dol.gov/dol/esa/public/whd_org.htm

Professional Organizations and Publications

Am. Society of Women Entrepreneurs (ASWE)
http://www.membership.com/aswe/

American Arbitration Association
http://www.adr.org/

American Institute of Small Business
http://www.accessil.com/aisb/home.htm

Association of Proposal Mgt. Professionals
http://www.apmp.org/

Association of Government Marketing Assistance Specialists (AGMAS)
http://www.agmas.org

Entrepreneurial Edge Online http://www.edgeonline.com/

Entrepreneurs and Small Business Information
http://www.lowe.org/

EntreWorld-Entrepreneurial Leadership
http://www.entreworld.org/

Front-Line Procurement Professional's Forum
http://www.arnet.gov/FLF/flfpg1f.htm

Home Office Association of America (HOAA)
http://www.hoaa.com/

Inc Online	http://www.inc.com/
InterActive Economic Development Network, Inc.	
	http://IEDN.com/IEDN/
Interagency Acquisition Internet Council	
	http://www.arnet.gov/IAIC/
Job Web--Nat. Assoc. of Colleges & Employers	
	http://www.jobweb.org//
Minority Business Entrepreneur (MBE) Magazine	
	http://www.mbemag.com/
National Association for Female Executives	
	http://www.nafe.com/
National Association of Black Procurement Professionals	
	http://www.bayside.net/nabpp/
National Association of Development Org.	
	http://www.nado.org/
National Association of Management and Technical Assistance Centers	
	http://www.namtac.com/
National Association of Purchasing Management	
	http://www.napm.org
Project Management Institute	http://www.pmi.org/
National Contract Management Association (NCMA)	
	http://www.ncmahq.org
National Council for Urban Economic Developmt.	
	http://CUED.org/cued/
National Foundation for Women Business Owners	
	http://www.nfwbo.org/
National Institute of Governmental Purchasing	
	http://www.nigp.org/nigp/
Northeast-Midwest Institute	http://www.nemw.org/
Project Management Institute	http://www.pmi.org/
Society of Cost Estimating and Analysis	
	http://www.erols.com/scea/
Trade Adjustment Assistance Program	
	http://www.tradeassistance.com/
Women Business Owners Corporation	
	http://www.wboc.org/
Women In Technology International	
	http://www.witi.com/
Women Organization Directory	http://www.feminist.org/gateway/womenorg.html
Women's Enterprise	http://www2.womens-enterprise.com/we/
WomenBiz	http://www.frsa.com/womenbiz
Women's Business Exclusive (WBE)	
	http://www.mbemag.com/html/WBEwelcome.html

Procurement Technical Assistance Centers (PTACs)

PTACs are an excellent resource to businesses trying to contract with the government. Since federal, state, and local funding resources support the PTACs, there is no fee to their clients for the basic services offered. Use them as your resident expert and counselor.

Many of the offices listed have field offices located in various locations in the area they cover. Contact them to locate the PTAC closest to you.

ALABAMA

University of Alabama at Birmingham
2800 Milan Court, Suite 124
Birmingham, AK 35211-6908
Point of Contact: Charles A. Hopson
Phone: 205-943-6750 Fax: 205-943-6752

ALASKA

University of Alaska Anchorage
SBDC
430 W 7th Ave Ste 100
Anchorage, AL 99501-3550
Point of Contact: Mike Taylor
Phone: 907-274-7232 Fax: 907-274-9524

ARIZONA

The National Center for AIED
National Center Headquarters
953 E Juanita Avenue
Mesa, AZ 85204
Point of Contact: Linda Alexius Hagerty
Phone: 602-545-1298 Fax: 602-545-4208

Aptan Inc
1435 N Hayden Rd
Scottsdale, AZ 85257-3773
Point of Contact: Paul Roddy
Phone: 602-945-5452 Fax: 602-945-4153
E-Mail: aptan@primenet.com
URL: www.aptan.com

ARKANSAS

Board Of Trustees, University of Arkansas
Cooperative Extension Service
103 E. Page
Malvern, AR 72104
Point of Contact: Toni Tosch
Phone: 501-337-5355 Fax: 501-337-5045
E-Mail: info@apacua.org
URL: www.apacua.org

CALIFORNIA

Riverside Community College District
4800 Magnolia Avenue
Riverside, CA 92501-3256
Point of Contact: Gail A. Zwart
Phone: 909-683-0194 Fax: 909-684-8369
E-Mail: zwart@rccd.cc.ca.us
URL: http://resources4u.com/pac/

Merced County Dept of Business-Economic Opportunities
3180 Collins Dr. Suite A
Merced, CA 95348
Point of Contact: Jane E. Mcginnis
Phone: 209-385-7686 Fax: 209-383-4959
E-Mail: cpc@cell2000.net
URL: www.cell2000.net/cpc

Contracting Opportunities Center
Southwestern College Foundation
3443 Camino Del Rio South, Suite 116
San Diego, CA 92108-3913
Point of Contact: J. Gunnar Schalin
Phone: 619-285-7020 Fax: 619-285-7030
E-Mail: sdcoc@pacbell.net
URL: home.pacbell.net/sdcoc

West Valley-Mission Community College District
Calptac/Economic Development Institute
14000 Fruitvale Ave.
Saratoga, CA 95070-5698
Point of Contact: Dr. Fred Prochaska
Phone: 408-741-2095

COLORADO
No PTA awarded in this state

CONNECTICUT
Southeastern Connecticut Enterprise Region (seCTer)
190 Governor Winthrop Blvd.\Suite 300
New London, CT 06320
Point of Contact: Arlene M. Vogel
Phone: 860 701-6056 or 1-888-6-secter Fax: 860-437-4662
E-mail: avogel@secter.org
Web Site: www.secter.org/ctptap.html

DELAWARE
University of Delaware
Small Business Development Center
Office of the Vice Provost for Research
Newark, DE 19716
Point of Contact: Geraldine Hobbs
Phone: 302-831-2136

DISTRICT OF COLUMBIA
No PTA awarded in this state

FLORIDA
University of West Florida
Florida PTA Program

19 W Garden St Ste 300
Pensacola, FL 32501
Point of Contact: Laura Subel
Phone: 850-595-6066 Fax: 850-595-6070
E-Mail: lsubel@uwf.edu

GEORGIA

Georgia Tech Research Corporation
Ga Institute of Technology
400 Tenth St Crb Rm 246
Atlanta, GA 30332-0420
Point of Contact: Zack Osborne
Phone: 912-953-1460 Fax: 912-953-3169
Web Site: http://www.edi.gatech.edu/gtpac/

HAWAII

No PTA awarded in this state

IDAHO

Idaho Department of Commerce
State of Idaho
700 West State Street
Boise, ID 83720-0093
Point of Contact: Larry Demirelli
Phone: 208-334-2470 Fax: 208-334-2631

ILLINOIS

State of Illinois
Dept of Commerce & Com Affairs
620 E Adams St Third Fl
Springfield, IL 62701
Point of Contact: Lois Van Meter
Phone: 217-557-1823 Fax: 217-785-6328
E-MAIL: ivanmete@commerce.state.il.us
Web Site: www.commerce.state.il.us

INDIANA

Indiana Small Business Development Corporation
Govt Marketing Asst Grp
One North Capitol Ave Ste 1275
Indianapolis, IN 46204-2026
Point of Contact: Judith A Jerome

Phone: 317-264-5600 Fax: 317-264-2806
Web Site: www.isbdcorp.org

Partners In Contracting Corporation
PTA Ctr
6100 Southport Road
Portage, IN 46368
Point of Contact: KATHY Deguilio-FOX
Phone: 219-762-8644 Fax: 219-763-1513

IOWA

Iowa State University of Science & Technology
Center for Industrial Research & Service
213 Beardshear Hall
Ames, IA 50011
Point of Contact: Bruce Coney
Phone: 515-242-4888 Fax: 515-242-4893
E-Mail: bruce.coney@ided.state.ia.us
Web Site: www.state.ia.us/sbro/ptac.htm

KANSAS

No PTA awarded in this state, but covered in part by Missouri program.

KENTUCKY

Kentucky Cabinet for Economic Development
Dept of Community Development
500 Mero St
22nd Fl Capital Plaza Tower
Frankfort, KY 40601
Point of Contact: James A. Kurz
Phone: 800-838-3266 Fax: 502-564-5932
E-mail: jkurz@mail.state.ky.us
Web Site: www.think-ky.com

LOUISIANA

Louisiana Productivity Center
University of Southwestern La.
PO Box 44172 241 E Lewis St
Lafayette, LA 70504-4172
Point of Contact: Sherrie Mullins
Phone: 318-482-6767 Fax: 318-262-5472
E-mail:sbm3321@usl.edu

Northwest Louisiana Government Procurement Center
Shreveport COC
400 Edwards St PO Box 20074
Shreveport, LA 71120-0074
Point of Contact: Kelly Ford
Phone: 318-677-2529 Fax: 318-677-2534
E-mail:kmford@iamerica.net

MAINE

Eastern Maine Development Corporation
Market Dev Ctr
One Cumberland Pl Ste 300/PO Box 2579
Bangor, ME 04402-2579
Point of Contact: Michael Robinson
Phone: 207-942-6389 Fax: 207-942-3548
E-mail: mrobinson@emdc.org
Web Site: www.mdcme.org

MARYLAND

Tri County Council for Western Maryland Inc
111 S George St
Cumberland, MD 21502
Point of Contact: Paul Riley
E-mail:priley1@mindspring.com
Phone: 301-777-2158 Fax: 301-777-2495

MASSACHUSETTS

University of Mass Amherst
MSBDC School of Mgmt
C/O Grant & Contract/408 Goodell
Amherst, MA 01003
Point of Contact: Maggie Vidrine
Phone: 413-545-6303

MICHIGAN

Genesee County Metropolitan Planning Commission
PTA Center
1101 Beach Street Room 223
Flint, MI 48502-1470
Point of Contact: Shelia A. Auten
Phone: 810-257-3010 Fax: 810-257-3185

The Enterprise Group of Jackson, Inc.
414 N Jackson St
Jackson, MI 49201
Point of Contact: Pennie Kay Southwell
Phone: 517-788-4680

West Michigan University
Business Development Bureau
346 West Michigan Avenue
Kalamazoo, MI 49007-3737
Point of Contact: Michael Black
Phone: 616-381-2977X3242 Fax: 616-343-1151
E-mail: swmitac@iserv.net

Schoolcraft College
18600 Haggerty Road
Livonia, MI 48152-2696
Point of Contact: Amy Reid
Phone: 734-462-4400X5309 Fax: 734-462-4439
E-Mail: 2382@softshare.com
Web Site: http://www.schoolcraft.cc.mi.us

Downriver Community Conference
Economic Development
15100 Northline
Southgate, MI 48195
Point of Contact: Paula Boase
Phone: 734-281-0700X129 Fax: 734-281-3418

Northwest Michigan Council of Governments
PTA Ctr
2194 Dendrinos Dr PO Box 506
Traverse City, MI 49685-0506
Point of Contact: James F. Haslinger
Phone: 231-929-5036 Fax: 231-929-5042
E-mail: jhasling@nwm.cog.mi.us

Warren, Center Line, Sterling Heights Chamber of Commerce
30500 Van Dyke Ave Ste 118
Warren, MI 48093
Point of Contact: Janet E. Masi
Phone: 810-751-3939 Fax: 810-751-3995
E-mail: jmasi@wcschamber.com
Web Site: www.michigantac.org

West Central Michigan Employment & Training Consortium
PTA Ctr
110 Elm St
Big Rapids, MI 49307
Point of Contact: Pamela Vanderlaan
Phone: 616-796-4891 Fax: 616-796-8316

MINNESOTA

Minnesota Project Innovation Inc
Procurement Technical Assistance Center
100 Mill Place
111 Third Ave South
Minneapolis, MN 55401-2551
Point of Contact: George Johnson
Phone: 612-347-6745 Fax: 612-349-2603
E-Mail: gjohnson@mpi.org
Web Site: http://www.mpi.org

MISSISSIPPI

Mississippi Contract Procurement Center Inc
1636 Popps Ferry Road, Suite 229
Biloxi, MS 39532
Point of Contact: Richard L. Speights
Phone: 228-396-1288 Fax: 228-396-2520
E-mail: mprogoff@aol.com
Web Site: www.mscpc.com

MISSOURI

Missouri Southern State College
3950 E Newman Rd
Joplin, MO 64801-1595
Point of Contact: Terri Bennett
Phone: 417-625-3001 Fax: 417-625-9782

The Curators of the University Of Missouri
Outreach & University Extension
310 Jesse Hall
Columbia, MO 65211
Point of Contact: Morris Hudson
Phone: 573-882-3597 Fax: 573-884-4297

MONTANA

Big Sky Economic Development Authority
222 North, 32 Street
Billings, MT 59101-1911
Point of Contact: Maureen Jewell
Phone: 406-256-6871 Fax: 406-256-6877
E-Mail: jewell@bigskyeda.org

NEBRASKA

Board of Regents of the University Of Nebraska
Nebraska Bus Development Ctr
1313 Farnam Street Suite 132
Omaha, NE 68182-0210
Point of Contact: Michael Hall
Phone: 402-595-3511 Fax: 402-595-3832
E-Mail: mh74736@alltell.net

NEVADA

State of Nevada
Commission on Econ Dev
5151 South Carson St
Carson City, NV 89701
Point of Contact: ROGER TOKARZ
Phone: 702-687-1813 Fax: 702-687-4450
E-Mail: cedpop@bizopp.state.nv.us

NEW HAMPSHIRE

State of New Hampshire
Ofc of Bus & Industrial Dev
PO Box 1856 172 Pembroke Rd
Concord, NH 03302-1856
Point of Contact: Joseph Flynn
Phone: 603-271-2591 Fax: 603-271-6784
E-mail: j_flynn@dred.state.nh.us
Web Site: www.ded.state.nh.us/obid/ptac

NEW JERSEY

Foundation at New Jersey Institute of Technology
PTA Center
240 Martin Luther King Boulevard
Newark, NJ 07102

Point of Contact: Dolcey Chaplin
Phone: 973-596-3105 Fax: 973-596-5806
E-mail chaplin@admin.njit.edu
Web Site: http://www.njit.edu/dptac/

Union County Economic Development Corporation
PTA Program
1085 Morris Ave Ste 531 Lib Hall Center
Union, NJ 07083
Point of Contact: John Fedkenheuer
Phone: 908-527-1166 Fax: 908-527-1207
E-mail johnf@ucedc.com
Web Site: http://www.ucedc.com

NEW MEXICO

State of New Mexico General Services Department
Procurement Assist Prog
1100 St Francis Dr Rm 2006
Santa Fe, NM 87503
Point of Contact: Charles Marquez
Phone: 505-827-0425 Fax: 505-827-0499
E-Mail: cmarquez@state.nm.us

NEW YORK

New York City Department of Business Services
Procurement Outreach Prog
110 William St 2nd Floor
New York, NY 10038
Point of Contact: Gordon Richards
Phone: 212-513-6472 Fax: 212-618-8899

Laguardia Community College/CUNY
Adult & Continuing Education
31-10 Thomson Avenue
Long Island City, NY 11101
Point of Contact: Judith L. McGaughey
Phone: 718-482-5300

Rockland Economic Development Corporation
Procurement
One Blue Hill Plaza Suite 1110
Pearl River, NY 10965-1575

Point of Contact: Roberta Rodriguez
Phone: 914-735-7040 Fax: 914-735-5736

Long Island Development Corporation
PTA Program
255 Executive Drive Suite 400
Plainview, NY 11803
Point of Contact: Solomon Soskin
Phone: 516-349-7800 Fax: 516-349-7881
E-mail: gov-contracts@lidc.org
Web Site: http://www.lidc.org

South Bronx Overall Economic Development Corporation
370 E 149th St
Bronx, NY 10455
Point of Contact: Dina Terry
Phone: 718-292-3113 Fax: 718-292-3115

Cattaraugus County
Dept of Econ Dev, Plan & Tour
303 Court St
Little Valley, NY 14755
Point of Contact: Thomas Livak
Phone: 716-938-9111 ext 307 Fax: 716-938-9431

NORTH CAROLINA

University of North Carolina at Chapel Hill
Small Bus & Tech Dev Ctr
Rm 300 Bynum Hall
Chapel Hill, NC 27599-4100
Point of Contact: Robert Truex
Phone: 919-715-7272 Fax: 919-715-7777
E-Mail: rtruex@sbtdc.org

NORTH DAKOTA

No PTA awarded in this state

OHIO

Lawrence Economic Development Corporation
Procure Outreach Ctr
216 Collins Ave / PO Box 488
South Point, OH 45680-0488
Point of Contact: Connie S. Freeman

Phone: 740-377-4550 Fax: 740-377-2091
E Mail: procure@zoomnet.net
Web Site: http://www.zoomnet.net/~procure/

Ohio Department Of Development
77 South High Street, 28th Floor/P. O. Box 1001
Columbus, OH 43216-1001
Point of Contact: Karen Shauri
Phone: 614-466-2711

Mahoning Valley Economic Development Corporation
4319 Belmont Avenue
Youngstown, OH 44505-1005
Point of Contact: Stephen J. Danyi
Phone: 330-759-3668

OKLAHOMA

Tribal Government Institute
421 East Comanche, Suite B
Norman, OK 73071
Point of Contact: Roy Robert Gann, Jr.
Phone: 405-329-5542 Fax: 405-329-5543

Oklahoma Department Of Vocational & Technical Education
Ok Bid Assistance Network
1500 W Seventh Ave
Stillwater, OK 74074-4364
Point of Contact: Guy M. Thomas
Phone: 405-743-6836 Fax: 405-743-6821
E-Mail: gthom@okvotech.org
Web Site: http://www.okvotech.org/business/oban/obanbeg.htm

OREGON

The Organization for Economic Initiatives
Govt Con Acquisition Prog
1144 Gateway Loop Suite 203
Springfield, OR 97477
Point of Contact: Jan Hurt
Phone: 541-736-1088 Fax: 541-736-1090

PENNSYLVANIA

NW Pennsylvania Regional Planning and Development Commission
395 Seneca Street

Oil City, PA 16301
Point of Contact: Richard A. Mihalic
Phone: 814 677-4800 Fax: 814-677-7663
E-Mail: nwpaptac@nwplan.org

Mon-Valley Renaissance
Ca Univ of Pa
250 University Ave
California, PA 15419
Point of Contact: Deborah S. Wojcik
Phone: 724-938-5881 Fax: 724-938-4575
E-Mail: wojcik@cup.edu

Southern Alleghenies Planning And Development Commission
Economic/Community Development
541 58th Street
Altoona, PA 16602
Point of Contact: Daniel R. Shade
Phone: 814-949-6528

Indiana University of Pennsylvania
650 South 13th Street/ Eberly College of Business
Indiana, PA 15705-1087
Point of Contact: Ron Moreau
Phone: 724-357-7824

Johnstown Area Regional Industries
Defense PAC
111 Market St
Johnstown, PA 15901
Point of Contact: Robert J. Murphy
Phone: 814-539-4951 Fax: 814-535-8677

Seda Council Of Governments
R R 1 Box 372
Lewisburg, PA 17837
Point of Contact: Chris Wilusz
Phone: 570-524-4491 Fax: 570-524-9190
E-Mail: sedapta@seda-cog.org
Web Site: http://www.seda-cog.org

University of Pennsylvania — Wharton
SE-PA PTAP
133 S 36th St Mezzanine Floor University of Philadelphia

Philadelphia, PA 19104-3246
Point of Contact: M. Clyde Stoltzfus
Phone: 215-898-1219 Fax: 215-573-2135

Economic Development Council of Northeast Pennsylvania
Local Dev District
1151 Oak St
Pittston, PA 18640
Point of Contact: David Kern
Phone: 570-655-5581
Fax: 570-654-5137

PUERTO RICO

Commonwealth of Puerto Rico
Econ Dev Admin
355 Roosevelt Ave
Hato Rey PR 00918
Point of Contact: Hilda Yunen
Phone: 787-753-6861 Fax: 787-751-6239

RHODE ISLAND

Rhode Island Development Corporation
Business Expansion Division
One West Exchange Street
Providence, RI 02903
Point of Contact: Michael H. Cunningham
Phone: 401-277-2601 Fax: 401-277-2102
E-Mail: mcunning@riedc.com

SOUTH CAROLINA

University of South Carolina
Frank L. Roddey Sbdc of Sc
College of Bus Admin
Columbia, SC 29208
Point of Contact: John M. Lenti
Phone: 803-777-4907 Fax: 803-777-4403

SOUTH DAKOTA

No PTA awarded in this state

TENNESSEE

Center For Industrial Services

Univ of Tennessee
226 Capitol Blvd Bldg Ste 606
Nashville, TN 37219-1804
Point of Contact: Becky Peterson
Phone: 615-532-4906 Fax: 615-532-4937

TEXAS

San Antonio Procurement Outreach Program
Econ Development Dept
PO Box 839966
San Antonio TX 78283
Point of Contact: Terri L. Williams
Phone: 210-207-3910 Fax: 210-207-3909

Del Mar College
Division of Business
101 Baldwin and Ayers
Corpus Christi, TX 78401
Point of Contact: Ms. Anne Matula
Phone: 361-698-1401

Angelina College Procurement Assistance Center
PO Box 1768
Lufkin, TX 75902-1768
Point of Contact: Thomas E. Brewer Jr.
Phone: 409-633-5424 Fax: 409-633-5478
E-Mail: acpac@lcc.net
Toll Free: 1-888-326-5223
Web Site: http://www.oecrc.org/acpac/

University of Texas at Brownsville/TSC
Center for Bus and Econ Dev
1600 E Elizabeth Street
Brownsville, TX 78520
Point of Contact: Rosalie Manzano
Phone: 956-548-8713 Fax: 956-548-8717
E-Mail: VPTAC@utb1.utb.edu

Texas Technical University
College of Bus Admin
203 Holder
Lubbock, TX 79409-1035
Point of Contact: Otilo Castellano
Phone: 806-745-1637 Fax: 806-745-6207

El Paso Community College
Resource Development
PO Box 20500
El Paso, TX 79998
Point of Contact: Frank Delgado
Phone: 915-831-4405 Fax: 915-831-4420

University of Texas at Arlington
Automation & Robotics Rsch Ins
Ofc of Pres Box 19125
Arlington, TX 76019
Point of Contact: Rogerio Flores
Phone: 817-272-5978 Fax: 817-272-5952

Panhandle Regional Planning Commission
Econ Dev Unit
PO Box 9257
Amarillo, TX 79105-9257
Point of Contact: Doug Nelson
Phone: 806-372-3381 Fax: 806-373-3268

Univ of Houston
TIPS (Texas Information Procurement Service)
2302 Fannin Suite 200
Houston, TX 77202
Point of Contact: Carey Joan White
Phone: 713 752-8466 Fax: 713-756-1515

UTAH

Utah Department of Community & Economic Development
Utah Procurement Technical Assistance Center (UPTAC)
324 South State St Ste 504
Salt Lake City, UT 84111
Point of Contact: Johnny C. Bryan
Phone: 801-538-8791 Fax: 801-538-8825

VERMONT

State of Vermont
Dept of Econ Development
National Life Building Drawer 20
Montpelier, VT 05609
Point of Contact: Greg Lawson
Phone: 802-828-5237 Fax: 802-828-3258

VIRGINIA

George Mason University
Entrepreneurship Ctr
4400 University Dr
Fairfax, VA 22030
Point of Contact: James Regan
Phone: 703-277-7750 Fax: 703-352-8195
E-Mail: ptap@gmu.edu
Web Site: www.gmu.edu/gmu/PTAP

Crater Planning District Commission
Crater Procurement Asst Ctr
1964 Wakefield St PO Box 1808
Petersburg, VA 23805
Point of Contact: John Fedkenheuer
Phone: 804-861-1667 Fax: 804-732-8972
E-Mail: jfedkenheuer@cpd.state.va.us
Web Site: www.cretepdc.state.va.us/PACmain.htm

Southwest Virginia Community College
Economic Development Div
PO Box SVCC
Richlands, VA 24641
Point of Contact: Glenda D. Calver
Phone: 540-964-7334 Fax: 540-964-7575
Web Site: www.sw.cc.va.us/pac.html

WASHINGTON

Economic Development Council of Snohomish County
728 134th Street SW
Building A, Ste 219
Everett, WA 98204
Point of Contact: Brent C. Helm
Phone: 425-743-4567 Fax: 425-745-5563
E-Mail: ptac@snoedc.org
Web Site: www.snoedc.org/patc.html

WEST VIRGINIA

Regional Contracting Assistance Center Inc
1116 Smith St Ste 202
Charleston, WV 25301
Point of Contact: R. Conley Salyer

Phone: 304-344-2546 Fax: 304-344-2574
Web Site: http://www.rcacwv.com

Mid-Ohio Valley Regional Council
PTA Ctr
PO Box 5528
Vienna, WV 26105
Point of Contact: Belinda Sheridan
Phone: 304-428-6889 Fax: 304-428-6891
E-Mail: ptac@access.mountain.net

WISCONSIN

Madison Area Technical College
SB PAC
211 North Carroll St
Madison, WI 53703
Point of Contact: Denise Kornetzke
Phone: 608-258-2350 Fax: 608-258-2329
Web Site: http://bpac.madison.tec.wi.us

Wisconsin Procurement Institute, Inc.
756 N Milwaukee St
Milwaukee, WI 53202
Point of Contact: Ms. Aina Vilumsons
Phone: 414-443-9744 Fax: 414-443-1122
E-Mail: wispro@execpc.com

WYOMING

University Of Wyoming
Wyoming Hall, Room 414
P. O. Box 3922
Laramie, WY 82071
Point of Contact: Diane Wolverton
Phone: (307) 766-3505

Federal Acquisition Regulation Outline

The following is the Table of Contents of the FAR, the "Bible" for federal procurement. By reviewing it, you can see that the regulations contained in the FAR are organized and presented in a way that will help you quickly locate the specific section you need to get the answer to your question.

Federal Acquisition Regulation
Table of Contents

Part 10 — Market Research

Part 11 — Describing Agency Needs

Part 12 — Acquisition of Commercial Items

FAR   Parts 13 - 18   Contracting Methods, Contract Types

Subchapter C   Contracting Methods and Contract Types

Part 13 — Simplified Acquisition Procedures

Part 14 — Sealed Bidding

Part 15 — Contracting by Negotiation

Part 16 — Types of Contracts

Part 17 — Special Contracting Methods

Part 18 — (Reserved)

FAR   Parts 19 - 26   Socioeconomic Programs

Subchapter D   Socioeconomic Programs

Part 19 — Small Business Programs

Part 20 — (Reserved)

Part 21 — (Reserved)

Part 22 — Application of Labor Laws to Government Acquisitions

Part 23 — Environment, Conservation, Occupational Safety, and Drug-Free Workplace

Part 24 — Protection of Privacy and Freedom of Information

Part 25 — Foreign Acquisition

Part 26 — Other Socioeconomic Programs

FAR   Parts 27 - 41   General Requirements, Special Categories

Subchapter E   General Contracting Requirements

Part 27 — Patents, Data, and Copyrights

Part 28 — Bonds and Insurance

Part 29 — Taxes

Part 30 — Cost Accounting Standards

Part 31 — Contract Price Principles and Procedures

Part 32 — Contract Financing

Part 33 — Protests, Disputes, and Appeals

Subchapter F   Special Categories Of Contracting

Part 34 — Major System Acquisition

Part 35 — Research and Development Contracting

Part 36 — Construction and Architect-Engineering Contracts

Part 37 — Service Contracting

Part 38 — Federal Supply Schedule Contracting

Part 39 — Acquisition of Information Resources

Part 40 — (Reserved)

Part 41 — Acquisition of Utility Services

FAR   Parts 42 - 51   Contract Management

Subchapter G   Contract Management

Part 42 — Contract Administration

Part 43 — Contract Modifications

Part 44 — Subcontracting Policies and Procedures

Part 45 — Government Property

Part 46 — Quality Assurance

Part 47 — Transportation

Part 48 — Value Engineering

Part 49 — Termination of Contracts

Part 50 — Extraordinary Contractual Actions

Part 51 — Use of Government Sources by Contractors

Federal Acquisition Regulation Outline

Common Contracting Forms

Following are the forms most commonly used in the federal procurement process.

Standard Form 18

REQUEST FOR QUOTATION *(THIS IS NOT AN ORDER)*		THIS RFQ ☐ IS ☐ IS NOT A SMALL BUSINESS SET-ASIDE		PAGE	OF	PAGES

1. REQUEST NO.	2. DATE ISSUED	3. REQUISITION/PURCHASE REQUEST NO.	4. CERT. FOR NAT. DEF. UNDER BDSA REG. 2 AND/OR DMS REG. 1	RATING

5a. ISSUED BY	6. DELIVER BY *(Date)*

5b. FOR INFORMATION CALL *(NO COLLECT CALLS)*

NAME	TELEPHONE NUMBER		7. DELIVERY ☐ FOB DESTINATION ☐ OTHER *(See Schedule)*
	AREA CODE	NUMBER	9. DESTINATION
			a. NAME OF CONSIGNEE

8. TO:

a. NAME	b. COMPANY	b. STREET ADDRESS
c. STREET ADDRESS		c. CITY
d. CITY	e. STATE	f. ZIP CODE	d. STATE	e. ZIP CODE

10. PLEASE FURNISH QUOTATIONS TO THE ISSUING OFICE IN BLOCK 5a ON OR BEFORE CLOSE OF BUSINESS *(Date)*	IMPORTANT: This is a request for information, and quotations furnished are not officers. If you are unable to quote, please so indicate on this form and return it to the address in Block 5a. This request does not commit the Government to pay any costs incurred in the preparation of the submission of this quotation or to contract for supplies or service. Supplies are of domestic origin unless otherwise indicated by quoter. Any representations and/or certifications attached to this Request for Quotation must be completed by the quoter.

11. SCHEDULE *(Include applicable Federal, State and local taxes)*

ITEM NO.	SUPPLIES/ SERVICES	QUANTITY	UNIT	UNIT PRICE	AMOUNT
(a)	(b)	(c)	(d)	(e)	(f)

12. DISCOUNT FOR PROMPT PAYMENT	a. 10 CALENDAR DAYS (%)	b. 20 CALENDAR DAYS (%)	c. 30 CALENDAR DAYS (%)	d. CALENDAR DAYS	
				NUMBER	PERCENTAGE

NOTE: Additional provisions and representations ☐ are ☐ are not attached.

13. NAME AND ADDRESS OF QUOTER	14. SIGNATURE OF PERSON AUTHORIZED TO SIGN QUOTATION	15. DATE OF QUOTATION
a. NAME OF QUOTER		
b. STREET ADDRESS	16. SIGNER	
	a. NAME *(Type or print)*	b. TELEPHONE
c. COUNTY		AREA CODE
d. CITY	e. STATE	f. ZIP CODE	c. TITLE *(Type or print)*	NUMBER

AUTHORIZED FOR LOCAL REPRODUCTION Previous edition not usable	FormFlow/Delrina Inc.	**STANDARD FORM 18** (REV. 6-95) Prescribed by GSA-FAR (48 CFR) 53.215-1(a)

Standard Form 26

AWARD/CONTRACT	1. THIS CONTRACT IS A RATED ORDER UNDER DPAS (15 CFR 350)	RATING	PAGE	OF	PAGES

2. CONTRACT (Proc. Inst. Ident.) NO.	3. EFFECTIVE DATE	4. REQUISITION/PURCHASE REQUEST/PROJECT NO.

5. ISSUED BY	CODE	6. ADMINISTERED BY (If other than Item 5)	CODE

7. NAME AND ADDRESS OF CONTRACTOR (No., street, county, State and ZIP Code)

8. DELIVERY

☐ FOB ORIGIN   ☐ OTHER (See below)

9. DISCOUNT FOR PROMPT PAYMENT

10. SUBMIT INVOICES (4 copies unless otherwise specified) TO THE ADDRESS SHOWN IN   ITEM

CODE		FACILITY CODE	

11. SHIP TO/MARK FOR	CODE	12. PAYMENT WILL BE MADE BY	CODE

13. AUTHORITY FOR USING OTHER THAN FULL AND OPEN COMPETITION:	14. ACCOUNTING AND APPROPRIATION DATA

☐ 10 U.S.C. 2304(c) (   )   ☐ 41 U.S.C. 253(c) (   )

15A. ITEM NO.	15B. SUPPLIES/SERVICES	15C. QUANTITY	15D. UNIT	15E. UNIT PRICE	15F. AMOUNT

15G. TOTAL AMOUNT OF CONTRACT ► $

16. TABLE OF CONTENTS

(X)	SEC.	DESCRIPTION	PAGE(S)	(X)	SEC.	DESCRIPTION	PAGE(S)
		PART I - THE SCHEDULE				**PART II - CONTRACT CLAUSES**	
	A	SOLICITATION/CONTRACT FORM			I	CONTRACT CLAUSES	
	B	SUPPLIES OR SERVICES AND PRICES/COSTS				**PART III - LIST OF DOCUMENTS, EXHIBITS AND OTHER ATTACH.**	
	C	DESCRIPTION/SPECS./WORK STATEMENT			J	LIST OF ATTACHMENTS	
	D	PACKAGING AND MARKING				**PART IV - REPRESENTATIONS AND INSTRUCTIONS**	
	E	INSPECTION AND ACCEPTANCE			K	REPRESENTATIONS, CERTIFICATIONS AND OTHER STATEMENTS OF OFFERORS	
	F	DELIVERIES OR PERFORMANCE					
	G	CONTRACT ADMINISTRATION DATA			L	INSTRS., CONDS., AND NOTICES TO OFFERORS	
	H	SPECIAL CONTRACT REQUIREMENTS			M	EVALUATION FACTORS FOR AWARD	

CONTRACTING OFFICER WILL COMPLETE ITEM 17 OR 18 AS APPLICABLE

17. ☐ CONTRACTOR'S NEGOTIATED AGREEMENT (Contractor is required to sign this document and return _____ copies to issuing office.) Contractor agrees to furnish and deliver all items or perform all the services set forth or otherwise identified above and on any continuation sheets for the consideration stated herein. The rights and obligations of the parties to this contract shall be subject to and governed by the following documents: (a) this award/contract, (b) the solicitation, if any, and (c) such provisions, representations, certifications, and specifications, as are attached or incorporated by reference herein. (Attachments are listedc herein.)

18. ☐ AWARD (Contractor is not required to sign this document.) Your offer on Solicitation Number _____ including the additions or changes made by you which additions or changes are set forth in full above, is hereby accepted as to the items listed above and on any condition sheets. this award consummates the contract which consists of the following documents: (a) the Government's solicitation and your offer, and (b) this award/contract. No further contractual document is necessary.

19A. NAME AND TITLE OF SIGNER (Type or print)	20A. NAME OF CONTRACTING OFFICER

19B. NAME OF CONTRACTOR	19C. DATE SIGNED	20B. UNITED STATES OF AMERICA	20C. DATE SIGNED
BY _____ (Signature of person authorized to sign)		BY _____ (Signature of Contracting Officer)	

NSN 7540-01-152-8069
Previous edition is unusable

STANDARD FORM 26 (REV. 4-85)
Prescribed by GSA - FAR (48 CFR) 53.214(a)

Standard Form 30 (front)

AMENDMENT OF SOLICITATION/MODIFICATION OF CONTRACT		1. CONTRACT ID CODE		PAGE OF PAGES
2. AMENDMENT/MODIFICAITON NO.	3. EFFECTIVE DATE	4. REQUISITION/PURCHASE REQ. NO.		5. PROJECT NO. (If applicble)
6. ISSUED BY CODE		7. ADMINISTERED BY (If other than Item 6)		CODE

8. NAME AND ADDRESS OF CONTRACTOR (No., street, county, State and ZIP Code)	(X)	9A. AMENDMENT OF SOLICIATION NO.
		9B. DATED (SEE ITEM 11)
		10A. MODIFICATION OF CONTRACT/ORDER NO.
		10B. DATED (SEE ITEM 11)
CODE FACILITY CODE		

11. THIS ITEM ONLY APPLIES TO AMENDMENTS OF SOLICITATIONS

☐ The above numbered solicitation is amended as set forth in Item 14. The hour and date specified for receipt of Offers ☐ is extended, ☐ is not extended.

Offers must acknowledge receipt of this amendment prior to the hour and date specified in the solicitation or as amended, by one of the following methods:

(a) By completing items 8 and 15, and returning _____ copies of the amendment; (b) By acknowledging receipt of this amendment on each copy of the offer submitted; or (c) By separate letter or telegram which includes a reference to the solicitation and amendment numbers. FAILURE OF YOUR ACKNOWLEDGMENT TO BE RECEIVED AT THE PLACE DESIGNATED FOR THE RECEIPT OF OFFERS PRIOR TO THE HOUR AND DATE SPECIFIED MAY RESULT IN REJECTION OF YOUR OFFER. If by virtue of this amendment your desire to change an offer already submitted, such change may be made by telegram or letter, provided each telegram or letter makes reference to the solicitation and this amendment, and is received prior to the opening hour and date specified.

12. ACCOUNTING AND APPROPRIATION DATA (If required)

13. THIS ITEM ONLY APPLIES TO MODIFICATION OF CONTRACTS/ORDERS. IT MODIFIES THE CONTRACT/ORDER NO. AS DESCRIBED IN ITEM 14.

CHECK ONE	
	A. THIS CHANGE ORDER IS ISSUED PURSUANT TO: (Specify authority) THE CHANGES SET FORTH IN ITEM 14 ARE MADE IN THE CONTRACT ORDER NO. IN ITEM 10A.
	B. THE ABOVE NUMBERED CONTRACT/ORDER IS MODIFIED TO REFLECT THE ADMINISTRATIVE CHANGES (such as changes in paying office, appropriation date, etc.) SET FORTH IN ITEM 14, PURSUANT TO THE AUTHORITY OF FAR 43.103(b).
	C. THIS SUPPLEMENTAL AGREEMENT IS ENTERED INTO PURSUANT TO AUTHORITY OF:
	D. OTHER (Specify type of modification and authority)

E. IMPORTANT: Contractor ☐ is not, ☐ is required to sign this document and return ——— copies to the issuing office.

14. DESCRIPTION OF AMENDMENT/MODIFICATION (Organized by UCF section headings, including solicitation/contract subject matter where feasible.)

Except as provided herein, all terms and conditions of the document referenced in Item 9A or 10A, as heretofore changed, remains unchanged and in full force and effect.

15A. NAME AND TITLE OF SIGNER (Type or print)	16A. NAME AND TITLE OF CONTRACTING OFFICER (Type or print)	
15B. CONTRACTOR/OFFEROR	16B. UNITED STATES OF AMERICA	16C. DATE SIGNED
(Signature of person authorized to sign) 15C. DATE SIGNED	(Signature of Contracting Officer)	

NSN 7540-01-152-8070
Previous edition unusable

STANDARD FORM 30 (REV. 10-83)
Prescribed by GSA FAR (48 CFR) 53.243

Standard Form 30 (back)

INSTRUCTIONS

Instructions for items other than those that are self-explanatory, are as follows:

(a) Item 1 (Contract ID Code). Insert the contract type identification code that appears in the title block of the contract being modified.

(b) Item 3 (Effective date).

(1) For a solicitation amendment, change order, or administrative change, the effective date shall be the issue date of the amendment, change order, or administrative change.

(2) For a supplemental agreement, the effective date shall be the date agreed to by the contracting parties.

(3) For a modification issued as an initial or confirming notice of termination for the convenience of the Government, the effective date and the modification number of the confirming notice shall be the same as the effective date and modification number of the initial notice.

(4) For a modification converting a termination for default to a termination for the convenience of the Government, the effective date shall be the same as the effective date of the termination for default.

(5) For a modification confirming the contacting officer's determination of the amount due in settlement of a contract termination, the effective date shall be the same as the effective date of the initial decision.

(c) Item 6 (Issued By). Insert the name and address of the issuing office. If applicable, insert the appropriate issuing office code in the code block.

(d) Item 8 (Name and Address of Contractor). For modifications to a contract or order, enter the contractor's name, address, and code as shown in the original contract or order, unless changed by this or a previous modification.

(e) Item 9, (Amendment of Solicitation No. - Dated), and 10, (Modification of Contract/Order No. - Dated). Check the appropriate box and in the corresponding blanks insert the number and date of the original solicitation, contract, or order.

(f) Item 12 (Accounting and Appropriation Data). When appropriate, indicate the impact of the modification on each affected accounting classification by inserting one of the following entries.

(1) Accounting classification
Net increase $ _____

(2) Accounting classification _____
Net decrease $ _____

NOTE: If there are changes to multiple accounting classifications that cannot be placed in block 12, insert an asterisk and the words "See continuation sheet".

(g) Item 13. Check the appropriate box to indicate the type of modification. Insert in the corresponding blank the authority under which the modification is issued. Check whether or not contractor must sign this document. (See FAR 43.103.)

(h) Item 14 (Description of Amendment/Modification).

(1) Organize amendments or modifications under the appropriate Uniform Contract Format (UCF) section headings from the applicable solicitation or contract. The UCF table of contents, however, shall not be set forth in this document

(2) Indicate the impact of the modification on the overall total contract price by inserting one of the following entries:

(i) Total contract price increased by $ _____

(ii) Total contract price decreased by $ _____

(iii) Total contract price unchanged.

(3) State reason for modification.

(4) When removing, reinstating, or adding funds, identify the contract items and accounting classifications.

(5) When the SF 30 is used to reflect a determination by the contracting officer of the amount due in settlement of a contract terminated for the convenience of the Government, the entry in Item 14 of the modification may be limited to --

(i) A reference to the letter determination; and

(ii) A statement of the net amount determined to be due in settlement of the contract.

(6) Include subject matter or short title of solicitation/contract where feasible.

(i) Item 16B. The contracting officer's signature is not required on solicitation amendments. The contracting offier's signature is normally affixed last on supplemental agreements.

STANDARD FORM 30 (REV. 10-83) BACK

Standard Form 33

SOLICITATION, OFFER AND AWARD	1. THIS CONTRACT IS A RATED ORDER UNDER DPAS (15 CFR 700)	RATING	PAGE	OF	PAGES

2. CONTRACT NUMBER	3. SOLICITATION NUMBER	4. TYPE OF SOLICITATION	5. DATE ISSUED	6. REQUISITION/PURCHASE NUMBER
		☐ SEALED BID (IFB) ☐ NEGOTIATED (RFP)		

7. ISSUED BY	CODE	8. ADDRESS OFFER TO (If other than Item 7)

NOTE: In sealed bid solicitations "offer" and "offeror" mean "bid" and "bidder".

SOLICITATION

9. Sealed offers in original and _____ copies for furnishing the supplies or services in the Schedule will be received at the place specified in Item 8, or if

handcarried, in the depository located in _____ until _____ local time _____

(Hour)   (Date)

CAUTION - LATE Submissions, Modifications, and Withdrawals: See Section L, Provision No. 52.214-7 or 52.215-1. All offers are subject to all terms and conditions contained in this solicitation.

10. FOR INFORMATION CALL:	A. NAME	B. TELEPHONE (NO COLLECT CALLS)			C. E-MAIL ADDRESS
		AREA CODE	NUMBER	EXT.	

11. TABLE OF CONTENTS

(X)	SEC.	DESCRIPTION	PAGE(S)	(X)	SEC.	DESCRIPTION	PAGE(S)
		PART I - THE SCHEDULE				PART II - CONTRACT CLAUSES	
	A	SOLICITATION/CONTRACT FORM			I	CONTRACT CLAUSES	
	B	SUPPLIES OR SERVICES AND PRICES/COSTS				PART III - LIST OF DOCUMENTS, EXHIBITS AND OTHER ATTACH.	
	C	DESCRIPTION/SPECS./WORK STATEMENT			J	LIST OF ATTACHMENTS	
	D	PACKAGING AND MARKING				PART IV - REPRESENTATIONS AND INSTRUCTIONS	
	E	INSPECTION AND ACCEPTANCE			K	REPRESENTATIONS, CERTIFICATIONS AND OTHER STATEMENTS OF OFFERORS	
	F	DELIVERIES OR PERFORMANCE					
	G	CONTRACT ADMINISTRATION DATA			L	INSTRS., CONDS., AND NOTICES TO OFFERORS	
	H	SPECIAL CONTRACT REQUIREMENTS			M	EVALUATION FACTORS FOR AWARD	

OFFER (Must be fully completed by offeror)

NOTE: Item 12 does not apply if the solicitation includes the provisions at 52.214-16, Minimum Bid Acceptance Period.

12. In compliance with the above, the undersigned agrees, if this offer is accepted within _____ calendar days (60 calendar days unless a different period is inserted by the offeror) from the date for receipt of offers specified above, to furnish any or all items upon which prices are offered at the price set opposite each item, delivered at the designated point(s), within the time specified in the schedule.

13. DISCOUNT FOR PROMPT PAYMENT (See Section I, Clause No. 52.232-8)	10 CALENDAR DAYS (%)	20 CALENDAR DAYS (%)	30 CALENDAR DAYS (%)	CALENDAR DAYS (%)

14. ACKNOWLEDGMENT OF AMEND-MENTS (The offeror acknowledges receipt of amendments to the SOLICITATION for offerors and related documents numbered and dated):	AMENDMENT NO.	DATE	AMENDMENT NO.	DATE

15A. NAME AND ADDRESS OF OFFER-OR	CODE	FACILITY	16. NAME AND TITLE OF PERSON AUTHORIZED TO SIGN OFFER (Type or print)

15B. TELEPHONE NUMBER			15C. CHECK IF REMITTANCE ADDRESS IS ☐ DIFFERENT FROM ABOVE - ENTER SUCH ADDRESS IN SCHEDULE.	17. SIGNATURE	18. OFFER DATE
AREA CODE	NUMBER	EXT.			

AWARD (To be completed by Government)

19. ACCEPTED AS TO ITEMS NUMBERED	20. AMOUNT	21. ACCOUNTING AND APPROPRIATION

22. AUTHORITY FOR USING OTHER THAN FULL AND OPEN COMPETITION: ☐ 10 U.S.C. 2304(c) ( ) ☐ 41 U.S.C. 253(c) ( )	23. SUBMIT INVOICES TO ADDRESS SHOWN IN (4 copies unless otherwise specified)	ITEM

24. ADMINISTERED BY (If other than Item 7)	CODE	25. PAYMENT WILL BE MADE BY	CODE

26. NAME OF CONTRACTING OFFICER (Type or print)	27. UNITED STATES OF AMERICA (Signature of Contracting Officer)	28. AWARD DATE

IMPORTANT - Award will be made on this Form, or on Standard Form 26, or by other authorized official written notice.

AUTHORIZED FOR LOCAL REPRODUCTION
Previous edition is unusable

STANDARD FORM 33 (REV. 9-97)
Prescribed by GSA - FAR (48 CFR) 53.214(c)

Standard Form 129 (front)

SOLICITATION MAILING LIST APPLICATION	1. TYPE OF APPLICATION ☐ INITIAL ☐ REVISION	2. DATE	OMB No.: 9000-0002 Expires: 10/31/97

NOTE: Please complete all items on this form. Insert N/A in items not applicable. See reverse for instruction.

Public reporting burden for this collection of information is estimated to average .58 hours per response, including the time for reviewing instructions, searching existing data sources, gathering and maintaining the data needed, and completing and reviewing the collection of information. Send comments regarding this burden estimate or any other aspect of this collection of information, including suggestions for reducing this burden, to the FAR Secretariat (MVR), Federal Acquisition Policy Division, GSA, Washington, DC 20405.

3. SUBMIT TO

a. FEDERAL AGENCY'S NAME

b. STREET ADDRESS

c. CITY   d. STATE   e. ZIP CODE

4. APPLICANT

a. NAME

b. STREET ADDRESS   c. COUNTY

d. CITY   e. STATE   e. ZIP CODE

5. TYPE OF ORGANIZATION *(Check one)*

☐ INDIVIDUAL   ☐ NON-PROFIT ORGANIZATION

☐ PARTNERSHIP   ☐ CORPORATION, INCORPORATED UNDER THE LAWS OF THE STATE OF:

6. ADDRESS TO WHICH SOLICITATIONS ARE TO BE MAILED *(If different than Item 4)*

a. STREET ADDRESS   b. COUNTY

c. CITY   d. STATE   e. ZIP CODE

7. NAMES OF OFFICERS, OWNERS, OR PARTNERS

a. PRESIDENT   b. VICE PRESIDENT   c. SECRETARY

d. TREASURER   e. OWNERS OR PARTNERS

8. AFFILIATES OF APPLICANT

NAME	LOCATION	NATURE OF AFFILIATION

9. PERSONS AUTHORIZED TO SIGN OFFERS AND CONTRACTS IN YOUR NAME *(Indicate if agent)*

NAME	OFFICIAL CAPACITY	TELEPHONE NUMBER	
		AREA CODE	NUMBER

10. IDENTIFY EQUIPMENT, SUPPLIES, AND/OR SERVICES ON WHICH YOU DESIRE TO MAKE AN OFFER *(See attached Federal Agency's supplemental listing and instruction, if any)*

11a. SIZE OF BUSINESS *(See defintions on reverse)* ☐ SMALL BUSINESS *(If checked, complete Items 11B and 11C)* ☐ OTHER THAN SMALL BUSINESS	11b. AVERAGE NUMBER OF EMPLOYEES *(Including affiliates)* FOR FOUR PRECEDING CALENDAR QUARTERS	11c. AVERAGE ANNUAL SALES OR RECEIPTS FOR PRECEDING THREE FISCAL YEARS $
12. TYPE OF OWNERSHIP *(See definitions on reverse)* *(Not applicable for other than small businesses)* ☐ DISADVANTAGED BUSINESS ☐ WOMAN-OWNED BUSINESS	**13. TYPE OF BUSINESS** *(See definitions on reverse)* ☐ MANUFACTURER OR PRODUCER ☐ SERVICE ESTABLISHMENT ☐ CONSTRUCTION CONCERN ☐ RESEARCH AND DEVELOPMENT	☐ SURPLUS DEALER
14. DUNS NO. *(If available)*	15. HOW LONG IN PRESENT BUSINESS?	

16. FLOOR SPACE *(SquareFeet/M²)*		**17. NET WORTH**	
a. MANUFACTURING	b. WAREHOUSE	a. DATE	b. AMOUNT $

18. SECURITY CLEARANCE *(If applicable, check highest clearance authorized)*

	FOR	TOP SECRET	SECRET	CONFIDENTIAL	c. NAMES OF AGENCIES GRANTING SECURITY CLEARANCES	d. DATES GRANTED
a.	KEY PERSONNEL					
b.	PLANT ONLY					

The information supplied herein *(including all pages attached)* is correct and neither the applicant nor any person *(or concern)* in any connection with the applicant as a principal or officer, so far as is known, is now debarred or otherwise declared ineligible by any agency of the Federal Government from making offers for furnishing materials, supplies, or services to the Government or any agency thereof.

19a. NAME OF PERSON AUTHORIZED TO SIGN *(Type or print)*	20. SIGNATURE	21. DATE SIGNED
19b. TITLE OF PERSON AUTHORIZED TO SIGN *(Type or print)*		

AUTHORIZED FOR LOCAL REPRODUCTION
Previous edition not usable

STANDARD FORM 129 (REV. 12-96)
Prescribed by GSA - FAR (48 CFR) 53.214(e)

Standard Form 129 (back)

INSTRUCTIONS

Persons or concerns wishing to be added to a particular agency's bidder's mailing list for supplies or services shall file this properly completed Solicitation Mailing List Application, together with such other lists as may be attached to this application form, with each procurement office of the Federal agency with which they desire to do business. If a Federal agency has attached a Supplemental Commodity list with instructions, complete the application as instructed. Otherwise, identify in Item 10 the equipment, supplies, and/or services on which you desire to bid. (Provide Federal Supply Class or Standard Industrial Classification codes, if available.) The application shall be submitted and signed by the principal as distinguished from an agent, however constituted.

After placement on the bidder's mailing list of an agency, your failure to respond (submission of bid, or notice in writing, that you are unable to bid on that particular transaction but wish to remain on the active bidder's mailing list for that particular item) to solicitations will be understood by the agency to indicate lack of interest and concurrence in the removal of your name from the purchasing activity's solicitation mailing for items concerned.

SIZE OF BUSINESS DEFINITIONS
(See Item 11A.)

a.   Small business concern - A small business concern for the purpose of Government procurement is a concern, including its affiliates, which is independently owned and operated, is not dominant in the field of operation in which it is competing for Government contracts, and can further qualify under the criteria concerning number of employees, average annual receipts, or the other criteria, as prescribed by the Small Business Administration. (See Code of Federal Regulations, Title 13, Part 121, as amended, which contains detailed industry definitions and related procedures.)

b. Affiliates - Business concerns are affiliates of each other when either directly or indirectly (i) one concern controls or has the power to control the other, or (ii) a third party controls or has the power to control both. In determining whether concerns are independently owned and operated and whether or not affiliation exists, consideration is given to all appropriate factors including common ownership, common management, and contractual relationship. (See Items 8 and 11A.)

c.   Number of employees - (Item 11B) In connection with the determination of small business status, "number of employees" means the average employment of any concern, including the employees of its domestic and foreign affiliates, based on the number of persons employed on a full-time, part-time, temporary or other basis during each of the pay periods of the preceding 12 months. If a concern has not been in existence for 12 months, "number of employees" means the average employment of such concern and its affiliates during the period that such concern has been in existence based on the number of persons employed during each of the pay periods of the period that such concern has been in business.

TYPE OF OWNERSHIP DEFINITIONS
(See Item 12.)

a.   "Disadvantaged business concern" - means any business concern (1) which is at least 51 percent owned by one or more socially and economically disadvantaged individuals; or, in the case of any publicly owned business, at least 51 percent of the stock of which is owned by one or more socially and economically disadvantaged individuals; and (2) whose management and daily business operations are controlled by one or more of such individuals.

b. "Women-owned business" - means a business that is at least 51 percent owned by a woman or women who are U.S. citizens and who also control and operate the business.

TYPE OF BUSINESS DEFINITIONS
(See Item 13.)

a.   "Manufacturer or producer" - means a person (or concern) owning, operating, or maintaining a store, warehouse, or other establishment that produces, on the premises, the materials, supplies, articles or equipment of the general character of those listed in Item 10, or in the Federal Agency's Supplemental Commodity List, if attached.

b. "Service establishment" - means a concern (or person) which owns, operates, or maintains any type of business which is principally engaged in the furnishing of nonpersonal services, such as (but not limited to) repairing, cleaning, redecorating, or rental of personal property, including the furnishing of necessary repair parts or other supplies as a part of the services performed.

• COMMERCE BUSINESS DAILY - The Commerce Business Daily, published by the Department of Commerce, contains information concerning proposed procurements, sales, and contract awards, For further information concerning this publication, contact your local Commerce Field Office.

STANDARD FORM 129 (REV. 12-96) **BACK**

Standard Form 1449 (front)

SOLICITATION/CONTRACT/ORDER FOR COMMERCIAL ITEMS *OFFEROR TO COMPLETE BLOCKS 12, 17, 23, 24, & 30*		1. REQUISITION NUMBER		PAGE 1 OF
2. CONTRACT NO.	3. AWARD/EFFECTIVE DATE	4. ORDER NUMBER	5. SOLICITATION NUMBER	6. SOLICIATION ISSUE DATE

7. FOR SOLICITATION INFORMATION CALL:	a. NAME	b. TELEPHONE NUMBER *(No collect calls)*	8. OFFER DUE DATE/ LOCAL TIME

9. ISSUED BY CODE	10. THIS ACQUISITON IS	11. DELIVERY FOR FOB DESTINATION UNLESS BLOCK IS MARKED	12. DISCOUNT TERMS

10. THIS ACQUISITON IS
- ☐ UNRESTRICTED
- ☐ SET ASIDE: _____ % FOR
  - ☐ SMALL BUSINESS
  - ☐ SMALL DISAV. BUSINESS
  - ☐ 8(A)

SIC:
SIZE STANDARD:

11. DELIVERY FOR FOB DESTINATION UNLESS BLOCK IS MARKED
- ☐ SEE SCHEDULE

☐ 13a. THIS CONTRACT IS A RATED ORDER UNDER DPAS (15 CFR 700)

13b. RATING

14. METHOD OF SOLICITATION
☐ RFQ ☐ IFB ☐ RFP

15. DELIVER TO CODE	16. ADMINISTERED BY CODE

17a. CONTRACTOR/ OFFEROR CODE FACILITY CODE	18a. PAYMENT WILL BE MADE BY CODE

TELEPHONE NO.

☐ 17b. CHECK IF REMITTANCE IS DIFFERENT AND PUT SUCH ADDRESS IN OFFER

18b. SUBMIT INVOICES TO ADDRESS SHOWN IN BLOCK 18a UNLESS BLOCK BELOW IS CHECKED
☐ SEE ADDENDUM

19. ITEM NO.	20. SCHEDULE OF SUPPLIES/SERVICES	21. QUANTITY	22. UNIT	23. UNIT PRICE	24. AMOUNT
	(Attach Additional Sheets as Necessary)				

25. ACCOUNTING AND APPROPRIATION DATA	26. TOTAL AWARD AMOUNT *(For Govt. Use Only)*

☐ 27a. SOLICITATION INCORPORATES BY REFERENCE FAR 52.212-1, 52.212-4. FAR 52.212-3 AND 52.212-5 ARE ATTACHED. ADDENDA ☐ ARE ☐ ARE NOT ATTACHED

☐ 27b. CONTRACT/PURCHASE ORDER INCORPORATES BY REFERENCE FAR 52.212-4. FAR 52.212-5 IS ATTACHED. ADDENDA ☐ ARE ☐ ARE NOT ATTACHED

28. CONTRACTOR IS REQUIRED TO SIGN THIS DOCUMENT AND RETURN _____ COPIES

29. AWARD OF CONTRACT: REFERENCE _____ OFFER

☐ TO ISSUING OFFICE. CONTRACTOR AGREES TO FURNISH AND DELIVER ALL ITEMS SET FORTH OR OTHERWISE IDENTIFIED ABOVE AND ON ANY ADDITIONAL SHEETS SUBJECT TO THE TERMS AND CONDITIONS SPECIFIED HEREIN.

☐ DATED _____. YOUR OFFER ON SOLICITATION (BLOCK 5, INCLUDING ANY ADDITIONS OR CHANGES WHICH ARE SET FORTH HEREIN, IS ACCEPTED AS TO ITEMS:

30a. SIGNATURE OF OFFEROR/CONTRACTOR	31a. UNITED STATES OF AMERICA *(SIGNATURE OF CONTRACTING OFFICER)*

30b. NAME AND TITLE OF SIGNER *(Type or print)*	30c. DATE SIGNED	31b. NAME OF CONTRACTING OFFICER *(Type or pint)*	31c. DATE SIGNED

32a. QUANTITY IN COLUMN 21 HAS BEEN
☐ RECEIVED ☐ INSPECTED ☐ ACCEPTED, AND CONFORMS TO THE CONTRACT, EXCEPT AS NOTED

33. SHIP NUMBER	34. VOUCHER NUMBER	35. AMOUNT VERIFIED CORRECT FOR
☐ PARTIAL ☐ FINAL		

32b. SIGNATURE OF AUTHORIZED GOVT. REPRESENTATIVE	32c. DATE

36. PAYMENT
☐ COMPLETE ☐ PARTIAL ☐ FINAL

37. CHECK NUMBER

38. S/R ACCOUNT NUMBER	39. S/R VOUCHER NUMBER	40. PAID BY

42a. RECEIVED BY *(Print)*

41a. I CERTIFY THIS ACCOUNT IS CORRECT AND PROPER FOR PAYMENT

41b. SIGNATURE AND TITLE OF CERTIFYING OFFICER	41c. DATE	42b. RECEIVED AT *(Location)*

42c. DATE REC'D *(YY/MM/DD)*	42d. TOTAL CONTAINERS

AUTHORIZED FOR LOCAL REPRODUCTION

SEE REVERSE FOR OMB CONTROL NUMBER AND PAPERWORK BURDEN STATEMENT

STANDARD FORM 1449 (10-95)
Prescribed by GSA - FAR (48 CFR) 53.212

Standard Form 1449 (back)

Public reporting burden for this collection of information is estimated to average 45 minutes per response including the time for reviewing instructions, searching existing data sources, gathering and maintaining the data needed, and completing and reviewing the collection of information. Send comments regarding this burden estimate or any other aspect of this collection of information, including suggestions for reducing this burden, to the FAR Secretariat (VRS), Office of Federal Acquisition Policy, GSA Washington, DC 20405.	OMBNO.: 9000-0136 Expires: 09/30/98

STANDARD FORM 1449 (10-95) BACK

Standard Form 254

<table>
<tr>
<td>STANDARD
FORM (SF)
254</td>
<td>Architect-Engineer
and Related Services
Questionnaire</td>
<td>Form Approved
OMB No. 9000-0004</td>
</tr>
</table>

Public reporting burden for this collection of information is estimated to average 1 hour per response, including the time for reviewing instructions, searching existing data sources, gathering and maintaining the data needed, and completing and reviewing the collection of information. Send comments regarding this burden estimate or any other aspect of this collection of information, including suggestions for reducing this burden, to the FAR Secretariat (VRS), Office of Federal Acquisition and Regulatory Policy, GSA, Washington, D.C. 20405; and to the Office of Management and Budget, Paperwork Reduction Project (9000-0004), Washington, D.C. 20503.

Purpose:

The policy of the Federal Government in acquiring architectural, engineering, and related professional services is to encourage firms lawfully engaged in the practice of those professions to submit annually a statement of qualifications and performance data. Standard Form 254, "Architect-Engineer and Related Services Questionnaire," is provided for that purpose. Interested A-E firms (including new, small, and/or minority firms) should complete and file SF 254's with each Federal agency and with appropriate regional or district offices for which the A-E is qualified to perform services. The agency head for each proposed project shall evaluate these qualification resumes, together with any other performance data on file or requested by the agency, in relation to the proposed project. The SF 254 may be used as a basis for selecting firms for discussions, or for screening firms preliminary to inviting submission of additional information.

Definitions:

"Architect-Engineer Services" are defined in Part 36 of the Federal Acquisition Regulation.

"Parent Company" is that firm, company, corporation, association or conglomerate which is the major stockholder or highest tier owner of the firm completing this questionnaire, i.e., Firm A is owned by Firm B which is, in turn, a subsidiary of Corporation C. The "parent company" of Firm A is Corporation C.

"Principals" are those individuals in a firm who possess legal responsibility for its management. They may be owners, partners, corporate offices, associates, administrators, etc.

"Discipline" as used in this questionnaire, refers to the primary technological capability of individuals in the responding firm. Possession of an academic degree, professional registration, certification, or extensive experience in a particular field of practice normally reflects an individual's primary technical discipline.

"Joint Venture" is a collaborative undertaking by two or more firms or individuals for which the participants are both jointly and individually responsible.

"Consultant," as used in this questionnaire, is a highly specialized individual or firm having significant input and responsibility for certain aspects of a project and possessing unusual or unique capabilities for assuring success of the finished work.

"Prime" refers to that firm which may be coordinating the concerted and complementary inputs of several firms, individuals or related services to produce a completed study or facility. The "prime" would normally be regarded as having full responsibility and liability for quality of performance by itself as well as by subcontractor professionals under its jurisdiction.

"Branch Office" is a satellite, or subsidiary extension, of a headquarters office of a company, regardless of any differences in name or legal structure of such a branch due to local or state laws. "Branch offices" are normally subject to the management decisions, bookkeeping, and policies of the main office.

Instructions of Filing (Numbers below correspond to numbers contained in form):

1. Type accurate and complete name of submitting firm, its address, and zip code.

1a. Indicate whether form is being submitted in behalf of a parent firm or a branch office. (Branch office submissions should list only personnel in, and experience of, that office.)

2. Provide date the firm was established under the name shown in question 1.

3. Show date on which form is prepared. All information submitted shall be current and accurate as of this date.

4. Enter type of ownership, or legal structure, of firm (sole proprietor, partnership, corporation, joint venture, etc.).

Check appropriate boxes indicating if firm is (a) a small business concern; (b) a small business concern owned and operated by socially and economically disadvantaged individuals; and (c) Woman-owned (See 48 CFR 19.101 and 52.219-9).

5. Branches of subsidiaries of large or parent companies, or conglomerates, should insert name and address of highest-tier owner.

5a. If present firm is the successor to, or outgrowth of, one or more predecessor firms, show name(s) of former entity(ies) and the year(s) of their original establishment.

6. List not more than two principals from submitting firm who may be contacted by the agency receiving this form. (Different principals may be listed on forms going to another agency.) Listed principals must be empowered to speak for the firm on policy and contractual matters.

7. Beginning with the submitting office, list name, location, total number of personnel, and telephone numbers for all associated or branch offices, (including any headquarters or foreign offices) which provide A-E and related services.

7a. Show total personnel in all offices. (Should be sum of all personnel, all branches.)

8. Show total number of employees, by discipline, in submitting office. (*If form is being submitted by main or headquarters office, firm should list total employees, by discipline, in all offices.) While some personnel may be qualified in several disciplines, each person should be counted only once in accord with his or her primary function. Include clerical personnel as "administrative." Write in any additional disciplines -- sociologists, biologists, etc. -- and number of people in each, in blank spaces.

NSN 7540-01-152-8073
Previous edition not usable

STANDARD FORM 254 (REV. 11-92)

Standard Form 254 (page 2)

STANDARD FORM (SF)
254

Architect-Engineer and Related Services Questionnaire

9. Using chart (below) insert appropriate index number to indicate range of professional services fees received by submitting firm each calendar year for last five years, most recent year first. Fee summaries should be broken down to reflect the fees received each year for (a) work performed directly for the Federal Government (not including grant and loan projects) or as a sub to other professionals performing work directly for the Federal Government; (b) all other domestic work, U.S. and possessions, including Federally-assisted projects, and (c) all other foreign work.

Ranges of Professional Services Fees

INDEX		INDEX	
1.	Less than $100,000	5.	$1 million to $2 million
2.	$100,000 to $250,000	6.	$2 million to $5 million
3.	$250,000 to $500,000	7.	$5 million to $10 million
4.	$500,000 to $1 million	8.	$10 million or greater

10. Select and enter, in numerical sequence, **not more than thirty** (30) "Experience Profile Code" numbers from the listing (next page) which most accurately reflect submitting firm's demonstrated technical capabilities and project experience. **Carefully review list**. (It is recognized some profile codes may be part of other services or projects contained on list; firms are encouraged to select profile codes which best indicate type and scope of services provided on past projects.) For each code number, show total number of projects and gross fees (in thousands) received for profile projects performed by firm during past few years. If firm has one or more capabilities not included on list, insert same in blank spaces at end of list and show numbers in question 10 on the form. In such cases, the filled-in listing **must** accompany the complete SF 254 when submitted to the Federal agencies.

11. Using the "Experience Profile Code" numbers in the same sequence as entered in item 10, give details of at least one recent (within last five years) representative project for each code number, up to a **maximum** of thirty (30) separate projects, or portions of projects, for which firm was responsible. (Project examples may be used more than once to illustrate different services rendered on the same job. Example: a dining hall may be part of an auditorium or educational facility.) Firms which select less than thirty "profile codes" may list two or more project examples (to illustrate specialization) for each code number so long as total of all project examples does not exceed thirty (30). After each code number in question 11, show: (a) whether firm was "P," the prime professional, or "C," a consultant, or "JV," part of a joint venture on that particular project (new firms, in existence less than five (5) years may use the symbol "IE" to indicate "Individual Experience" as opposed to firm experience); (b) provide name and location of the specific project which typifies firm's (or individual's) performance under that code category; (c) give name and address of the owner

of that project (if government agency indicate responsible office); (d) show the estimated construction cost (or other applicable cost) for that portion of the project for which the firm was primarily responsible. (Where no construction was involved, show approximate cost of firm's work); and (e) state year work on that particular project was, or will be, completed.

12. The completed SF 254 should be signed by a principal of the firm, preferably the chief executive officer.

13. Additional data, brochures, photos, etc. should not accompany this form unless specifically requested.

NEW FIRMS (not reorganized or recently-amalgamated firms) are eligible and encouraged to seek work from the Federal Government in connection with performance of projects for which they are qualified. Such firms are encouraged to complete and submit Standard Form 254 to appropriate agencies. Questions on the form dealing with personnel or experience may be answered by citing experience and capabilities of individuals in the firm, based on performance and responsibility while in the employe of others. In so doing, notation of this fact should be made on the form. In question 9, write in "N/A" to indicate "not applicable" for those years prior to firm's organization.

STANDARD FORM 254 PAGE 2 (REV. 11-92)

Standard Form 254 (page 3)

Experience Profile Code Numbers
for use with questions 10 and 11

001	Acoustics; Noise Abatement
002	Aerial Photogrammetry
003	Agricultural Development; Grain Storage; Farm Mechanization
004	Air Pollution Control
005	Airports; Navaids; Airport Lighting; Aircraft Fueling
006	Airports; Terminals & Hangars; Freight Handling
007	Arctic Facilities
008	Auditoriums & Theatres
009	Automation; Controls; Instrumentation
010	Barracks; Dormitories
011	Bridges
012	Cemeteries (Planning & Relocation)
013	Chemical Processing & Storage
014	Churches; Chapels
015	Codes; Standards; Ordinances
016	Cold Storage; Refrigeration; Fast Freeze
017	Commercial Building (low rise); Shopping Centers
018	Communication Systems; TV; Microwave
019	Computer Facilities; Computer Service
020	Conservation and Resource Management
021	Construction Management
022	Corrosion Control; Cathodic Protection; Electrolysis
023	Cost Estimating
024	Dams (Concrete; Arch)
025	Dams (Earth; Rock); Dikes; Levees
026	Desalination (Process & Facilities)
027	Dining Halls; Clubs; Restaurants
028	Ecological & Archeological Investigations
029	Educational Facilities; Classrooms
030	Electronics
031	Elevators; Escalators; People-Movers
032	Energy Conservation; New Energy Sources
033	Environmental Impact Studies; Assessments or Statements
034	Fallout Shelters; Blast-Resistant Design
035	Field Houses; Gyms; Stadiums
036	Fire Protection
037	Fisheries; Fish Ladders
038	Forestry & Forest Products
039	Garages; Vehicle Maintenance Facilities; Parking Decks
040	Gas Systems (Propane; Natural, Etc.)

041	Graphic Design
042	Harbors; Jetties; Piers, Ship Terminal Facilities
043	Heating; Ventilating; Air Conditioning
044	Health Systems Planning
045	Highrise; Air-Rights-Type Buildings
046	Highways; Streets; Airfield Paving Parking Lots
047	Historical Preservation
048	Hospital & Medical Facilities
049	Hotels; Models
050	Housing (Residential, Multi-Family; Apartments; Condominiums)
051	Hydraulics & Pneumatics
052	Industrial Buildings; Manufacturing Plants
053	Industrial Processes; Quality Control
054	Industrial Waste Treatment
055	Interior Design; Space Planning
056	Irrigation; Drainage
057	Judicial and Courtroom Facilities
058	Laboratories; Medical Research Facilities
059	Landscape Architecture
060	Libraries; Museums; Galleries
061	Lighting (Interiors; Display; Theatre, Etc.)
062	Lighting (Exteriors; Streets; Memorials; Athletic Fields, Etc.)
063	Materials Handling Systems; Conveyors; Sorters
064	Metallurgy
065	Microclimatology; Tropical Engineering
066	Military Design Standards
067	Mining & Mineralogy
068	Missile Facilities (Silos; Fuels; Transport)
069	Modular Systems Design; Pre-Fabricated Structures or Components
070	Naval Architecture; Off-Shore Platforms
071	Nuclear Facilities; Nuclear Shielding
072	Office Building; Industrial Parks
073	Oceanographic Engineering
074	Ordnance; Munitions; Special Weapons
075	Petroleum Exploration; Refining
076	Petroleum and Fuel (Storage and Distribution)
077	Pipelines (Cross-Country - Liquid & Gas)
078	Planning (Community, Regional, Areawide and State)
079	Planning (Site, Installation, and Project)
080	Plumbing & Piping Design
081	Pneumatic Structures, Air-Support Buildings
082	Postal Facilities
083	Power Generation, Transmission, Distribution
084	Prisons & Correctional Facilities

085	Product, Machine & Equipment Design
086	Radar; Sonar; Radio & Radar Telescopes
087	Railroad; Rapid Transit
088	Recreation Facilities (Parks, Marinas, Etc.)
089	Rehabilitation (Buildings; Structures; Facilities)
090	Resource Recover; Recycling
091	Radio Frequency Systems & Shieldings
092	Rivers; Canals; Waterways; Flood Control
093	Safety Engineering; Accident Studies; OSHA Studies
094	Security Systems; Intruder & Smoke Detection
095	Seismic Designs & Studies
096	Sewage Collection, Treatment and Disposal
097	Soils & Geologic Studies; Foundations
098	Solar Energy Utilization
099	Solid Wastes; Incineration; Land Fill
100	Special Environments; Clean Rooms. Etc.
101	Structural Design; Special Structures
102	Surveying; Platting; Mapping; Flood Plain Studies
103	Swimming Pools
104	Storm Water Handling & Facilities
105	Telephone Systems (Rural; Mobile; Intercom, Etc.)
106	Testing & Inspection Services
107	Traffic & Transportation Engineering
108	Towers (Self-Supporting & Guyed Systems)
109	Tunnels & Subways
110	Urban Renewals; Community Development
111	Utilities (Gas & Steam)
112	Value Analysis; Life-Cycle Costing
113	Warehouses & Depots
114	Water Resources; Hydrology; Ground Water
115	Water Supply; Treatment and Distribution
116	Wind Tunnels; Research/Testing Facilities Design
117	Zoning; Land Use Studies
201	_____
202	_____
203	_____
204	_____
205	_____

STANDARD FORM 254 PAGE 3 (REV. 11-92)

Standard Form 254 (page 4)

STANDARD FORM (SF) **254** Architect-Engineer and Related Services Questionnaire	1. Firm Name/Business Address:		2. Year Present Firm Established	3. Date Prepared:
			4. Specify type of ownership and check below, if applicable.	
			A. Small Business	
			B. Small Disadvantaged Business	
	1a. Submittal is for ☐ Parent Company ☐ Branch or Subsidiary Office		C. Woman-owned Business	

5. Name of Parent Company, if any:	5a. Former Parent Company Name(s), if any, and Year(s) Established:

6. Names of not more than Two Principals to Contact: Title/Telephone
1)
2)

7. Present Offices: City / State / Telephone / No. Personnel Each Office   7a. Total Personnel _____

8. Personnel by Discipline: (List each person only once, by primary function.)

1111 Administrative	____ Electrical Engineers	____ Oceanographers
1111 Architects	____ Estimators	____ Planners: Urban/Regional
____ Chemical Engineers	____ Geologist	____ Sanitary Engineers
____ Civil Engineers	____ Hydrologists	____ Soils Engineers
____ Construction Inspectors	____ Interior Designers	____ Specification Writers
____ Draftsmen	____ Landscape Architects	____ Structural Engineers
____ Ecologists	____ Mechanical Engineers	____ Surveyors
____ Economists	____ Mining Engineers	____ Transportation Engineers

9. Summary of Professional Services Fees Received: (Insert index number)

Last 5 Years (most recent year first)

19____ 19____ 19____ 19____ 19____

Direct Federal contract work, including overseas ____ ____ ____ ____ ____
All other domestic work ____ ____ ____ ____ ____
All other foreign work* ____ ____ ____ ____ ____

*Firms interested in foreign work, but without such experience, check here: ☐

Ranges of Professional Services Fees
INDEX
1. Less than $100,000
2. $100,000 to $250,000
3. $250,000 to $500,000
4. $500,000 to $1 million
5. $1 million to $2 million
6. $2 million to $5 million
7. $5 million to $10 million
8. $10 million or greater

STANDARD FORM 254 PAGE 4 (REV. 11-92)

Standard Form 254 (page 5)

Profile of Firm's Project Experience, Last 5 Years

Profile Code	Number of Projects	Total Gross Fees (in thousands)	Profile Code	Number of Projects	Total Gross Fees (in thousands)	Profile Code	Number of Projects	Total Gross Fees (in thousands)
1)			11)			21)		
2)			12)			22)		
3)			13)			23)		
4)			14)			24)		
5)			15)			25)		
6)			16)			26)		
7)			17)			27)		
8)			18)			28)		
9)			19)			29)		
10)			20)			30)		

11. Project Examples, Last 5 Years

Profile Code	"P," "C," "JV," or "IE"	Project Name and Location	Owner Name and Address	Cost of Work (in thousands)	Completion Date (Actual or Estimated)
		1			
		2			
		3			
		4			
		5			
		6			
		7			

STANDARD FORM 254 PAGE 5 (REV. 11-92)

Standard Form 254 (page 6)

		8			
		9			
		10			
		11			
		12			
		13			
		14			
		15			
		16			
		17			
		18			
		19			

STANDARD FORM 254 PAGE 6 (REV. 11-92)

Standard Form 254 (page 7)

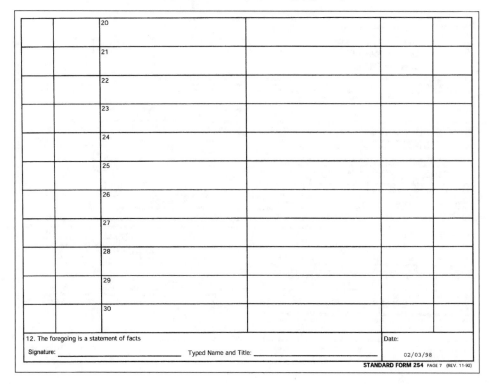

		20			
		21			
		22			
		23			
		24			
		25			
		26			
		27			
		28			
		29			
		30			

12. The foregoing is a statement of facts

Signature: _____   Typed Name and Title: _____

Date:

02/03/98

STANDARD FORM 254 PAGE 7 (REV. 11-92)

Standard Form 255

STANDARD FORM (SF) **255**	**Architect-Engineer and Related Services Questionnaire for Specific Project**	Form Approved OMB No. 9000-0005

Public reporting burden for this collection of information is estimated to average 1.2 hours per response, including the time for reviewing instructions, searching existing data sources, gathering and maintaining the data needed, and completing and reviewing the collection of information. Send comments regarding this burden estimate or any other aspect of this collection of information, including suggestions for reducing this burden, to the FAR Secretariat (VRS), Office of Federal Acquisition and Regulatory Policy, GSA, Washington, D.C. 20405; and to the Office of Management and Budget, Paperwork Reduction Project (9000-0005), Washington, D.C. 20503.

Purpose:

This form is a supplement to the "Architect-Engineer and Related Services Questionnaire" (SF 254). Its purpose is to provide additional information regarding the qualifications of interested firms to undertake a specific Federal A-E project. Firms, or branch offices of firms, submitting this form should enclose (or already have on file with the appropriate office of the agency) a current (within the past year) and accurate copy of the SF 254 for that office.

The procurement official responsible for each proposed project may request submission of the SF 255 "Architect-Engineer and Related Services Questionnaire for Specific Project" in accord with applicable civilian and military procurement regulations and shall evaluate such submissions, as well as related information contained on the Standard Form 254, and any other performance data on file with the agency, and shall select firms for subsequent discussions leading to contract award in conformance with Public Law 92-582. This form should only be filed by an architect-engineer or related services firm when requested to do so by the agency or by a public announcements. Responses should be as complete and accurate as possible, contain data relative to the specific project for which you wish to be considered, and should be provided, by the required due date, to the office specified in the request or public announcement.

This form will be used only for the specified project. Do not refer to this submittal in response to other requests or public announcements.

Definitions:

"Architect-Engineer Services" are defined in Part 36 of the Federal Acquisition Regulation.
"Principals" are those individuals in a firm who possess legal responsibility for its management. They may be owners, partners, corporate officers, associates, administrators, etc.
"Discipline," as used in this questionnaire, refers to the primary technological capability of individuals in the responding firm. Possession of an academic degree, professional registration, certification, or extensive experience in a particular field of practice normally reflects an individual's primary technical discipline.
"Joint Venture" is a collaborative undertaking by two or more firms or individuals for which the participants are both jointly and individually responsible.
"Key Persons, Specialists, and Individual Consultants, " as used in this questionnaire, refer to individuals who will have major project responsibility or will provide unusual or unique capabilities for the project under consideration.

Instructions for Filing (Numbers below correspond to numbers contained in form):

1. Give name and location of the project for which this form is being submitted.
2. Provide appropriated data from the Commerce Business Daily (CBD) identifying the particular project for which this form is being filed.
   2a. Give the date of the Commerce Business Daily in which the project announcement appeared, or indicate "not applicable" (N/A) if the source of the announcement is other than the CBD.
   2b. Indicate Agency identification or contract number as provided in the CBD announcement.
3. Show name and address of the individual or firm (or joint venture) which is submitting this form for the project.
   3a. List the name, title, and telephone number of that principal who will serve as the point of contact. Such an individual must be empowered to speak for the firm on policy and contractual matters and should be familiar with the programs and procedures of the agency to which this form is directed.
   3b. Give the address of the specific office which will have responsibility for performing the announced work.
4. Insert the number of consultant personnel by discipline proposed for subject project on line (A). Insert the number of in-house personnel by discipline proposed for subject project on line (B). While some personnel may be qualified in several disciplines, each person should be counted only once in accord with his or her primary function. Include clerical personnel as "administrative." Write in any additional disciplines -- sociologists, biologists, etc. -- and number of people in each, in blank spaces.
5. Answer only if this form is being submitted by a joint venture of two or more collaborating firms. Show the names and addresses of all individuals or organizations excepted to be included as part of the joint venture and describe their particular areas of anticipated responsibility (ie., technical disciplines, administration, financial, sociological, environment, etc.).
   5a. Indicate, by checking the appropriate box, whether this particular joint venture has worked together on other projects.
Each firm participating in the joint venture should have a Standard Form 254 on file with the contracting office receiving this form. Firms which do not have such forms on file should provide same immediately along with a notation at the top of page 1 of the form regarding their association with this joint venture submittal.

NSN 7540-01-152-8074
Previous edition not usable.

STANDARD FORM 255 (REV. 11-92)
Prescribed by GSA - FAR (48 CFR) 53.236-2(2)

Standard Form 255 (page 2)

STANDARD FORM (SF) **255**	**Architect-Engineer and Related Services Questionnaire for Specific Project**	Standard Form 255 General Services Administration Washington, D.C. 20405

6. If respondent is not a joint venture, but intends to use outside (as opposed to in-house or permanently and formally affiliated) consultants or associates, he should provide names and addresses of all such individuals or firms, as well as their particular areas of technical/professional expertise, as it relates to this project. Existence of previous working relationships should be noted. If more eight than outside consultants or associates are anticipated, attach an additional sheet containing requested information.

7. Regardless of whether respondent is a joint venture or an independent firm, provide brief resumes of key personnel expected to participate on this project. Care should be taken to limit resumes to only those personnel and specialists who will have major project responsibilities. Each resume must include: (a) name of each key person and specialist and his or her title, (b) the project assignment or role which that person will be expected to fulfill in connection with this project, (c) the name of the firm or organization, if any, with whom that individual is presently associated, (d) years of relevant experience with present firm and other firms, (e) the highest academic degree achieved and the discipline covered (if more than one highest degree, such as two Ph.D.'s, list both), the year received and the particular technical/professional discipline which that individual will bring to the project, (f) if registered as an architect, engineer, surveyor, etc., show only the field of registration and the year that such registration was first acquired. If registrered in several states, do not list states, and (g) a synopsis of experience, training, or other qualities which reflect individual's potential contribution to this project. Include such data as: familiarity with Government or agency procedures, similar type of work performed in the past, management abilities, familiarity with the geographic area, relevant foreign language capabilities, etc. Please limit synopsis of experience to directly relevant information.

8. List up to ten projects which demonstrate the firm's or joint venture's competence to perform work similar to that likely to be required on this project. The more recent such projects, the better. Prime consideration will be given to projects which illustrate respondent's capability for performing work similar to that being sought. Required information must include: (a) name and location of project, (b) brief description of type and extent of services provided for each project (submissions by joint ventures should indicate which member of the joint venture was the prime on that particular project and what role it played), (c) name and address of the owner of that project (if Government agency, indicate responsible office), and name and phoone number of individual to contact for reference (preferably the project manager), (d) completion date (actual when available, otherwise estimated), (e) total construction cost of completed project (or where no construction was involved, the approximate cost of your work) and that portion of the cost of the project for which the named firm was/is responsible.

9. List only those projects which the A-E firm or joint venture, or members of the joint venture, are currently performing under direct contract with an agency or department of the Federal Government. Exclude any grant or loan projects being financed by the Federal Government but being performed under contract to other non-Federal Government entities. Information provided under each heading is similar to that requested in the preceding Item 8, except for (d) "Percent Complete." Indicate in this item the percentage of A-E work completed upon filing this form.

10. Through narrative discussion, show reason why the firm or joint venture submitting this questionnaire believes it is especially qualified to undertake the project. Information provided should include, but not be limited to, such data as: specialized equipment available for this work, any awards or recognition received by a firm or individuals for similar work, required security clearances, special approaches or concepts developed by the firm relevant to this project, etc. Respondents may say anything they wish in support of their qualifications. When appropriate, respondents may supplement this proposal with graphic material and photographs which best demonstrate design capabilities of the team proposed for this project.

11. Completed forms should be signed by the chief executive officer of the joint venture (thereby attesting to the concurrence and commitment of all members of the joint venture), or by the architect-engineer principal responsible for the conduct of the work in the event it is awarded to the organization submitting this form. Joint ventures selected for subsequent discussions regarding this project must make available a statement of participation signed by a principal of each member of the joint venture. ALL INFORMATION CONTAINED IN THE FORM SHOULD BE CURRENT AND FACTUAL.

STANDARD FORM 255 PAGE 2 (REV.11-92)

Standard Form 255 (page 3)

STANDARD FORM (SF) **255** Architect-Engineer and Related Services Questionnaire for Specific Project	1. Project Name/Location for which Firm is Filing:	2a. Commerce Business Daily Announcement Date, if any:	2b. Agency Identification Number, if any:

3. Firm (or Joint-Venture) Name & Address

3a. Name, Title & Telephone Number of Principal to Contact

3b. Address of office to perform work, if different from Item 3

4. Personnel by Discipline: (List each person only once, by primary function.) Enter proposed consultant personnel <u>to be utilized</u> on this project on line (A) and in-house personnel on line (B).

(A)	(B)	Administrative	(A)	(B)	Electrical Engineers	(A)	(B)	Oceanographers	(A)	(B)	
(A)	(B)	Architects	(A)	(B)	Estimators	(A)	(B)	Planners: Urban/Regional	(A)	(B)	
(A)	(B)	Chemical Engineers	(A)	(B)	Geologists	(A)	(B)	Sanitary Engineers	(A)	(B)	
(A)	(B)	Civil Engineers	(A)	(B)	Hydrologists	(A)	(B)	Soils Engineers	(A)	(B)	
(A)	(B)	Construction Inspectors	(A)	(B)	Interior Designers	(A)	(B)	Specification Writers	(A)	(B)	
(A)	(B)	Draftsmen	(A)	(B)	Landscape Architects	(A)	(B)	Structural Engineers	(A)	(B)	
(A)	(B)	Ecologists	(A)	(B)	Mechanical Engineers	(A)	(B)	Surveyors	(A)	(B)	
(A)	(B)	Economists	(A)	(B)	Mining Engineers	(A)	(B)	Transportation Engineers	(A)	(B)	Total Personnel

5. If submittal is by JOINT-VENTURE list participating firms and outline specific areas of responsibility (including administrative, technical and financial) for each firm: (Attach SF 254 for each if not on file with Procuring Office.)

5a. Has this Joint-Venture previously worked together? ☐ Yes ☐ No

STANDARD FORM 255 PAGE 3 (REV.11-92)

Standard Form 255 (page 4)

6. If respondent is not a joint-venture, list outside key Consultants/Associates anticipated for this project (Attach SF 254 for Consultants/Associates listed, if not already on file with the Contracting Office).

Name & Address	Specialty	Worked with Prime before (Yes or No)
1)		
2)		
3)		
4)		
5)		
6)		
7)		
8)		

STANDARD FORM 255 PAGE 4 (REV.11-92)

Standard Form 255 (page 5)

7. Brief resume of key persons, specialists, and individual consultants anticipated for this project.	
a. Name & Title:	a. Name & Title:
b. Project Assignment:	b. Project Assignment:
c. Name of Firm with which associated:	c. Name of Firm with which associated:
d. Years experience: With this Firm _____ With Other Firms _____	d. Years experience: With this Firm _____ With Other Firms _____
e. Education: Degree(s)/Year/Specialization	e. Education: Degree(s)/Year/Specialization
f. Active Registration: Year First Registered/Discipline	f. Active Registration: Year First Registered/Discipline
g. Other Experience and Qualifications relevant to the proposed project:	g. Other Experience and Qualifications relevant to the proposed project:

STANDARD FORM 255 PAGE 5 (REV. 11-92)

Standard Form 255 (page 6)

7. Brief resume of key persons, specialists, and individual consultants anticipated for this project.	
a. Name & Title:	a. Name & Title:
b. Project Assignment:	b. Project Assignment:
c. Name of Firm with which associated:	c. Name of Firm with which associated:
d. Years experience: With this Firm .... With Other Firms	d. Years experience: With this Firm .... With Other Firms ....
e. Education: Degree(s)/Year/Specialization	e. Education: Degree(s)/Year/Specialization
f. Active Registration: Year First Registered/Discipline	f. Active Registration: Year First Registered/Discipline
g. Other Experience and Qualifications relevant to the proposed project:	g. Other Experience and Qualifications relevant to the proposed project:

STANDARD FORM 255 PAGE 6 (REV.11-92)

Standard Form 255 (page 7)

7. Brief resume of key persons, specialists, and individual consultants anticipated for this project.	
a. Name & Title:	a. Name & Title:
b. Project Assignment:	b. Project Assignment:
c. Name of Firm with which associated:	c. Name of Firm with which associated:
d. Years experience: With this Firm ...... With Other Firms	d. Years experience: With this Firm ...... With Other Firms ....
e. Education: Degree(s)/Year/Specialization	e. Education: Degree(s)/Year/Specialization
f. Active Registration: Year First Registered/Discipline	f. Active Registration: Year First Registered/Discipline
g. Other Experience and Qualifications relevant to the proposed project:	g. Other Experience and Qualifications relevant to the proposed project:

STANDARD FORM 255 PAGE 7 (REV.11-92)

Standard Form 255 (page 8)

7. Brief resume of key persons, specialists, and individual consultants anticipated for this project.	
a. Name & Title:	a. Name & Title:
b. Project Assignment:	b. Project Assignment:
c. Name of Firm with which associated:	c. Name of Firm with which associated:
d. Years experience: With this Firm _____ With Other Firms _____	d. Years experience: With this Firm _____ With Other Firms _____
e. Education: Degree(s)/Year/Specialization	e. Education: Degree(s)/Year/Specialization
f. Active Registration: Year First Registered/Discipline	f. Active Registration: Year First Registered/Discipline
g. Other Experience and Qualifications relevant to the proposed project:	g. Other Experience and Qualifications relevant to the proposed project:

STANDARD FORM 255 PAGE 8 (REV.11-92)

Standard Form 255 (page 9)

8. Work by firms or joint-venture members which best illustrates current qualifications relevant to this project (list not more than 10 projects).					
			d. Completion Date (actual or estimated)	e. Estimated Cost (in Thousands)	
a. Project Name & Location	b. Nature of Firm's Responsibility	c. Project Owner's Name& Address and Project Manager's Name & Phone Number		Entire Project	Work for Which Firm Was/Is Responsible
(1)					
(2)					
(3)					
(4)					
(5)					
(6)					
(7)					
(8)					
(9)					
(10)					

STANDARD FORM 255 PAGE 9 (REV. 11-92)

Standard Form 255 (page 10)

a. Project Name & Location	b. Nature of Firm's Responsibility	c. Agency (Responsible Office) Name and Address and Project Manager's Name & Phone Number	d. Percent Complete	e. Estimated Cost (in Thousands)	
9. All work by firms or joint-venture members currently being performed directly for Federal agencies.				Entire Project	Work for Which Firm Is Responsible

STANDARD FORM 255 PAGE 10 (REV11-92)

Standard Form 255 (page 11)

10. Use this space to provide any additional information or desciption of resources (including any computer design capabilities) supporting your firm's qualifications for the proposed project

11. The foregoing is a statement of facts.

Signature: _____

Typed Name and Title:_____

Date:

STANDARD FORM 255 PAGE 11 (REV11-92)

Form DD 1707

INFORMATION TO OFFERORS OR QUOTERS
SECTION A - COVER SHEET

Form Approved
OMB No. 9000-0002
Expires Sep 30, 2000

The public reporting burden for this collection of information is estimated to average 35 minutes per response, including the time for reviewing instructions, searching existing data sources, gathering and maintaining the data needed, and completing and reviewing the collection of information. Send comments regarding this burden estimate or any other aspect of this collection of information, including suggestions for reducing the burden, to Department of Defense, Washington Headquarters Services, Directorate for Information Operations and Reports (9000-0002), 1215 Jefferson Davis Highway, Suite 1204, Arlington VA 22202-4302. Respondents should be aware that notwithstanding any other provision of law, no person shall be subject to any penalty for failing to comply with a collection of information if it does not display a currently valid OMB control number.

PLEASE DO NOT RETURN YOUR FORM TO THE ABOVE ADDRESS. RETURN COMPLETED FORM TO THE ADDRESS IN BLOCK 4 BELOW.

1. SOLICITATION NUMBER	2. *(X one)*	3. DATE/TIME RESPONSE DUE
	a. INVITATION FOR BID (IFB)	
	b. REQUEST FOR PROPOSAL (RFP)	
	c. REQUEST FOR QUOTATION (RFQ)	

INSTRUCTIONS

NOTE: The provision entitled "Required Central Contractor Registration" is applicable to most solicitations.

1. If you are not submitting a response, complete the information in Blocks 9 through 11 and return to the issuing office in Block 4 unless a different return address is indicated in Block 7.

2. Responses must set forth full, accurate, and complete information as required by this solicitation (including attachments). "Fill-ins" are provided on Standard Form 18, Standard Form 33, and other solicitation documents. Examine the entire solicitation carefully. The penalty for making false statements is prescribed in 18 U.S.C. 1001.

3. Responses must be plainly marked with the Solicitation Number and the date and local time set forth for bid opening or receipt of proposals in the solicitation document.

4. Information regarding the timeliness of response is addressed in the provision of this solicitation entitled either "Late Submission, Modification and Withdrawal of Bid" or "Instructions to Offerors - Competitive Acquisitions".

4. ISSUING OFFICE *(Complete mailing address, including ZIP Code)*	5. ITEMS TO BE PURCHASED *(Brief description)*

6. PROCUREMENT INFORMATION *(X and complete as applicable)*

a. THIS PROCUREMENT IS UNRESTRICTED	
b. THIS PROCUREMENT IS _____ % SET-ASIDE FOR SMALL BUSINESS. THE APPLICABLE SIC CODE IS:	
c. THIS PROCUREMENT IS _____ % SET-ASIDE FOR HUB ZONE CONCERNS. THE APPLICABLE SIC CODE IS:	
d. THIS PROCUREMENT IS RESTRICTED TO FIRMS ELIGIBLE UNDER SECTION 8(a) OF THE SMALL BUSINESS ACT.	

7. ADDITIONAL INFORMATION

8. POINT OF CONTACT FOR INFORMATION

a. NAME *(Last, First, Middle Initial)*	b. ADDRESS *(Include Zip Code)*
c. TELEPHONE NUMBER *(Include Area Code and Extension)*	d. E-MAIL ADDRESS	

9. REASONS FOR NO RESPONSE *(X all that apply)*

a. CANNOT COMPLY WITH SPECIFICATIONS	d. DO NOT REGULARLY MANUFACTURE OR SELL THE TYPE OF ITEMS INVOLVED
b. UNABLE TO IDENTIFY THE ITEM(S)	e. OTHER *(Specify)*
c. CANNOT MEET DELIVERY REQUIREMENT	

10. MAILING LIST INFORMATION *(X one)*

WE [ ] DO [ ] DO NOT DESIRE TO BE RETAINED ON THE MAILING LIST FOR FUTURE PROCUREMENT OF THE TYPE INVOLVED.

11a. COMPANY NAME	b. ADDRESS *(Include Zip Code)*

c. ACTION OFFICER

(1) TYPED OR PRINTED NAME *(Last, First, Middle Initial)*	(2) TITLE

(3) SIGNATURE	(4) DATE SIGNED *(YYYYMMDD)*

DD FORM 1707, FEB 1999 (EG)   PREVIOUS EDITION IS OBSOLETE.   WHS/DIOR, Feb 99

CCR Registration Form

Central Contractor Registration Form

Please type or print legibly in black ink. Information must be legible for registration to be processed in a timely manner. **This form is to be printed out and faxed or mailed to the fax number or address at the bottom of the form.** **(M) = Mandatory field. Data must be entered for registration to be complete.**

General Information

DUNS Number[1] **(M)**:_____ CAGE Code[2] **(M)** if foreign:_____

Legal Business Name **(M)**:_____

Doing Business As:_____

Tax ID #[3] **(M)**:_____ **OR** Social Security Number:_____

Division Name:_____ Division Number:_____

Street Address **(M)**:_____

Street Address 2:_____

City **(M)**:_____ State **(M)**:_____

Zip/Postal Code **(M)**:_____ Country **(M)**:_____

Business Start Date **(M)**:_____ Number of Employees **(M)**:_____

Fiscal Year Close Date **(M)**:_____ Annual Revenue **(M)**:_____

Type of Organization (M):

☐ Sole Proprietorship ☐ Partnership ☐ Corporate Entity (Tax Exempt)

☐ Corporate Entity (Not Tax Exempt) ☐ Federal, State or Local Government ☐ Foreign Government

☐ International Organization ☐ Other

State of Incorporation **(M)**:_____ or Country:_____

Business Type(s) (M):

☐ Tribal Government	☐ S Corporation	☐ Research Institute
☐ Municipality	☐ Educational Institution	☐ Emerging Business/Other Unlisted Type
☐ Nonprofit Institution	☐ Sheltered Workshop	☐ Historically Black College/University
☐ Federal, State, County or City Facility	☐ Construction Firm	☐ Federal Agency
☐ 8(a) Program Participant	☐ Foreign Supplier	☐ Service Location
☐ Woman Owned Business	☐ Minority Owned Business	☐ Small Business
☐ Surplus Dealer	☐ Manufacturer of Goods	☐ Small Disadvantaged Business
☐ American Indian Owned	☐ Veteran Owned	☐ Subgroup
	☐ Labor Surplus Area Firm	☐ Limited Liability Company

1. Data Universal Numbering System (DUNS)– Call Dun & Bradstreet at 1-800-333-0505 or 1-610-882-7000 if unsure.
2. Commercial and Government Entity (CAGE) Code – If you do not have a CAGE Code, one will be assigned to you, call DLIS – Defense Logistics Information Services at 1-888-352-9333 Option 3 if unsure, or check CAGE search web <http://www.dlis.dla.mil/CAGESearch/>.
3. Taxpayer Identification Number (TIN) – Call the IRS at 1-800-829-1040 if unsure. The TIN may be used by the Government to collect and report on any delinquent amounts arising out of the offeror's relationship with the Government (31 U.S.C. 7701 (c) (3)).

Version 4
07/28/2000

Page 1 of 4
CCR Registration Form

CCR Registration Form (page 2)

Goods and Services:

SIC Codes[4] **(M)** Standard Industrial Classification Codes identify what type of activity your business performs.

SIC Code:_____   SIC Code:_____   SIC Code: _____

SIC Code:_____   SIC Code:_____   SIC Code:_____

SIC Code:_____   SIC Code:_____   SIC Code:_____

SIC Code:_____   SIC Code:_____   SIC Code:_____

PSC Codes (Optional) Product Service Codes are similar to SIC Codes. PSC Codes are used only to identify services.

PSC Code:_____   PSC Code:_____   PSC Code:_____

PSC Code:_____   PSC Code:_____   PSC Code:_____

FSC Codes (Optional) Federal Supply Classification Codes, FSC Codes are used to identify products.

FSC Code:_____   FSC Code:_____   FSC Code:_____

FSC Code:_____   FSC Code:_____   FSC Code:_____

Electronic Funds Transfer (EFT) Information:

Financial Institution Name **(M)**:_____

ABA Routing Number **(M)**:_____

Must indicate type of account **(M)**

Account Number **(M)**:_____ ☐ Checking OR ☐ Savings

Lockbox Number:_____ Authorization Date **(M)**:_____

Automated Clearing House (ACH=Bank) **(M)** at least one method of contact must be entered

ACH Phone Number:_____ ACH Fax:_____

ACH International Phone:_____Ext._____

ACH Email:_____

Do you (the Registrant) use or accept Credit Cards   ☐ Yes   ☐ No
as a method of Purchase of Payment? **(M)**:

4.   Contact your regional Electronic Commerce Resource Center (ECRC) to determine your SIC, PSC, or FSC. Call San Diego ECRC 1-800-400-
     4207 for assistance or check web addresses <http://www.ecrc.camp.org>, see EC Tools or <http://www.osha.gov/oshstats/sicser.html>
     To contact Procurement Technical Assistance Center Call 1-703-767-1650 to locate your regional PTAC http://www.dla.mil/ddas/ .

CCR Registration Form (page 3)

Address Information:

Remittance Address **(M)** (If EFT is unavailable, where would you like the check mailed?)

Name:_____

Address:_____

City, State, Zip/Postal Code_____

Country:_____

Mailing Address Information **(M)** if other than your legal address identified on the General Information Page. P.O. Box is acceptable here.

Name:_____

Address:_____

City, State, Zip/Postal Code:_____

Country:_____

Party Performing Certification **(M)** if approved by Small Business Administration (SBA) for Section 8(a) Program.

Name:_____

Address:_____

City, State, Zip/Postal Code:_____

Country:_____

Registration Acknowledgement and Point of Contact Information:

Note: The Registrant acknowledges that the information provided is current, accurate, and complete.

Registrant Name **(M)**:_____

Phone Number **(M)**:_____ Ext.:_____

International Phone Number:_____ Ext.:_____

Please check method of preferred contact for CCR-related issues:
☐ Us mail

☐ Fax:_____

☐ Email:_____

Version 4
07/28/2000

Page 3 of 4
CCR Registration Form

CCR Registration Form (page 4)

Registration Acknowledgement and Point of Contact Information continued:

Alternate Contact Information **(M)**:

Name **(M)**:_____

Phone Number **(M)**:_____ Ext.:_____

International Phone Number:_____ Ext.:_____

Accounts Receivable Contact **(M)**:

Name **(M)**:_____

Phone Number **(M)**:_____ Ext.:_____

International Phone Number:_____ Ext.:_____

Fax:_____ Email:_____

Owner Information **(M)** if Sole Proprietorship:

Name:_____

Phone Number:_____ Ext.:_____

International Phone Number:_____ Ext.:_____

Fax:_____ Email:_____

You may enter directly on the web at **www.ccr.dlsc.dla.mil**

For Electronic Data Interchange (EDI) registrations, please contact your Value Added Network (VAN) Service Provider.

You may mail or fax completed registration to:
Department of Defense
Central Contractor Registration
74 Washington Avenue N Ste. 7
Battle Creek, MI 49017-3084

FAX: 616-961-7243

For registration assistance call 1-888-227-2423 or 1-616-961-4725 (outside USA)

Version 4
07/28/2000

Page 4 of 4
CCR Registration Form

SBA PRO-*Net* Registration Instructions

How to Register with PRO-Net

Privacy Statement

If your company is a small business, as defined in the SBA's online size standard reference, and you have not been debarred from furnishing materials, supplies or services to the the Federal Government, you are eligible to be on PRO-Net.

Press the "Register New Profile" button below. We suggest that you print the blank profile form to use as a guide to assemble the information needed to complete the form. We have provided hot links to help you look up codes which may be unfamiliar to you. The more information you provide, the more likely your company will be found in searches.

Be sure to fill in the MANDATORY fields and use the formats shown on the right side of the form. The MANDATORY fields are:

- Name of Firm: Up to 80 characters

- EIN: In this format: 99-9999999 - Questions on EIN numbers can be obtained from the IRS at - http://www.irs.ustreas.gov/prod/bus_info/pub1635.html. Be very careful entering your EIN because, once entered, **you cannot change it without contacting the SBA.**

- Main Office or Branch Office: You can have only one main office in PRO-Net, but you can register multiple branch offices with different addresses, phone numbers, etc. If you're not sure whether or not you're already registered in PRO-Net, you can search before registering. Be very careful entering whether the profile is for a main or branch office because, once entered, **you cannot change it without contacting the SBA.**

- Address, line 1: Up to 60 characters

- City: Up to 30 characters

- State: Select from the drop down list on the form

- Zip Code: 999999 or 99999-9999

- Phone Number: 999-999-9999

- Fax Number (Either Fax Number or E-mail Address): 999-999-9999

- E-mail Address (Either Fax Number or E-mail Address): up to 50 characters

- SIC Codes: Up to 25 SIC codes, 4 numeric digits, separated by commas. To look up codes pertinent to your business, see the first paragraph, above. SIC codes are often used to search for companies.

SBA PRO-*Net* Registration Instructions (page 2)

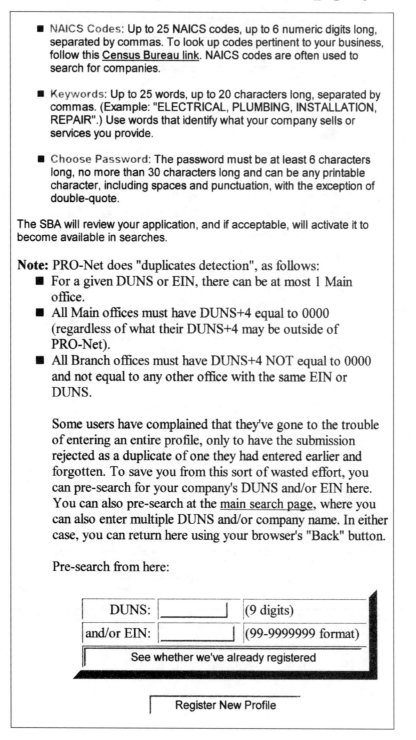

- NAICS Codes: Up to 25 NAICS codes, up to 6 numeric digits long, separated by commas. To look up codes pertinent to your business, follow this <u>Census Bureau link</u>. NAICS codes are often used to search for companies.

- Keywords: Up to 25 words, up to 20 characters long, separated by commas. (Example: "ELECTRICAL, PLUMBING, INSTALLATION, REPAIR".) Use words that identify what your company sells or services you provide.

- Choose Password: The password must be at least 6 characters long, no more than 30 characters long and can be any printable character, including spaces and punctuation, with the exception of double-quote.

The SBA will review your application, and if acceptable, will activate it to become available in searches.

Note: PRO-Net does "duplicates detection", as follows:
- For a given DUNS or EIN, there can be at most 1 Main office.
- All Main offices must have DUNS+4 equal to 0000 (regardless of what their DUNS+4 may be outside of PRO-Net).
- All Branch offices must have DUNS+4 NOT equal to 0000 and not equal to any other office with the same EIN or DUNS.

Some users have complained that they've gone to the trouble of entering an entire profile, only to have the submission rejected as a duplicate of one they had entered earlier and forgotten. To save you from this sort of wasted effort, you can pre-search for your company's DUNS and/or EIN here. You can also pre-search at the <u>main search page</u>, where you can also enter multiple DUNS and/or company name. In either case, you can return here using your browser's "Back" button.

Pre-search from here:

DUNS:	_____	(9 digits)
and/or EIN:	_____	(99-9999999 format)

See whether we've already registered

Register New Profile

Standard Form 1403 (front)

PREAWARD SURVEY OF PROSPECTIVE CONTRACTOR (GENERAL)	1. SERIAL NO. *(For surveying activity use)*	OMB NO.:**9000-0011** Expires: 10/31/97

Public reporting burden for this collection of information is estimated to average 24 hours per response, including the time for reviewing instructions, searching existing datasources, gathering and maintaining the data needed, and completing and reviewing the collection of information. Send comments regarding this burden estimate or any other aspect of this collection of information, including suggestions for reducing this burden, to the FAR Secretariat (VRS), Office of Federal Acquisition and Regulatory Policy, GSA, Washington, DC 20405; and to the Office of Management and Budget, Paperwork Reduction Project (9000-0011), Washington, DC 20503.

SECTION I - REQUEST *(For Completion by Contracting Office)*

2. NAME AND ADDRESS OF SURVEYING ACTIVITY	3. SOLICITATION NO.	4. TOTAL OFFERED PRICE $
	5. TYPE OF CONTRACT	

6A. NAME AND ADDRESS OF SECONDARY SURVEY ACTIVITY *(For surveying activity use)*	7A. NAME AND ADDRESS OF PROSPECTIVE CONTRACTOR

6B. TELEPHONE NO. *(Include AUTOVON, WATS, or FTS, if available)*	7B. FIRM'S CONTACT	7C. TELEPHONE NO. *(with area code)*

8. WILL CONTRACTING OFFICE PARTICIPATE IN SURVEY? ☐ YES ☐ NO	13. NAME AND ADDRESS OF PARENT COMPANY *(If applicable)*

9. DATE OF REQUEST	10. DATE REPORT REQUIRED

11. PROSPECTIVE CONTRACTOR REPRESENT THAT IT ☐ IS, ☐ IS NOT A SMALL BUSINESS CONCERN.

12. WALSH-HEALY CON ACT *(Check applicable box(es))*	A. IS NOT APPLICABLE	14A. PLANT AND LOCATION *(If different from Item 7, above)*
	B. IS APPLICABLE AND PROSPECTIVE CONTRACTOR REPRESENTS HIS CLASSIFICATION AS: ☐ MANUFACTURER ☐ REGULAR DEALER ☐ OTHER *(Specify)*	

15A. NAME OF REQUESTING ACTIVITY CONTRACTING OFFICER	14B. POINT OF CONTACT	14C. TELEPHONE NO. *(with area code)*

15B. SIGNATURE	16A. NAME OF CONTACT POINT AT REQUESTING ACTIVITY *(If different from Item 15A)*

15C. TELEPHONE NO. *(Include AUTOVAN, WATS or FTS, if available)*	

17. RETURN PREAWARD SURVEY TO THIS ADDRESS:	16B. TELEPHONE NO. *(Include AUTOVON, WATS, or FTS, if available)*

ATTN:

SECTION II - DATA *(For Completion by Conracting Office)*

18A. ITEM NO.	18B. NATIONAL STOCK NUMBER (NEW) AND NOMENCLATURE		18C. TOTAL QUANTITY	18D. UNIT PRICE	18E. DELIVERY SCHEDULE				
					(a)	(b)	(c)	(d)	(e)
		SOLICITED							
		OFFERED		$					
		SOLICITED							
		OFFERED		$					
		SOLICITED							
		OFFERED		$					
		SOLICITED							
		OFFERED		$					
		SOLICITED							
		OFFERED		$					
		SOLICITED							
		OFFERED		$					
		SOLICITED							
		OFFERED		$					
		SOLICITED							
		OFFERED		$					

AUTHORIZATION FOR LOCAL REPRODUCTION
Previous edition is usable.

STANDARD FORM 1403 (REV. 9-88)
Prescribed by GSA FAR (48 CFR) 53.209-1(a)

Standard Form 1403 (back)

SECTION III - FACTORS TO BE INVESTIGATED

19. MAJOR FACTORS	CHK. (a)	SAT. (b)	UN-SAT. (c)	20. OTHER FACTORS (Provide specific requirements in Remarks)	CHK. (a)	SAT. (b)	UN-SAT. (c)
A. TECHNICAL CAPABILITY				A. GOVERNMENT PROPERTY CONTROL			
B. PRODUCTION CAPABILITY				B. TRANSPORTATION			
C. QUALITY ASSURANCE CAPABILITY				C. PACKAGING			
D. FINANCIAL CAPABILITY				D. SECURITY			
E. ACCOUNTING SYSTEM				E. SAFETY			

21. IS THIS A SHORT FORM PREAWARD REPORT? *(For completion by surveying activity)*

☐ YES ☐ NO

22. IS A FINANCIAL ASSISTANCE PAYMENT PROVISION IN THE SOLICITATION? *(For completion by contracting activity)*

☐ YES ☐ NO

	CHK. (a)	SAT. (b)	UN-SAT. (c)
F. ENVIRONMENTAL/ENERGY CONSIDERATION			
G. FLIGHT OPERATIONS/FLIGHT SAFETY			
H. OTHER *(Specify)*			

23. REMARKS *(For Contracting Activity Use)*

SECTION IV - SURVEYING ACTIVITY RECOMMENDATIONS

24. RECOMMEND	25A. NAME AND TITLE OF SURVEY APPROVING OFFICIAL	25B. TELEPHONE NO.
☐ A. COMPLETE AWARD ☐ B. PARTIAL AWARD (Quantity _____) ☐ C. NO AWARD	25C. SIGNATURE	25D. DATE

STANDARD FORM 1403 (REV. 9-88) **BACK**

Standard Form 1404

PREAWARD SURVEY OF PROSPECTIVE CONTRACTOR TECHNICAL	SERIAL NO. *(For surveying activity use)*	OMB NO.: **9000-0011** Expires: 10/31/97
	PROSPECTIVE CONTRACTOR	

Public reporting burden for this collection of information is estimated to average 24 hours per response, including the time for reviewing instructions, searching existing data sources, gathering and maintaining the data needed, and completing and reviewing the collection of information. Send comments regarding this burden estimate or any other aspect of this collection of information, including suggestions for reducing this burden, to the FAR Secretariat (VRS), Office of Federal Acquisition and Regulatory Policy, GSA, Washington, DC 20405; and to the Office of Management and Budget, Paperwork Reduction Project (9000-0011), Washington, DC 20503.

1. RECOMMENDED

☐ a. COMPLETE AWARD ☐ b. PARTIAL AWARD (Quantity: _____) ☐ c. NO AWARD

2. NARRATIVE *(Include the following information concerning key personnel who will be involved with the prospective contract: (1) Names, qualifications/experience and length of affiliation with prospective contractor; (2) Evaluate technical capabilities with respect to the requirements of the proposed contract or item classifications); (3) Description of any technical capabilities which the prospective contractor lacks. Comment on the prospective contractor's efforts to obtain the needed technical capabilites.)*

IF CONTINUATION SHEETS ☐
ATTACHED - MARK HERE

3. FIRM HAS AND/OR UNDERSTANDS *(Give explanation for any items marked "NO" in 2. Narrative)*

a. SPECIFICATIONS ☐ YES ☐ NO	b. EXHIBITS ☐ YES ☐ NO
c. DRAWINGS ☐ YES ☐ NO	d. TECHNICAL DATA REQUIREMENTS ☐ YES ☐ NO

4. SURVEY MADE BY	a. SIGNATURE AND OFFICE *(Include typed or printed name)*	b. TELEPHONE NO. *(include area code)*	c. DATE SIGNED
5. SURVEY REVIEWING OFFICIAL	a. SIGNATURE AND OFFICE *(Include typed or printed name)*	b. TELEPHONE NO. *(include area code)*	c. DATE REVIEWED

AUTHORIZED FOR LOCAL REPRODUCTION
Previous edition is usable.

STANDARD FORM 1404 (REV. 9-88)
Prescribed by GSA - FAR (48 CFR) 53.209-1(b)

Standard Form 1405

PREAWARD SURVEY OF PROSPECTIVE CONTRACTOR PRODUCTION	SERIAL NO. *(For surveying activity use)*	OMB No.: 9000-0011 Expires: 09/30/91
	PROSPECTIVE CONTRACTOR	

Public reporting burden for this collection of information is estimated to average 24 hours per response, including the time for reviewing instructions, searching existing data sources, gathering and maintaining the data needed, and completing and reviewing the collection of information. Send comments regarding this burden estimate or any other aspect of this collection of information, including suggestions for reducing this burden, to the FAR Secretariat (VRS), Office of Federal Acquisition and Regulatory Policy, GSA, Washington, DC 20405; and to the Office of Management and Budget, Paperwork Reduction Project (9000-0011), Washington, DC 20503.

SECTION I - RECOMMENDATION

1. RECOMMENDED

☐ COMPLETE AWARD ☐ b. PARTIAL AWARD *(Quantity: ————)* ☐ c. NO AWARD

2. NARRATIVE *(Cite those sections of this report which substantiate the recommendations. List any other backup information in this space or on attached sheet if necessary. Identify any formal systems reviews and state results.)*

IF CONTINUATION SHEETS ATTACHED - MARK HERE ☐

3. SURVEY MADE BY	a. SIGNATURE AND OFFICE *(Include typed or printed name)*	b. TELEPHONE NUMBER *(Include are code)*	c. DATE SIGNED
4. SURVEY REVIEWING OFFICIAL	a. SIGNATURE AND OFFICE *(Include typed or printed name)*	b. TELEPHONE NUMBER *(Include are code)*	c. DATE REVIEWED

AUTHORIZED FOR LOCAL REPRODUCTION
Previous edition not usable

STANDARD FORM 1405 (REV. 9-88)
Prescribed by GSA-FAR (48 CFR) 53.209-1(c)

Standard Form 1405 (page 2)

SECTION II - PLANT FACILITIES

1. SIZE OF TRACT		4. DESCRIPTION AND TYPE OF BUILDING(S)
		☐ OWNED
2. SQUARE FEET UNDER ROOF	3. NO. OF BUILDINGS	☐ LEASED *(Give expiration date)*

5. SPACE					6. MISCELLANEOUS PLANT OBSERVATIONS *(Explain any items marked "NO" on an attached sheet.)*	YES	NO
	TYPE	SQUARE FEET	ADE-QUATE	INADE-QUATE			
MANUFAC-TURING	a. TOTAL MANUFACTURING SPACE				a. GOOD HOUSEKEEPING MAINTAINED		
	b. SPACE AVAILABLE FOR OFFERED ITEM				b. POWER AND FUEL SUPPLY ADEQUATE TO MEET PRODUCTION		
STORAGE	c. TOTAL STORAGE SPACE				c. ALTERNATE POWER AND FUEL SOURCE AVAILABLE		
	d. FOR INSPECTION LOTS				d. ADEQUATE MATERIAL HANDLING EQUIPMENT AVAILABLE		
	e. FOR SHIPPING QUANTITIES				e. TRANSPORTATION FACILITIES AVAILABLE FOR SHIPPING PRODUCT		
	f. SPACE AVAILABLE FOR OFFERED ITEM				OTHER *(Specify)* f.		
	g. AMOUNT OF STORAGE THAT CAN BE CONVERTED FOR MANUFAC-TURING, IF REQUIRED				g.		
					h.		

SECTION III - PRODUCTION EQUIPMENT

	LIST MAJOR EQUIPMENT REQUIRED *(Include GFP and annotate it as such)* (a)	QUANTITY REQUIRED FOR PROPOSED CONTRACT (b)	TOTAL QTY. REQD. DUR-ING LIFE OF PROPOSED CONTRACT (c)	QUANTITY ON HAND (d)	CONDI-TION (e) G F P	QUANTITY SHORT* *(Col. (c) minus (d))* (f)	SOURCE, IF NOT ON HAND (g)	VERIFIED DELIVERY DATE (h)
MANUFACTURING	1.							
SPECIAL TOOLING	2.							
SPECIAL TEST	3.							

*Coordinate shortage information for financial implications.

STANDARD FORM 1405 (REV. 9-88) **PAGE 2**

Standard Form 1405 (page 3)

SECTION IV - MATERIALS, PURCHASED PARTS AND SUBCONTRACTS

1. PARTS/MATERIALS/SUBCONTRACTS WITH LONGEST LEAD TIME OR CRUCIAL ITEMS

DESCRIPTION (a)	SOURCE (b)	VERIFIED DELIVERY DATE. TO MEET PROD. (c)

2. DESCRIBE THE MATERIAL CONTROL SYSTEM, INDICATING WHETHER IT IS CURRENTLY OPERATIONAL, AND EVALUATE ITS ABILITY TO MEET THE NEEDS OF THE PROPOSED ACQUISITION.

SECTION V - PERSONNEL

1. NUMBER AND SOURCE OF EMPLOYEES

2. SHIFTS ON WHICH WORK IS TO BE PERFORMED

☐ FIRST ☐ SECOND ☐ THIRD

3. UNION AFFILIATION

TYPE OF EMPLOYEES	NO. ON BOARD	ADD. NO. REQUIRED	AVAIL. YES	AVAIL. NO	SOURCE
a. SKILLED PRODUCTION					
b. UNSKILLED PRODUCTION					
c. ENGINEERING					
d. ADMINISTRATIVE					
e. TOT. (Lines A thru D)					

AGREEMENT EXPIRATION DATE ▶

4. RELATIONSHIP WITH LABOR INDICATES PROBLEMS AFFECTING TIMELY PERFORMANCE OF PROPOSED CONTRACT (If "Yes," explain on attached sheet)

☐ YES ☐ NO

SECTION VI - DELIVERY PERFORMANCE RECORD

STANDARD FORM 1405 (REV. 9-88) PAGE 3

Standard Form 1405 (page 4)

SECTION VII - RELATED PREVIOUS PRODUCTION *(Government)*						
PAST YEAR PRODUCTION		GOVERNMENT CONTRACT NUMBER* (c)	PERFORMANCE		QUANTITY (f)	DOLLAR VALUE ($000) (g)
ITEM NOMENCLATURE (a)	NATIONAL STOCK NO. (NSN) (b)		ON SCHED. (d)	DELIN-QUENT (e)		

* Identify identical items by an asterisk(*) after the Government contract number.

SECTION VIII - CURRENT PRODUCTION
(Government and civilian concurrent production schedule using same equipment and/or personnel as offered item)

ITEM(S) (Include Government Contract No., if applicable. Identify unsatisfactory performance with asterisk(*).)	MONTHLY SCHEDULE OF CONCURRENT DELIVERIES *(Quantity)*										
	1st	2nd	3rd	4th	5th	6th	7th	8th	9th	10th	BAL.
BEING PRODUCED 1.											
PENDING AWARD 2.											

SECTION IX - ORGANIZATION AND MANAGEMENT DATA

Provide the following information in SECTION NARRATIVE:

1. Describe the relationship between management production, and inspection. Attach an organization chart, if available.

2. Describe the prospective contractor's production control system. State whether or not it is operational.

3. Evaluate the prospective contractor's production control system in terms of (a) historical effectiveness, (b) the proposed contract, and (c) total production during performance of the proposed contract.

4. Comment on or evaluate other areas unique to this survey (include all special requests by the contracting office and any other information pertinent to the proposed contractor item classification).

STANDARD FORM 1405 (REV. 9-88) PAGE 4

Standard Form 1406

PREAWARD SURVEY OF PROSPECTIVE CONTRACTOR	SERIAL NO. *(For surveying activity use)*	OMB No.:9000-0011 Expires: 10/31/2000
QUALITY ASSURANCE	PROSPECTIVE CONTRACTOR	

Public reporting burden for this collection of information is estimated to average 24 hours per response, including the time for reviewing instructions, searching existing data sources, gathering and maintaining the data needed, and completing and reviewing the collection of information. Send comments regarding this burden estimate or any other aspect of this collection of information, including suggestions for reducing this burden, to the FAR Secretariat (MVR), Federal Acquisition Policy Division, GSA, Washington, DC 20405.

SECTION I - RECOMMENDATION

1. RECOMMEND: ☐ AWARD ☐ NO AWARD *(Provide full substantiation for recommendation in 4. NARRATIVE)*

2. IF PROSPECTIVE CONTRACTOR RECEIVES AWARD, A POST AWARD CONFERENCE IS RECOMMENDED. ☐ YES ☐ NO

3. AN ON-SITE SURVEY WAS PERFORMED. ☐ YES ☐ NO

4. NARRATIVE

IF CONTINUATION SHEETS ATTACHED - MARK HERE ☐

5. SURVEY MADE BY		6. SURVEY REVIEWING OFFICIAL	
A. SIGNATURE	B. DATE SIGNED	A. SIGNATURE	B. DATE REVIEWED
C. NAME		C. NAME	
D. OFFICE		D. OFFICE	
E. AREA CODE F. TELEPHONE NUMBER G. EXT.		E. AREA CODE F. TELEPHONE NUMBER G. EXT.	

AUTHORIZED FOR LOCAL REPRODUCTION
Previous edition is not usable.

STANDARD FORM 1406 (REV. 11-97)
Prescribed by GSA FAR (48 CFR) 53.209-1(d)

Standard Form 1406 (page 2)

SECTION II - COMPANY AND SOLICITATION DATA

1. BRIEFLY DESCRIBE HOW QUALITY ASSURANCE RESPONSIBILITIES ARE ACCOMPLISHED.

2. QUALITY ASSURANCE OFFICIALS CONTACTED

A. NAME	B. TITLE	C. YEARS OF QUALITY ASSURANCE EXPERIENCE

3. APPLICABLE CONTRACT QUALITY REQUIREMENTS

A. NUMBER	B. TITLE	C. TAILORING (If any)

4. ☐ IDENTICAL OR ☐ SIMILAR ITEMS HAVE BEEN ☐ PRODUCED, ☐ SUPPLIED, OR ☐ SERVICED BY PROSPECTIVE CONTRACTOR

(If similar items, identify:)

SECTION III - EVALUATION CHECKLIST

STATEMENTS			YES	NO
1. These items (where applicable to the contract) are understood by the prospective contractor.	A.	Exhibits, technical data, drawings, specifications, and approval requirements.		
	B.	Preservation, packaging, packing, and marking requirements.		
	C.	Other (Specify)		
2. Records available indicate that the prospective contractor has a satisfactory quality performance record during the past twelve (12) months for similar items.				
3. Used, reconditioned, or remanufactured material and former Government surplus material will be furnished by the prospective contractor. (If Yes, explain in Section I NARRATIVE)				
4. Prospective contractor will require unusual assistance from the Government. (If Yes, explain in Section I NARRATIVE)				
5. Did prospective contractor fulfill commitments to correct deficiencies, as proposed on previous surveys, when awarded that contract? (If No, explain in Section I NARRATIVE)				
6. Quality verification personnel	NUMBER SKILLED	NUMBER SEMI-SKILLED		
7. Quality verification to production personnel ratio.		RATIO :		
THE FOLLOWING ARE AVAILABLE AND ADEQUATE. (If not applicable, show "N/A" in "Yes" column.)				
8. Inspection and test equipment, gauges, and instruments for first article and production (including solicitation specified equipment).				
9. Calibration/metrology program.				
10. Quality system procedures and controls.				
11. Control of specifications, drawings, changes and modifications, work/process instructions.				
12. System for determining inspection, test, and measurement requirements.				
13. Purchasing: Processes for selecting qualified suppliers and assuring the quality of purchased materials.				
14. Product identification, segregation, traceability, and maintenance.				
15. Government furnished property controls.				
16. Process controls.				
17. Nonconforming product: System for timely identification, disposition, correction of deficiencies, and corrective and preventative action.				
18. Preservation, storage, packaging, packing, marking, and delivery controls.				
19. Records (such as: inspection, test, status, corrective actions, calibration, etc.)				
20. Controls for investigation of customer complaints and correction of deficiencies.				
21. Design controls system.				
22. Computer software (deliverable and/or non-deliverable) quality assurance program.				
23. Management review and internal quality audits.				
24. Quality assurance training program.				
25. Installation and servicing quality assurance program.				
26. Statistical techniques.				

STANDARD FORM 1406 (REV. 11-97) **BACK**

Standard Form 1407

PREAWARD SURVEY OF PROSPECTIVE CONTRACTOR FINANCIAL CAPABILITY	SERIAL NO. *(For surveying activity use)*	OMB No.:**9000-0011** Expires: 09/30/91
	PROSPECTIVE CONTRACTOR	

Public reporting burden for this collection of information is estimated to average 24 hours per response, including the time for reviewing instructions, searching existing data sources, gathering and maintaining the data needed, and completing and reviewing the collection of information. Send comments regarding this burden estimate or any other aspect of this collection of information, including suggestions for reducing this burden, to the FAR Secretariat (VRS), Office Federal Acquisition and Regulatory Policy, GSA, Washington, DC 20405; and to the Office of Management and Budget, Paperwork Reduction Project (9000-0011), Washington, DC 20503.

SECTION I - RECOMMENDATION

1. RECOMMENDED

☐ a. COMPLETE AWARD   ☐ b. PARTIAL AWARD (Quantity: _____)   ☐ c. NO AWARD

2. TOTAL OFFERED PRICE

3. NARRATIVE *(Cite those sections of the report which substantiate the recommendation. Give any other backup information in this space or on an additional sheet, if necessary.)*

IF CONTINUATION SHEETS
ATTACHED - MARK HERE ☐

4. SURVEY MADE BY	a. SIGNATURE	b. TELEPHONE NUMBER *(Include area code)*	c. DATE SIGNED
5. SURVEY REVIEWING OFFICIAL	a. SIGNATURE	b. TELEPHONE NUMBER *(Include area code)*	c. DATE REVIEWED

AUTHORIZED FOR LOCAL REPRODUCTION
Previous edition is usable.

STANDARD FORM 1407 (REV. 9-88)
Prescribed by GSA - FAR (48 CFR) 53.209-1(e)

Standard Form 1407 (page 2)

SECTION II - GENERAL	
1. TYPE OF COMPANY ☐ CORPORATION ☐ PARTNERSHIP ☐ SUBSIDIARY ☐ DIVISION ☐ PROPRIETORSHIP ☐ OTHER *(Specify)* **2. YEAR ESTABLISHED:**	**3. NAME AND ADDRESS OF:** a. PARENT CO. b. SUBSIDIARIES

SECTION III - BALANCE SHEET/PROFIT AND LOSS STATEMENT

PART A - LATEST BALANCE SHEET		PART B - LATEST PROFIT AND LOSS STATEMENT		
1. DATE	**2. FILED WITH**	**1. CURRENT PERIOD**		**2. FILED WITH**
		a. FROM	b. TO	

3. FINANCIAL POSITION

a. Cash	$	**3. NET SALES**	a. CURRENT PERIOD	$
b. Accounts Receivable			b. First prior fiscal year	
c. Inventory			c. Second prior fiscal year	
d. Other Current Assets		**4. NET PROFITS BEFORE TAXES**	a. CURRENT PERIOD	$
e. Total Current Assets			b. First prior fiscal year	
f. Fixed Assets			c. Second prior fiscal year	
g. Current Liabilities				
h. Long Term Liabilities		**PART C - OTHER**		
i. Total Liabilities		**1. FISCAL YEAR ENDS** *(Date)*:		
j. Net Worth		**2. BALANCE SHEETS AND PROFIT AND LOSS STATEMENTS HAVE BEEN CERTIFIED**	a. THROUGH *(Date)*	b. BY *(Signature)* ▶
4. WORKING CAPITAL *(Current Assets less Current Liabilities)*		**3. OTHER PERTINENT DATA**		

5. RATIOS

a. CURRENT ASSETS TO CURRENT LIABILITIES	b. ACID TEST *(Cash, temporary Investments held in lieu of cash and current receivables to current liabilities)*	c. TOTAL LIABILITIES TO NET WORTH

SECTION IV - PROSPECTIVE CONTRACTOR'S FINANCIAL ARRANGEMENTS

Mark "X" in appropriate column.	YES	NO	4. INDEPENDENT ANALYSIS OF FINANCIAL POSITION SUPPORTS THE STATEMENTS SHOWN IN ITEMS 1, 2, AND 3 ☐ YES ☐ NO *(If "NO", explain)*
1. USE OF OWN RESOURCES			
2. USE OF BANK CREDITS			
3. OTHER *(Specify)*			

SECTION V - GOVERNMENT FINANCIAL AID

1. TO BE REQUESTED IN CONNECTION WITH PERFORMANCE OF PROPOSED CONTRACT	2. EXPLAIN ANY "YES" ANSWERS TO ITEMS 1a, b, AND c.

Mark "X" in appropriate column.	YES	NO
a. PROGRESS PAYMENT(S)		
b. GUARANTEED LOAN		
c. ADVANCE PAYMENTS		

3. FINANCIAL AID CURRENTLY OBTAINED FROM THE GOVERNMENT

Complete items below only if Item a., is marked "YES."

a. PROSPECTIVE CONTRACTOR RECEIVES GOVERNMENT FINANCING AT PRESENT ☐ YES ☐ NO	b. IS LIQUIDATION CURRENT? ☐ YES ☐ NO	c. AMOUNT OF UNLIQUIDATED PROGRESS PAYMENTS OUTSTANDING $	DOLLAR AMOUNTS	(a) AUTHORIZED	(b) IN USE
			a. Guaranteed loans	$	$
			b. Advance payments	$	$

4. LIST THE GOVERNMENT AGENCIES INVOLVED	5. SHOW THE APPLICABLE CONTRACT NOS.

STANDARD FORM 1407 (REV. 9-88) **PAGE 2**

Standard Form 1407 (page 3)

SECTION VI - BUSINESS AND FINANCIAL REPUTATION

1. COMMENTS OF PROSPECTIVE CONTRACTOR'S BANK

2. COMMENTS OF TRADE CREDITORS

3. COMMENTS AND REPORTS OF COMMERCIAL FINANCIAL SERVICES AND CREDIT ORGANIZATIONS *(Such as, Dun & Bradstreet, Standard and Poor, etc.)*

4. MOST RECENT CREDIT RATING	a. DATE	b. BY

5. DOES PRICE APPEAR UNREALISTICALLY LOW? ☐ YES ☐ NO *(If Yes, explain in Section I NARRATIVE)*

6. DESCRIBE ANY OUTSTANDING LIENS OR JUDGMENTS

SECTION VII - SALES (000'S) FOR NEXT SIX QUARTERS

CATEGORY	1	2	3	4	5	6	TOTAL
1. CURRENT CONTRACT SALES (Backlog)	$	$	$	$	$	$	$
A. GOVERNMENT (Prime & Subcontractor)							
B. COMMERCIAL							
2. ANTICIPATED ADDITIONAL SALES							
A. GOVERNMENT (Prime & Subcontractor)							
B. COMMERCIAL							
3. TOTALS							

STANDARD FORM 1407 (REV. 9-88) PAGE 3

Standard Form 1408

PREAWARD SURVEY OF PROSPECTIVE CONTRACTOR ACCOUNTING SYSTEM	SERIAL NO. *(For surveying activity use)*	OMB No.:9000-0011 Expires: 10/31/97
	PROSPECTIVE CONTRACTOR	

Public reporting burden for this collection of information is estimated to average 24 hours per response, including the time for reviewing instructions, searching existing data sources, gathering and maintaining the data needed, and completing and reviewing the collection of information. Send comments regarding this burden estimate or any other aspect of this collection of information, including suggestions for reducing this burden, to FAR Secretariat (VRS), Office of Federal Acquisition and Regulatory Policy, GSA, Washington, DC 20405; and to the Office of Management and Budget, Paperwork Reduction Project (9000-0011), Washington, DC 20503.

SECTION I - RECOMMENDATION

1. PROSPECTIVE CONTRACTOR'S ACCOUNTING SYSTEM IS ACCEPTABLE FOR AWARD OF PROSPCTIVE CONTRACT

☐ YES   ☐ NO *(Explain in 2. NARRATIVE)*

☐ YES, WITH A RECOMMENDATION THAT A FOLLOW ON ACCOUNTING SYSTEM REVIEW BE PERFORMED AFTER CONTRACT AWARD *(Explain in 2. NARRATIVE)*

2. NARRATIVE *(Clarification of deficiencies, and other pertinent comments,. If additional space is required, continue on plain sheets of paper.)*

IF CONTINUATION SHEETS ATTACHED - MARK HERE ☐

3. SURVEY MADE BY	a. SIGNATURE AND OFFICE *(Include typed or printed name)*	b. TELEPHONE NO. *(include area code)*	c. DATE SIGNED
4. SURVEY REVIEWING OFFICIAL	a. SIGNATURE AND OFFICE *(Include typed or printed name)*	b. TELEPHONE NO. *(Include area code)*	c. DATE REVIEWED

AUTHORIZED FOR LOCAL REPRODUCTION
Previous edition usable

STANDARD FORM 1408 (REV. 9-88)
Prescribed by GSA
FAR (48 CFR) 53.209-1(f)

Standard Form 1408 (page 2)

SECTION II - EVALUATION CHECKLIST			
MARK"X" IN THE APPROPRIATE COLUMN *(Explain any deficiencies in SECTION I NARRATIVE)*	YES	NO	NOT APPLIC-CABLE
1. EXCEPT AS STATED IN SECTION I NARRATIVE, IS THE ACCOUNTING SYSTEM IN ACCORD WITH GENERALLY ACCEPTED ACCOUNTING PRINCIPLES APPLICABLE IN THE CIRCUMSTANCES?			
2. ACCOUNTING SYSTEM PROVIDES FOR:			
a. Proper segregation of direct costs from indirect costs.			
b. Identification and accumulation of direct costs by contract.			
c. A logical and consistent method for the allocation of indirect costs to intermediate and final cost objectives. (A contract is a final cost objective.)			
d. Accumlation of costs under general ledger control.			
e. A timekeeping system that identifies employees' labor by intermediate or final cost objectives.			
f. A labor distribution system that charges direct and indirect labor to the appropriate cost objectives.			
g. Interim (at least monthly) determination of costs charged to a contract through routine posting of books of account.			
h. Exclusion from costs charged to government contracts of amounts which are not allowable in terms of FAR 31, Contract Cost Principles and Procedures, or other contract provisions.			
i. Identification of costs by contract line item and by units (as if each unit or line item were a separate contract) if required by the proposed contract.			
j. Segregation of preproduction costs from production costs.			
3. ACCOUNTING SYSTEM PROVIDES FINANCIAL INFORMATION:			
a. Required by contract clauses concerning limitation of cost (FAR 52.232-20 and 21) or limitation on payments (FAR 52.216-16).			
b. Required to support requests for progress payments.			
4. IS THE ACCOUNTING SYSTEM DESIGNED, AND ARE THE RECORDS MAINTAINED IN SUCH A MANNER THAT ADEQUATE, RELIABLE DATA ARE DEVELOPED FOR USE IN PRICING FOLLOW-ON ACQUISITONS?			
5. IS THE ACCOUNTING SYSTEM CURRENTLY IN FULL OPERATION? (If not, describe in Section I Narrative which portions are (1) in operation, (2) set up, but not yet in operation, (3) anticipated, or (4) nonexistent.)			

GSA FORM 1408 (REV. 9-88) BACK

Sample Request for Quotation

REQUEST FOR QUOTATION (THIS IS NOT AN ORDER)

DLA, DEFENSE SUPPLY CENTER COLUMBUS
3990 EAST BROAD STREET
P.O. BOX 16704
COLUMBUS, OH 43216-5010

REQUEST NO.	DATE ISSUED	RETURN BY	DELIVER BY:	PURCHASE REQUEST NUMBER
SP075000QA331	03/07/00	03/21/00	AWD DT + 90	YPC99347001065

BUYER CODE	BUYER NAME	BUYER PHONE	BUYER FAX
LDAC3	Julie Brill	(614) 692-1278	(614) 693-1574

NSN or Part Number	Unit of Issue	Quantity
2910-01-263-3224	EA	65

Rating	FOB	Standard Industrial Classification Code	Small Business Size Standard
DOA4	DESTINATION	3714	0

```
SEE CONTINUATION SHEETS TO COMPLETE QUOTE INFORMATION.
Quoters may respond:  (1) electronically via the DSCC Internet
Bid Board System (DIBBS) at http://dibbs.dsccols.com;  by
facsimile to the buyer's fax number, or (2) by hard copy via
mail or other physical delivery to the address listed above.
Quoter must also complete the following:

a.  Quotation is valid for 90 days from return quote date unless otherwise
    indicated:_____.

b.  FOB Point ____   Destination
               ____   Origin         Shipping Point (City,State)_____

c.  If delivery period shown above is unacceptable, provide
    best possible delivery:  _____

d.  Quoter's CAGE Code:  _____
    Quoter's Address (Name, Street, City, State, ZIP):

    _____
    _____
    _____
    _____

e.  Remittance Address (Name, Street, City, State, ZIP):  applicable
    only if EFT does not apply.

    _____
    _____
    _____
    _____

f.  Vendor FAX Number:
    Vendor Telephone Number:
    Vendor E-Mail Number:
```

Sample Request for Quotation (page 2)

ITEM DESCRIPTION

```
NSN or Part Number: 2910-01-263-3224

TANK, FUEL, ENGINE
"CLASS I OZONE DEPLETING CHEMICALS ARE NOT TO BE
USED NOR INCORPORATED IN ANY ITEMS TO BE
DELIVERED UNDER THIS CONTRACT.  THIS PROHIBITION
SUPERSEDES ALL SPECIFICATION REQUIREMENTS BUT
DOES NOT ALLEVIATE ANY PRODUCT REQUIREMENTS.
SUBSTITUTE CHEMICALS MUST BE SUBMITTED FOR
APPROVAL UNLESS THEY ARE AUTHORIZED BY THE
SPECIFICATION REQUIREMENTS."
IF AQLS ARE LISTED IN THE SPECIFICATION(S)
OR DRAWING(S) THEY MAY BE USED TO ESTABLISH THE
AUTHORIZED SAMPLE SIZE, HOWEVER, THE ACCEPTANCE
NUMBER FOR THIS CONTRACT IS ZERO; I.E., THIS
CONTRACT REQUIRES A SAMPLING PLAN THAT ACCEPTS
ON ZERO DEFECTS AND REJECTS ON ONE OR MORE
DEFECT(S).
DLAD 52.246-9004, PRODUCT VERIFICATION TESTING,
APPLIES.  THIS CLAUSE IS A GOVERNMENT OPTION
THAT CAN ONLY BE INVOKED UPON THE COGNIZANT
CONTRACT ADMINISTRATION OFFICE NOTIFYING THE
CONTRACTOR THAT PVT SAMPLES ARE TO BE SELECTED.
I/A/W DWG NR 19207 12338583
REFNO DTD 01/22/86
AMEND NR  C DTD 10/16/90
"DETAILED DRAWING (ONE ITEM)"
I/A/W DWG NR 19207 12338588
BASIC DTD 07/29/86
AMEND NR  E DTD 10/07/92
"DETAILED DRAWING (ONE ITEM)"
I/A/W DWG NR 19207 12338588
REFNO DTD 08/18/87
AMEND NR  A DTD 09/26/90
SUPPLEMENTAL QUALITY ASSURANCE PROVISIONS
(SQAP) ALL TYPES.
I/A/W DWG NR 19207 12339975
REFNO DTD 07/23/86
"DETAILED DRAWING (ONE ITEM)"
```

LINE ITEM 0001

PURCHASE REQUEST	QUANTITY	UNIT OF ISSUE	UNIT PRICE
YPC99347001065	50	EA	

PACKAGING DATA

```
PREP FOR DELIVERY

    PKGING DATA - MIL-STD-2073-1C, 01 OCT 1996
    QUP = 001: PRES MTHD = AE: CLNG/DRY = 1: PRESV MAT = 00:
    WRAP MAT = XX: CUSH/DUNN MAT = XX: CUSH/DUNN THKNESS = X:
    UNIT CONT = D3: OPI = O:
    INTRMDTE CONT = YY: INTRMDTE CONT QTY = AAA:
    PACK CODE = U:
```

Sample Request for Quotation (page 3)

```
        MARKING SHALL BE IN ACCORDANCE WITH MIL-STD-129.
        SPECIAL MARKING CODE: 00 - NO SPECIAL MARKING.
        PALLETIZATION SHALL BE IN ACCORDANCE WITH DC1636P001 REV B
        DATED 99238
        SUPPLEMENTAL INSTRUCTIONS


        DOD BAR CODE MARKING REQUIRED IN ACCORDANCE WITH
        MIL-STD-129 (LATEST REVISION) MARKING AND BAR
        CODING IN ACCORDANCE WITH AIM BC1.
```

SHIPPING DATA

```
FREIGHT SHIPPING ADDRESS

SW3108
TRANSPORTATION OFFICER
DDSP - NEW CUMBERLAND FACILITY
BUILDING MISSION   DOOR 113-134
NEW CUMBERLAND PA      17070-5002

NON-MILSTRIP
RDD: 04/04/00
```

LINE ITEM 0002

PURCHASE REQUEST	QUANTITY	UNIT OF ISSUE	UNIT PRICE
YPC99347001065	15	EA	

PACKAGING DATA

```
PREP FOR DELIVERY

    PKGING DATA - MIL-STD-2073-1C, 01 OCT 1996
    MIL-STD-2073 PACKAGING DATA SAME AS PRIOR LINE
```

SHIPPING DATA

```
PARCEL POST ADDRESS

SW3200
DEF DIST DEPOT SAN JOAQUIN
SAN JOAQUIN   TRACY
PO BOX    96001
STOCKTON CA      95296-0130


FREIGHT SHIPPING ADDRESS

SW3200
DEF DIST DEPOT SAN JOAQUIN
SAN JOAQUIN   TRACY
25600 S CHRISMAN ROAD RECV WHS 10
TRACY CA      95376-5000

NON-MILSTRIP
```

Sample Request for Quotation (page 4)

RDD: 04/04/00

PROCUREMENT HISTORY FOR NSN: 2910012633224

TYPE	CAGE	CONTRACT NUMBER	QUANTITY	UNIT COST	AWD DATE
STK	32783	SP075000V0436	000040	360.00000	10/19/99
STK	9R012	SP075099M2671	000030	369.28000	09/07/99
STK	32783	SP075099M2486	000024	392.10000	04/30/99

APPLICABLE CLAUSES

All clauses and provisions listed within this individual
solicitation are contained in the DSCC Master Solicitation
(S9C/S9E) dated JUNE 1999. This document can be found at (
www.dscccols.com) . Current changes to the aforementioned
Master Solicitation are contained within this solicitation and
will supersede any outdated information contained in the Master
Solicitation. The clauses/provisions incorporated by reference
have the same force and effect as if they were in full text;
however, those having no bearing on the instant acquisition
become self-deleting. In the event of an inconsistency between
the Master Solicitation and the individual solicitation, the
provision of the individual solicitation shall govern.
For Simplified Acquisitions (under $100,000) quoters may respond
electronically via the DSCC Internet Bid Board System (DIBBS) at
http://dibbs.dscccols.com or by facsimilie to the buyer's fax
number.

SECTION B

B02 -
QUANTITY BREAK (DLAD 52.213-9000) (MAR 1988)

B03 - DSCC WEB SITE
     The DSCC Master Solicitation is available on the Internet
via the DSCC Web Site at
http://dibbs.dscccols.com/Refs/ProvClauses/.
Also, the full text of FAR/DFARS/DLAD clauses incorporated by
reference may be accessed electronically at
http://www.procregs.hq.dla.mil/icps.htm .

BO4 - ALTERNATE DISPUTE RESOLUTION (ADR)

B15 - ADVANCE NOTICE OF DELIVERY TO CONSIGNEES (OTHER THAN AIR
OR WATER TERMINALS (AUG 1985)

B30 - MANUFACTURER'S PART NUMBER
Prior to or at the time the offer is submitted, the contractor
shall inform the buyer if any discrepancy exists between the
physical/functional description and the specifications/drawings.
ALL OFFERS MUST PROVIDE THE FOLLOWING INFORMATION:
Offer based on:

Sample Request for Quotation (page 5)

```
Manufacturer's Name:

Manufacturer's P/N:

Actual Bare Item Part Number Marking:



SECTION C

C - Y2K
COMPLIANT NOTICE


SECTION D

D02a -
PACKAGING AND MARKING REQUIREMENTS (DSCC 52.246-9C41)
(AUG 1999)


D03 - PACKING LIST/INVOICE/SHIPPING DOCUMENTS (AUG 1999) (DSCC
52.211-9C17)


D07 - LABELS (AUG 1999) (DSCC 52.211-9C18)


D08 - SPECIAL HANDLING DATA/ACKNOWLEDGEMENT (AUG 1999)
(DSCC 52.211-9C20)


SECTION E

E01 -
CLAUSES INCORPORATED BY REFERENCE (FAR 52.252-2) (FEB
1998)


E02 - INSPECTION OF SUPPLIES-FIXED PRICE (FAR 52.246-2)
(AUG 1996)


E03 - INSPECTION AT ORIGIN (DSCC 52.246-9C01) (FEB 1993)
     (c)  Inspection Points:
          SUPPLIES
CLIN(s)
          ( )  Same as Offeror
          ( )  Other (CAGE, Name, Street Address, City,
             State and Zip Code)
          ( )


          ( )


          PACKAGING
CLIN(s)
          ( )  Same as Offeror
          ( )  Same as above
          ( )  Other (CAGE, Name, Street Address, City,
             State and Zip Code)
          ( )
```

Sample Request for Quotation (page 6)

```
              ( )



E04 - ACCEPTANCE AT ORIGIN (DSCC 52.246-9C02) (NOV 1995)


E06 - MATERIAL INSPECTION AND RECEIVING REPORT
(DFARS 252.246-7000) (DEC 1991)


E15 - CERTIFICATE OF CONFORMANCE (FAR 52.246-15) (APR 1984)


E18 - PRODUCT VERIFICATION TESTING (DLAD 52.246-9004) (AUG
1997)


E21 - WARRANTY - ACCEPTANCE OF SUPPLIES (DSCC 52.246-9C10)
(JUN 1989)


E23 - SUBSTITUTION OF ITEM AFTER AWARD (DSCC 52.246-9C13)
(JAN 1999)


E28 - DOCUMENTATION OF PART NUMBER CHANGE (DSCC 52.246-9C30)
(JUN 1997)
The offer certifies that the part number (P/N) requested in the
Request for Quotation (RFQ) has been changed from CAGE -
P/N                   to P/N                  and that this is
a part number change
only.
Reason for change is



E32 - RECORDS RETENTION REQUIREMENTS (DSCC 52.204-9C01)
(JUN 1980)


SECTION F

F01 -
SOLICITATION CLAUSES INCORPORATED BY REFERENCE
(FAR 52.252-2) (FEB 1998)


F05 - SHIPPING INSTRUCTIONS (DOMESTIC) (DSCC 52.247-9C02)
(JUN 1999)


F20 - REQUIRED DELIVERY WITH DELIVERY EVALUATION FACTOR
(DSCC 52.211-9C09) (OCT 1999)
     (a)  This clause applies to CLIN(s) ALL            .
The Government's intent is to meet the Required Delivery Schedule
at the best possible price.  Offers will be evaluated in
accordance with Provision M26, Delivery Evaluation Factor (DEF).
The Government requires delivery to be made according to the
following schedule:
          REQUIRED DELIVERY SCHEDULE
```

Sample Request for Quotation (page 7)

```
        (Contracting Officer to insert specific details)
ITEM NO.    QUANTITY    WITHIN DAYS AFTER DATE OF CONTRACT
ALL         65          90
```

It is intended to award without discussions regarding delivery; therefore, it is in the offeror's best interest to provide the best delivery. If the offeror proposes no other delivery schedule below, the Required Delivery Schedule will apply.
        OFFEROR'S PROPOSED DELIVERY SCHEDULE

```
ITEM NO.    QUANTITY    WITHIN DAYS AFTER DATE OF CONTRACT
```

(b) Application of the Delivery Evaluation Factor set forth below in (c) may result in award to other than the lowest priced acceptable offeror. (e.g., award to an offeror with a higher offered price and a better/shorter delivery schedule). The formula reflected below is used in DEF calculations and is for evaluation purposes only. This calculation is applied to each line (CLIN and subCLIN) for which an offer has been made. The total amount for each line (CLIN and subCLIN) is added together for each offer received.

[Total Offered Price per line x Evaluation Factor] x [Offered Delivery per line - Govt's Required Delivery] + Price Adjustment per line = Evaluated Offer per Line
(c) If a DEF award is made based on paying a DEF price differential and the delivery/ship date is made after the contract due date (CDD) because of a contractor-caused delay, the award price may be automatically reduced for late delivery using the Award Reduction Formula reflected below. In this circumstance, recoupment/consideration may also be required. When calculating the recoupment/consideration amount, the applicable DEF factor reflected in the solicitation will be used.
Unit Price x Evaluation Factor (See Clause F20a) x Delinquent Quantity x Number of Days Delinquent + Administrative Costs (when applicable)
Reductions may be up to, but not exceeding 25% of the total contract price or 150% of the price differential, whichever is greater, plus the administrative cost(s) of modifying the contract to provide for a revised delivery schedule.
(d) This clause does not affect or limit the Government's right under the Default Clause of this contract.
(e) Attention is directed to the contract award provision of the solicitation which provides that a written award or acceptance of an offer mailed or otherwise furnished to the successful offeror results in a binding contract. The Government will mail or otherwise furnish to the offeror an award or notice of award not later than the day the award is dated. Therefore, the offeror shall compute the time available for performance beginning with the award date on the contract, in lieu of the date the written notice of award is received from the Contracting Officer through the ordinary mails. The Government will evaluate an offer that proposes delivery based on the Contractor's date of receipt of the contract or notice of award by adding five days for delivery of the award through the ordinary mails.

Sample Request for Quotation (page 8)

```
NOTE:   Unless otherwise specified in the individual solicitation
or contract, ACCELERATED DELIVERY is acceptable and desired at no
additional cost to the Government.


SECTION I

I01 -
CLAUSES INCORPORATED BY REFERENCE (FAR 52.252-2)
(FEB 1998)
The following changes have been made to the Master Solicitation:
FAR 52.223-2  Clean Air and Water  (Deleted)
FAR 52.225-8  Duty-Free Entry (FEB 2000)
FAR 52.225-13 Restriction on Certain Foreign Purchases (FEB 2000)
FAR 52.225-14 Inconsistency between English and Translation
              of Contract (FEB 2000)
FAR 52.225-15 Sanctioned European Union Country End
              Products (FEB 2000)
FAR 52.226-1  Utilization of Indian Organizations and
              Indian-Owned Economic Enterprises (FEB 2000)
FAR 52.248-1  Value Engineering (FEB 2000)


I17 - The following must be completed for offers/quotations
based on supplying surplus materials:
     GOVERNMENT SURPLUS MATERIAL (MAY 1999) - DLAD 52.211-9000
(a)  With respect to the surplus supplies being offered, the
Offeror represents that:
     (1)  The supplies are unused and in good condition.
     (2)  The supplies were purchased by the Offeror from the
Government selling agency or other source contract date, and the
contract number.  If the supplies were purchased from the
Government by a source other than the Offeror, also identify that
source and its address.  If complete information is not
available, attach an explanation as to when, where, and how the
property was acquired.)
Government Selling Agency or Other Source:

Contract Date (Month, Year):
Contract Number:
     (3)  The supplies ( ) have ( ) have not been
altered, modified, or refurbished, and (ii) ( ) do ( )
do not contain cure dated components.  (If the supplies are to be
reconditioned or altered, attach a complete description of the
work to be done.
     (4)  The Offeror ( ) has ( ) does not have the
supplies.  (If the Offeror does not have the supplies, attach an
explanation as to how the offered quantities will be secured.)
     (5)  If items have data plates attached, the Offeror has
furnished a copy of information contained thereon, which is
stated below:


     (6)  The offered item(s) ( ) are ( ) are not in
their original package.  (If the original package is being used,
state here all markings and data including contract number, cited
on the package, and provide a copy or facsimile of package
markings.)
Contract Number:
NSN:
Cage Code:
Part Number:
Other Markings/Data:
(b)  The Offeror agrees that in the event of award and
```

Sample Request for Quotation (page 9)

notwithstanding the provisions of this solicitation, inspection and acceptance of the surplus supplies will be performed at origin or destination subject to all applicable provisions for origin or destination inspection.
(c) Failure to provide the information requested by this clause may result in rejection of the offer for failure to meet the requirements of the solicitation.

I58 - HAZARDOUS MATERIAL IDENTIFICATION AND MATERIAL SAFETY DATA (FAR 52.223-3) (JAN 1997)
     MATERIAL IDENTIFICATION NO. (If none, insert "None")

I63 - HAZARD WARNING LABELS (DFARS 252.223-7001) (DEC 19961)
     MATERIAL (If none, insert "None") ACT

I64 - MATERIAL SAFETY DATA SHEETS AND HAZARD WARING LABELS (DLAD 52.223-9000) (MAR 1992)
          (2) Check here ( ) if an MSDS accompanies your offer. Where this is the case, the MSDS must be identified to the offer, and must cite the solicitation number and the applicable CAGE code of the manufacturer, the part number, and, where so identified, the National Stock Number (NSN).

I74 - SUBCONTRACTS FOR COMMERCIAL ITEMS AND COMMERCIAL COMPONENTS (far 52.244-6) (APR 1998)

I78 - CONFIGURATION CONTROL - ENGINEERING CHANGES, DEVIATIONS AND WAIVERS (DSCC 52.248-9C01)(APR 1996)

I89 - NOTICE OF TOTAL SMALL BUSINESS SET-ASIDE (FAR 52.219-6) (JUL 1996)
( ) Alternate I (OCT 1995)

SECTION K

K01
- SOLICITATIONS PROVISIONS INCORPORATED BY REFERNCE (FAR 52.252-1) (FEB 1998)

K06 - TAXPAYER IDENTIFICATION (FAR 52.204-3) (OCT 1998)
     (d) Taxpayer Identification Number (TIN).
          ( ) TIN: .
          ( ) TIN has been applied for.
          ( ) TIN is not required because:
               ( ) Offeror is a nonresident alien, foreign corporation, or foreign partnership that does not have income effectively connected with the conduct of a trade or business in the U.S. and does not have an office or place of business or a

Sample Request for Quotation (page 10)

```
fiscal paying agent in the U.S.;
            ( )  Offeror is an agency or instrumentality
of a foreign government;
            ( )  Offeror is an agency or instrumentality
of a Federal, state, or local government;
            ( )   Other.  State basis.

    (e)  Type of Organization.
            ( )  Sole proprietorship;
            ( )  Partnership;
            ( )  Corporate entity (not tax-exempt);
            ( )  Corporate entity (tax-exempt);
            ( )  Foreign government;
            ( )  International organization per 26 CFR
1.6049-4;
            ( )  Other
    (f)  Common Parent.
            ( )  Offeror is not owned or controlled by a
common parent as defined in paragraph (a) of this provision.
            ( )  Name and TIN of common parent:
Name:
TIN:


K08 - DATA UNIVERSAL NUMBERING SYSTEM (DUNS) NUMBER
(FAR 52.204-6) (JUN 1999)


K27 - SMALL BUSINESS PROGRAM REPRESENTATION (FAR 52.219-1)
(MAY 1999)
    (a)(1) The standard industrial classification (SIC) code for
this acquisition is 3714   (insert SIC code).
        (2) The small business size standard is 500      (insert
size standard).
        (3) The small business size standard for a concern which
submits an offer in its own name, other than on a construction or
service contract, but which proposes to furnish a product which
it did not itself manufacture, is 500 employees.
    (b) Representations. (1) The offeror represents as part of
its offer that it ( ) is, ( ) is not a small business
concern.
        (2) (Complete only if offeror represented itself as a
small business concern in paragraph (b)(1) of this provision.)
The offeror represents, for general statistical purposes, that it
( ) is, ( ) is not a small disadvantaged business
concern as defined in 13 CFR 124.1002.
        (3) (Complete only if offeror represented itself as a
small business concern in paragraph (b)(1) of this provision.)
The offeror represents as part of its offer that it ( ) is,
( ) is not a women-owned small business concern.
(X) ALTERNATE I (NOV 1999)
The
offeror represents
(i)  It ( ) is, ( ) is not a HUBZone small
business concern
(ii)  It ( ) is, ( ) is not a joint venture
that complies with the requirements of 13 CFR part 126,
The offeror shal enter
the name or names of the HUBZone small business concern or
concerns that are participating in the joint venture:

ALTERNATE II (NOV 1999)
        (5)  (Complete if offeror represented itself as
disadvantaged in paragraph (b)(2) of this provision).  (The
```

Sample Request for Quotation (page 11)

offeror shall check the category in which its ownership falls):
    ( ) Black American.
    ( ) Hispanic American.
    ( ) Native American (American Indians, Eskimos,
Aleuts, or Native Hawaiians).
    ( ) Asian-Pacific American (persons with origins from
Burma, Thailand, Malaysia, Indonesia, Signapore, (Kampuchea),
Vietnam, Korea, The Philippines, U.S. Trust Territory of the
Pacific Islands (Republic of Palau), Republic of the Marshall
Islands, Federated States of Micronesia, the Commonwealth of the
Northern Marianna Islands, Guam, Samoa, Macao, Hong Kong, Fiji,
Tonga, Kiribati, Tuvalu, or Nauru).
    ( ) Subcontinent Asian (Asian-Indian) American
(persons with origins from India, Pakistan, Bangladesh, Sri
Lanka, Bhutan, the Maldives Islands, or Nepel).
    ( ) Individual/concern, other than one of the
preceding.

K33 - PREVIOUS CONTRACTS AND COMPLIANCE REPORTS (FAR 52.222-22)
(FEB 1999)
The offeror represents that --
    (a) It ( ) has, ( ) has not participated in a
previous contract or subcontract subject to the Equal Opportunity
clause of this solicitation;
    (b) It ( ) has, ( ) has not filed all required
compliance reports

K34 - AFFIRMATIVE ACTION COMPLIANCE (FAR 52.222-25)
(APR 1984)
The offeror represents that
    (a) it ( ) has developed and has on file, ( ) has
not developed and does not have on file, at each establishment,
affirmative action programs required by the rules and regulations
of the Secretary of Labor (41 CFR 60-1 and 60-2), or
    (b) it ( ) has not previously had contracts subject to
the written affirmative action programs requirement of the rules
and regulations of the Secretary of Labor.

K39 - INFORMATION FOR DUTY-FREE ENTRY EVALUATION
(DFARS 252.225-7003) (MAR 1998)
    (a) Is the offer based on furnishing any supplies (i.e.,
end items, components, or material) of foreign origin other than
those for which duty-free entry is to be accorded pursuant to the
Duty-Free Entry -- Qualifying Country End Products and Supplies
clause of this solicitation?
        ( ) Yes   ( ) No
    (b) If the answer in paragraph (a) is yes, answer the
following questions:
        (1) Are such foreign supplies now in the United
States?   ( ) Yes   ( ) No
        (2) Has the duty on such foreign supplies been paid?
            ( ) Yes   ( ) No
        (3) If the answer to paragraph (b)(2) is no, what
amount is included in the offer to cover such duty?
            $

SECTION L

L01
- SOLICITATION PROVISIONS INCORPORATED BY REFERENCE

Sample Request for Quotation (page 12)

```
(FAR 52.252-1) (FEB 1998)
The following changes have been made to the Master Solicitation:
FAR 52.225-10  Notice of Buy American Act/Balance of Payments
               Program Requirement Construction
               Materials (FEB 2000)
FAR 52.225-12  Notice of Buy American Act/Balance of Payments
               Program Requirement-Construction Materials under
               Trade Agreements (FEB 2000)


L03 - AVAILABILITY OF SPECIFICATIONS LISTED IN THE DOD INDEX OF
SPECIFICATIONS AND STANDARDS (DODISS) AND DESCRIPTIONS LISTED IN
THE ACQUISITION MANAGEMENT SYSTEMS AND DATA REQUIREMENTS CONTROL
LIST, DoD 5010.12-L. (FAR 52.211-2) (DEC 1999)


L07 - AVAILABILITY OF DRAWINGS, PURCHASE DESCRIPTIONS OR
DEVIATIONS LISTS (DSCC 52.211-9C13) (OCT 1996)


L09 - CONDITIONS FOR EVALUATION OF OFFERS OF SURPLUS MATERIAL
(DLAD 52.211-9003) (JUN 1999)
The Agency will evaluate offers of surplus material when
the contracting officer determines the offeror is
otherwise in line for award, after adding the cost of evaluation
($200 for internal evaluation and, if applicable, an additional
$500 for Engineering Support Activity (ESA) evaluation plus any
additional fees required for special testing and/or
inspection).


L25 - AGENCY PROTESTS (DLAD 52.233-9000) (SEP 1999)


SECTION M


M01 - SOLICITATION PROVISIONS INCORPORATED BY REFERENCE
(FAR 52.252-1) (FEB 1998)


M07 - AUTOMATED BEST VALUE SYSTEM (ABVS) (DSCC 52.215-9C10)
(FEB 2000)
(a)  Award against this solicitation shall be made based on a
comparative assessment of offerors' prices, quoted deliveries,
and past performance.  Award may be made to other than the
low-priced, technically acceptable, responsible offeror.  The
Government retains the right to award to the offeror with the
lowest quoted or lowest evaluated price.  Price, quoted delivery,
and past performance will be evaluated equally when making a
comparative analysis of offers.  The past performance factor
considers quality performance and delivery performance to be of
equal value.
(b) Past Performance:
     (1)  Past performance information is maintained for
performance under all procurements with the Defense Logistics
Agency (DLA).  Overall performance is evaluated as is performance
in each Federal Supply Class (FSC).  This information is used to
generate ABVS ratings which are based on the following
indicators:
Delivery Delinquencies
- Number
- Severity
- Contractor caused Terminations, Cancellations, and Withdrawals
```

Sample Request for Quotation (page 13)

For administrative purposes, the delivery rating period excludes the most recent 60 days. For ABVS purposes, delinquent lines represent shipments not shipped and/or received in their entirety by the Contract Delivery Date (CDD).
Quality Complaints
- Product Nonconformances/Laboratory Test Failures
- Packaging Nonconformances
For administrative purposes, the quality rating period excludes the most recent 30 days.
NOTE: The above 60 and 30 day offset periods are NOT grace periods.
   (2) An offeror's past performance is an indicator of performance risk and will be evaluated first on the basis of past performance in the same Federal Supply Class (FSC) as the supplies being solicited. The Contracting Officer may consider the volume of business on which the performance score is based as a measure of confidence in the FSC score. A vendor's overall score may be evaluated when a satisfactory measure of confidence cannot be obtained from the FSC score or if a vendor has no FSC score. The Contracting Officer may also take into consideration any other available and relevant past performance data.
   (3) An offeror with no performance history in any FSC procured by DLA will be identified as a new offeror and will not be scored by ABVS on performance. However, any other available and relevant past performance data may be considered in rendering an award decision. Regardless, the status of being a new offeror will not be grounds for disqualification for an award. New offerors may be considered more favorably than scored offerors with a poor performance record. Also, the desirability of expanding the supplier base and possible competition enhancement in future procurements will be considered in the source selection decision when new offerors are present.
   (4) ABVS ratings do not determine an offeror's award eligibility, or technical acceptability, nor does it constitute a responsibility or non-responsibility determination.
   (5) By accessing the DSCC Internet Bid Board System (DIBBS), (http://dibbs.dscccols.com/), each offeror will be provided the opportunity to review their ABVS scores and negative historical performance data. For any questions or challenges to negative performance data, please forward requests/challenges to an ABVS Administrator at the below cited address, or telephone/fax an Administrator at one of the provided numbers:
Mail requests to: Defense Supply Center, Columbus
                              ATTN: DSCC-PAMB
                              P. O. Box 3990
                              Columbus OH   43216-5010
Telephone Numbers: (614) 692-1381
                              (614) 692-3383
Facsimile (FAX) Number: (614) 692-4170
   (6) When a discrepancy between contractor data and Government data occurs, the Government will make every effort to resolve the discrepancy expeditiously. However, the Government may make an award decision despite the existence of an unresolved challenge. The Government is the final authority for resolution of disputed data and its use in the source selection process.
(c) Price. In making an award decision, the Government may consider price as follows:
   (1) Offered Price - The Government will evaluate the reasonableness of the offered price after a price analysis of offers is performed.
   (2) Evaluated Price - If required, the evaluation process may include the Factor (DEF), the Small Disadvantaged Business Concerns (SDBC) preference, and/or any other applicable price

Sample Request for Quotation (page 14)

evaluation factor(s).
(d) Delivery. The quoted delivery will be evaluated in comparison with the delivery required on the solicitation.
(e) General Basis for Award. Award will be made to the offeror whose proposal conforms to the terms and conditions of the solicitation and which represents the best value to the Government. In making the best value determination, the Government will make a comparative assessment of the proposals with regard to price, delivery, and past performance. The following considerations may affect the trade-off determination:
- Whether or not an item is used in a weapons system or is a personnel support item
- Item delivery and quality history
- Inventory status
- Delivery schedule/urgency of the item
- Limited number of supply sources
- Benefits from obtaining new sources
- Difference in price

M26 - DELIVERY EVALUATION FACTOR (DEF) (DSCC 52.211-9C12) (OCT 1999)

(a) Offers will be evaluated based upon the delivery offered in DSCC Clause F20, Required Delivery with Delivery Evaluation Factor, and the formula set forth below in paragraph (c) of this provision. The Evaluated Price may include additive CLIN(s) and/or the value of any option CLIN(s). Calculations of the Evaluated Price are made on a line-by-line (CLIN-by-CLIN, subCLIN-by-subCLIN) basis for which an offer has been received. However, offers could be awarded on a total price basis only or by a CLIN/line basis.
For evaluation purposes only:
7 Offers with a Proposed Delivery Schedule which meets/is the same as the Required Delivery Schedule will be evaluated without an adjustment to their offered price.
7 Offers with a Proposed Delivery Schedule shorter/earlier than the Required Delivery Schedule will also be evaluated without an adjustment to their offered price.
7 Offers with a Proposed Delivery Schedule longer/later than the Required Delivery Schedule will have the evaluation factor adjustment added to their offered price.

(b) The DEF is based upon separate Center factors for Construction (S9C) FSCs/items and Electronic (S9E) FSCs/items. Currently, the factor for S9C FSCs/items is .00118; while for S9E FSCs/items, it is .00256. The factor represents the day/cost ratio (the cost per day due to late delivery) and is expressed as a portion of the overall contract cost.
(c) For DEF evaluation purposes only, the formula reflected below is used for this acquisition to calculate the DEF Price Adjustment and the Evaluated Price per line/CLIN.
[Total Offered Price per line x Evaluation Factor]   x
[Offered Delivery per line - Govt's Required Delivery] +
Price Adjustment per line = Evaluated Price per line

Example:
DEF Factor: .00256 per day
Total Quantity: 30 ea   CLIN 0001 - 20 ea;   CLIN 0002 - 10 ea
Option Quantity: 30 ea
Govt's Required Delvy: CLIN 0001 - 90 days; CLIN 0002 - 60 days
FAT Delivery and Approval Time: 180 days

(a)	(b)	(c)	(d)	(e)
			Govt's	Total

Sample Request for Quotation (page 15)

CLIN	Quantity	Offered Unit Price	Offered Delivery	Required Delivery	Evaluation Factor
0001	20	$1,375.00	60	90	$27,500.00
0002	10	$1,500.00	60	60	$15,000.00
5001AA	20	$1,375.00	60	90	$27,500.00
5001AB	10	$1,500.00	60	60	$15,000.00
9907	1	$1,000.00	180	180	---
(f)		(g)		(h)	(i)

Evaluation Factor	Difference in Offered and Govt's Required Delivery (d-c)	Price Adjustment (exfxg)	Evaluated Price (Per Line) (e+h)
.00256	-30	0	$27,500.00
.00256	0	0	$15,000.00
.00256	-30	0	$27,500.00
.00256	0	0	$ 1,000.00
	Total Evaluated Price		$86,000.00

PART VII MASTER SOLICITATION - PALLETIZATION NO. DC1636P001 -
96150 - APPLIES

Numbered Notes

One of the main ways that you can find out about contracting opportunities is to religiously read the *Commerce Business Daily* (*CBD*). The *CBD* lists notices of proposed government procurement actions, contract awards, and other procurement information.

When you read a notice in the *CBD*, you will often see references to numbered notes within the text. (For example, you may see such phrases as "Notes 12 and 26 apply" or "See Note(s) 22 and 23.") The purpose of these numbered notes, which are similar to footnotes, is to avoid the unnecessary repetition of information that appears in various announcements. Whenever a numbered note is included in a notice, the note referred to must be read as part of the item or section in which it appears.

Following is a listing of numbered notes and their meaning.

Numbered Notes

1. The proposed contract is 100 percent set aside for small business concerns.

2. A portion of the acquisition is set aside for small business concerns.

3. The proposed contract is a labor surplus area set-aside. (This note is deleted as of 7/21/99.)

4. The proposed contract is 100 percent set aside for small disadvantaged business concerns (SDB). Offers from concerns other than SDBs will not be considered. (This note is deleted as of 11/24/99.)

5. The proposed contract is 100 percent set aside for Historically Black Colleges and Universities (HBCUs) and Minority Institutions (MIs). Offers from other than HBCUs and MIs will not be considered.

6. The proposed contract is a total small disadvantaged business set aside or is being considered as a total small disadvantaged business set aside. (This note is deleted as of 11/24/99.)

7. The proposed contract is 100 percent set aside for Historically Black Colleges, Universities and Minority Institutions or is partially set aside for Historically Black Colleges, Universities and Minority Institutions.

8. The solicitation document contains information that has been designated as "Militarily Critical Technical Data." Only businesses that have been certified by the Department of Defense, United States/Canada Joint Certification Office, and have a valid requirement may have a copy of the solicitation document. All requests for copies of the solicitation document must include a certified copy of DD Form 2345, Militarily Critical Technical Data Agreement. To obtain certification, contact: Commander, Defense Logistics Information Service (DLIS), ATTN: U.S./Canada Joint Certification Office, 74 Washington Avenue North, Battle Creek, MI 49017-3084 or call the DLIS at (800)-352-3572. The DLIS Unites States/Canada Joint Certification Lookup service is available via the Internet at: http://www.dlis.dla.mil/ccal/.

9. Interested parties may obtain copies of Military and Federal Specifications and Standards, Qualified Product Lists, Military Handbooks, and other standardization documents from the DoD Single Stock Point (DODSSP), in Philadelphia, PA. Most documents are available in Adobe PDF format from the ASSIST database via the Internet at http://assist.daps.mil.

    Users may search for documents using the ASSIST-Quick Search and, in most cases, download the documents directly via the Internet using standard browser software.

    Documents not available for downloading from ASSIST can be ordered from the DODSSP using the ASSIST Shopping Wizard, after establishing a DODSSP Customer Account by following the registration procedures or by phoning the DoDSSP Special Assistance Desk at (215) 697-2179 (DSN: 442-2179).

    Users not having access to the Internet may contact the DODSSP Special Assistance Desk at (215) 697-2179 (DSN: 442-2179) or mail requests to the DODSSP, Bldg. 4/D, 700 Robbins Avenue, Philadelphia, PA 19111-5094. Patterns, Drawings, Deviations Lists, Purchase Descriptions, etc., are not stocked at the DODSSP.

10. Reserved.

11. Reserved

12. One or more of the items under this acquisition may be subject to an Agreement on Government Procurement approved and implemented in the United States by the Trade Agreements Act of 1979. All offers shall be in the English language and in U.S. dollars. All interested suppliers may submit an offer.

13. The proposed contract is restricted to domestic sources under the authority of FAR 6.302-3. Accordingly, foreign sources, except Canadian sources, are not eligible for award.

14. Reserved

15. Reserved

16. Reserved

17. Reserved

18. Reserved

19. Reserved

20. Reserved

21. Reserved

22. The proposed contract action is for supplies or services for which the Government intends to solicit and negotiate with only one source under the authority of FAR 6.302. Interested persons may identify their interest and capability to respond to the requirement or submit proposals. This notice of intent is not a request for competitive proposals. However, all proposals received within forty-five days (thirty days if award is issued under an existing basic ordering agreement) after date of publication of this synopsis will be considered by the Government. A determination by the Government not to compete with this proposed contract based upon responses to this notice is solely within the discretion of the Government. Information received will normally be considered solely for the purpose of determining whether to conduct a competitive procurement.

23. Award will be made only if the offeror, the product/service or the manufacturer meets qualification requirement at time of award, in accordance with FAR clause 52.209-1 or 52.209-2. The solicitation identifies the office where additional information can be obtained concerning qualification requirements and is cited in each individual solicitation.

24. Architect-Engineer firms which meet the requirements described in this announcement are invited to submit: (1) a Standard Form 254, Architect-Engineer and Related Services Questionnaire, (2) a Standard Form 255, Architect-Engineer and Related Services Questionnaire for Specific Project, when requested, and (3) any requested supplemental data to the procurement office shown. Firms having a current Standard Form 254 on file with the procurement office shown are not required to register this form. Firms desiring to register for consideration for future projects administered by the procurement office (subject to specific requirements for individual projects) are encouraged to submit annually, a statement of qualifications and performance data, utilizing Standard Form 254, Architect-Engineer and Related Services Questionnaire. Firms responding to this announcement before the closing date will be considered for selection, subject to any limitations indicated with respect to size and geographic location of firm, specialized technical expertise or other requirements listed. Following an initial evaluation of the qualification and performance data submitted, three or more firms that are considered to be the most highly qualified to provide the type of services required, will be chosen for negotiation. Selection of firms for negotiation shall be made through an order of preference based on demonstrated competence and qualifications necessary for the satisfactory performance of the type of professional services required, that include: (1) professional capabilities; (2) specialized experience and technical competence, as required; (3) capacity to accomplish the work in the required time; (4) past performance on contracts with respect to cost control, quality of work, and compliance with performance schedules; (5) geographical location and knowledge of the locality of the project, provided that application of the criterion leaves an appropriate number of qualified firms, given the nature and size of the project; (6) any other special qualification required under this announcement by the contracting activity. In addition to the above qualifications, special qualifications in the Department of Defense include the volume of work previously awarded to the firm by the Department of Defense, with the object of effecting an equitable distribution of Department of Defense architect engineer contracts among qualified architect-engineer firms including small and small disadvantaged business firms, and firms that have not had prior Department of Defense contracts.

25. Information submitted should be pertinent and specific in the technical area under consideration, on each of the following qualifications: (1) Experience: An outline of previous projects, specific work previously performed or being

performed and any in-house research and development effort; (2) Personnel: Name, professional qualifications and specific experience of scientist, engineers and technical personnel who may be assigned as a principal investigator and/or project officer; (3) Facilities: Availability and description of special facilities required to perform in the technical areas under consideration. A statement regarding industry security clearance. Any other specific and pertinent information as pertains to this particular area of procurement that would enhance our consideration and evaluation of the information submitted.

26. Based upon market research, the Government is not using the policies contained in Part 12, Acquisition of Commercial Items, in its solicitation for the described supplies or services. However, interested persons may identify to the contracting officer their interest and capability to satisfy the Government's requirement with a commercial item within 15 days of this notice.

27. The proposed contract is set aside for HUBZone small business concerns. Offers from other than HUBZone small business concerns will not be considered.

28. The proposed contract is set-aside for Very Small Business Concerns (VSB). A VSB is a small business concern whose headquarters is located within the geographic area served by a district designated by SBA; and which, together with its affiliates, has no more than 15 employees and has average anual receipts that do not exceed $1 million. Offers from other than very small business concerns will not be considered.

Appendix **8**

Using the Freedom of Information Act

Requesting and getting information from the government may seem like a daunting task, but current federal law spells out exactly how to do it. What's more, if you follow the rules, the government is bound by law to get you the information you need, unless there is an specific reason not to (which is also specified in the law). It's all explained below:

A Citizen's Guide on Using The Freedom of Information Act and The Privacy Act Of 1974 to Request Government Records

First Report by The House Committee on Government Operations Subcommittee on Information, Justice, Transportation, and Agriculture, 1993 Edition, House Report 103-104, 103rd Congress, 1st Session, Union Calendar No. 53

CONTENTS

I. PREFACE

In 1977, the House Committee on Government Operations issued the first Citizen's Guide on how to request records from federal agencies.[1] The original Guide was reprinted many times and widely distributed. The Superintendent of Documents at the Government Printing Office reported that almost 50,000 copies were sold between 1977 and 1986 when the guide went out of print. In addition, thousands of copies were distributed by the House Committee on Government Operations, Members of Congress, the Congressional Research Service, and other federal agencies. The original Citizen's Guide is one of the most widely read congressional committee reports in history.

In 1987, the Committee issued a revised Citizen's Guide.[2] The new edition was prepared to reflect changes to the Freedom of Information Act made during 1986. As a result of special efforts by the Superintendent of Documents at the Government Printing Office, the availability of the new Guide was well publicized. The 1987 edition appeared on GPO's "Best Seller" list in the months following its issuance.

During the 100th Congress, major amendments were made to the Privacy Act of 1974. The Computer Matching and Privacy Protection Act of 1988[3] added new provisions to the Privacy Act and changed several existing requirements. None of the changes affects a citizen's rights to request or see records held by federal agencies. However, some of the information in the 1987 Guide became outdated as a result, and a third edition was issued in 1989.[4]

During the 101st Congress, the Privacy Act of 1974 was amended through further adjustments to the Computer Matching and Privacy Protection Act of 1988. The changes do not affect access rights. This fourth edition of the Citizen's Guide reflected all changes to the FOIA and Privacy Act made through the end of 1990.[5] The current edition version is the fifth edition and includes an expanded bibliography and editorial changes.

II. INTRODUCTION

"A popular Government without popular information or the means of acquiring it, is but a Prologue to a Farce or a Tragedy or perhaps both. Knowledge will forever govern ignorance, and a people who mean to be their own Governors, must arm themselves with the power knowledge gives." James Madison[6]

The Freedom of Information Act (FOIA) establishes a presumption that records in the possession of agencies and departments of the Executive Branch of the United States government are accessible to the people. This was not always the approach to federal information disclosure policy. Before enactment of the FOIA in 1966, the burden was on the individual to establish a right to examine these government records. There were no statutory guidelines or procedures to help a person seeking information. There were no judicial remedies for those denied access.

With the passage of the FOIA, the burden of proof shifted from the individual to the government. Those seeking information are no longer required to show a need for information. Instead, the "need to know" standard has been replaced by a "right to know" doctrine. The government now has to justify the need for secrecy.

The FOIA sets standards for determining which records must be disclosed and which records can be withheld. The law also provides administrative and judicial remedies for those denied access to records. Above all, the statute requires federal agencies to provide the fullest possible disclosure of information to the public.

The Privacy Act of 1974 is a companion to the FOIA. The Privacy Act regulates federal government agency record keeping and disclosure practices. The Act allows most individuals to seek access to federal agency records about themselves. The Act requires that personal information in agency files be accurate, complete, relevant, and timely. The subject of a record may challenge the accuracy of information. The Act requires that agencies obtain information directly from the subject of the record and that information gathered for one purpose not be used for another purpose. As with the FOIA, the Privacy Act provides civil remedies for individuals whose rights have been violated.

Another important feature of the Privacy Act is the requirement that each federal agency publish a description of each system of records maintained by the agency that contains personal information. This prevents agencies from keeping secret records.

The Privacy Act also restricts the disclosure of personally identifiable information by federal agencies. Together with the FOIA, the Privacy Act permits disclosure of most personal files to the individual who is the subject of the files. The two laws restrict disclosure of personal information to others when disclosure would violate privacy interests.

While both the FOIA and the Privacy Act support the disclosure of agency records, both laws also recognize the legitimate need to restrict disclosure of some information. For example, agencies may withhold information properly classified in the interest of national defense or foreign policy, trade secrets, and criminal investigatory files. Other specifically defined categories of confidential information may also be withheld.

The essential feature of both laws is that they make federal agencies accountable for information disclosure policies and practices. While neither law grants an absolute right to examine government documents, both laws establish the right to request records and to receive a response to the request. If a record cannot be released, the requester is entitled to be told the reason for the denial. The requester also has a right to appeal the denial and, if necessary, to challenge it in court.

These procedural rights granted by the FOIA and the Privacy Act make the laws valuable and workable. As a result, the disclosure of federal government information cannot be controlled by arbitrary or unreviewable actions.

III. RECOMMENDATIONS

The Committee recommends that this Citizen's Guide be made widely available at low cost to anyone who has an interest in obtaining documents from the federal government. The Government Printing Office and federal agencies subject to the Freedom of Information Act and the Privacy Act of 1974 should distribute this report widely.

The Committee also recommends that this Citizen's Guide be used by federal agencies in training programs for government employees who are responsible for administering the Freedom of Information Act and the Privacy Act of 1974. The Guide should also be used by those government employees who only occasionally work with these two laws.

IV. HOW TO USE THIS GUIDE

This report explains how to use the Freedom of Information Act and the Privacy Act of 1974. It reflects all changes to the laws made since 1977. Major amendments to the Freedom of Information Act passed in 1974 and 1986. A major addition to the Privacy Act of 1974 was enacted in 1988. Minor amendments to the Privacy Act were made in 1989 and 1990.

This Guide is intended to serve as a general introduction to the Freedom of Information Act and the Privacy Act.[7] It offers neither a comprehensive explanation of the details of these Acts nor an analysis of case law. The Guide will enable those who are unfamiliar with the laws to understand the process and to make a request. In addition, the complete text of each law is included in an appendix.

Readers should be aware that FOIA litigation is a complex area of law. There are thousands of court decisions interpreting the FOIA.[8] These decisions must be considered in order to develop a complete understanding of the principles governing disclosure of government information. Anyone requiring more details about the FOIA, its history, or the case law should consult other sources. There has been less controversy and less litigation over the Privacy Act, but there is nevertheless a considerable body of case law for the Privacy Act as well. There are other sources of information on the Privacy Act as well.

However, no one should be discouraged from making a request under either law. No special expertise is required. Using the Freedom of Information Act and the Privacy Act is as simple as writing a letter. This Citizen's Guide explains the essentials.

V. WHICH ACT TO USE

The access provisions of the FOIA and the Privacy Act overlap in part. The two laws have different procedures and different exemptions. As a result, sometimes information exempt under one law will be disclosable under the other.

In order to take maximum advantage of the laws, an individual seeking information about himself or herself should normally cite both laws. Requests by an individual for information that does not relate solely to himself or herself should be made only under the FOIA.

Congress intended that the two laws be considered together in the processing of requests for information. Many government agencies will automatically handle requests from individuals in a way that will maximize the amount of information that is disclosable. However, a requester should still make a request in a manner that is most advantageous and that fully protects all available legal rights. A requester who has any doubts about which law to use should always cite both the FOIA and the Privacy Act when seeking documents from the federal government.

VI. THE FREEDOM OF INFORMATION ACT

A. The Scope Of The Freedom of Information Act

The federal Freedom of Information Act applies to documents held by agencies in the executive branch of the federal government. The executive branch includes cabinet departments, military departments, government corporations, government controlled corporations, independent regulatory agencies, and other establishments in the executive branch.

The FOIA does not apply to elected officials of the federal government, including the President[9], Vice President, Senators, and Congressmen.[10] The FOIA does not apply to the federal judiciary. The FOIA does not apply to private companies; persons who receive federal contracts or grants; tax-exempt organizations; or state or local governments.

All States and some localities have passed laws like the FOIA that allow people to request access to records. In addition, there are other federal and state laws that may permit access to documents held by organizations not covered by the federal FOIA.[11]

B. What Records Can Be Requested Under the FOIA?

The FOIA requires agencies to publish or make available for public inspection several types of information. This includes: (1) descriptions of agency organization and office addresses; (2) statements of the general course and method of agency operation; (3) rules of procedure and descriptions of forms; (4) substantive rules of general applicability and general policy statements; (5) final opinions made in the adjudication of cases; and (6) administrative staff manuals that affect the public. This information must either be published in the Federal Register or made available for inspection and copying without the formality of an FOIA request.

All other "records" of a federal agency may be requested under the FOIA. However, the FOIA does not define "record". Any item containing information that is in the possession, custody, or control of an agency is usually considered to be an agency record under the FOIA. Personal notes of agency employees may not be agency records. A document that is not an "record" will not be available under the FOIA.

The form in which a record is maintained by an agency does not affect its availability. A request may seek a printed or typed document, tape recording, map, photograph, computer printout, computer tape or disk, or a similar item.

Of course, not all records that can be requested must be disclosed. Information that is exempt from disclosure is described below in the section entitled "Reasons Access May Be Denied Under the FOIA".

The FOIA carefully provides that a requester may ask for records rather than information. This means that an agency is only required to look for an existing record or document in response to an FOIA request. An agency is not obliged to create a new record to comply with a request. An agency is not required to collect information it does not have. Nor must an agency do research or analyze data for a requester.[12]

Requesters must ask for existing records. Requests may have to be carefully written in order to obtain the desired information. Sometimes, an agency will help a requester identify a specific document that contains the information being sought. Other times, a requester may need to be creative when writing an FOIA request in order to identify an existing document or set of documents containing the desired information.

There is a second general limitation on FOIA requests. The law requires that each request must reasonably describe the records being sought. This means that a request must be specific enough to permit a professional employee of the agency who is familiar with the subject matter to locate the record in a reasonable period of time.

Because agencies organize and index records in different ways, one agency may consider a request to be reasonably descriptive while another agency may reject a similar request as too vague. For example, the Federal Bureau of Investigation has a central index for its primary record system. As a result, the FBI is able to search for records about a specific person. However, agencies that do not maintain a central name index may be unable to conduct the same type of search. These agencies may reject a similar request because the request does not describe records that can be identified.

Requesters should make requests as specific as possible. If a particular document is required, it should be identified precisely, preferably by date and title. However, a request does not always have to be that specific. A requester who cannot identify a specific record should clearly explain his or her needs. A requester should make sure, however, that a request is broad enough to include all desired information.

For example, assume that a requester wants to obtain a list of toxic waste sites near his home. A request to the Environmental Protection Agency for all records on toxic waste would cover many more records than are needed. The fees for such a request might be very high, and it is possible that the request might be rejected as too vague.

A request for all toxic waste sites within three miles of a particular address is very specific. But it is unlikely that EPA would have an existing record containing data organized in that fashion. As a result, the request might be denied because there is no existing record containing the information.

The requester might do better to ask for a list of toxic waste sites in his city, county, or state. It is more likely that existing records might contain this information. The requester might also want to tell the agency in the request letter exactly what information is desired. This additional explanation may help the agency to find a record that meets the request.

Many people include their telephone number with their requests. Some questions about the scope of a request can be resolved quickly when an agency employee and the requester talk. This is an efficient way to resolve questions that arise during the processing of FOIA requests.

It is to everyone's advantage if requests are as precise and as narrow as possible. The requester benefits because the request can be processed faster and cheaper. The agency benefits because it can do a better job of responding to the request. The agency will also be able to use its resources to respond to more requests. The FOIA works best when both the requester and the agency act cooperatively.

C. Making an FOIA Request

The first step in making a request under the FOIA is to identify the agency that has the records. An FOIA request must be addressed to a specific agency. There is no central government records office that services FOIA requests.

Often, a requester knows beforehand which agency has the desired records. If not, a requester can consult a government directory such as the United States Government Manual.[13] This manual has a complete list of all federal agencies, a description of agency functions, and the address of each agency. A requester who is uncertain about which agency has the records that are needed can make FOIA requests at more than one agency.

Agencies normally require that FOIA requests be in writing. Letters requesting records under the FOIA can be short and simple. No one needs a lawyer to make an FOIA request. Appendix 1 of this Guide contains a sample request letter.

The request letter should be addressed to the agency's FOIA Officer or to the head of the agency. The envelope containing the written request should be marked "Freedom of Information Act Request" in the bottom left-hand corner.[14]

There are three basic elements to an FOIA request letter. First, the letter should state that the request is being made under the Freedom of Information Act. Second, the request should identify the records that are being sought as specifically as possible. Third, the name and address of the requester must be included.

Under the 1986 amendments to the FOIA, fees chargeable vary with the status or purpose of the requester. As a result, a requester may have to provide additional information to permit the agency to determine the appropriate fees. Different fees can be charged to commercial users, representatives of the news media, educational or noncommercial scientific institutions, and individuals. The next section explains the fee structure in more detail.

There are several optional items that are often included in an FOIA request. The first is the telephone number of the requester. This permits an agency employee processing a request to speak with the requester if necessary.

A second optional item is a limitation on the fees that the requester is willing to pay. It is common for a requester to ask to be notified in advance if the charges will exceed a fixed amount. This allows the requester to modify or withdraw a request if the cost may be too high. Also, by stating a willingness to pay a set amount of fees in the original request letter, a requester may avoid the necessity of additional correspondence and delay.

A third optional item sometimes included in an FOIA request is a request for a waiver or reduction of fees. The 1986 amendments to the FOIA changed the rules for fee waivers. Fees must be waived or reduced if disclosure of the information is in the public interest because it is likely to contribute significantly to public understanding of the operations or activities of the government and is not primarily in the commercial interest of the requester. Decisions about granting fee waivers are separate from and different than decisions about the amount of fees that can be charged to a requester.

A requester should keep a copy of the request letter and related correspondence until the request has been finally resolved.

> D. Fees and Fee Waivers

FOIA requesters may have to pay fees covering some or all of the costs of processing their requests. As amended in 1986, the law establishes three types of fees that may be charged. The 1986 law makes the process of determining the applicable fees more complicated. However, the 1986 rules reduce or eliminate entirely the cost for small, non-commercial requests.

First, fees can be imposed to recover the cost of copying documents. All agencies have a fixed price for making copies using copying machines. A requester is usually charged the actual cost of copying computer tapes, photographs, and other nonstandard documents.

Second, fees can also be imposed to recover the costs of searching for documents. This includes the time spent looking for material responsive to a request. A requester can minimize search charges by making clear, narrow requests for identifiable documents whenever possible.

Third, fees can be charged to recover review costs. Review is the process of examining documents to determine whether any portion is exempt from disclosure. Before the 1986 amendments took effect, no review costs were charged to any requester. Effective on April 25, 1987, review costs may be charged to commercial requesters only. Review charges only include costs incurred during the initial examination of a document. An agency may not charge for any costs incurred in resolving issues of law or policy that may arise while processing a request.

Different fees apply to different requesters. There are three categories of FOIA requesters. The first includes representatives of the news media, and educational or noncommercial scientific institutions whose purpose is scholarly or scientific research. A requester in this category who is not seeking records for commercial use can only be billed for reasonable standard document duplication charges. A request for information from a representative of the news media is not considered to be for commercial use if the request is in support of a news gathering or dissemination function.

The second category includes FOIA requesters seeking records for commercial use. Commercial use is not defined in the law, but it generally includes profit making activities. A commercial user can be charged reasonable standard charges for document duplication, search, and review.

The third category of FOIA requesters includes everyone not in the first two categories. People seeking information for personal use, public interest groups, and non-profit organizations are examples of requesters who fall into the third group. Charges for these requesters are limited to reasonable standard charges for document duplication and search. Review costs may not be charged. The 1986 amendments did not change the fees charged to these requesters.

Small requests are free for a requester in the first and third categories. This includes all requesters except commercial users. There is no charge for the first two hours of search time and for the first 100 pages of documents. A non-commercial requester who limits a request to a small number of easily found records will not pay any fees at all.

In addition, the law also prevents agencies from charging fees if the cost of collecting the fee would exceed the amount collected. This limitation applies to all requests, including those seeking documents for commercial use. Thus, if the allowable charges for any FOIA request are small, no fees are imposed.

Each agency sets charges for duplication, search, and review based on its own costs. The amount of these charges is listed in agency FOIA regulations. Each agency also sets its own threshold for minimum charges.

The 1986 FOIA amendments also changed the law on fee waivers. Fees now must be waived or reduced if disclosure of the information is in the public interest because it is likely to contribute significantly to public understanding of the operations or activities of the government and is not primarily in the commercial interest of the requester.

The 1986 amendments on fees and fee waivers have created some confusion. Determinations about fees are separate and distinct from determinations about fee waivers. For example, a requester who can demonstrate that he or she is a news reporter may only be charged duplication fees. But a requester found to be a reporter is not automatically entitled to a waiver of those fees. A reporter who seeks a waiver must demonstrate that the request also meets the standards for waivers.

Normally, only after a requester has been categorized to determine the applicable fees does the issue of a fee waiver arise. A requester who seeks a fee waiver should ask for a waiver in the original request letter. However, a request for a waiver can be made at a later time. The requester should describe how disclosure will contribute to public understanding of the operations or activities of the government. The sample request letter in the appendix includes optional language asking for a fee waiver.

Any requester may ask for a fee waiver. Some will find it easier to qualify than others. A news reporter who is only charged duplication costs may still ask that the charges be waived because of the public benefits that will result from disclosure. A representative of the news media, a scholar, or a public interest group are more likely to qualify for a waiver of fees. A commercial user may find it difficult to qualify for waivers.

The eligibility of other requesters will vary. A key element in qualifying for a fee waiver is the relationship of the information to public understanding of the operations or activities of government. Another important factor is the ability of the requester to convey that information to other interested members of the public. A requester is not eligible for a fee waiver solely because of indigence.

E. Requirements for Agency Responses

Each agency is required to determine within ten days (excluding Saturdays, Sundays, and legal holidays) after the receipt of a request whether to comply with the request. The actual disclosure of documents is required to follow promptly thereafter. If a request is denied in whole or in part, the agency must tell the requester the reasons for the denial. The agency must also tell the requester that there is a right to appeal any adverse determination to the head of the agency.

The FOIA permits an agency to extend the time limits up to ten days in unusual circumstances. These circumstances include the need to collect records from remote locations, review large numbers of records, and consult with other agencies. The agency is supposed to notify the requester whenever an extension is invoked.[15]

The statutory time limits for responses are not always met. An agency sometimes receives an unexpectedly large number of FOIA requests at one time and is unable to meet the deadlines. Some agencies assign inadequate resources to FOIA offices. The Congress does not condone the failure of any agency to meet the law's time limits. However, as a practical matter, there is little that a requester can do about it. The courts have been reluctant to provide relief solely because the FOIA's time limits have not been met.

The best advice to requesters is to be patient. The law allows a requester to consider that his or her request has been denied if it has not been decided within the time limits. This permits the requester to file an administrative appeal or file a lawsuit in federal district court. However, this is not always the best course of action. The filing of an administrative or judicial appeal will not necessarily result in any faster processing of the request.

Each agency generally processes requests in the order of receipt. Some agencies will expedite the processing of urgent requests. Anyone with a pressing need for records should consult with the agency FOIA officer about how to ask for expedited treatment of requests.

F. Reasons Access May Be Denied Under the FOIA

An agency may refuse to disclose an agency record that falls within any of the FOIA's nine statutory exemptions. The exemptions protect against the disclosure of information that would harm national defense or foreign policy, privacy of individuals, proprietary interests of business, functioning of the government, and other important interests. A document that does not qualify as an "agency record" may be denied because only agency records are available under the FOIA. Personal notes of agency employees may be denied on this basis. However, most records in the possession of an agency are "agency records" within the meaning of the FOIA.

An agency may withhold exempt information, but it is not always required to do so. For example, an agency may disclose an exempt internal memorandum because no harm would result from its disclosure. However, an agency is not likely to agree to disclose an exempt document that is classified or that contains a trade secret.

When a record contains some information that qualifies as exempt, the entire record is not necessarily exempt. Instead, the FOIA specifically provides that any reasonably segregable portions of a record must be provided to a requester after the deletion of the portions that are exempt. This is a very important requirement because it prevents an agency from withholding an entire document simply because one line or one page is exempt.

1. Exemption 1: Classified Documents

The first FOIA exemption permits the withholding of properly classified documents. Information may be classified in the interest of national defense or foreign policy.

The rules for classification are established by the President and not the FOIA or other law. The FOIA provides that, if a document has been properly classified under a presidential Executive Order, the document can be withheld from disclosure.

Classified documents may be requested under the FOIA. An agency can review the document to determine if it still requires protection. In addition, the Executive Order on Security Classification establishes a special procedure for requesting the declassification of documents.[16] If a requested document is declassified, it can be released in response to an FOIA request. However, a document that is declassified may be still be exempt under other FOIA exemptions.

2. Exemption 2: Internal Personnel Rules and Practices

The second FOIA exemption covers matters that are related solely to an agency's internal personnel rules and practices. As interpreted by the courts, there are two separate classes of documents that are generally held to fall within exemption two.

First, information relating to personnel rules or internal agency practices is exempt if it is trivial administrative matter of no genuine public interest. A rule governing lunch hours for agency employees is an example.

Second, an internal administrative manual can be exempt if disclosure would risk circumvention of law or agency regulations. In order to fall into this category, the material will normally have to regulate internal agency conduct rather than public behavior.

3. Exemption 3: Information Exempt Under Other Laws

The third exemption incorporates into the FOIA other laws that restrict the availability of information. To qualify under this exemption, a statute must require that matters be withheld from the public in such a manner as to leave no discretion to the agency. Alternatively, the statute must establish particular criteria for withholding or refer to particular types of matters to be withheld.

One example of a qualifying statute is the provision of the Tax Code prohibiting the public disclosure of tax returns and tax return information.[17] Another qualifying Exemption 3 statute is the law designating identifiable census data as confidential.[18] Whether a particular statute qualifies under Exemption 3 can be a difficult legal question.

4. Exemption 4: Confidential Business Information

The fourth exemption protects from public disclosure two types of information: trade secrets and confidential business information. A trade secret is a commercially valuable plan, formula, process, or device. This is a narrow category of information. An example of a trade secret is the recipe for a commercial food product.

The second type of protected data is commercial or financial information obtained from a person and privileged or confidential. The courts have held that data qualifies for withholding if disclosure by the government would be likely to harm the competitive position of the person who submitted the information. Detailed information on a company's marketing plans, profits, or costs can qualify as confidential business information. Information may also be withheld if disclosure would be likely to impair the government's ability to obtain similar information in the future.

Only information obtained from a person other than a government agency qualifies under the fourth exemption. A person is an individual, a partnership, or a corporation. Information that an agency created on its own cannot normally be withheld under exemption four.

Although there is no formal requirement under the FOIA, many agencies will notify a submitter of business information that disclosure of the information is being considered.[19] The submitter then has an opportunity to convince the agency that the information qualifies for withholding. A submitter can also file suit to block disclosure under the FOIA. Such lawsuits are generally referred to as "reverse" FOIA lawsuits because the FOIA is being used in an attempt to prevent rather than to require the disclosure of information. A reverse FOIA lawsuit may be filed when the submitter of documents and the government disagree whether the information is confidential.

5. Exemption 5: Internal Government Communications

The FOIA's fifth exemption applies to internal government documents. An example is a letter from one government department to another about a joint decision that has not yet been made. Another example is a memorandum from an agency employee to his supervisor describing options for conducting the agency's business.

The purpose of the fifth exemption is to safeguard the deliberative policy making process of government. The exemption encourages frank discussion of policy matters between agency officials by allowing supporting documents to be withheld from public disclosure. The exemption also protects against premature disclosure of policies before final adoption.

While the policy behind the fifth exemption is well- accepted, the application of the exemption is complicated. The fifth exemption may be the most difficult FOIA exemption to understand and apply. For example, the exemption protects the policy making process, but it does not protect purely factual information related to the policy process. Factual information must be disclosed unless it is inextricably intertwined with protected information about an agency decision.

Protection for the decision making process is appropriate only for the period while decisions are being made. Thus, the fifth exemption has been held to distinguish between documents that are pre-decisional and therefore may be protected, and those which are post-decisional and therefore not subject to protection. Once a policy is adopted, the public has a greater interest in knowing the basis for the decision.

The exemption also incorporates some of the privileges that apply in litigation involving the government. For example, papers prepared by the government's lawyers can be withheld in the same way that papers prepared by private lawyers for clients are not available through discovery in civil litigation.

6. Exemption 6: Personal Privacy

The sixth exemption covers personnel, medical, and similar files the disclosure of which would constitute a clearly unwarranted invasion of personal privacy. This exemption protects the privacy interests of individuals by allowing an agency to withhold intimate personal data kept in government files. Only individuals have privacy interests. Corporations and other legal persons have no privacy rights under the sixth exemption.

The exemption requires agencies to strike a balance between an individual's privacy interest and the public's right to know. However, since only a clearly unwarranted invasion of privacy is a basis for withholding, there is a perceptible tilt in favor of disclosure in the exemption. Nevertheless, the sixth exemption makes it harder to obtain information about another individual without the consent of that individual.

The Privacy Act of 1974 also regulates the disclosure of personal information about an individual. The FOIA and the Privacy Act overlap in part, but there is no inconsistency. An individual seeking records about himself or herself should cite both laws when making a request. This ensures that the maximum amount of disclosable information will be released. Records that can be denied to an individual under the Privacy Act are not necessarily exempt under the FOIA.

7. Exemption 7: Law Enforcement

The seventh exemption allows agencies to withhold law enforcement records in order to protect the law enforcement process from interference. The exemption was amended slightly in 1986, but it still retains six specific subexemptions.

Exemption (7)(A) allows the withholding of a law enforcement record that could reasonably be expected to interfere with enforcement proceedings. This exemption protects an active law enforcement investigation from interference through premature disclosure.

Exemption (7)(B) allows the withholding of information that would deprive a person of a right to a fair trial or an impartial adjudication. This exemption is rarely used.

Exemption (7)(C) recognizes that individuals have a privacy interest in information maintained in law enforcement files. If the disclosure of information could reasonably be expected to constitute an unwarranted invasion of personal privacy, the information is exempt from disclosure. The standards for privacy protection in Exemption 6 and Exemption (7)(C) differ slightly. Exemption (7)(C) protects against an unwarranted invasion of personal privacy while Exemption 6 protects against clearly an unwarranted invasion. Also, Exemption (7)(C) allows the withholding of information that "could reasonably be expected to "invade" someone's privacy. Under Exemption 6, information can be withheld only if disclosure "would" invade someone's privacy.

Exemption (7)(D) protects the identity of confidential sources. Information that could reasonably be expected to reveal the identity of a confidential source is exempt. A confidential source can include a state, local, or foreign agency or authority, or a private institution that furnished information on a confidential basis. In addition, the exemption protects information furnished by a confidential source if the data was compiled by a criminal law enforcement authority during a criminal investigation or by an agency conducting a lawful national security intelligence investigation.

Exemption (7)(E) protects from disclosure information that would reveal techniques and procedures for law enforcement investigations or prosecutions or that would disclose guidelines for law enforcement investigations or prosecutions if disclosure of the information could reasonably be expected to risk circumvention of the law.

Exemption (7)(F) protects law enforcement information that could reasonably be expected to endanger the life or physical safety of any individual.

8. Exemption 8: Financial Institutions

The eighth exemption protects information that is contained in or related to examination, operating, or condition reports prepared by or for a bank supervisory agency such as the Federal Deposit Insurance Corporation, the Federal Reserve, or similar agencies.

9. Exemption 9: Geological Information

The ninth FOIA exemption covers geological and geophysical information, data, and maps about wells. This exemption is rarely used.

G. FOIA Exclusions

The 1986 amendments to the FOIA gave limited authority to agencies to respond to a request without confirming the existence of the requested records. Ordinarily, any proper request must receive an answer stating whether there is any responsive information, even if the requested information is exempt from disclosure.

In some narrow circumstances, acknowledgement of the existence of a record can produce consequences similar to those resulting from disclosure of the record itself. In order to avoid this type of problem, the 1986 amendments established three "record exclusions".

The exclusions allow an agency to treat certain exempt records as if the records were not subject to the FOIA. An agency is not required to confirm the existence of three specific categories of records. If these records are requested, the agency may respond that there are no disclosable records responsive to the request. However, these exclusions do not broaden the authority of any agency to withhold documents from the public. The exclusions are only applicable to information that is otherwise exempt from disclosure.

The first exclusion may be used when a request seeks information that is exempt because disclosure could reasonably be expected to interfere with a current law enforcement investigation (exemption (7)(A)). There are three specific prerequisites for the application of this exclusion. First, the investigation in question must involve a possible violation of criminal law. Second, there must be reason to believe that the subject of the investigation is not already aware that the investigation is underway. Third, disclosure of the existence of the records -- as distinguished from the contents of the records -- could reasonably be expected to interfere with enforcement proceedings.

When all of these conditions exist, an agency may respond to an FOIA request for investigatory records as if the records are not subject to the requirements of the FOIA. In other words, the agency's response does not have to reveal that it is conducting an investigation.

The second exclusion applies to informant records maintained by a criminal law enforcement agency under the informant's name or personal identifier. The agency is not required to confirm the existence of these records unless the informant's status has been officially confirmed. This exclusion helps agencies to protect the identity of confidential informants. Information that might identify informants has always been exempt under the FOIA.

The third exclusion only applies to records maintained by the Federal Bureau of Investigation which pertain to foreign intelligence, counterintelligence, or international terrorism. When the existence of these types of records is classified, the FBI may treat the records as not subject to the requirements of FOIA.

This exclusion does not apply to all classified records on the specific subjects. It only applies when the records are classified and when the existence of the records is also classified. Since the underlying records must be classified before the exclusion is relevant, agencies have no new substantive withholding authority.

In enacting these exclusions, congressional sponsors stated that it was their intent that agencies must inform FOIA requesters that these exclusions are available for agency use. Requesters who believe that records were improperly withheld because of the exclusions can seek judicial review.

H. Administrative Appeal Procedures

Whenever an FOIA request is denied, the agency must inform the requester of the reasons for the denial and the requester's right to appeal the denial to the head of the agency. A requester may appeal the denial of a request for a document or for a fee waiver. A requester may contest the type or amount of fees that were charged. A requester may appeal any other type of adverse determination including a rejection of a request for failure to describe adequately the documents being requested. A requester can also appeal because the agency failed to conduct an adequate search for the documents that were requested.

A person whose request was granted in part and denied in part may appeal the part that was denied. If an agency has agreed to disclose some but not all requested documents, the filing of an appeal does not affect the release of the documents that are disclosable. There is no risk to the requester in filing an appeal.

The appeal to the head of the agency is a simple administrative appeal. A lawyer can be helpful, but no one needs a lawyer to file an appeal. Anyone who can write a letter can file an appeal. Appeals to the head of the agency often result in the disclosure of some records that had been withheld. A requester who is not convinced that the agency's initial decision is correct should appeal. There is no charge for filing an administrative appeal.

An appeal is filed by sending a letter to the head of the agency. The letter must identify the FOIA request that is being appealed. The envelope containing the letter of appeal should be marked in the lower left hand corner with the words "Freedom of Information Act Appeal."[20]

Many agencies assign a number to all FOIA requests that are received. The number should be included in the appeal letter, along with the name and address of the requester. It is a common practice to include a copy of the agency's initial decision letter as part of the appeal, but this is not required. It can also be helpful for the requester to include a telephone number in the appeal letter.

An appeal will normally include the requester's arguments supporting disclosure of the documents. A requester may include any facts or any arguments supporting the case for reversing the initial decision. However, an appeal letter does not have to contain any arguments at all. It is sufficient to state that the agency's initial decision is being appealed. Appendix 1 includes a sample appeal letter.

The FOIA does not set a time limit for filing an administrative appeal of an FOIA denial. However, it is good practice to file an appeal promptly. Some agency regulations establish a time limit for filing an administrative appeal. A requester whose appeal is rejected by an agency because it is too late may refile the original FOIA request and start the process again.

A requester who delays filing an appeal runs the risk that the documents could be destroyed. However, as long as an agency is considering a request or an appeal, the agency must preserve the documents.

An agency is required to make a decision on an appeal within twenty days (excluding Saturdays, Sundays, and federal holidays). It is possible for an agency to extend the time limits by an additional ten days. Once the time period has elapsed, a requester may consider that the appeal has been denied and may proceed with a judicial appeal. However, unless there is an urgent need for records, this may not be the best course of action. The courts are not sympathetic to appeals based solely on an agency's failure to comply with the FOIA's time limits.

I. Filing a Judicial Appeal

When an administrative appeal is denied, a requester has the right to appeal the denial in court. An FOIA appeal can be filed in the United States District Court in the district where the requester lives. The requester can also file suit in the district where the documents are located or in the District of Columbia. When a requester goes to court, the burden of justifying the withholding of documents is on the government. This is a distinct advantage for the requester.

Requesters are sometimes successful when they go to court, but the results vary considerably. Some requesters who file judicial appeals find that an agency will disclose some documents previously withheld rather than fight about disclosure in court. This does not always happen, and there is no guarantee that the filing of a judicial appeal will result in any additional disclosure.

Most requesters require the assistance of an attorney to file a judicial appeal. A person who files a lawsuit and substantially prevails may be awarded reasonable attorney fees and litigation costs reasonably incurred. Some requesters may be able to handle their own appeal without an attorney. Since this is not a litigation guide, details of the judicial appeal process have been not included. Anyone considering filing an appeal can begin by reading the provisions of the FOIA on judicial review.[21]

VII. THE PRIVACY ACT OF 1974

A. The Scope of the Privacy Act of 1974

The Privacy Act of 1974 provides safeguards against an invasion of privacy through the misuse of records by federal agencies. In general, the Act allows a citizen to learn how records are collected, maintained, used, and disseminated by the federal government. The Act also permits an individual to gain access to most personal information maintained by federal agencies and to seek amendment of any incorrect or incomplete information.

The Privacy Act applies to personal information maintained by agencies in the executive branch of the federal government. The executive branch includes cabinet departments, military departments, government corporations, government controlled corporations, independent regulatory agencies, and other establishments in the executive branch. Agencies subject to the Freedom of Information Act (FOIA) are also subject to the Privacy Act. The Privacy Act does not generally apply to records maintained by state and local governments or private companies or organizations.[22]

The Privacy Act only grants rights to United States citizens and to aliens lawfully admitted for permanent residence. As a result, a foreign national cannot use the Act's provisions. However, a foreigner may use the FOIA to request records about himself or herself.

In general, the only records subject to the Privacy Act are records that are maintained in a system of records. The idea of a "system of records" is unique to the Privacy Act and requires explanation.

The Act defines a "record" to include most personal information maintained by an agency about an individual. A record contains individually identifiable information, including but not limited to information about education, financial transactions, medical history, criminal history, or employment history. A "system of records" is a group of records from which information is actually retrieved by name, social security number, or other identifying symbol assigned to an individual.

Some personal information is not kept in a system of records. This information is not subject to the provisions of the Privacy Act, although access may be requested under the FOIA. Most personal information in government files is subject to the Privacy Act.

The Privacy Act also establishes general records management requirements for federal agencies. In summary, there are five basic requirements that are most relevant to individuals.

First, each agency must establish procedures allowing individuals to see and copy records about themselves. An individual may also seek to amend any information that is not accurate, relevant, timely, or complete. The rights to inspect and to correct records are the most important provisions of the Privacy Act. This guide explains in more detail how an individual can exercise these rights.

Second, each agency must publish notices describing all systems of records. The notices include a complete description of personal-data record keeping policies, practices, and systems. This requirement prevents the maintenance of secret record systems.

Third, each agency must make reasonable efforts to maintain accurate, relevant, timely, and complete records about individuals. Agencies are prohibited from maintaining information about how individuals exercise rights guaranteed by the First Amendment to the U.S. Constitution unless maintenance of the information is specifically authorized by statute or relates to an authorized law enforcement activity.

Fourth, the Act establishes rules governing the use and disclosure of personal information. The Act specifies that information collected for one purpose may not be used for another purpose without notice to or the consent of the subject of the record. The Act also requires that each agency keep a record of some disclosures of personal information.

Fifth, the Act provides legal remedies that permit an individual to seek enforcement of the rights granted under the Act. In addition, federal employees who fail to comply with the Act's provisions may be subjected to criminal penalties.

B. The Computer Matching and Privacy Protection Act

The Computer Matching and Privacy Protection Act of 1988 (Public Law 100-503) amended the Privacy Act by adding new provisions regulating the use of computer matching. Records used during the conduct of a matching program are subject to an additional set of requirements.

Computer matching is the computerized comparison of information about individuals for the purpose of determining eligibility for federal benefit programs. A matching program can be subject to the requirements of the Computer Matching Act if records from a Privacy Act system of records are used during the program. If federal Privacy Act records are matched against state or local records, then the state or local matching program can be subject to the new matching requirements.

In general, matching programs involving federal records must be conducted under a matching agreement between the source and recipient agencies. The matching agreement describes the purpose and procedures of the matching and establishes protections for matching records. The agreement is subject to review and approval by a Data Integrity Board. Each federal agency involved in a matching activity must establish a Data Integrity Board.

For an individual seeking access to or correction of records, the computer matching legislation provides no special access rights. If matching records are federal records, then the access and correction provisions of the Privacy Act apply. There is no general right of access or correction for matching records of state and local agencies. It is possible that rights are available under state or local laws.

There is, however, a requirement that an individual be notified of agency findings prior to the taking of any adverse action as a result of a computer matching program. An individual must also be given an opportunity to contest such findings. The notice and opportunity-to-contest provisions apply to matching records whether the matching was done by the federal government or by a state or local government. Section 7201 of Public Law 101-508 modified the due process notice requirement to permit the use of statutory or regulatory notice periods.

The matching provisions also require that any agency -- federal or non-federal -- involved in computer matching must independently verify information used to take adverse action against an individual. This requirement was included in order to protect individuals from arbitrary or unjustified denials of benefits. Independent verification includes independent investigation and confirmation of information. Public Law 101- 508 also modified the independent verification requirement in circumstances in which it was unnecessary.

Most of the provisions of the Computer Matching and Privacy Protection Act of 1988 were originally scheduled to become effective in July 1989. Public Law 101-56 delayed the effective date for most matching programs until January 1, 1990.

C. Locating Records

There is no central index of federal government records about individuals. An individual who wants to inspect records about himself or herself must first identify which agency has the records. Often, this will not be difficult. For example, an individual who was employed by the federal government knows that the employing agency or the Office of Personnel Management maintains personnel files.

Similarly, an individual who receives veterans' benefits will normally find relevant records at the Department of Veterans Affairs or at the Defense Department. Tax records are maintained by the Internal Revenue Service, social security records by the Social Security Administration, passport records by the State Department, etc.

For those who are uncertain about which agency has the records that are needed, there are several sources of information. First, an individual can ask an agency that might maintain the records. If that agency does not have the records, it may be able to identify the proper agency.

Second, a government directory such as the United States Government Manual[23] contains a complete list of all federal agencies, a description of agency functions, and the address of the agency and its field offices. An agency responsible for operating a program normally maintains the records related to that program.

Third, a Federal Information Center can help to identify government agencies, their functions, and their records. These Centers, which are operated by the General Services Administration, serve as clearinghouses for information about the federal government. There are Federal Information Centers throughout the country.

Fourth, every two years, the Office of the Federal Register publishes a compilation of system of records notices for all agencies. These notices contain a complete description of each record system maintained by each agency. The compilation -- which is published in five large volumes -- is the most complete reference for information about federal agency personal information practices.[24] The information that appears in the compilation also appears sometimes in the Federal Register.[25]

The compilation -- formally called Privacy Act Issuances -- may be difficult to find and hard to use. It does not contain a comprehensive index. Copies will be available in some federal depository libraries and possibly in other libraries as well. Although the compilation is the best single source of detailed information about personal records maintained by federal agencies, it is not necessary to consult the compilation before making a Privacy Act request. A requester is not required to identify the specific system of records that contains the information being sought. It is sufficient to identify the agency that has the records. Using information provided by the requester, the agency will determine which system of records has the files that have been requested.

Those who request records under the Privacy Act can help the agency by identifying the type of records being sought. Large agencies maintain hundreds of different record systems. A request can be processed faster if the requester tells the agency that he or she was employed by the agency, was the recipient of benefits under an agency program, or had other specific contacts with the agency.

D. Making a Privacy Act Request for Access

The fastest way to make a Privacy Act request is to identify the specific system of records. The request can be addressed to the system manager. Few people do this. Instead, most people address their requests to the head of the agency that has the records or to the agency's Privacy Act Officer. The envelope containing the written request should be marked "Privacy Act Request" in the bottom left-hand corner.[26]

There are three basic elements to a request for records under the Privacy Act. First, the letter should state that the request is being made under the Privacy Act. Second, the letter should include the name, address, and signature of the requester. Third, the request should describe the records as specifically as possible. Appendix 1 includes a sample Privacy Act request letter.

It is a common practice for an individual seeking records about himself or herself to make the request under both the Privacy Act of 1974 and the Freedom of Information Act. See the discussion in the front of this guide about which act to use.

A requester can describe the records by identifying a specific system of records, by describing his or her contacts with an agency, or by simply asking for all records about himself or herself. The broader and less specific a request is, the longer it may take for an agency to respond.

It is a good practice for a requester to describe the type of records that he or she expects to find. For example, an individual seeking a copy of his service record in the Army should state that he was in the Army and include the approximate dates of service. This will help the Defense Department narrow its search to record systems that are likely to contain the information being sought. An individual seeking records from the Federal Bureau of Investigation may ask that files in specific field offices be searched in addition to the FBI's central office files. The FBI does not routinely search field office records without a specific request.

An agency will generally require a requester to provide some proof of identity before records will be disclosed. Agencies may have different requirements. Some agencies will accept a signature; others may require a notarized signature. If an individual goes to the agency to inspect records, standard personal identification may be acceptable. More stringent requirements may apply if the records being sought are especially sensitive.

An agency will inform requesters of any special identification requirements. Requesters who need records quickly should first consult agency regulations or talk to the agency's Privacy Act Officer to find out how to provide adequate identification.

An individual who visits an agency office to inspect a Privacy Act record may bring along a friend or relative to review the record. When a requester brings another person, the agency may ask the requester to sign a written statement authorizing discussion of the record in the presence of that person.

It is a crime to knowingly and willfully request or obtain records under the Privacy Act under false pretenses. A request for access under the Privacy Act can only be made by the subject of the record. An individual cannot make a request under the Privacy Act for a record about another person. The only exception is for a parent or legal guardian who can request records for a minor or a person who has been declared incompetent.

E. Fees

Under the Privacy Act, fees can only be charged for the cost of copying records. No fees may be charged for the time it takes to search for records or for the time it takes to review the records to determine if any exemptions apply. This is a major difference from the FOIA. Under the FOIA, fees can sometimes be charged to recover search costs and review costs.[27] The different fee structure in the two laws is one reason many requesters seeking records about themselves cite both laws. This minimizes allowable fees.

Many agencies will not charge fees for making a copy of a Privacy Act file, especially when the file is small. If paying the copying charges is a problem, the requester should explain in the request letter. An agency can waive fees under the Privacy Act.

F. Requirements for Agency Responses

Unlike the FOIA, there is no fixed time when an agency must respond to a request for access to records under the Privacy Act. It is good practice for an agency to acknowledge receipt of a Privacy Act request within ten days and to provide the requested records within thirty days.

At many agencies, FOIA and Privacy Act requests are processed by the same personnel. When there is a backlog of requests, it takes longer to receive a response. As a practical matter, there is little that a requester can do when an agency response is delayed. Requesters should be patient.

Agencies generally process requests in the order in which they were received. Some agencies will expedite the processing of urgent requests. Anyone with a pressing need for records should consult with the agency Privacy Act officer about how to ask for expedited treatment of requests.

G. Reasons Access May Be Denied Under the Privacy Act

Not all records about an individual must be disclosed under the Privacy Act. Some records may be withheld to protect important government interests such as national security or law enforcement.

The Privacy Act exemptions are different than the exemptions of the FOIA. Under the FOIA, any record may be withheld from disclosure if it contains exempt information when a request is received. The decision to apply an FOIA exemption is made only after a request has been made. In contrast, Privacy Act exemptions apply not to a record but to a system of records. Before an agency can apply a Privacy Act exemption, the agency must first issue a regulation stating that there may be exempt records in that system of records.

Without reviewing system notices or agency regulations, it is hard to tell whether particular Privacy Act records are exempt from disclosure. However, it is a safe assumption that any system of records that qualifies for an exemption has been exempted by the agency.

Since most record systems are not exempt, the exemptions are not relevant to most requests. Also, agencies do not always rely upon available Privacy Act exemptions unless there is a specific reason to do so. Thus, some records that could be withheld will nevertheless be disclosed upon request.

Because Privacy Act exemptions are complex and used infrequently, most requesters need not worry about them. The exemptions are discussed here for those interested in the Act's details and for reference when an agency withholds records. Anyone needing more information about the Privacy Act's exemptions can begin by reading the relevant sections of the Act. The complete text of the Act is reprinted in an appendix to this guide.[28]

The Privacy Act's exemptions differ from those of the FOIA in another important way. The FOIA is mostly a disclosure law. Information exempt under the FOIA is exempt from disclosure only. The Privacy Act, however, imposes many separate requirements on personal records. Some systems of records are exempt from the disclosure requirements, but no system is exempt from all Privacy Act requirements.

For example, no system of records is ever exempt from the requirement that a description of the system be published. No system of records can be exempted from the limitations on disclosure of the records outside of the agency. No system is exempt from the requirement to maintain an accounting for disclosures. No system is exempt from the restriction against the maintenance of unauthorized information on the exercise of First Amendment rights. All systems are subject to the requirement that reasonable efforts be taken to assure that records disclosed outside the agency be accurate, complete, timely, and relevant. Each agency must maintain proper administrative controls and security for all systems. Finally, the Privacy Act's criminal penalties remain fully applicable to each system of records.

1. General Exemptions

There are two general exemptions under the Privacy Act. The first applies to all records maintained by the Central Intelligence Agency. The second applies to selected records maintained by an agency or component whose principal function is any activity pertaining to criminal law enforcement. Records of criminal law enforcement agencies can be exempt under the Privacy Act if the records consist of (A) information compiled to identify individual criminal offenders and which consists only of identifying data and notations of arrests, the nature and disposition of criminal charges, sentencing, confinement, release, and parole and probation status; (B) criminal investigatory records associated with an identifiable individual; or (C) reports identifiable to a particular individual compiled at any stage from arrest through release from supervision.

Systems of records subject to the general exemptions may be exempted from many of the Privacy Act's requirements. Exemption from the Act's access and correction provisions is the most important. An individual has no right under the Privacy Act to ask for a copy of or to seek correction of a record subject to the general exemptions.

In practice, these exemptions are not as expansive as they sound. Most agencies that have exempt records will accept and process Privacy Act requests. The records will be reviewed on a case-by-case basis. Agencies will often disclose any information that does not require protection. Agencies also tend to follow a similar policy for requests for correction.

Individuals interested in obtaining records from the Central Intelligence Agency or from law enforcement agencies should not be discouraged from making requests for access. Even if the Privacy Act access exemption is applied, portions of the record may still be disclosable under the FOIA. This is a primary reason individuals should cite both the Privacy Act and the FOIA when requesting records.

The general exemption from access does prevent requesters from filing a lawsuit under the Privacy Act when access is denied. The right to sue under the FOIA is not changed because of a Privacy Act exemption.

2. Specific Exemptions

There are seven specific Privacy Act exemptions that can be applied to systems of records. Records subject to these exemptions are not exempt from as many of the Act's requirements as are the records subject to the general exemptions. However, records exempt under the specific exemptions are likely to be exempt from the Privacy Act's access and correction provisions. Nevertheless, since the access and correction exemptions are not always applied when available, those seeking records should not be discouraged from making a request. Also, the FOIA can be used to seek access to records exempt under the Privacy Act.

The first specific exemption covers record systems containing information properly classified in the interest of national defense or foreign policy. Classified information is also exempt from disclosure under the FOIA and will normally be unavailable under either the FOIA and Privacy Acts.

The second specific exemption applies to systems of records containing investigatory material compiled for law enforcement purposes other than material covered by the general law enforcement exemption. The specific law enforcement exemption is limited when -- as a result of the maintenance of the records -- an individual is denied any right, privilege, or benefit to which he or she would be entitled by federal law or for which he or she would otherwise be entitled. In such a case, disclosure is required except where disclosure would reveal the identity of a confidential source who furnished information to the government under an express promise that the identity of the source would be held in confidence. If the information was collected from a confidential source before the effective date of the Privacy Act (September 27, 1975), an implied promise of confidentiality is sufficient to permit withholding of the identity of the source.[29]

The third specific exemption applies to systems of records maintained in connection with providing protective services to the President of the United States or other individuals who receive protection from the Secret Service.

The fourth specific exemption applies to systems of records required by statute to be maintained and used solely as statistical records.

The fifth specific exemption covers investigatory material compiled solely to determine suitability, eligibility, or qualifications for federal civilian employment, military service, federal contracts, or access to classified information. However, this exemption applies only to the extent that disclosure of information would reveal the identity of a confidential source who provided the information under a promise of confidentiality.

The sixth specific exemption applies to systems of records that contain testing or examination material used solely to determine individual qualifications for appointment or promotion in federal service, but only when disclosure would compromise the objectivity or fairness of the testing or examination process. Effectively, this exemption permits withholding of questions used in employment tests.

The seventh specific exemption covers evaluation material used to determine potential for promotion in the armed services. The material is only exempt to the extent that disclosure would reveal the identity of a confidential source who provided the information under a promise of confidentiality.

3. Medical Records

Medical records maintained by federal agencies -- for example, records at Veterans Administration hospitals -- are not formally exempt from the Privacy Act's access provisions. However, the Privacy Act authorizes a special procedure for medical records that operates, at least in part, like an exemption.

Agencies may deny individuals direct access to medical records, including psychological records, if the agency deems it necessary. An agency normally reviews medical records requested by an individual. If the agency determines that direct disclosure is unwise, it can arrange for disclosure to a physician selected by the individual or possibly to another person chosen by the individual.

4. Litigation Records

The Privacy Act's access provisions include a general limitation on access to litigation records. The Act does not require an agency to disclose to an individual any information compiled in reasonable anticipation of a civil action or proceeding. This limitation operates like an exemption, although there is no requirement that the exemption be applied by regulation to a system of records before it can be used.

H. Administrative Appeal Procedures For Denial of Access

Unlike the FOIA, the Privacy Act does not provide for an administrative appeal of the denial of access. However, many agencies have established procedures that will allow Privacy Act requesters to appeal a denial of access without going to court. An administrative appeal is often allowed under the Privacy Act, even though it is not required, because many individuals cite both the FOIA and Privacy

Act when making a request. The FOIA provides specifically for an administrative appeal, and agencies are required to consider an appeal under the FOIA.

When a Privacy Act request for access is denied, agencies usually inform the requester of any appeal rights that are available. If no information on appeal rights is included in the denial letter, the requester should ask the Privacy Act Officer. Unless an agency has established an alternative procedure, it is possible that an appeal filed directly with the head of the agency will be considered by the agency.

When a request for access is denied under the Privacy Act, the agency explains the reason for the denial. The explanation must name the system of records and explain which exemption is applicable to the system. An appeal may be made on the basis that the record is not exempt, that the system of records has not been properly exempted, or that the record is exempt but no harm to an important interest will result if the record is disclosed.

There are three basic elements to a Privacy Act appeal letter. First, the letter should state that the appeal is being made under the Privacy Act of 1974. If the FOIA was cited when the request for access was made, the letter should state that the appeal is also being made under the FOIA. This is important because the FOIA grants requesters statutory appeal rights.

Second, a Privacy Act appeal letter should identify the denial that is being appealed and the records that were withheld. The appeal letter should also explain why the denial of access was improper or unnecessary.

Third, the appeal should include the requester's name and address. It is a good practice for a requester to also include a telephone number when making an appeal.

Appendix 1 includes a sample letter of appeal.

I. Amending Records Under the Privacy Act

The Privacy Act grants an important right in addition to the ability to inspect records. The Act permits an individual to request a correction of a record that is not accurate, relevant, timely, or complete. This remedy allows an individual to correct errors and to prevent incorrect information from being disseminated by the agency or used unfairly against the individual.

The right to seek a correction extends only to records subject to the Privacy Act. Also, an individual can only correct errors contained in a record that pertains to himself or herself. Records disclosed under the FOIA cannot be amended through the Privacy Act unless the records are also subject to the Privacy Act. Records about unrelated events or about other people cannot be amended unless the records are in a Privacy Act file maintained under the name of the individual who is seeking to make the correction.

A request to amend a record should be in writing. Agency regulations explain the procedure in greater detail, but the process is not complicated. A letter requesting an amendment of a record will normally be addressed to the Privacy Act officer of the agency or to the agency official responsible for the maintenance of the record system containing the erroneous information. The envelope containing the request should be marked "Privacy Act Amendment Request" on the lower left corner.

There are five basic elements to a request for amending a Privacy Act record.

First, the letter should state that it is a request to amend a record under the Privacy Act of 1974.

Second, the request should identify the specific record and the specific information in the record for which an amendment is being sought.

Third, the request should state why the information is not accurate, relevant, timely, or complete. Supporting evidence may be included with the request.

Fourth, the request should state what new or additional information, if any, should be included in place of the erroneous information. Evidence of the validity of the new or additional information should be included. If the information in the file is wrong and needs to be removed rather than supplemented or corrected, the request should make this clear.

Fifth, the request should include the name and address of the requester. It is a good idea for a requester to include a telephone number.

Appendix 1 includes a sample letter requesting amendment of a Privacy Act record.

J. Appeals and Requirements For Agency Responses

An agency that receives a request for amendment under the Privacy Act must acknowledge receipt of the request within ten days (not including Saturdays, Sundays, and legal holidays). The agency must promptly rule on the request.

The agency may make the amendment requested. If so, the agency must notify any person or agency to which the record had previously been disclosed of the correction.

If the agency refuses to make the change requested, the agency must inform the requester of: (1) the agency's refusal to amend the record; (2) the reason for refusing to amend the request; and (3) the procedures for requesting a review of the denial. The agency must provide the name and business address of the official responsible for conducting the review.

An agency must decide an appeal of a denial of a request for amendment within thirty days (excluding Saturdays, Sundays, and legal holidays), unless the time period is extended by the agency for good cause. If the appeal is granted, the record will be corrected.

If the appeal is denied, the agency must inform the requester of the right to judicial review. In addition, a requester whose appeal has been denied also has the right to place in the agency file a concise statement of disagreement with the information that was the subject of the request for amendment.

When a statement of disagreement has been filed and an agency is disclosing the disputed information, the agency must mark the information and provide copies of the statement of disagreement. The agency may also include a concise statement of its reasons for not making the requested amendments. The agency must also give a copy of the statement of disagreement to any person or agency to whom the record had previously been disclosed.

K. Filing a Judicial Appeal

The Privacy Act provides a civil remedy whenever an agency denies access to a record or refuses to amend a record. An individual may sue an agency if the agency fails to maintain records with accuracy, relevance, timeliness, and completeness as is necessary to assure fairness in any agency determination and the agency makes a determination that is adverse to the individual. An individual may also sue an agency if the agency fails to comply with any other Privacy Act provision in a manner that has an adverse effect on the individual.

The Privacy Act protects a wide range of rights about personal records maintained by federal agencies. The most important are the right to inspect records and the right to seek correction of records. Other rights have also been mentioned here, and still others can be found in the text of the Act. Most of these rights can become the subject of litigation.

An individual may file a lawsuit against an agency in the federal district court in which the individual lives, in which the records are situated, or in the District of Columbia. A lawsuit must be filed within two years from the date on which the basis for the lawsuit arose.

Most individuals require the assistance of an attorney to file a judicial appeal. An individual who files a lawsuit and substantially prevails may be awarded reasonable attorney fees and litigation costs reasonably incurred. Some requesters may be able to handle their own appeal without an attorney. Since this is not a litigation guide, details about the judicial appeal process have not been included. Anyone considering filing an appeal can begin by reviewing the provisions of the Privacy Act on civil remedies.[30]

Footnotes

[1] A Citizen's Guide on How to Use the Freedom of Information Act and the Privacy Act in Requesting Government Documents, House Report No. 95-796, 95th Cong., 1st Sess. (1977).

[2] A Citizen's Guide on Using the Freedom of Information Act and the Privacy Act of 1974 To Request Government Records, House Report No. 100-199, 100th Cong., 1st Sess. (1987)

[3] Public Law 100-503.

[4] A Citizen's Guide on Using the Freedom of Information Act and the Privacy Act of 1974 To Request Government Records, House Report No. 101-193, 101st Cong., 1st Sess. (1989).

[5] A Citizen's Guide on Using the Freedom of Information Act and the Privacy Act of 1974 To Request Government Records, House Report No. 102-146, 102d Cong., 1st Sess. (1991).

[6] Letter to W.T. Barry, August 4, 1822, in G.P. Hunt, ed., IX The Writings of James Madison 103 (1910). The Committee wishes to acknowledge the assistance of Harold C. Relyea, Specialist, American National Government, Government Division, Congressional Research Service, in the preparation of this report.

[7] This Guide is primarily intended to help the general public. It includes a complete explanation of the basics of the two laws. In the interest of producing a guide that would be both simple and useful to the intended audience, the Committee deliberately avoided addressing some of the issues that are highly controversial. The Committee cautions against treating the neutrally written descriptions contained in this report as definitive expressions of the Committee's views of the law or congressional intent. The Committee has expressed its views on some of these issues in other reports. See, for example, Security Classification Policy and Executive Order 12356, House Report No. 97-731, 97th Cong., 2d Sess. (1982); Who Cares About Privacy? Oversight of the Privacy Act of 1974 by the Office of Management and Budget and by the Congress, House Report 98-455, 98th Cong., 1st Sess.(1983); Electronic Collection and Dissemination of Information by Federal Agencies: A Policy Overview, House Report 99-560, 99th Cong., 2d Sess. (1986); Freedom of Information Act Amendments of 1986, House Report 99-832, 99th Cong., 2d Sess. (1986) (report to accompany H.R. 4862). The latter report is a legislative report for a bill reforming the business procedures of the FOIA. The bill did not become law. The 1986 amendments to the FOIA were made by the Freedom of Information Reform Act of 1986, Public Law 99-570. There were no committee reports in either House or Senate accompanying the Freedom of Information Reform Act.

[8] See, e.g., U.S. Department of Justice, Freedom of Information Case List (published annually).

[9] The Presidential Records Act of 1978, 44 U.S.C. §2201-2207 (1982), does make the documentary materials of former Presidents subject to the FOIA in part.

Presidential papers and documents generated after January 20, 1981, will be available -- subject to certain restrictions and delays -- under the general framework of the FOIA.

[10]Virtually all official records of the Congress are available to the public. The Congressional Record, all bills introduced in the House and the Senate, and all committee reports (except for those containing classified information) are printed and disseminated. Most committee hearings are also printed and available. Copies of most congressional publications are available at federal depository libraries throughout the county. Historical records of the Congress are made available in accordance with procedures established by House and Senate rules.

In addition, almost all activities of the Congress take place in public. The sessions of the House and Senate are normally open to the public and televised. Most committee hearings and markups are open to the public, and some are televised.

[11]See, e.g., the Federal Fair Credit Reporting Act, 15 U.S.C. §1681 et seq. (1982) (providing for access to files of credit bureaus); the Federal Family Educational Rights and Privacy Act of 1974, 20 U.S.C. §1232g (1982) (providing for access to records maintained by schools and colleges). Some states have enacted laws allowing individuals to have access to personnel records maintained by employers. See, e.g., Michigan Compiled Laws Annotated §423.501.

[12]When records are maintained in a computer, an agency is required to retrieve information in response to an FOIA request. The process of retrieving the information may result in the creation of a new document when the data is printed out on paper or written on computer tape or disk. Since this may be the only way computerized data can be disclosed, agencies are required to provide the data even if it means a new document must be created.

[13]The United States Government Manual is sold by the Superintendent of Documents of the U.S. Government Printing Office. Virtually every public library should have a copy on its shelves.

[14]All agencies have issued FOIA regulations that describe the request process in greater detail. For example, large agencies may have several components each of which has its own FOIA rules. A requester who can find agency FOIA regulations in the Code of Federal Regulations (available in many libraries) might find it useful to check these regulations before making a request. A requester who follows the agency's specific procedures may receive a faster response. However, the simple procedures suggested in this guide will be adequate to meet the minimum requirements for an FOIA request.

[15]Agencies that take more than ten days to respond to a request do not always notify each requester that an extension has been invoked.

[16]At the time that this guide was prepared, the current Executive Order on Security Classification was E.O. 12356 which was promulgated by President Reagan on April 2, 1982. The text of the order can be found at 47 Federal Register 14874-84 (April 6, 1982). The rules for mandatory review for declassification are in Section 3.4 of the Executive Order.

[17]26 U.S.C. §6103 (1982).

[18]13 U.S.C. §9 (1982).

[19]See Predisclosure Notification Procedures for Confidential Commercial Information, Executive Order 12600 (June 23, 1987).

[20]Agency FOIA regulations will normally describe the appeal procedures and requirements with more specificity. At some agencies, decisions on FOIA appeals have been delegated to other agency officials. Requesters who have an opportunity to review agency regulations in the Code of Federal Regulations (available in many libraries) may be able to speed up the processing of the appeal. However, following the simple procedures described in this Guide will be sufficient to maintain a proper appeal.

[21]More information on judicial review under the FOIA and Privacy Act can be found in Adler, Litigation Under the Federal Freedom of Information Act and Privacy Act (American Civil Liberties Union Foundation) (published annually).

[22]The Privacy Act applies to some records that are not maintained by an agency. Subsection (m) of the Act provides that, when an agency provides by contract for the operation of a system of records on its behalf, the requirements of the Privacy Act apply to those records. As a result, some records maintained outside of a federal agency are subject to the Privacy Act. Descriptions of these systems are published in the Federal Register. However, most records maintained outside of federal agencies are not subject to the Privacy Act.

[23]The United States Government Manual is sold by the Superintendent of Documents of the U.S. Government Printing Office. Virtually every public library should have a copy.

[24]Each system notice contains the name of the system; its location; the categories of individuals covered by the system; the categories of records in the system; the legal authority for maintenance of the system; the routine disclosures that may be made for records in the system; the policies and practices of storing, retrieving, accessing, retaining, and disposing of records; the name and address of the manager of the system; procedures for requesting access to the records; procedures for requesting correction or amendment of the records; the source of the information in the system; and a description of any disclosure exemptions that may be applied to the records in the system.

[25]Agencies are required to publish in the Federal Register a description of each system of records when the system is established or amended. In the past, agencies were required to publish an annual compilation in the Federal Register, but that requirement was eliminated in 1982. As a result, for most agencies it will be difficult to find a complete list of all systems of records in the Federal Register. Some agencies do, however, reprint all system notices from time to time. An agency's Privacy Act officer may be able to provide more information about the agency's publication practices.

[26]All agencies have Privacy Act regulations that describe the request process in greater detail. Large agencies may have several components, each of which has its own Privacy Act rules. Requesters who can find agency Privacy Act regulations in the Code of Federal Regulations (available in many libraries) might read these regulations before making a request. A requester who follows the agency's specific procedures may receive a faster response. However, the simple procedures suggested in this guide are adequate to meet the minimum statutory requirements for a Privacy Act request.

[27]An individual seeking records about himself or herself under the FOIA should not be charged review charges. The only charges applicable under the FOIA are search and copy charges.

[28]In 1975, the Office of Management and Budget issued guidance to federal

agencies on the Privacy Act of 1974. Those guidelines are a good source of commentary and explanation for many of the provisions of the Act. The OMB guidelines can be found at 40 Federal Register 28948 (July 9, 1975).

[29]This distinction between express and implied promises of confidentiality is repeated throughout the specific exemptions of the Privacy Act.

[30]See note 21.

APPENDIX 1: SAMPLE REQUEST AND APPEAL LETTERS

A. Freedom of Information Act Request Letter

Agency Head [or Freedom of Information Act Officer]
Name of Agency
Address of Agency
City, State, Zip Code

Re: Freedom of Information Act Request

Dear :

This is a request under the Freedom of Information Act.

I request that a copy of the following documents [or documents containing the following information] be provided to me: [identify the documents or information as specifically as possible]. In order to help to determine my status to assess fees, you should know that I am (insert a suitable description of the requester and the purpose of the request. Sample requester descriptions below)

— a representative of the news media affiliated with the _____ newspaper (magazine, television station, etc.), and this request is made as part of news gathering and not for a commercial use.

— affiliated with an educational or noncommercial scientific institution, and this request is made for a scholarly or scientific purpose and not for a commercial use.

— an individual seeking information for personal use and not for a commercial use.

— affiliated with a private corporation and am seeking information for use in the company's business.]

[Optional] I am willing to pay fees for this request up to a maximum of $_____. If you estimate that the fees will exceed this imit, please inform me first.

[Optional] I request a waiver of all fees for this request. Disclosure of the requested information to me is in the public interest because it is likely to contribute significantly to public understanding of the operations or activities of the government and is not primarily in my commercial interest. [Include a specific explanation.]

Thank you for your consideration of this request.

Sincerely,

Name
Address
City, State, Zip Code
Telephone number [Optional]

B. Freedom of Information Act Appeal Letter

Agency Head or Appeal Officer
Name of Agency
Address of Agency
City, State, Zip Code

Re: Freedom of Information Act Appeal

Dear :

This is an appeal under the Freedom of Information Act.

On (date), I requested documents under the Freedom of Information Act. My request was assigned the following identification number: _____. On (date), I received a response to my request in a letter signed by (name of official). I appeal the denial of my request.

[Optional] The documents that were withheld must be disclosed under the FOIA because....

[Optional] I appeal the decision to deny my request for a waiver of fees. I believe that I am entitled to a waiver of fees. Disclosure of the documents I requested is in the public interest because the information is likely to contribute significantly to public understanding of the operations or activities of government and is not primarily in my commercial interest. (Provide details)

[Optional] I appeal the decision to require me to pay review costs for this request. I am not seeking the documents for a commercial use. (Provide details)

[Optional] I appeal the decision to require me to pay search charges for this request. I am a reporter seeking information as part of news gathering and not for commercial use.

Thank you for your consideration of this appeal.

Sincerely,

Name
Address
City, State, Zip Code
Telephone Number [Optional]

C. Privacy Act Request for Access Letter

Privacy Act Officer [or System of Records Manager]
Name of Agency
Address of Agency
City, State, Zip Code

Re: Privacy Act Request for Access

Dear :

This is a request under the Privacy Act of 1974.

I request a copy of any records [or specifically named records] about me maintained at your agency.

[Optional] To help you to locate my records, I have had the following contacts with your agency: [mention job applications, periods of employment, loans or agency programs applied for, etc.].

[Optional] Please consider that this request is also made under the Freedom of Information Act. Please provide any additional information that may be available under the FOIA.

[Optional] I am willing to pay fees for this request up to a maximum of $_____. If you estimate that the fees will exceed this limit, please inform me first.

[Optional] Enclosed is [a notarized signature or other identifying document] that will verify my identity.

Thank you for your consideration of this request.

Sincerely,

Name
Address
City, State, Zip Code
Telephone number [Optional]

D. Privacy Act Denial of Access Appeal

Agency Head or Appeal Officer
Name of Agency
Address of Agency
City, State, Zip Code

Re: Appeal of Denial of Privacy Act Access Request

This is an appeal under the Privacy Act of the denial of my request for access to records.

On (date), I requested access to records under the Privacy Act of 1974. My request was assigned the following identification number: _____. On (date), I received a response to my request in a letter signed by (name of official). I appeal the denial of my request.

[Optional] The records that were withheld should be disclosed to me because .....

[Optional] Please consider that this appeal is also made under the Freedom of Information Act. Please provide any additional information that may be available under the FOIA.

Thank you for your consideration of this appeal.

Sincerely,

Name
Address
City, State, Zip Code
Telephone Number [Optional]

E. Privacy Act Request to Amend Records

Privacy Act Officer [or System of Records Manager]
Name of Agency
Address of Agency
City, State, Zip Code

Re: Privacy Act Request to Amend Records

Dear :

This is a request under the Privacy Act to amend records about myself maintained by your agency.

I believe that the following information is not correct: [Describe the incorrect information as specifically as possible].

The information is not (accurate) (relevant) (timely) (complete) because ....

[Optional] Enclosed are copies of documents that show that the information is incorrect.

I request that the information be [deleted] [changed to read:].

Thank you for your consideration of this request.

Sincerely,

Name
Address
City, State, Zip Code
Telephone Number [Optional]

F. Privacy Act Appeal of Refusal to Amend Records

Agency Head or Appeal Officer
Name of Agency
Address of Agency
City, State, Zip Code

Re: Privacy Act Appeal of Refusal to Amend Records

Dear :

This is an appeal under the Privacy Act of the refusal of your agency to amend records as I requested.

On (date), I requested that records about me be amended. My request was assigned the following identification number _____. On (date), I was informed by (name of official) that my request was rejected. I appeal the rejection of my request.

The rejection of my request for amendment was wrong because ......

[Optional] I enclose additional evidence that shows that the records are incorrect and that the amendment I requested is appropriate.

Thank you for your consideration of this appeal.

Sincerely,

Name
Address
City, State, Zip Code
Telephone Number [Optional]

Index

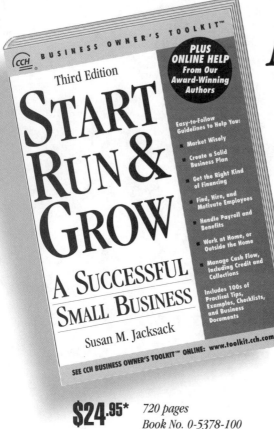

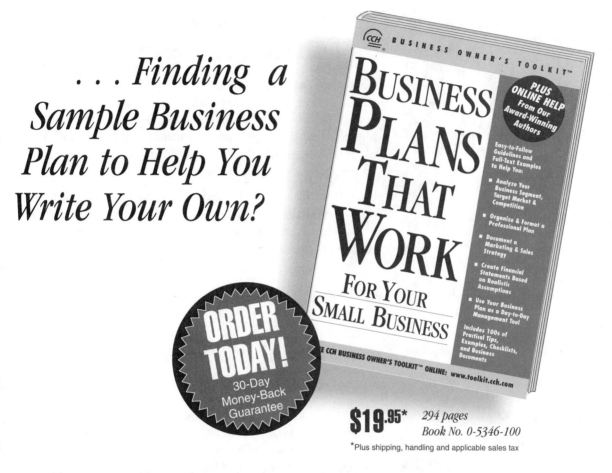

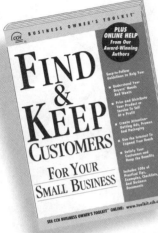
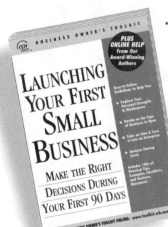

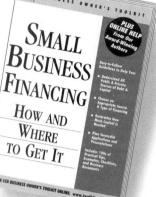